THE PUDDING IS IN THE PROOF

Recipes for Surviving and Thriving

Sandra Hartley

T0381499

AuthorHouse™ UK Ltd.
500 Avebury Boulevard
Central Milton Keynes, MK9 2BE
www.authorhouse.co.uk
Phone: 08001974150

First published by AuthorHouse 11/15/08

ISBN: 978-1-4389-0642-3 (sc)

Printed in the United States of America
Bloomington, Indiana

This book is printed on acid-free paper.

Dedicated to my sons Daniel and Ben with all my love

Acknowledgments

To Andrew for the title! To Lora for fishing the subtitle out of the text and for proofreading. To Louise and Val for more proofreading. To Mike for his computer expertise and saving me from the pdf horrors. To Linda, Cami and Glenn, Angela, and Liz for reading some of it and giving me invaluable feedback. To my son Ben for saying 'Go on Mum. You never do anything by halves. Just do it', when I was wobbling about publishing, and for the wonderful message he sent on first looking at the emailed version, which meant so much to me. To all my teachers, who always popped up at the right time, and all my friends, who have endlessly supported and encouraged me. And to John for the years writing in Andalucia, to Swithin for leaving at the right time(!), and Glenn and Cami for their Divine Window in Vermont.

CONTENTS

INGREDIENTS

There are a squillion tools for surviving and thriving out there. These are just some of the ingredients of my recipes for surviving and thriving. They were what crossed my path and I clutched them with gratitude and used them. The thing is…. to USE them. To walk the talk, not read about it….

Beginnings	Meditation
	Watching Brief
To New Worlds	Celtic Wheel of the Year
	Spring Equinox meditation
	Toning
	Chakras
The Power of Focus	Focus
	Sacred space
	Divination cards
	Personal ritual
The Power of Dreams	Summer solstice
	Labyrinths
	Dreams
Exploration	Ley lines
	Dowsing
Harvest	Sacred sensuality
	The Divine Feminine
Challenge	Resistance
	The Divine Masculine
To a Place of Power	Sacred spiral
	Power of Writing
	Number 13
	Solitude
	Mindfulness
	Backward Circle
	'Peace to all Beings'
	Ho'oponopono healing
	Metaphor
Confrontation	Recipe for Dealing with Fear on the Hoof
	Ego – sticky stuff
	Darkness
	Projection
	Therapy
Hawaii	Pele Goddess of Fire

RECIPES – for eating!

Food has been a source of pleasure all my life. From macaroni cheese as a student to the most exotic food I ever cooked as a restaurateur, it is a mainstay of life for me. As I put my story together I realised each stage had foods associated with it, and so here are some of them. My father, a master baker, said 'Don't go into the food industry'....and I proceeded to run restaurants for many years. I still LOVE to cook.

Beginnings	White sauce....the foundation
To New Worlds	Jelka's soup, Cevapcic, Paprikash
The Power of dreams	Miro's Steak, Steak au Poivre, Watercress Stilton and Mushroom Pate and Melba Toast
Challenge	Beef Strogonof, Sole for Angels, Grape and Ginger Syllabub
Exploration	Pan Haggerty, Half hour 'Stews'
Harvest	Crab in Tarragon Cream, Noisettes of lamb with Duxelles topping, Grape and Ginger Syllabub
Challenge	Watercress, Stilton and Mushroom Pate, Beef Strogonof, Sole for Angels, One Pot Motorhome cooking
Stepping into Magic	One bowl salads, Comforting Potatoes, More Comforting Potatoes Yugoslav style
Cleaning up	Glenn's Tuna pie, Rabbit Stew or Pie off the road, Beef stew or Cobbler
Stability	Recipes for Dropping the pounds, and Veggie dishes: Nettle soup, Roast Veggies, Griddled veggies with goats cheese, Crudites
Abundance	Mum's Recipes: Cheese Souffle, Fruit Fools, Junket, Cream Caramel
Opening	Sweet Things: Chocolate and Grand Marnier Mousse, Caramel Bananas, Champagne Jelly, Honeyed Apricots
Epilogue	Tiramisu – the ultimate dolcissimo?

PROLOGUE

From a Window in Vermont   February 08

At last, I sit here in the still silent white world of winter Vermont surrounded by papers and old journals and disks and I write. The pale sun shafts across the shadowed Adirondack Mountains and spreads itself in glimmering silver on the lake below me. The world is holding it's breath before it jumps into spring.

I have carved a month out of my life in England to finally finish putting this book together. I am now nearly 62 and I feel an urgency to finish this account of myself and of my experience of life. The book was conceived at St Michael's Mount in spring 1998, Part One was written in the Colorado Rockies USA later that year, Part Two in the mountains of Andalucia Spain 2004-6, and is now virtually complete, here at this window in Vermont.

It has been a long journey since I wrote the first Prologue in Colorado – it follows on from this one – and I am leaving it just as it was written then, rather raw, jagged, and angry. I ask that you read my story without trying to work it all out, just stay with me, accept the confusions and the jumps in time and space. I have written *as it came to me and I think it is best left like that*. It has *insisted* on being written, it has its own life, I will not now try to make it 'perfect'. I also suggest that you just read through the story, reading the framed boxes later or if you feel a need to for clarification of something. I hope this is book you can USE, use as a divination tool, to go on dipping into.

Well, that said, we all have a book in us, and this is mine.

It is a very personal and candid tale of Great Change. It is about how I stopped playing victim and started to Feast on my Life. How I climbed out of all the shit and found it had grown a lot of flowers.

When I started writing it in Colorado in October 1998, from my old journals, I sat on the top deck at the top of the world, and I wrote. *'Well, it's grown dark as I sit here scribbling. I have nearly two months to get this book written. It is so hard to know where to start when there is so much to say and I'm overflowing with it all and I just wish I could put it all down at once. But I'll just start, just see what comes. Let it write itself. What I want is to show you my personal vision of the world and of life and my recipes for surviving and thriving (and they taste pretty damn good), and of my own story, as I chronicle this year of 1998.'*

It occurs to me now at this divine window that I have always worked on this book amid mountains. My life has felt like a mountain to climb, but no longer.

I have reached my Meadow. God willing.

This account is for my sons Daniel and Ben, and it is for my family and friends. But also true is that I wrote it primarily just for me. No agenda, no needs, no expectations, no need for response. I just had to express myself. It is also in honour of all the teachers - who have always popped up at just the right time.

It is the story of my journey this lifetime, and my testament to the power of faith and surrender.......as we learn to live consciously in the Mystery.... and to consciously create our own lives.

And from a Deck in Colorado   October 1998

First Came The Questions......

I have been asking apparently unanswerable questions about life and myself from the earliest age. And I guess my life has been dedicated to seeking the answers. It seems, looking back, that I did this by living as fully as I possibly could, by diving into deep ends and trusting I would know how to swim....and swim I did, despite the seas being tumultuous at times.

But in the deep winter of early 1997 I experienced a tragedy I would never have dreamt I could survive.

My son Daniel, who was 29, committed suicide.

He was schizophrenic like his Yugoslav father, whom I had finally divorced some 5 years before. I was married for 25 years, not knowing about the mental illness, just aware that it was often so difficult, impossible really. I was a naïve and vulnerable very sheltered girl who had innocently dropped herself right into the unspeakable torments of the Eastern European psyche. I thought it was all my fault (actually I was right but it took my lifetime to understand in what way) and kept adjusting myself to try to improve things.

The helplessness in the face of their agony was worse than the sadism of my deeply wounded husband. My life had been one of considerable suffering in many ways and my self-esteem was nearing zero. Through those years I kept long journals of my soul searching, my pain and also the joy that my mum said I 'brought with me'. But by the end of my marriage my joy, optimism, and my sense of God were under severe threat and I wept ....

WHY ?   I pleaded with God

'Why is my life so dreadful? Other people don't seem to have such a hard time'
'Why do terrible traumas keep on happening to me?'
'What have I done to deserve all this?'
'I've tried everything. I despair. What on earth does God want of me?'

I battled with guilt, shame, helplessness, resentment, bitterness, exhaustion.....love and hate...

There came a point when I knew I had to free myself from my marriage or I would go under myself and be no use to anyone, and with the aid of intensive psychotherapy and blind faith I divorced my husband and set to work on both the business and financial mess and more importantly myself....and began to find answers....

But then when Dan died 5 years later, all those despairing questions reared up again and I sat in the bleak little room in the Psychiatric Hospital and I cried 'Can I survive **THIS**? Will this finally be the breaking of me?' Every emotion there is raged through me.

But by then I had been a free woman for five years and felt empowered by a far greater understanding of the patterns in my life, and a year later, still alive and kicking, saved by my viewpoint on Daniel's story, the support of family and friends, and my passion for my work, I began to ask questions of myself about my own future.

Which I could see could end at any time. Around the time of Dan's death there were several other deaths in my larger circle. Highlighting for me the sense of gratitude for being alive and a certain generalised urgency for *something*.....

I thought furiously 'I can either let this ruin my life too, or I can say with a good strong healthy anger 'well, fuck it, I'm NOT going to let his inability to live ruin MY life too....

But also, 'Dan did such an immense thing' I said, 'It feels like a challenge to me, asking me to match it in my *life* so that somehow his death has an immense effect, a positive effect.'

It already had led to a tide of healing and forgiveness in my small family, between my younger son Ben, my mother, and I, as we huddled together in our grief. Ben's instinctive understanding that it was the right thing that had happened, that Dan was at peace, helped a lot. Ben has a natural deep wisdom about human nature and one day this will come through and he will take up his position in life as a leader of the way. It was as if somehow Dan had with his action, cleared a lot of the family karma.
 'I feel the greater the positive effect of his death, the greater the benefit to his soul wherever he is. There has to be a reason for all this.'

And I remembered questions I had come across in various teachings over the years:

A VERY DIFFERENT SET OF QUESTIONS

'What would I do if I only had a year to live?'

'What would I do if I couldn't fail?'

'What would I *pay* to do?'

'What do I *really* want to do? If this is my last chance.'

And 'What would LOVE do now'

And questions of my own:

'If I die soon what will I really regret not doing?'

'What would I do if I was thinking only of myself'

'If my life is a novel I'm reading,(and I love novels), what do I want to read when I turn the page? What do I want to happen next? How do I want it to end?'

'What would I do even if I knew it would never "impress", be rewarded or recognized?'

'What would I be proud of, and would make Daniel proud of me?'

So I asked them and watched the train of events that was set in motion. It began at New Year, when it came to me clearly that I needed to LIVE AS IF THIS YEAR WAS MY LAST and make a series of PILGRIMAGES TO SACRED SITES, AS A KIND OF HONOURING OF DANIEL. And.... that I needed to WRITE DOWN OUR STORY

I had no idea of what was to come. I had in mind Chartres and Iona. Maybe Greece.

My mother had bought me some suitcases for Christmas.

SO I SET OFF ON MY QUEST
WITH A WATCHING BRIEF.....

Just Looking, not Looking For. Looking at the world and looking at me and my world and Remembering.

My series of pilgrimages turned, step by guided step, into journeys to Cornwall, Cape Cod and Colorado in the USA, the Scilly Isles, Chartres, and Portugal, and then a journey alone all the way around the world and a ten week stay in a Sacred Valley in the Rockies.

And no, I didn't have lots of money, I just trusted it was the right thing and did it.

PART ONE

1998
THE YEAR I LIVED AS IF
IT WAS MY LAST

'Pilgrimage…'

12 yrs old

Daniel at 14

Mum and Dad

On the Jersey Battle of Flowers Float

Chapter 1
New Years Eve 1997/8...... Beginnings

This is one year I am not sorry to see end.

My mother and I sit in the dim winter light, a candle lit, and remember Daniel.

We talk about his strength, energy and humour, his style and swagger, and his intelligence. He was so beautiful. Golden. When he arrived from wherever there was always a huge inflow of warmth. He used to say with a twitch of his lips 'hello mummy' and swing me up and around as if I was a leaf.

We tell stories of him. How he tied a borrowed horse to a long wooden seat outside the moorland restaurant we ran and the horse clopped off across the square trailing the seat. How he loved the restaurant and washed up when he could barely reach the sink, and longed to be tall enough to wait tables. How the customers loved his service with a flourish. How he came on the ferry to Santander to meet us on one of our long motorhome jaunts and even though we weren't at all sure he was coming I felt the bond like a thick white tendon-like cord and I knew he was on board.

I thought I had done what was needed. I had tried so hard, worked so hard, to transform the life I had so misguidedly and innocently created, and myself. HOW could this happen? And to my mum, my poor mum, living quietly in her little life, it was just not right. What WAS I supposed to do?

In the deep dark of midwinter, we take turns to read aloud my father's most powerful sermon. My mother carried this sermon with her for years after he died. I have copied it in, just as he, Jack Hedley wrote it. Mum and I sit in silence while my father's words wrap us in strength, and then with difficulty we get up, make a cup of tea and I go. Driving along the empty A30, between the years, I remember painfully the day Dan died.

---

18 February 1997

It was about 10am on a Monday morning and I was drinking tea and laughing with my colleague in the Arts and Therapy Centre I founded in Exeter.

I will never forget the moment when I looked up to see, standing in anguish in the door, the sagging staring figure of my long estranged ex- husband. I knew what he would say before he said it. It's come, I thought. It's happened. 'Daniel has taken his life' he said, his eyes staring. Our beloved beautiful 29 year old son Daniel had been in a far distant Psychiatric Hospital in Cambridge for nearly six months. He had attempted suicide before, and told me it really would be better for him and us if he succeeded. The appalling helplessness of watching and listening to his agony was without a doubt the worst pain I have ever known.

'The Brook that Dried Up'   1 kings Chap 17 V 2-3, 7-9

There is no stronger story on the lips of men and women than the story of God's Providence.

Sometimes it is very clear in its workings, sometimes very obscure, but despite the fact that sometimes He seems to have deserted us, always full of love, always working out for the best, always right in the end.

It is one thing to be in God's hands- as we most surely are- it's another to know this is so.

God does not stamp all his gifts with the broad seal of Heaven – the Divine Mark is put where you wont see it unless you look for it – inside a ring.

God is always helping us to help ourselves, working through and around our human efforts till sometimes we don't know where one finished and the other began. It is too easy to say 'I alone did it'.

But sometimes, like Elijah, we come face to face with a famine. In a land where bread and water were failing fast, Elijah was sent to the brook at Chereth and told 'God will supply all needs'.

But the brook dried up. It failed. God knew it would fail. He meant it to fail.   This second part of Providence is harder. Elijah watched the brook dwindle day by day., perhaps he thought ' God has forgotten me'. He is in despair. He has been sent here. WHY would the brook dry up when he was sent here?

The brook dried up.

This aspect of Providence is hard to take. We can easily recognise a Love that gives, but not a Love that takes away. 'How providential' we say when we hear the brook running and babbling in our ears, when the prayer is answered, when a need is met.

But hunger, suffering, death, hard times, grey days, bleak nights, broken hopes and hearts, severed fellowships……

The education of our faith is not enough if we have not learned the Providence of Loss, the Gift of Emptiness, the Ministry of Failing and Fading things.

A desperate situation may prove a great blessing.

We have to learn the difference between trusting in the gift and trusting in the Giver.

'Hide thyself by the brook Chereth' the Lord told Elijah. The Brook dried up.

Elijah came to the end of his resources, but the Providence of God leads us into some hard places but it never leaves us there. 'Get thee to Zaraphath'….Chereth is a stopping place not a destination.

We need tomorrow to explain today. We must get to the end before we find the meaning of the beginning. When Elijah reached the widow's cottage at Zaraphath, the meal on the table, God's explanation was clear as daylight.

God does not mean us to see Zaraphath before we have been brought face to face with our despair, and with the mercy that knows no bounds.

We look into the eyes of suffering then upward into the eyes of God, and we are brought from the brook that failed to the meal and the oil that failed not.

When the comforting and pleasant babble of the brook falls silent, it is only then that we might hear the low deep murmur of the River of God that is full of water, the unfaltering message of the Eternal.

God grant us the strength to hear it, to know our faith in full, and to come through to the wonders of life.
AMEN
.

I remember driving through storms fog rain and M25 paralysis. It wasn't me driving the car, I know. Some higher power held that wheel. I had had that experience before, driving under intense emotional pain.

I remember Daniel's tall frame motionless and waxen and swelling, tubes and wires and flickering machines and monitors, grave faces, long vigils, tea and blankets.

Talking to him, holding his hand, stroking his marble-like forehead. His father and I, either side of him, standing in silence. Somehow for a moment my tormented husband, also long mentally ill, seemed the charismatic young Serbian I had fallen in love with thirty years ago. And I stood and felt the full weight of the responsibility of what had come of our love. I could only say 'I'm so sorry, Dan, I'm so sorry.' Telling him we were all there for him, his Dad and I and Ben. I know he heard us, saw us, in some way. We had time to take our leave of each other, and I knew when he was gone, though the machines flickered on.

Then the slowing, slowing and finally still, screens. The howling, the brokenness. A nurse holding me and weeping with me. My husband and Ben standing numbly. Miro said he wished he could weep like that too. Sitting alone in silent shock in the chapel. Then out into the cold night air, a wind sprung from nowhere, a bird singing, the racing clouds.

His father and brother in their long coats, carrying his bags out of the Mental Hospital. The groups of sad faces huddled in the cold smoking and watching. Their spokeswoman saying 'You must be Dan's mother. We are so sorry'. The bleak little room where we met the doctors. 'Am I going to be able to bear this one?' I asked myself as I sat there. Thirty years of such suffering. There has been so much to bear.

But at least Dan's out of his pain now. And it was that of course that made it possible to bear it. But still as I type this, I weep. And the pain comes behind my eyes. And I remember how it was. The dark red pain filling my throat and heart, belly like lead and pierced by knives so heavy sharp and hot. Feeling numbed dead, finished, empty. The shaking which would not stop.

His death was achieved effectively, against the odds, and there was even humour. He had taken anti-freeze, (we were told he had seen that done on 'Casualty' that week) and covered the smell by getting drunk. So he was left to sleep it off by the nurses and even hours later he semi-woke and laughed and joked about too many beers. By the time the staff realised there was something wrong it was too late.

At the inquest they said he was ' a highly intelligent young man with great insight into his illness who has chosen not to live with it any longer'. I feel proud of his courage.

These were the poems he wrote while at the Norfolk Institute of Art and Design. He was doing so well there, as a mature student, well thought of by his tutors, and on course to go out to Africa to help dig wells for six months. He was raising money for it. When things got so good, suddenly he seemed to be unable to cope with that....and he left, said he needed a break. Nobody could help. It was all downhill then. He wanted to be in an East Anglian hospital because it was so far, and Ben said he really really really didn't want me to have to care for him any more or to suffer any more. He insisted I mustn't go.

I read the poems out at his funeral.

DAWN

Silence is removed from stillness
by notes beyond the branches
the awakening of
by the days that have drowned
the distraction of dream
something
fluttering from the chrysalis
searching for wings

SCHIZOPHRENIA

If you have so much character
that you don't know who you are
corridors can be safe
striplighted to the halls
with chessboard floors
always walk on the right
there is no sign to tell you so
but you will be told if you are not.

I am nearing my temporary home now, which has thrown up some interesting challenges for me. My dark room in this strange shared house faces, very closely, a bulky dark church tower. In the courtyard there is a crow in a cage. My best friend here is a nervy black cat called Luther. In the midst of all this darkness and ancient powerful symbols of metamorphosis I have met some dark places in myself. One night recently I was tormenting myself as usual when Dan's picture appeared to fling itself to the floor. I knew he was saying 'Don't Mum, don't. Don't do what I did' I picked up his picture and told him I would not, and that I would soon be gone from here.

As I was. On Christmas Day at Eaglehurst House on Dartmoor I heard that I would be able to move back to my beloved Old Meadow, and I asked whether as Caroline was travelling for four months I could have her room.

This was my best Christmas present: asked to go back to Old Meadow, where I had house-sat for friends Caroline and Marcus for some months in the autumn. I never needed to leave when my friends returned from their travels, but I had not dared to say I would like to stay, so I put myself through the Fitzpaine horror. (Fitz*paine*!)

Christmas Day, Caroline led a meditation high up on Meldon Hill, vast sweeping moor all around us, and afterwards there was sherry and mince pies at Eaglehurst. It was all very satisfying, and as I drank my sherry, looking at that view, and admiring the house, Caroline said 'I'm off abroad for four months. Would you like to come back and share with Marcus?' I said 'I would love to, but if you are going for so long, could I have your room while you're gone?'

It seems my ability to ask for what I need had grown somewhat with the Fitzpaine experience....

It was a lovely time there, Marcus was very easy to share with, and we supported each other, taking it in turns to cook and wash up and clean. I adored the space and the sunroom and watching the garden grow that spring was my first connection to the gardening I have come to love so passionately. I found I just had to walk around it each early morning to see what had come up overnight, what had happened. There was always something new.

I got later and later at the Centre, as the rural idyll captivated and held me. The land had claimed me. Dartmoor rose purple and brown and empty above me, the village chimneys smoked below me. I adored it and savoured every moment. I longed to be able to move the Centre out of the city. This had begun when I sold my flat at River Meadows on the quay in Exeter, writing on my whiteboard 'off to the hills' with a drawing beneath. And now, I think my spirit had left the city and was needing to manifest a change, how, I had no idea.

So with this need for change sitting in my heart, my year of pilgrimages was beginning and I had two large suitcases as another important Christmas present. It was part of the big letting go. I had let go of

My marriage
My house
My teaching jobs
My apartment
And I was forced to let go of my son

And now it might be time to let go of the leased Queen Street properties in Exeter - a relic of my marriage - one way or another, and also my attachment to pleasing my mother, who feared my travelling spirit.

The last stretch of my drive back to my temporary home that New Year's Eve.... I let the tears fall, the clouds cleared, and when I reached the top of a ridge of hills, there before me hanging in the luminescent sky was the new moon and Venus.

It was like an offering of new beginnings and I stopped the car to stand in grateful silence.

I offered the sight to one of my housemates, who seemed truly pleased. And then I went up to shower and change and write a poem for a New Year's Eve Ceremony with my friends.

NEW YEAR'S EVE 97/8

tonight I was yet again
given all I could wish to receive

the New Moon and Venus beside her
hang still
in the blue
electric and deepening and sublime

poised between two years
the most special of years
our Universe Goddess and God
God and Goddess
give us
a moment of grace

beginnings and beauty
suspended in time

dark disc edged with the
curl of new light

the Dark met in the year past
the comet the herald of freedom
and peace
but first the roar and the fire and the twisting ache
the head thrown back and the burning tears
The night wind and the birds and the flying soul
the beseeching

the soft flows and the stroking
and the arms and the eyes
the seals and the horses
the butterflies and the child
the rocks and the skies and the pouring rain

and power and peace come hand in hand

and compassion wraps the steel of strength

And the black cat called Luther is my friend
between the Tower and the Crow

The Choices are made
and let go

let go

there is only the moment
holding me, wide open

safe in the sublime
at rest in the not knowing

and the Knowing

It is a very special evening. My friend Rachel - tall, classy, very emotionally articulate-has prepared the top floor of her house as a ceremonial space. We sit in a circle and are silent in meditation.

We each speak about our intentions for the year to come. We offer our creations. Rachel sings to her harmonium of the death of her lover. I read my poem. Glenn (he's an earth energy researcher at my Arts and Therapy Centre in the leased Exeter properties) gives us all 2 stones each, to strike together as we say our intention, so that the impact fixes the intention in the stones. We take cards for the year. My animal card is a Squirrel. Gathering time. My angel is Patience. It will all come in due course. I voice deep envy of others; more dramatic cards - hawks etc. but then I remember I am giving up my addiction to drama and am grateful for my quiet cards.

Merriment and champagne and the chimes of Big Ben. Loving faces around me. Hugs and kisses and out into the starlit night.

It is a new year, and I lift my arms to the stars in the crystalline dark.

I set off home, driving through the poised black of the midwinter night, and I remember our meditation. It is the first and main ingredient for survival recipes, and I was taught to do it following the Zen tradition.

I drive home, thinking about how far I have come, to have such a circle of beautiful friends. I remember the anxious, earnest, shy and lonely girl and wife I was. The knowing and not-knowing that always made me different. It has been a long road, but a rich one too, through suffering and out the other side....

The Only Child

This self-searching started early. I have a clear memory of myself at 11 years old, walking up the steep hill home from school in St Helier in Jersey in the Channel Islands, with the little Gideon New Testament that we had just been given, studying the fault-finding chart at the back. All my life I have wanted to know what was wrong with me so that I could put it right. The Christian aim - to be like Christ. This may well originate partly from trying to find out why I was not popular! But of course such concerns were probably part of the reason so it was a self-perpetuating cycle.

I have few memories before that age, but my first is as a child of nearly five, I had found a purse and been asked to take it around all the classrooms. This was not a possibility for the terrified child I was, so I hid it. When this emerged I was not of course believed. I was misjudged and had no means of protecting myself. I see now that this theme followed me through my marriage. I once read of an unusual psychological trait whereby someone has such weak boundaries of self that they take on all guilt and show it even when not at all guilty. This understandably confused people all my life until I began to deal with it at last in my forties. My other first memory is of playing alone in the playground, pretending to watching teachers that I was playing with others. Ashamed of my rejection, my loneliness, yet strangely self sufficient too. They say these first memories set the theme for our lives. (What are yours?)

I was a frail child, bronchitic to the extent that the doctors sent us from the smogs of Southall in London to the sea and my father got a job in Jersey. I remember feeling I had come alive as we sailed there, and the excitement of passing and naming all the bays I had read about. Reading was my greatest pleasure. I guess that cut me off too.

My mother told me in the last months of her lucidity that I'd been seen as 'stuck-up' by the church youngsters. I couldn't make real contact with any of them. I was too thoughtful, too open AND I was cut off. At my small highly disciplined girls grammar school I was both picked on and cruelly overlooked as a newcomer to the island of Jersey, unfortunately both intelligent and pretty.

The Methodist church with its emphasis on sin, shame and the glorification of suffering had stamped me deeply its own. Home was colourless, no rows allowed by my lay preacher father, no emotion, certainly no excesses, very much always the same. Dad was a lay preacher, a good man terrified of his own anger. Mum was a mass of anxiety, who also liked things her own way and used her weakness to get them. (The recognition of the many positives of my background came all too late in life…!!!)

There was no other life. Church and Girls Grammar School. No wonder really that I chose such a challenging but colourful life for myself as soon as I was free. I headed quite unconsciously for the Wild…….

First experiments were with the drifter beatniks who lounged on the island's beaches playing guitars. I was an outsider but I enjoyed sitting on the fringes watching, and sitting in Royal Square or beery floored clubs in bare feet and fringed flared hipsters and long hair, trying desperately to be cool and causing my parents endless anguish.. My more forward friends all found beatnik boyfriends and I was deeply ashamed of being unwanted.

I look at photos now and see an agonisingly shy girl lovely but a little stooped hiding behind her unfashionably bushy long blonde hair, eyes downcast- especially when in what I perceived to be 'superior' company. Then I see photos of myself in church groups and see

MEDITATION

Sit
Either in a chair, or kneeling with cushions under feet and between thighs
and calves, or crosslegged on edge of cushion
Breathe out, softly, like a sigh, all your breath...
straighten the shoulders and back,fold your hands left over right on your
belly......relax
let go of everything that has gone before this moment
and that is to come
relax more with every outbreath, consciously
letting go
bring the attention to the belly
sit straight, head level, eyes closed
watch the breath
rising and falling in the belly
until you hear the bell
This is the simplest, like a cat purring
when thoughts and feelings come
note them and return the attention to the breath
which is light and natural
when there are noises or pains or distractions
note them and return undisturbed
to the breathing
relax
if the mind is very busy count the outbreaths slowly down from 10 to 1
or use a simple mantra
perhaps 'love' on the inbreath and 'free from fear' on the outbreath
keep the attention in the belly just below the navel
not in the head
relax
breathe
and rest in your meditation
sit in groups or alone
at home, just dropping to the floor where you are
or in a special spot
in a temple or on a bus.
wherever, whenever, you need to

23

the other side of myself, cool and aloof, my growing defence system against loneliness. Oh the pain of comparison, of feeling inferior/superior. Fragile ego.

It was to take a lifetime to let go of the insecurity of these ego games and simply be me and love my life.

I failed my Chemistry A-level (why on earth was I told to take Chemistry when I never managed to pass Maths O level??? We were all on a conveyor belt, and seemed to have little choice what we studied. I longed for Art School but had been shunted along the academic route.) So I was unable to go to Aberystwyth University. It meant that I stayed on a year and was a guinea pig (one of only 3!) in the first days of co-education with the boys' grammar. It was different there and I had glimpses of confidence. I was immediately made a prefect, where at the girls school they said I was too rebellious . There was a boy called Perce who was I think 20 and re-sitting for the second time, who took me under his wing and protected me. Bless him. There were no female dragons to push me mercilessly down and I enjoyed some real respect and some compliments from staff - 'our PreRaphaelite prefect' .

Though there was a master who almost seduced me - I remember clearly the intense pleasure he gave me, during 'private' lessons in his home...... (there had been many examples of low level 'abuse' in my life which it never occurred to me to report, after all, such things were unmentionable, it was clearly my fault, and this was a big factor shaping in my life as it unfolded) ... I remember when I was much younger, about 10, when a flasher exposed himself to a friend and me. She was dragging me away, but I felt so sorry for him, didn't want to hurt his feelings. 'What do you call that, what he showed us?' my friend asked her mum. 'Oh, botty, dear' she said unhappily. Such were the times.

The headmaster said I was a 'student they were really glad to have had'. It helped. My results were excellent, and I successfully applied (the Girls Grammar saying 'you'll never get in there') to The London School of Economics: I chose it because it was London, it sounded exciting, and I could read Geography with Sociology there, which felt glamorous and different.

That was my first experience of how things apparently not good actually are. But for my bad results I would have been stuck in Aberystwyth, (apologies to that splendid University) which was I guess all I felt I deserved...instead, I was heading for the centre of London and the world's foremost School of the Social, Economic and Political Sciences.....

My parents paid for a holiday as a reward. There was no one to go with, so I went alone; I chose a Ramblers Association trip, not that I'd had anything do with it or with rambling for that matter. First I chose painting in Austria. That would have most likely been quite 'safe'.

At the last minute I for some unknown reason changed to 'Sailing in Dalmatia'...a romantic Mediterranean destination and definitely NOT so safe....and set the course of my life.

I never understood why I was sent off to the Mediterranean all alone, a total innocent of 19, lovely, lonely and with a longing for passion… I used to say 'what did they expect???' But slowly, the charge of the accusation has gone, as love and forgiveness seeps through my memories…

And so at 19 I headed out into the world unconsciously but determinedly in search of full colour living – unbridled excitement, passion and desire.

1965 Yugoslavia

I stood on the quay gazing with rapture at the Mediterranean. 'If you go around looking like that you'll end up in trouble' said the Welsh ship's captain nastily. It was the first time that I experienced my bliss interpreted as a come-on and it was a deep shock. I stared at him in confusion. I was a gazelle in those days, long and lithe, tanned pale gold, swinging a long and thick blonde plait. I look back and like everyone wish I'd been aware of all that at the time. In a way I was, and was at a loss to understand why I was so unwanted, so unloved. It is a syndrome that haunted me all my life and only began to clear in my fifties, believe it or not….

PERSPECTIVES FROM NOW - FROM A WINDOW IN VERMONT February 2008

As I sit here putting this book together at this divine window in Vermont, almost ten years after I started to write it (!!!!) I reflect wryly that I'm still working on it at over sixty – but NOT by 'working' – by allowing it, accepting, forgiving, loving, it's all we can do!!!!!…. loving ourselves as we are even without understanding – that seems to then be reflected in our world, and I have indeed felt loved since I practiced this discipline and began accepting the mystery of it all. I remember how Spiritual Teacher Andrew Cohen says 'Just Stop. Stop trying to work it out'…he sees 'just one person stopping' as a of huge benefit to world….because we are all one, the cosmos is a hologram and we are a piece of it that contains the whole. What happens in a piece affects all. The Divine Mystery. When we Know this, we are never alone again, and we know the power and glory of the small shifts towards peace and bliss in ourselves.

What we think about and feel becomes our world and my focus on the troubles, and my fears, and my judgments, all created exactly what I was afraid of ....it has taken me a lifetime to work out how to create a great life, but the secrets are all out there now and no one needs to spend so long. We can turn things around much faster now!! We just need to watch our thoughts and feelings moment by moment....make sure they match what we want in our life.

The world weary ship's captain was right, of course, and the trouble in question was posing nonchalantly on the side of the converted fishing boat, smoking a cigarette, little knowing he was destined to trouble me profoundly as a husband for nearly twenty five years.

That was the beginning of my love affair with Yugoslavia and Miro. Miro was a seriously handsome and even more seriously charming Philosophy and English student, working for the summer on the boat...

It was a sturdy converted fishing boat –the 'Duzac'- and it raised its brown sails and threaded its way gracefully southwards among the myriad islands. We floated across milky seas at dawn, along clean baked white rocky shores at the toes of the barren mountains..... We swam in turquoise and gold waters and grilled lamb over herby fires. .....We climbed the scented hillsides to collect cheeses...... We danced under vines in lamplit restaurants in blue dusk beside the moonlit water and wandered the polished pale stone streets of exquisite little walled cities.

I was enchanted and there was no chance of resistance. I was being touched and warmed. I was alive and living and drinking in beauty and romance as if I'd come out of the desert. Which in a sense I had. And I have never since returned to the sensual desert of propriety and Methodism and convention that I thirsted in as a child.

1998 is dawning and I am going to live it, fully, live it as if it is the last year of my life. Most of those close to me: my father, my mother, my husband and my elder son, didn't or don't want to live, let alone fully, but I DO.

I DO. It is a vow to myself, an inner marriage.

I DO.

I DOOOOOOOOOO

And I am conscious of this choice, and I give myself a **Watching Brief** to not only Live but Live Consciously as my own witness.

I AM.

I am alive and I know it, moment by moment I watch my aliveness, my awareness, I watch and feel the suchness of each moment

**SO I AM OFF ON A
WATCHING BRIEF.......**

I hold my arms up, determinedly, powerfully, to the Universe on New Years' Day and I punch the air and shout as loud as I can to the Gods

I AM

And louder

I AM

And still louder

I AM

Try it. Go on. Shout it to the skies. Say Yes to Life.

YES.....

YESSSSSSSSSS

It's the start of the way out of suffering.

**Suffering - I've done one hell of a lot of it.
My meditation teacher Roshi John Garrie used to say 95% of it's unnecessary.
I agree.**

Now, I would say that that there is 'positive pain' –pain met in the present moment, felt, faced and allowed, and 'negative' pain - pain dwelt on and indulged, or denied or resisted. Sorting out which is which and why helps a lot.
It cuts right down the hell of suffering.

It is said that the main difference between more evolved beings and ourselves is that they OBSERVE MORE.

So, watch, look, see, accept, …

And love

....within and without

YES.... 95% of Suffering is UNNECESSARY, we CAN let it go, and this book is about my journey doing that.

WATCHING BRIEF

watching our own thoughts, emotions, instincts,
behaviour and motives
watching for ego messing up the works
watching all the events, ailments, people, in our
lives for their message to us
watching for metaphor, symbol and sign in the
world
watching for the times we slip out of NOW into
the pain of the past or fear of the future
watching the world in gratitude
watching our own boundaries
watching without judgement
watching with love and compassion
This is consciousness
This is spirituality.
Spirituality only starts with daily practice
sessions, it is making ALL of daily life fully
alive.
In the moment of consciousness we simply
CANNOT act out of baser instincts.
As we bring consciousness to more moments our
lives purify and we live more and more from our
higher selves. We put our soul in charge.

I call it
SOUL CONTROL

In Yugoslavia at 20

Chapter 2
To America via Cornwall   Into New Worlds

January 1998

Its definitely a new year. New Worlds beckon. Not only was I off back to Old Meadow, but….

'Do you want to come to America?' says Glenn, coming into the reception at the Convergence Centre. (Another of those questions that changed my life.) 'It'll be your birthday there!' Pause. Poverty consciousness kicking in and being kicked out. 'YES OF COURSE I DO!' I beam.

Later: 'If I'm going to America I need to be able to wear my jeans'…. 'I read something about Princess Diana's diet' Glenn offers, and brings in a double page spread cutting about the 'Kensington diet', which is based on the well established Hay Food Combining Diet. I began, and the weight began dropping off. Nothing like a real motive….

February 1 comes, and brings Imbolc, the Celtic Festival of the First Light, when the land begins faintly to stir in response to the growing light. I love these Festivals. Celebrating them brings a connection with our indigenous culture and with nature, an awareness of the natural cycles, and of the Divine in Nature, and most importantly the time to pause and reflect. I first learned of them in 1994, and have celebrated them ever since.

We celebrate at first in darkness, and in silence, and one by one the candles light in a circle, and we speak of the first stirrings of new life, of what seeds have been dormant in our lives over the winter, what we will grow in our lives this year. We speak from open hearts of how the darkness has been for us, and then the

energy grows as we begin to see our year ahead. I am feeling growing excitement as I prepare myself for America.

February

On the anniversary of Dan's death Ben and I go to sit on the bench I arranged to be placed in Bellevue Park beside the river in Exeter. This was where, from the footbridge, Miro and Ben scattered his ashes, and Ben had a strong sense of his freedom now. The seat is in a fabulous spot, raised, looking down the river. On it I put a plaque with Dan's name and dates, all our love, and a quote, from Julian of Norwich. 'All shall be well, and all shall be well, and all manner of things shall be well'. It was amazing, I picked the spot, but the Council said they couldn't put it there it had to be further back. But then, when I went to see, there it was and they had built a special mound for it too.

March

It's Spring equinox, March 21 – the Celtic Festival the Church calls Easter. My personal 'Getting out the Sunbed' Festival. Resurrection. In our ceremony we talk of the insights of the introspection of the winter, and let go of the dark as the sun gains in power. We come to stillness with the balance of light and dark, as the Sun pauses at the Equator, before it appears to climb the sky until it is overhead at the Tropic of Cancer at Solstice and at its nearest to us in the Northern hemisphere. We talk of where we are in balance and where out of it...

I know I need to keep my balance as I fly west in ten days. I feel nearly ready now.

By the end of March, a stone lighter and much swimming, aquarobics, walking, horse-riding later I feel ready for the New World.

I have a week in Cornwall, long booked, in delicious Vine Cottage - owned by local character Basil Bolitho who lives in a miniscule lean-to attached to the cottage. The cottage has unaccountably sprouted an American flag in the sitting room – I looked at it bemused. I sat on the cliffs at the Marconi monument and gazed disbelieving across the ocean to its equivalent the other side. Was I really going there...? I even managed to stick to my diet all week, with my friend Ros's support.

In two days I fly.

But first I go to see clairvoyant Dorothy Chitty. 'I see a lot of change around you' she says, sprightly. My face falls. 'Oh its for the better' she hastily adds, and is flattering in a superficial way. I am wanting her to see deeper, and she senses this and there is

MONEY IS NOT THE PRIME FACTOR

When deciding whether to do something, or not do something, Money is not the Prime Factor.
If it feels that doing something is for the highest good, then the money will come to enable you to do it.
But if you do something, like work, ' Just for The Money', it will not work, will not give you the satisfaction. Do something for the passion and rightness of it – though it may feel passionately right to simply earn money honourably! The key is being in touch with signs and intuition and knowing whether it is right.

silence. A lot later she suddenly looks agitated and crumples and is silent again and then whispers 'I see a lost child'. **'yes'** 'You are asking for forgiveness' **'yes'** 'he is saying none is needed' **'Ah'**. I sigh. She listens then says…. '*and* he says to tell you that he is sorry - *he made the loneliness worse'* she looks at me sadly 'does that mean anything to you' **'Oh yes'.** Only Daniel knew that I felt that perhaps my deepest motive for having and wanting him –right in the middle of my LSE degree course- was my loneliness – he had asked for a true answer. So I know it *is* Daniel speaking to me. I walk out of that room with perhaps the last shreds of guilt and shame dissolving and flowing away. I float, in fact.

So….I come out of Dorothy Chitty's house that spring day in 1998 very shakily. But, I realise as I drive away, 'I FEEL FREE'. Ready indeed for the US of A….. ready to fly…..

1965 London School of Economics

And so a shy grammar school girl, philosophical and poetical daughter of a Methodist lay preacher, came to New Worlds, to the London School of Economics in the Sixties with a clear intention to be more outgoing, fortified by her Dalmatian love affair…

It was not long before I had something approaching a new almost wild image. My intelligence was totally overlooked as I took on my sexuality. I remember at reunions people assuming I only got a third, and I strongly reminded them that actually I got a 2:2, amazing in the circumstances…I know I would have got a 2:1 in normal ones.

Because even though, having had no reply to my letters, I had put my Yugoslav love affair behind me, destiny was having none of it. Our year was off to Finland in September to study glacial moraines. I was uninterested in cold climates. I wanted heat. Then at the last minute it was realised the study had been done and a chance to camp on a Yugoslav island and study the impact of tourism was offered by a lecturer with a contact there. 'You'll want to come now won't you' they said. 'Contact that man you met there, he can help us with the language'.

Fate, I thought. Obviously meant to be. I can only surmise now that this relationship was as they say 'karmic', a 'soul contract'…that our spirits had decided, pre incarnation, that this would happen? How else to explain the wild coincidence that took me back to Miro?? It's all a mystery and I look forward to finding out when I die…

Simultaneously with the Expedition change of destination a letter came from 'that man' inviting me for the summer. After a year of no contact at all, despite long missives from me at the beginning…. And so there I was back in the idyll, being taken to meet the nonplussed family and neglecting my studies shamefully. (Though I did later put the report together and get it printed)

I remember how we stood entwined by the harbour in Zadar, and he said, rather desperately, I noticed his need even then, 'do you love me?' somewhere dimly a flicker of thought and feeling 'but what about me? Isn't this supposed to be the other way round?'

I came back pregnant and terrified, unable (incomprehensibly to me now) to consider either abortion or actually looking after the baby. My mother wrote me a wholly predictable, vicious and utterly condemning letter. I believe I had Daniel out of my fear of loneliness, but for months I was sure I would have him adopted and this belief protected me from total terror at my situation. I always said 'it will all work out'. I was known for it. But this was the 60s and babies out of wedlock were still just not on. Hard to imagine the disgrace now.

But I was actually weirdly quite proud. I felt connected to the human race by the baby inside me. It proved, in my strange mind, that I was wanted. One of my ex-boyfriends, Ed, a really great guy, said to me 'are you really sure about this…..' and 'I was in love with you, you know'. Oh what a different path my life would have taken. I believe Ed went to Canada and was a great academic success.

I revised for my Sociology finals in the maternity hospital and took the exam successfully ten days after the appalling and protracted birth of my exceptionally beautiful baby Daniel in May. I took him back to my decrepit shared house on Clapham Common and everyone enjoyed him. Lee, Diana, and Patsy, Gill and Caroline were all wonderful…. Mum stayed awhile, bless her, and tells how she cleared 50 largely unwashed milk bottles from the corners of the kitchen. I couldn't go home to Jersey in the summer (as a shamed unmarried mother) and my mum's twin sister Betty and her large family welcomed me very warmly to their home, and saved the day. Dan was a good baby at first and fortunately mostly slept through the whole summer, so the household was relatively undisturbed.

Then when term restarted I took a flat in Wimbledon, an attic with a lidded bath in the large kitchen and a bed in the sitting room for the princely sum of £6 a week, and awaited Miro's arrival, which was endlessly delayed. A postcard came saying he had to go to the dentist. Nowadays I would look at the symbolism – teeth are about decisions, what you bite off in life.

He was obviously very frightened at what he was biting off but of course I was oblivious to that and just got very desperate. I remember when he eventually did set off he was due to arrive at Victoria Station at 7pm and ……… he wasn't there. For ages I scanned the crowds, my heart and stomach dropping and dropping. Then I went dejectedly, despairingly, home to where my poor mum was waiting with 6 month old Dan. Later we had a phone call from Customs in Dover: Miro was there, being held because he had only £5. We guaranteed him and he arrived later, peering sheepishly but still with a smile of charming bravado over the landlord's shoulder at two in the morning.

MEDITATION FOR SPRING EQUINOX

The Wheel of the Celtic Year turns on....the waking Earth turns its greening face to the Sun, and it pauses.
We feel the Poise before the Sun begins to soar to Solstice. All is still, soft, delicate; Light and Dark held in exquisite Balance. This is the Time of Balance.

We wait, breathing out gently, a sigh of relief for the end of the dark. Breathing out and letting go of all that has gone before. Coming into this Moment with full vibrating consciousness of its purity. We are still, in the space between, in the gap. The Place of Power and of Potential.

We wait and in the space the Light floods in and nature dances in celebration of all that is to come: the flowerdecked Beltane frolics of Mayday when creativity pours forth, the sumptuous Solstice at the peak of the Sun's climb, and the first fruits of harvest at lammas....round and round the wheel turns

But Now, Now it is the beginning of the Light- filled time, and juices are running faster, and the pace of Life quickens and leaps and all is growth and expansion.

We reflect on what may or may not be in balance in our lives and on how we can make adjustments to come to equilibrium and stability, before we start on the time of expansion.

This is thus a foundation time of the year, and this work is all important in determining the harvest we reap as the year begins to wane.

Breathe out the dark, breathe in the Light and the Love, and feel the Power in the pause, in the stillness, at the end of each long, long outbreath......feel the Spring Equinox in your body, and sing aloud to its glory.

2008

And now, nearly sixty two years old, I look back with such pleasure to that August day in 2004 standing with John at the huge floor-ceiling window of a hotel room looking down at that same railway station, while he massaged my shoulders and I felt his desire and mine, after twelve and a half years of celibacy due to both working relentlessly on myself and my fear of men and my sexuality, plus beliefs of being unwanted ... It was as if that old memory was being healed, and old beliefs and pains being broken through. This man was here, when he said he would be, and he had means. And we were looking down at the past together. He will always be of the most enormous importance to me, and just two weeks ago he showed me his city, New York City, with great pride and enjoyment. We had not seen each other for some 18 months, but the bond —as he said- will always remain. With me he went up the Empire State building for the first time and looked down on his home town.....!

And so, in 1966, began my marriage to Miro, for we were soon married, at my mother's insistence. She said I could divorce him soon, but I must get married. He had already struck me, to my total shock, but I believed I loved him no matter what. 'It must have been my fault.' Anyway I was stuck with my choice, there seemed no way out, so I chose to ignore it, told no one and went ahead with the wedding, which was a sad registry office affair of course. I believed my love could 'conquer all'...!!!! Oh poor foolish girl. We loved and struggled on.

I bought him a book. Inside I wrote 'Thankyou for letting me love you'. I remember feeling I couldn't add 'thankyou for loving me'. I didn't dare.

I loved cooking for him. I had always cooked. Mum taught me how to make white sauce...a roux is the basis for so much. See the recipe. I used to make chicken in cream and wine sauce for dinner parties at home, and now I cooked it for Miro.

After I finished my degree – and mum and dad offered to take Dan to Jersey for 6 months so I could do this, a truly brave action - I flew out to Yugoslavia, taking a year-old Daniel and my hopeful, foolish, excited and oversensitive self into the remote mountains inland from Zadar. To Knin. The bitter Hotbed of Serbian nationalism. A wild and robust land darkened and heavy with past and future atrocities. A brutal land. Searing heat in summer and way below zero in winter. A million miles from the Jersey Methodist church...

THE ART OF THE ROUX

My mum, Freda Hedley, nee Connelly, taught me to make white sauce or bechamel, and it is I think a basic of cooking to master and ring the changes on.

Melt a big knob of good yellow salted butter in a non stick pan, until it sizzles, then stir in briskly over a high heat enough flour (white, Self raising or plain are both fine) to absorb all the butter – cook a moment, stirring, but don't burn. This is the roux. Then gradually add milk, stirring strongly, still on high heat – to make this sauce well needs fire!!!...no pussy footing around. Keep adding until the sauce is smooth and the consistency you want. Then lower heat right down and simmer very gently for a minute or two. Season...I like not just salt and WHITE pepper but dried mustard, cayenne too.

That is the basic. You can play with that. ...

Add white wine and stock instead of some of the milk for a wine and cream sauce to go with chicken,
add chopped parsley for parsley sauce to go with fish or broad beans or gammon.,
add grated hard cheese for cheese sauce for pasta, or vegetables.
Add sliced fried mushrooms, or avocado, or even tomatoes and some tomato puree, to go with anything
add chopped hard boiled egg to go with fish (my mum's invalid food which I remember so fondly)

To make cream soups add stock instead of some of the milk, plus pureed or chopped vegetables– make it thinner of course by using more liquid.. and blend if you want to, and swirl cream on the top , and/or croutons and chopped parsley... etc ...etc...etc...
some unusual cream soups are : lettuce, young nettles (the most nutritious thing in the world in spring...try it, you need a whole carrier bag stuffed with nettle tips) , watercress, broad bean growing tips, celery leaf
and it's the same idea, to make **thick stews and curries**, melt butter and oil, sauté onions and garlic, and stir in flour till absorbed, then liquid of choice...stock, red wine, marsala, sherry...for curry stir curry paste into onions,(you don't need to add flour if you don't want to)
if you want to thicken with a roux AFTERwards, just mix soft butter and flour till blended, then work in small lumps of this as you stir on a medium heat, till it is all thickened to the consistency you want....this is called **beurre manie** because French chefs do it with their hands

the thing is....PLAY!!!!!!

Miro had felt overwhelmed by everything and gone on ahead. I remember sitting outside in the sun on the grass looking at the view at Alexandra Palace during finals, talking with Dick, my friend. He asked me courageously why I had let myself go so much since I got married.

I realised this was true. I was no longer taking care of myself. But I was powerless to do so, and I didn't begin to really do it until the end of my marriage. I disappeared. I was submerged in the caretaking of my sons and husband, and later in businesses, in a maelstrom of emotion. **I had put my self into another prison**, *out of fear at the sensuous and passionate Sandra only unleashed once let out of her other childhood prisons.* **Deceptively safe places - prisons.**

April 1 to April 19 To the New World

Next day in the morning, despite the fact that we are due to catch the train at midday, I rush off to town, 'I HAVE to have some PALE clothes'.   Someone has recently said to me 'why do you wear so much black and dark red?' I couldn't at the time, ever since Dan died actually, think of any other colour I could wear!!!!! (it seems natural now I think about it). So I walk into a shop and walk out wearing stone coloured trousers and sweater and a pinky gold shirt. I guess I have to reflect the new lightness I am feeling.

Rachel's Angels…… (We will all always remember them). She appears unexpectedly with huge smiles at the railway station and bestows upon each of the ten of us, with great ceremony, an 'angel' each. She'd picked an angel card for each of us to represent the quality we offer and written its name in thick gold pen on angel shaped lilac card. Mine is 'Inspiration'. Philippa unearths a pack of safety pins (classic Philippa!) and we all wear our angels for the whole journey!!! We fly American Airlines, so we enter America as we board the plane. We are bemused, amazed. The flight is party party party all the way, the atmosphere aboard is incredible. We are all over the place, and other people join in the fun. Chloe (4) has found a friend and they are running up and down the plane. Laughing stewards are literally throwing us Toblerones and little bottles of sparkling wine and gin and tonic. Are all long haul flights like this???

I am enthralled, stunned, by what must be Greenland(?) below us, the endless arctic wastes, the pack ice and floes. All glittering in the sun. Ice scoured rock juts cruelly from the blinding white. I marvel at where life has brought me.

Boston airport is in the spell too. The security men are open, warm, full of bounce, throwing compliments. I am quite dazed with the unexpectedness of the welcome, at this meeting with the American warmth. And so at baggage claim, I stand there and announce, to much laughter 'I'm going to be living here one day'. And so I will.

So sad now America has taken the path of fear and that wondrous warmth and welcome and ebullience is gone from its borders. Contraction and paranoia have taken the place of that extrovert expansiveness, and the warmth feels more shallow now especially in the cities. The US was always so self contained that it needed no one else, and few Americans went abroad (only 7% have passports?? Forgotten the figure), but now they are isolated in their fear, resorting to attacking. But, having said this, I feel a new expectancy of change there this time, as elections approach and Barack Obama gains more and more support.

But this is 1998 and dear Nancy is there to meet us all with two cars. What a feat. Soon we are drawing into a fabulous clapboard beach house on Cape Cod. This is 'Jay's house'- a friend of Nancy's has lent it to some of us. The others will stay with Nancy. Two cars and two houses for the ten of us. Philippa and Louise and I walk through and when we step out onto the deck there is the white empty beach and the ocean, right there. Wooden steps lead down onto the powdery sand. Next morning, we fully realise the peace and space of this place. There is no-one in sight on the white-gold beach stretching away forever, fringed by dune grasses and weathered wooden steps. I sink into the space and know I will write no more for a while.

Memories of Cape Cod, a glorious tapestry in my mind's eye….

The dunes on the spit opposite turning turquoise in the sunset. Sleeping on the beach and waking to find a large black Labrador lying right beside me. Making a spiral in the sand with Philippa – dear, clear, direct, the best of friends and a Zen student with the same teacher as me -and walking it. The Cape Cod houses. Provincetown. The Café Heaven. Marconi monument – so special after being so often at the one on the Lizard in Cornwall- I've got to the other side! First Encounter beach, where Nancy's parents had their house.

Driving into Boston – a faint red haze on the maples – 'the promise of red'. Finding the ONLY space in the multi-storey. My first Skyscrapers! The tallest one soaring bluely out of the square in front of the library. We sat and gazed up. Then gazed at the beautiful faces of the statues on the library steps. Quincy market – food stalls from around the world. Getting SUCH a haircut on Newbury Street. The gold dome on the civic centre. The extraordinary sunset from the car park when we left.

And oh the coffee!! And the huge everything…cookers, teaspoons, fridges, traffic cones, sandwiches. And everywhere the warmth.

Walking Peter the dog by myself , all day, along the beach – I loved how he came to me when I called. Cuddled up in a big bed in blankets with little Chloe watching some amazing film about the earth, her talking non stop then suddenly mid word fast asleep. I deliberately passed on several events because I needed a quiet week before what I knew would be very intense experience….and I just loved being in that beach house!!!

Memories of Colorado….the experience here shot up the scale of intensity. It was in the Colorado Rockies that America showed me that **anything is possible**. My concept of what my life could contain expanded exponentially. This was a pivotal time, a kind of molecular change or vibrational shift throughout my body about who I was.

We stood on the pass into the great alpine valleys of the Rockies, and the unspeakable vastness and the sorrow of all the ancient conflicts here, hit me like an earthquake and sent tremors coursing through me. Tears gushed, and we stood in a close circle hugging each other, shaking, and toning. Unearthly sound hung above us – it was hard to believe we had made it as it seemed quite separate from us.

I shook uncontrollably until we reached Crestone.

I know now that shaking is often the way the body changes. It can happen at times when life will never be the same again. I remember many times when this has happened to me. Even now, I go to the States for that expansion that I first experienced on that pass. A pass into a new land.

Crestone is a tiny community surrounded in shimmering flat khaki and ochre desert in a Secret Valley 7000' up in the Rockies. Like the Secrets of Life it is an Open Secret but relatively unsought. Look at even the smallest relief map of the USA and there it is, clearly visible in the southern Colorado Rockies, the San Luis valley, vast and empty. 100 miles long N-S, up to 60 miles wide, drained by the mighty Rio Grande, walled by 14,000 ft mountains. It is an ancient rift valley, 30000 ft deep, in-filled with layers of sediment and aquifers.

It is a Sacred Valley, the Bloodless Valley of the Native Americans, who have never fought or hunted here. It is the place of Vision Quest and Ceremony for several tribes, and spoken of with awe. It is utterly sublime and untouched as yet. Eagles still soar and bears, lynx and mountain lions roam the wilderness, sometimes coming down to the village....

Something of its energy and clarity protects it; a very high pure energy, Crown Chakra energy, and it seems that it's relentless and insistent honesty reveals all too much to those who come here, and less honest visitors flee to murkier and more comfortable lands (or go quite mad...).

I said to Philippa some way through that immensely powerful ten days 'I am astonished at our capacity for momentousness'. There was somehow too much to ever write down afterwards and I have only the briefest summary of what we did. I am distraught to realise that I cannot do this time justice in words. One of the most exciting times of my life till then and not a moment to write. So the details got rather lost, and I realise now how valuable all my journals are.

High points that spring to mind ....

The atmosphere of the Sacred Valley and of Crestone's unique spiritual community, in which dozens of different spiritual centres co-exist, in mutual respect. The waterfall in the sacred cave with Shaman Naomi, with the Wolf rock silhouetted above. The Mexican restaurant in Alamosa and the gorgeous Desert Sage restaurant. The circle of maybe 100 people out in the desert meditating and chanting for Easter Sunday. How I didn't have a coat or hat and they were given me, plus a white flower to wear.

Lying in the steaming hot water of the natural hotsprings, snow all around, and later the flakes settling softly on us as we lay, gazing up at the mountains. Those majestic

TONING

Stand up tall, opening the chest and throat, and breathe in deeply and simply open the mouth and let a sound flow out with the breath, slowly, any sound, any pitch. Aaaaah, ooohhhh, eehhhh, aaayyyeee, any sound....let it out, at different pitches and different volumes, just let it out freely, sending the sound to the sky or the rocks, wherever. Try it alone or stand together in a circle. And the harmonies will begin by themselves. Try it in caves, dolmens, cathedrals, beaches or on top of hills....it is heavenly...as you lose inhibition you will find the experience more and more moving, and it will free up communication and speech in your life

VISION QUEST

Native American tribes have long undergone this ceremonial test. Alone in the desert, the participant dives deeply into himself, into the stillness and silence, to connect with Great Spirit. Visions come, new perceptions and understandings well up, signs are seen. The weather, happenings and animals that visit are seen as messages

CHAKRAS

Chakras are the centres where vital life force or 'chi' enters the human body from the universal subtle energy field that underlies everything, to sustain the individual's energy field. The power source is so strong it needs to be transformed down to a usable level, and the chakras do this.

The state of our energy field and the efficiency of each chakra determines how we feel. Each chakra – seven basic ones are ranged down the body- transmits and transforms certain vibrations of energy. The planetary 'body' is thought to also possess chakras.

and solemn mountains, the Sangre de Christo (Blood of Christ), flaring red in the sunset on my birthday. The Zen Mountain Centre's Lindisfarne Dome Chapel, lying there in that unearthly peace. Toning there felt so light and full of spirit. The richness and colour of the Earthship and Temple at the Hindu Ashram. Delectable Taos. The pink curvy adobe buildings of Santa Fe. The blizzard on the long long road back. Buying my Turquoise Eagle pendant. Walking up the trail in the snow (signs telling you what to do if a bear appears – sing!!!) and driving the big car. My fabulous fabulous birthday party- chocolate dipped strawberries, dancing, and beautiful presents.

I was transported, I underwent some kind of vibrational shift, and my life expanded beyond all recognition, in that sacred valley in spring….. I saw just how good life can get. I sensed the 'field of infinite possibilities'.

Philippa gave me Thich Nhat Hanh's little book 'The Long Road Turns to Joy'. He is a Zen Master, Peace activist and Nobel Peace Prize nominee, and he says

> I have arrived
> I am home
> In the here
> In the now
> I am solid
> I am free
> In the Ultimate
> I dwell

That is how I feel, and that is a good place to explore from.

When I met Swithin in autumn 2007, he took me to Thich Nhat Hanh's retreat centre in the Dordogne: Plum Village. The Pure Land. The sublime beginning of something very deeply special.

When we return from The States I know very surely I have to return to Crestone.

A few days later, Glenn says 'do you really want to go back? Because if you do, Vince and Mary say that Joan is looking for a lodger. It's a fabulous house. AND, they say that maybe they could swap cars with you because they are coming to the UK this summer AND you could use their computer too. You could go for three months – that's the maximum you are allowed to stay as a visitor'. So there doesn't seem to be much doubt about what I am meant to do….who am I to argue.

And Beltane is upon us, festival of creativity and growth. It is also the Festival of sexuality but my life in that direction is a self sufficient one sadly. But the energies are there, all channelled excitedly into these new possibilities.

Brimming with them, I dropped into a local travel agency to see about fares. I was horrified. 'Well, that is summer' said the young man. '*But, if you spend another £200 you could go around the world.*' '*I'll do that then*' I said.

He consulted his screen: 'Singapore, Bali, Australia, New Zealand, Los Angeles?...'. 'sounds good to me?' I replied, and felt a bemused smile form itself on my face. 'plus….plus the South Pacific and Hawaii I think……?'

I know this plan is going to be very unpopular at the Convergence Centre, (an Arts and Therapy Centre in Exeter that I set up and run, but I feel a Knowing about it, that it is right and for everybody's Highest Good. I have been 'mummy' there for 4 years and it is time for the centre to have a go at growing up. If it is truly the right thing for me, it is right for everyone. It will all fall into place I know. And indeed it does, though not without some tears and harsh words.

I have recently had the alarming thought that if the centre is not making real money now, it can't. It is full and thriving. Every room over 5 floors of the two seven story Regency properties I manage is occupied. Every evening/weekend the attic rooms are used for groups and workshops. Yet I barely clear £400 a month, and I am working full time. I survive well on it, living so cheaply in a shared house, but that is not the point.

Also, stirring in me is a deep barely acknowledged feeling that I do not want to work in the city any more. The hills have been calling for so long, and I am adoring living among them, lifting my eyes to their peaks each day, watching the smoke curl from cottage chimneys in dusk. I wish I could move the Centre out to them. I really do not know what is going to happen, just that it is right for me to go on this trip around the world while I can – while I am well, while I have no place of my own to pay mortgage or rent on, and while there is the little bit of money from my flat sale- and spend time in the transformational atmosphere of Crestone in the mountains and the big big energies of America.

Information and suggestions about my trip flood in. A Ghandian Ashram in Bali, a friend of a friend in Sydney, my friend in San Francisco, someone called Joan Ocean in Hawaii. But in between my continuing trips(!) all my energy goes to preparing the Centre to leave. Wonderful Dawn says she would love the chance to run it for four months. We work together to make the handover as smooth as possible. It is all coming together.

And meanwhile the pilgrimages continue.

Miro Daniel and I

Chapter 3
To the Scillies...... The Power of Focus

7 June St Michael's Mount

I sit in my car looking across at St Michael's Mount. I am on my way to the magical Scillies, waiting for Philippa to join me next day. A seagull struts on the bonnet and pecks at the windscreen wipers, eyeing my fish and chips with first one eye and then the other.

'I'm going to fly off too' I tell the seagull. I watch the racing clouds. 'I'm going round the world' I add. 'This year I'm living as if I only have this year to live.'

I eat another squidgy fingersful of fish in batter. I am peering between some half a dozen hopeful gulls now ranged on my bonnet. **'That's the book' I announce 'A Diary of a Year Lived As If It's The Only One I've Got. Following the signs I'm given and my intuition'**

There is a huge certainty and energy flowing through me. I laugh at myself, used to my fondness for dramatics, but trust it nevertheless, and, picking up my notebook, I go and sit atop the rocks out of the wind with my thermos and a packet of chocolate hobnobs. I sip, dip and scribble.

Then I find myself slowly walking the emerging causeway, and it is suddenly important to cross. The crisscrossing wavelets still look deep and I stand still patiently, speaking to the sea and the stones and myself as I do. Then the waters are parting at my feet and the path is clear and shining ahead. As I walk slowly, savouring the sensation, even the deepest part is revealed and I cross over with strong images of the children of Israel and the Promised Land.

It is as if I am being shown that for my idea the paths would open even as I follow in faith. And that I would be the first to tread that particular path.

Voices. Two sailing people with lovely faces. 'We've been watching you. It was like the Children of Israel'. 'I know' I say in delight, and then recall my conversations with myself out there. But they seem unconcerned and speak of how happily marooned they were in their catamaran, and how well the fishermen were looking after them. They too are bound for the Scillies. There is something quite otherworldly about the encounter.

Later in my hotel room overlooking the Mount (I always go for rooms with views) I watch a television programme, idly at first, then gripped. It is Wycliffe, and is the story of a man who was naturally full of joy, who made a tormented man so jealous he let him fall to his death while they climbed the Cornish cliffs. It brings to mind my troubled marriage, how he found my joy so intolerable, and - not entirely unconsciously - tried so hard to destroy it….. and I shivered. And said a prayer of gratitude for having escaped despite severe odds.

1968 Yugoslavia

I wrote an article about my year living in Yugoslavia, so I have copied some extracts about it here.

'In the mountains hemming the Dalmatian coast, a region of raw and savage beauty, the ancient traditions have ruled for centuries, a heady mix of influences from the Turkish, French, Austrian and Italian invaders of the past. This is part of the tormented 'shatter belt' of Europe, the land of the South Slavs,(Yug = south) a wild and angry land, and the stones and the faces, the hearts and minds, store painfully the agonies of the past, from a thousand years ago to the unspeakable atrocities of the Second World War. There is a small dirty railway town called Knin, near the borders of Croatia, Serbia and Bosnia, which has long been the Hotbed of Serbian nationalism.

I came to this town, in the late sixties, as a young woman with a baby, and lived as a part of a Yugoslav family for a year. I also visited for long periods many times later, and I sensed the evil, the darkness, which ruled the town. I did not then understand, but the atmosphere was evident.

Over these dark undertones was a timeless, warm and passionate way of life. Habits of close extended family life, strenuous work in extreme conditions, fierce loyalties, colourful ceremony and extravagant celebration form a bond so strong it has resisted a thousand years of invaders. But cars and television were doing what the invaders failed to do. In my earnest enthusiasm, I felt privileged to observe the last days of a rich traditional society about to die from contact with American consumerism, and it was one of my life's great experiences.

I learned to love Yugoslavia passionately. I would sit on the balcony and watch it go noisily by under its great hot sun. The dust, the donkeys, wooden carts, the leathery skinned peasants, the barefoot brown children leaping, the colourful gypsies, the chickens everywhere – chickens on railway stations and in streets and tied to gas stoves in kitchens...

I remember taking the train in deep winter somewhere remote, the great steam train roaring in over the white spaces, true Dr Zhivago style; I struggled to climb up from the snowy ground...no platform... the wooden seats, the noise, the assorted caged livestock amid the groups of people with their picnics of bread, cheese, whole salamis and a knife, and bottles of rough wine... the interest in us...oh so much smiling I had to do.

I walked miles pushing the pushchair over the rough stony paths through rocky gorges of sharp white limestone where cold green water rushed between towering crags under a bronze sky, and along jungly river valleys with red soil and tall cornfields, and often I struggled up to the castle on its great crag to look over the dry red and ochre polje. I walked with gypsies from time to time, and was once given tea by their fire. Such horror when I spoke of it to the family. What a strange thing for those gypsies, the beautiful young English girl with her baby in an English pushchair wandering the wild places....

I savoured the raucous family life, loved that there were so many arms and laps and eyes to hold and watch Daniel. I loved sitting round huge tables with wine or liqueurs and the great dishes of food which the women of the house took all morning to make. I loved the hugs and the affectionate nicknames; mine was cetcom, which means broomhandle. I was a Twiggy in those days. I loved my neighbour Jelka, who taught me to make soup, and stews, and gave me walnut brandy (once at 9am!!) that she had made on her balcony in the sun, just walnuts in a bottle of cheap brandy ... I could always go to her. She was my saviour.

I loved the honesty, authenticity. I read Ethel Mannin, who says 'Mental honesty....would always seem ...too starkly naked to be decent...the English character had got over its aversion to physical nakedness but it still jibbed at mental nakedness. We were made humbug ridden, part of the cause of our intolerable smugness. We were altogether too sure of our own integrity.' I had rebelled against just this, and here I was in a real world, no humbug here.

One weekend, after a wedding in a remote village, we climbed a loose rocky slope for an hour or two to a stone hut. Goats and mountain sheep grazed outside on the thorny scrub, and chickens ran in and out, scratching the earth floor. In the dark smoky interior were three old widows; one of them was dying, and she had asked to see the bride brought from

47

so far. A brushwood fire smouldered on a stone slab, and on a makeshift bed under a pile of goatshair rugs was a shrivelled figure. She was barely visible, her voice scarcely audible, and yet, amid all this decay and degradation I could feel her dignity and that of her companions. They must have represented the last of a generation living remote even from the village, which itself was hours of walk from the train station. I was struck by a feeling of both peace and vitality in that hut'.

So, enormous learnings and experiences, but always overshadowed by my fear of Miro's always simmering and sometimes exploding violence and by not enough food. I became ill by the end of the year and we went back to Jersey with my parents who came to visit, and who nearly died of shock. And they were already in deep shock after driving the precipitous coast road south...

My husband, I now know, carried in his psyche the wounds of this place, and his body must have remembered being carried as a small child through the mountains by his mother in the war, fleeing unimaginable horrors... he was full of both collective and personal fear. He was paralysed by the responsibility for me and for Daniel, and instead of studying to complete his degree and running his family restaurant, he drank and took out his angry fear on me...... it was bad enough to make any sane girl go home within the month - he hit me on the concrete stairs of the block of flats one day, while I held Daniel. A saner girl would have seen that to leave was the kindest thing to do for him and for herself and their baby. I see now how his madness and violence distracted me from my own madness. Because I must have been mad in some way to tolerate it. And I went on tolerating it. But my incomprehensible choices also brought a great richness into my life for so long, and his too, and I can't regret them. I know he didn't either.

It was a passionate marriage, we adored each other so. Reaching hopelessly really across the chasms of culture, language and history that separated us, connecting mysteriously through some deep place in ourselves. 'Such closeness' my mother observed, after it ended. 'You were such a tight unit. I couldn't come in'. Yet so little tenderness towards me from him, so little caring.

'There is too much love there' said my stony faced father- in- law. But later on he was to tell Miro to 'listen to her because she understands things'. One of my favourite compliments ever. What a strange mixture of wisdom and madness I was, and he was the same... my charismatic, beautiful, man.

2008
Yugoslavia was at war again by the end of my marriage, and yet more unspeakable atrocities were lashing its peoples. I said to Miro 'if you can't

CEVAPCICI

You need for 4, 2lb mixed beef, lamb and pork, 1 onion, few fat cloves garlic, salt & pepper, some chopped parsley and oregano, 1 tsp each of cumin & paprika, good pinch cayenne.

Put it all in a food processor & whiz till bound...shape into little oval meatballs no more than 2" long, and grill for few minutes on each side. Pass though gas flame if you can, it vastly improves them, so it's fabulous on barbecues....

JELKA'S SOUP

I have been grateful all my life for this.

Boil bones of a roast chicken or beef bones from the butcher with one halved unskinned onion (nice to char it in the gas flame first if you can) some carrots and sprigs of parsley and bay leaves. Simmer for ages....at least a couple of hours.

Then strain it, remove the meat from the bones, the carrot and disintegrated onion, chop them and add them to the soup. Stir in several dollops of tomato puree and seasonings.

I like a bit of cayenne too.

Reheat, sprinkle with fresh chopped parsley and there you are...

And you can add some pasta, or rice, or potatoes...

PAPRIKASH

Brown some stewing beef (rolled in plenty of well-seasoned flour) and onions in oil, stir in several tbsp of paprika. Let the oil absorb the flour to make a roux, cook gently for minute or two then add beef stock, plenty of tomato puree, a tin of tomatoes, charred red peppers (use a jar if you need to though I remember how they used to stand charring the peppers on the flames), potatoes in big chunks or small whole ones, and bay leaves. Bring to boil and simmer for at least an hour and a half, then check seasoning and eat it with hot crusty bread to dip in the sauce and lots of napkins.

detach somehow from all of this, it will destroy you'. But he couldn't and became ever more psychotic.

When I read pieces now that I wrote about the early years of my marriage –I always wrote– I feel astonishment and horror not only at what I chose and then allowed, which was a measure of the depth of my desperation to be married, and to live an exciting life, but also at the hidden conviction no one 'decent' would want me. I am dismayed at what I saw then as his and see NOW as also MY obsession and fear of a terrifying degree, and which we called love. Though it WAS love, no doubt of that, but love taken because of fear to the excess and distortion of possessiveness and codependency.

Yet always, too, it was love that brought me through, love for life, for the experiences parading themselves before my wondering eyes.

I reached out and embraced all aspects of experience.

And now I know that Self cannot be damaged by experience, it all contributes to our awakening to consciousness of ourselves.

I have been looked after indeed, despite throwing myself with such innocence into the tortured breeding place of some of the world's worst atrocities as a naïve 21 year old woman with a baby... my friend Ros, clever, generous, terrier-like Ros, who has studied the country and lived there albeit in cities, says I did well to survive.

The energy surge and the full moon shining in on my hotel bed keep me awake. I walk out in the windy moonlit grounds, jumping as security lights fly on. I am nervous from my rememberings. The Mount is black against dark blue, and the moon casts molten silver in a wide sweep. I breathe out. Yes. I am alive and I am still adventuring. Yes.

I remember, what we focus on is what we create in the future. And probably my focus on envying the 'wild, colourful and free' created my exotic marriage. And focussing on the suffering created more of it. Fear is always self-fulfilling. Focus, changing it, is a big part of how I changed my life. It is necessary to engage the will to do this- but only after the feelings have been felt and faced.

Which of course is the tricky bit.....to allow ourselves to see ourselves, as reflected in the world around us. It is the fear of ourselves. The greatest fear. The key to being able to face this one is to know we aren't meant to be and don't have to be perfect, we are who we are, that that is fine, it is all a great journey, every stage of it is as important as the end of it. We can love ourselves as we are, no matter what we've done, and just do the best we can. Self compassion enables authenticity.

Perhaps for me to live fully has been the great thing, and now, to do that consciously.

I slide back into the sleeping hotel and into the warm bed, and lie in the moonlight, watching......

8 June   Bryher in the Scillies

The symbolism still flows next morning as I eat breakfast to the strains of 'Sail Away, Sail Away' under a ship's figurehead of a woman in a turquoise (my current colour - representing speaking my truth) dress with a rose (a recurrent symbol of truth for me) at her breast. Feeling very on course and pleased I nobly eat fish instead of my usual full works. And go to meet Philippa.

Am extremely glad of my nobility at breakfast later when the Scillonian is pushing robustly into huge Atlantic swells in a howling gale and sheets of rain. The turquoise bow wave is clean cut and immense. Saturated but ecstatic I gaze down into it, I could fly dive fly again. The bliss of being.

Landing on Bryher on Anneka Rice's jetty, dripping up the beach carrying our bags. Then another kind of bliss, in the warm and friendly Fraggle Rock Cafe on Bryher. The owner takes one look at us and says 'Hot coffee? Hot soup? Hot whisky...?' Exhilaration. Smiles. Pulling on dry clothes. A big soppy dog warming my feet.

It actually stopped raining for us to put up our tents.

In the corner of my borrowed tent is a jar of honeysuckle. And a feather, a heart shaped stone, a twist of driftwood. And my Power Deck Cards, Angel Cards, and Animal Medicine Cards in red silk squares all on a shawl my son gave me. Incense burns and outside in the cold the full moon flies out of the clouds and seems suddenly lonely in the dark.

I heat up water for hot chocolate and the indispensible hot water bottle. We sit outside for a little while huddled in blankets watching the moon in silence. The Bishop Rock Lighthouse flashes its light every 10 seconds out in the maelstrom of ocean and rock.

9 June

Sun! A sparrow is sitting on my toe, warm under the rug - (toe not sparrow) advancing every now and again up my leg towards the plate of nutmeggy scone and Hartley's (!) jam from the bakery beside the beach. Up the hills to north and south of the saddle the camp site straddles are seas of purple foxgloves, to the east the glittering calm of the Tresco Lagoon, to the west the roar of the Atlantic.

Gathering backpacks we rather reluctantly head from the shelter of the tents up onto Shipman Head. But once we find ourselves up there looking down over the wild vistas of crashing seas and being-like rocks, roaring wind and sun lighting it all with metallic shifting slivers of silvers and golds, we are transported.

And then climbing up and down and up again and we are on this high and extraordinary hill. Flat topped, steep sided with 3 sides plunging to the tumult below: it is a natural altar or offering place, it feels a Sacred Place. On the top flat slabs of shiny and glittering pale granite. A central pool of still clear water reflecting the clouds. Beside it a teardrop shape of very lush grass.

Philippa is deep in meditation part way down amid the tangled rocks and spray. I stretch out flat on my back on the grass and feel myself an offering. Surrendered. The bliss of will aligned with the Divine - a sense of glory all around. Honouring in gratitude and humility the numinous, the ineffable. I stand arms outstretched and turn slowly to each of the four directions. I bow to each, speak whatever words come to me, of praise and thanks and surrender

We come home to the camp, running with the wind and laughing. We make supper and then we go to the pub. Hell Bay Hotel...!!

As we drink our pints it comes onto rain torrents of it and we worry about getting wet. No joke when in a flimsy tent….on a site with virtually no facilities. But….aaaah….we are saved from our foolishness….Some people we are talking to lend us wonderful yellow cycling capes. In the morning Philippa (who is fit!) ran down to the jetty with them to return them to their owners. There is so often this sense of always being protected even when we make mistakes.

I look up the special place. It is, interestingly, called Badplace Hill.... was it a sacrifical place, or was it a very powerful spot named to keep it protected? I would love to know. It has a wonderful feeling. It is off to the west of the major ley line that runs from the Hebrides to the Scillies (Tresco and the Old Man of Gugh on St Agnes) and thence to Spain. Who knows....another mystery.

I am sitting on the beach, bare-legged but in a jumper, with pen and notebook, flask of tea, and a picnic of hard boiled egg and salt, some cheese, a fresh roll from the bakery, and an apple. Grasses are stirring behind me in a silky breeze, glittery sand sparkles on my legs and feet. I am gazing out at bare abandoned Samson Island, and remembering how it was once a living community and how everyone was forced to leave…I wish I knew more. I feel the echoes of past suffering. I drop into sadness, theirs and mine, waves of melancholy and longing passing though my spirit and body, causing me to droop and my cheese to lose its taste. I am remembering my despair, still so near the surface.. The light of the fresh day dims.

(Curiously the computer dims as I type this in Andalucia - from that very notebook- the battery is low! I must turn on the generator! I am often unable to do that, the Romanians from the building site nearby usually do it for me...!!)

My eyes close. But then I find myself in an unsought meditation and into the black soft void come the words Paradox and Sacred Witness. I straighten my back and with my out-breath wells up a wordless knowing of the grander picture beyond our understanding….

…..shimmering through the fabric of our world
in the weave of time and places
the Power resting in the spaces…

FOCUS

If we focus on the beauty of everything our worlds change to reflect that Beauty

This is the **Beauty Way** of the Native Americans. And an aspect of ancient wisdoms and new age thinking alike, that
What we Focus on Expands.

This does not mean denying the negative but simply not choosing to dwell on it or fill our minds with it

Just as we choose what food to put into our bodies we can choose what thoughts and images to put into our minds.

It's a kind of mental hygiene and involves at first an effort of will.

Those thoughts and the feelings they induce are what create our lives.....we need to notice what thoughts and feelings serve us well...and which don't and can be let go of

SACRED SPACE

Everything is sacred
everywhere everyone and everywhen
we can honour this
and remind ourselves of it by creating Sacred Space
a personal Altar to the Divine
in any place we find ourselves living working or playing
and taking care of our living space
keeping it clear, beautiful and loved in our own way
And we must take care not to judge....it all has its place
So creating sacred space and beauty in our world
without judging how others do things
seems to be the way that works.....

DIVINATION CARDS

Can be fun, comforting, helpful, directional, reassuring, thought provoking, uncannily accurate, educational, exciting, revelatory, and also terrifying and very confrontational....!

They are especially great as you start to change your life.

You can pick a card at random casually or with ceremony. You can do whole readings of a whole selection of cards. You can do it yourself as a daily routine or get a professional to do a reading for you. There are loads of kinds, from high powered stuff like the tarot to tiny angel cards. Some are very beautiful. Some are text only.

Ask them a specific question, or ask for what quality you need right now, or what a given situation will bring you, or what the angels want to give you....

When you acquire a pack, wrap them in silky stuff, keep them in a special place, and bless them.

Be sure to be the first person to choose a card from them.

You will enjoy offering the positive only cards for people to pick a gift card from you.

Write down readings and special cards picked, and look back in times to come....

I think cards show us what is deep down in our souls, in our 'Higher self'.

They help us contact that part of ourselves for guidance.

How we can live as Sacred Witness suspended in created reality, in duality, how each quality of creation is expanded from its singularity into its whole spectrum, and how we can hold the Paradoxes that flow as creation happens. Creation blossoming forth in Divine Exuberance from Zero. To One, to Two, to the multitude. The nearer we come to Truth or to the One, the more Paradoxes we encounter and hold.

To surrender and to never give up. To expect nothing and everything. To be self-centred and also selfless. To be totally impressed and totally unimpressed. To feel the compassionate and the stern face at the same time. To relax in total alertness. To allow everything and resist nothing but be in moment by moment watchfulness of thought and feeling. To be proud and humble. Gentle and fierce….

Living with the Sacred Witness within us, endlessly allowing and forgiving, endlessly disciplining and endlessly surrendering…. moment upon moment working to open to the Divine in us. Bringing healing Distance through Sacred Connection. Connected, we are free in the Beauty and the Love. Disconnected we drown in duality, in the Terror of Creation, in Fear.

I come to, feel myself held in the shimmering afternoon, suspended in that Glittering and Glowing Sea of Energy that underpins our world, and shines out through the spaces….and I breathe out in gratitude

and pick up my cheese again

to Taste it.

PERSONAL RITUAL

is whatever comes, feels right
it does not have to be slick or perfect or orchestrated, just
sincere
the intent to honour the Source of All is all
to honour the moment
it is conscious reverent and loving
it may be planned or spontaneous
simple or elaborate
at home before your personal Altar to the Sacred
or anywhere at all
out in wilderness or a sudden moment of joy on a city
street
Ritual Form can derive from such varied traditions as
Celtic, Native American, Christian, Buddhist, New Age
Goddess Worship.....
I like to create my own, drawing from the richness of all and
from my imagination and intuition
it's like cooking! recipes start you off and then you can be
creative....
out in nature we can find special stones, feathers, shells or
leaves which can hold the energy of that moment for us and
be placed on our Altar or around the house or car
life becomes Sacred Ritual
Ritual is a prayer and communion, and wherever we are we
can feel the connection to the Divine
and honour it within ourselves,
perhaps pausing ,and letting words form a tribute to the
pleasure of living with the
flow of Spirit

Outside the Old Inn

With Ben as a baby

Ben now 4, Dan 11

Chapter 4
Chartres for Summer Solstice……
The Power of Dreams

June

The wonders of Chartres Cathedral and its labyrinth are popping up everywhere in my reading and conversations and I begin to dream of going there. It would be a most important pilgrimage. I read that at Solstice the sunlight shone in a rapier-like ray through a purpose built slit high in the wall, to hit a tenon, or brass nail head, in the floor at the true midday, and I know it is important to witness this and to walk the labyrinth before I set off around the world.....

So I dream up a trip there for Solstice, and Rachel, Louise and Sarah come with me. Rachel books fabulous B&Bs and I book my old but willing blue Polo onto the ferry, going via my childhood home of Jersey just for the fun of it.

June 21

Such memories. Sitting by a lake in the night-time singing and counting shooting stars, swinging high on a swing in a rose filled garden, French cafes, hearing French spoken all around, first sight of Chartres cathedral high above the roofs of the town, entering the immense dim numinous blue space, thick with holiness.

Watching the point of light travel across the floor to the tenon and then the collective sigh from the waiting crowd as it strikes the tenon and the brass bursts into life as the precise peak of the sun's annual journey is reached. As it has every solstice since the cathedral was built. The labyrinth is covered by chairs to our dismay, then suddenly, when we leave the cathedral, we see it is cleared, and crowds of people are walking it.....we rush to join the queue.

THREE HOURS later, after pacing so slowly we were barely moving at all, we reached the centre and each knelt in one petal of the rose. This was truly a meditation, a journey to stillness through 'the dirt on the road', watching it all as it surfaced and letting it be. A purification. It was a pilgrimage through and to self.

Afterwards.... exhausted, enthralled, satisfied and proud, we sink down laughing into a café beside the cathedral and order beers....and talk about making dreams come true....

Yes I always Dreamed, but oh how far have I come now from the days of the first Dreams....

1975 The First Dream - a Restaurant on a Moor

It was back in 1975 that I began consciously dreaming up futures. (can't in all honesty say 'we'......in fact after the divorce at the one amicable lunch we shared Miro said 'what I miss is making the dreams come true' 'can't you dream your own?' I said, 'no' he said sadly.)

Ben had been born by then, a planned and celebrated and gloriously easy and speedy birth. I glowed with health and wellbeing. We bought a house. Miro had progressed from washing up in a Waterloo pub to being manager of the Yvonne Arnaud Theatre Restaurant in Guildford. He was good at his job.

But things began to deteriorate; Miro was not so well as I was, he was being taunted at work and soon was cruelly taking it out on me, with physical and verbal abuse. I asked my

58

LABYRINTHS

Are a beautiful and very ancient transformational tool for those on the spiritual path, which for me is the search for the way out of unnecessary suffering and into peace and bliss.
They are convoluted spiral paths which represent a journey or ceremonial pathway to our own centre and back again out into the world,
On the journey in, one cleanses the dirt from the road.
On the journey out, one is born anew to consciously dwell in a human body,
made holy by having received a taste of the Infinite, of the Sacred, at the Centre.
In ancient days, they replaced long pilgrimages for those unable to make them. People believed that if you walked the labyrinth with the full dedication of a pilgrim, you would be transformed, the old you would be grounded at the threshold stone, a purified you emerging, ready to tackle new directions in your life's journey...

SUMMER SOLSTICE

The year is in it's fullness: it is the juicy climax of the natural year when the sun is at its peak. Nature is rampant, ripe, succulent, blazing with colour. The element associated here is fire, and the celebration is of passion and ecstasy. Dance around a fire in a large mature garden, a wild place, on the beach or on the hills. Take off clothes and swim naked in the sea or walk naked in the warm air.
Juices flow, there is a feeling of overspilling, of abandon. Let in it, feel it, feel its dance and its glorious beauty

father if I could come home, I actually told him what was happening. He said no, it would upset the fragile peace he had created at home with my very neurotic mum. 'I've opted for peace at a price' he said sadly to me as we walked down the road. I have never understood how he could leave his daughter in an abusive marriage. He seemed to think I deserved it, that I had made my bed and must lie in it. Maybe he did. Though I see now that he was ultimately right in that I was not ready to be alone. But I wish he'd kept tabs on how I was…. I felt so alone with it all, so unsupported.

I was talking to John about this recently, and he said 'why didn't you ask your mother?' Oh wise man. Well, he was right, I should have done, but Dad was there, he came to see us at that time, Mum rarely did, and she always got so agitated, but I now see that deep deep down I must have been setting myself up for betrayal, so I could say 'you see, men betray me'.

Anyway, back to dreams. I had this strong vision of a restaurant on a moor…… Miro said my cooking was 'better than the chefs'. The bank manager looked at us patronisingly and said 'Save'. We thought 'yes, like forever?' I saw a small ad in the Caterer magazine looking for a couple with capital to run a mid-Devon restaurant, so I wrote a good letter and we went to see Ron Yates in North Tawton. He quickly sussed our penniless state but was impressed with us and four months later he rang us out of the blue to offer us the chance to run his restaurant high up on Dartmoor for a % of turnover.

How about that?

So, at the end of my school term – I was teaching (more in the deep end stuff) – we put the cot on the roof rack – Ben was one - and the cat in a basket and went to run The Muzle Patch in Moretonhampstead. It was charming. And it was killing.

One day I was teaching, next day standing in the kitchen wondering what I should do to prepare for lunch. I hesitantly put some eggs to hard boil, because I saw egg mayonnaise on the menu. (Yes it was that bad) Then the doorbell started clanging and in came hordes of tourists. I whizzed about desperately for a few hours and that was the beginning of my catering career: fourteen years of whizzing around desperately. Before long we were getting booked up, even in winter, and offering such exotic delights as Medieval Nights complete with Miro dressed as Henry 8th and whole roast suckling pigs on the bar fire. Symposiums were riotous nights of excessive food and overheated debate; Yugoslav nights were famed for even more excessive food and drink. We were featured a lot in the press.

Ben was used to sitting on the stairs of an evening watching proceedings, and customers were used to stepping around him and his strewn toys. He was uncontainable from a very early age, rolling around at three months, walking at ten. There was no chance of keeping him in bed. The Ladies was our bathroom, full of ducks and boats. We were a bizarre enterprise. Often we sat up all night with our favourite customers, until the milkman

DREAMS

Dreams keep us moving, evolving, developing, learning, loving. They fill us with enthusiasm, which means 'God within'.

They are desires, full of passion and love and energy, coming from a feeling of excitement not from a yearning or sense of lack or dissatisfaction.

We don't HAVE to do anything. Just follow our bliss, in the time honoured but very valid phrase.

If that is environmental or social work, great, but don't do it because you think you should.

Dreams come from deep within and are a driving force and a raison d'etre.

Commitment to a dream brings into being loads of support from the universe.

And then again....some of the best things in my life have been undreamed-of! ...I guess it's the Quality that manifests itself and we can leave the details to the universe.

clanked into the square. I remember doing cartwheels one night outside (in a skirt). I don't think I ever stopped, barely slept.

At about the same time my parents came back to England from Jersey. Dad was, amazingly, baking bread from organically grown wheat for the farmer, who had bought a village bakery. Then they started making Essene bread from a recipe in the Dead Sea Scrolls! Mum was busy transforming the bakery's shop into a wholefood and crafts shop to which people came from miles and miles. It was her great achievement. Soon it was all so successful that the farmer bought a factory instead, Dad hated it, but was nearing retirement and hung on. Mum was offered a shop in a town nearby but bottled out, which was a huge pity.

Dad in the new 'factory'

Master baker Jack Hedley checks the baking temperature

At this stage I knew I had to find out more about Hugh Coates, his background and how he found his way to 'baking with a difference,' and who helps him in his business. He described himself by saying: 'I'm a rare bird to find involved in baking at all as I have no formal bakery training. What training I have is what I have picked up from the master baker I am fortunate enough to have working with me, that is Jack Hedley, who has a wealth of experience and is a charmer to go with it.
 'Having worked alongside him for some

*After four years the bank was so impressed with us they lent us half the money to buy the lease of The Old Inn in Drewsteignton. **Our wonderful customers lent us the rest** –an amazing thing really now I think about it, and off we went, to our own restaurant on a moor, dream fully realised against all the odds. I was captivated by the immaculate kitchen, all the guest rooms, the old barn, stables and cellars, land and views, not to mention the exquisite village atop the hill above Fingle Bridge and the dramatic Teign Gorge ....it was an enormous property and all in spotless order. We proceeded to be the village cabaret for 6 years. It is easy to write that now but we went through serious tragedy as well as farce.*

But nevertheless our time there remains a nostalgically recalled legend in the Drewsteignton community. Lots of laughter and lots of warmth. Miro always had that gift of making people feel special. He remembered their stories and always knew what to say. I barely knew anyone. People still terrified me. I was so self centred in my fears I could not take an interest in others. I thought they weren't interested in me, so I hid. It was really the other way round.

MIRO'S STEAK

A sirloin or fillet steak cooked a million times on the flambé lamp in our restaurants.

Pepper the steaks a little. Melt a little butter and oil in a heavy frying pan, brown the steaks on a high heat, pour in a good splash of brandy for each steak and swirl the pan to let the flame catch it alight and mix with the juices. Add a glass of red wine for two steaks, turn down the heat, and cook until done to your fancy. If it's too hot the sauce will evaporate and separate. If it does add water. At the last minute stir in a good knob of parsley and garlic butter. Let the sauce bubble up and then serve. Its great with sauté potatoes and salad.

STEAK AU POIVRE

Probably my favourite meal.

Coat the steaks well with crushed black peppercorns (use a tea towel and rolling pin or mallet). Brown and flame them with brandy. Lower the heat and add at least half a cup of double cream for two steaks and let it blend with the juices.. Bubble it for a minute, till the steak is done to your liking, if you like it well done you may need to add more cream, and then stir in a nut of butter to enrich, thicken and gloss the sauce.

.......OR YOU CAN

Add chopped onion and sliced mushroom to the oil and butter before adding the steaks, and cook till soft, then cook as for Miro's steak. For the Au Poivre, add wholegrain mustard or horseradish or stilton to the cream...(less pepper of course!) Serve the steak on a crouton of fried bread , top it with pate, and pour the sauce over.

POHOVANI SIR

This is a Yugoslav dish, cooked at home a lot with many variations. It is cheese fried in a spicy coating. For two: first mix the coating, with 3 eggs, salt, black pepper, a tsp each of chopped parsley and oregano, tbsp paprika, a good dash of cayenne, a tbsp of flour, a tbsp of breadcrumbs. Take four slices of hard cheese (our cheddar works well) and place a filling of caramelised onion relish or sliced mushrooms or tomatoes, (or bacon or ham for a non vegetarian dish) between slices, to make two 'sandwiches'. Flour these well, then coat with the egg mixture. Fry in hot shallow oil till golden. Not too long or the cheese melts too much. Try this coating on pork or chicken, lamb or aubergines too. Try mixing lamb and aubergines, or pork and apricots, or chicken and asparagus.

Ben adored it. He was four. 'I'm having a garden for Christmas'. As soon as we arrived all the village children appeared at the door and off he went, scarcely to be seen again. He had a childhood running around the countryside with bikes and tents. No mobile phones in those days...

Soon after we moved there, just before Christmas 1979 as we were very very busy getting ready for two functions happening on one evening (ouch), I answered the phone in mid-flight, and my dad's boss was there and my spinning world was wrenched to a halt ...

'No no. That can't be true, this isn't real, it isn't is it, I am dreaming, no. No. No.....NO'. My father had dropped dead, suddenly, at work, on the eve of retirement. He was 64. My mother had asked his boss to call me. Asked his boss to call me. 'ASKED HIM TO CALL ME'. I said in disbelief, 'she asked HIM to call me to tell me THAT'.

I had to get on a train and travel through the night, to and through London and up to Buckinghamshire. I sat on the empty cold train paralysed, frozen in horror, I bought a brandy but nothing touched the disbelief. Lights flashed past my unseeing gaze, as I sped through the dark. My mother was sitting neatly, drinking tea with my aunt. I came flying in awash with tears to this gentility and stopped in confusion. There never were real tears that I saw. No real grief or mourning. Just the preoccupation with being nice, refined... and the neediness. The raw grief I could have supported with real love and presence, but I could never get through to the real. Only the mask, the pretence. I thought later, this was why I ran away from safety TO the horrors of the world, to get REAL

My father had said six months before 'You'll look after your mother won't you, if anything happens to me.' 'Of course' I said, as I always did to any request from anyone. He said this, knowing he had not taken out any life insurance, they had never saved, he had always refused to buy a home, their home and the car belonged to his boss, and my mother could neither drive nor write a cheque.....So, from then on, my apparently helpless mother was left effectively homeless and almost penniless.....and I was responsible for her. My father died on the eve of retirement, he could not face being at home without work to go to, all day with my mother's anxiety.

My anger at my father, my husband, my elder son, at the males in my life, erupted in Spain with my first lover after my marriage- over twelve years after. It is as if John came into my life to embody all their qualities (it was extraordinary) and let me express this anger. I screamed at him, I opened my mouth and I screamed.... I yelled at him to FUCK OFF again and again. I had never been able to do that safely...I had no model for safe anger. I bellowed my fury and incomprehension, my frustration and my disbelief, my grief. He stood solidly and held me.

My perception was that I have been betrayed by all the men in my life. Over and over again. John (my father's name and their birthdays are within 2 days of each other !!) showed me what it could be like to be loved by a man and a really male man, and then proved to be unavailable. (quite a story there!) The absent male again. My dad had never been there, he hid at work. I was betrayed again and my anger knew no bounds. And one day amidst all this fury a probably poisonous snake was on my worktop beside the tiles I bought John- was this a poisonous situation or was it a symbol of shedding skin and transformation? Maybe both. In a leap from here could I be free of all this? But the place held me, it was so divine. It felt like a gift from all these betraying men and I wanted to love and cherish it and not go until my instinct was clear, which, eventually, it was....

I now know how all my life I have set myself up for these experiences...creating situations which reinforced my belief that men betray me. It was clear to anyone else from the start.....

I did the same thing with my beloved Swithin (his choice of pseudonym), my Magician, in 2007....set myself up. But we will never ever regret what proved to be for us both the most exquisite experience, I later called it 'the time of my life'. We were so joyful, so playful, so harmonious and happy. We laughed until it hurt, we danced and danced, and we were in still silences together, and we were also awestruck at what happening for us. It was a gift. S said much later 'It was all so beautiful, no words can express or challenge what happened'. But I already had the information that told me it could not last, and the end should not have been such a shock... but that is another story, not for this book. I know now it was best ended, and he did that for me....I could not have done it. Thankyou Swithin. He and John, and Woody too, were blessings and steps along the way.

Interestingly, my mother, whom my father said he would never leave because she would be helpless (though he also admitted in his cups to knowing he would never be able to live alone...)

... went on to live very capably albeit in her needy way for another twenty three years. Of course there was a miracle...dad had died at work and there was insurance. Miro saw a flat near us for £11000, which was exactly what the insurance paid out... The ground floor flat in a big old house was coated in nicotine, and she would not go in, but my cousins and I cleaned it out and she finally moved in. Which left the problem of income...

...... and miraculously it was soon discovered by a complete fluke that she was entitled to a Jersey pension too, and so she had sufficient income, which she supplemented by working for the National Trust at Castle Drogo for 50 pence an hour. What a disgrace. But she loved 'being on the door' and pretending she was welcoming people to her own castle. She lived in Flat 2 Monte Rosa, Chagford, (she called it Corners, because it was oddly shaped and she said she just wanted to crawl into a corner) complaining, pleading weakness, manipulating me until I sussed it long long after, for the rest of her life, saving, and managing very well indeed. My father would have been amazed.

I didn't master the bitterness about my mother till two years before she died. But I DID master it and I am proud and pleased that we healed our relationship and came to acceptance, forgiveness and the tremendous love and the gratitude and respect that lay beneath.

The years of crippling overwork in the restaurants passed, a blur of breakfasts, coffees, lunches, teas, dinners, functions, cooking, publicising, cleaning, dishwashing, chambermaiding. Not to mention motherhood! I felt I had to. People said 'She does EVERYTHING'. Mrs Drewe at Castle Drogo (a customer) was mystified by me 'Why don't you go on strike?' she said.

My resentment ate away at my innate joy. Sourness threatened to fill me. Exhaustion failed to stop me driving myself relentlessly. I felt I had no choice. No-one else would do it.... And staff cost......I had such a fear of spending on staff, and absolutely no concept of caring for myself. But I did have a huge fury that no one cared for me.

But those years were not without their joys. And it was all a great achievement – our barn, where every weekend in a rustic and bohemian atmosphere that H&S would never for a minute tolerate now we roasted half a lamb or a pig or a whole sirloin over a vast fire, and fed hordes of people. Kids played in the wilderness of garden, while our German help Sabine's goat grazed......and was brought through the barn if it began to rain! It was wonderful, and is still remembered. What is missed because of over-regulation!

One Christmas Day I cooked for 35 in the restaurant and 60 in the Wine Barn, and had 12 staying and five fires to keep lit...but they were also such amazing times. Speaking of fires... sometimes we had a chimney fire, we lit such big fires... and the firemen in their yellow jackets and helmets would come charging happily though the packed restaurant and put it out, then get their beers at the bar. But once, when I had my first ever week off and was at my aunt's, Dan burned a cushion and put it still smouldering in an outbuilding and there was a major fire. I came home rapidly in shock to charred remains of all the back outbuildings and unspeakable mess.   But fortunately the insurance paid for lovely new loos and storage out there, a big improvement on the previously primitive facilities.

The boys grew, running wild in the countryside with their friends, camping, biking...a trail of cereal bowls marked their passage. I do wish (this is my main regret in life) I had had more time just to be with them, but at least we were there, physically, if busy. Dan loved to help and was great at it. Ben was wiser and kept his distance from the whole riotous world that was Miro's Restaurant. They had a wonderful time altogether, and both said so later. These days children don't get that freedom to roam, explore, make mistakes and learn and grow.

The dark side to all of this was that occasionally, Miro's psychological pain would overwhelm him, he would get very drunk and lash out at me, and at the restaurant...... I was a fool, I cowered, shrank, wept. Many times I took the boys to safety and came back in the morning to clear up. But it wasn't often enough to drive me away. I just kept trying to help, believing love could solve anything. I read the Bible 'not seven times do you forgive, but seventy times seven'.... 'turn the other cheek'.....aaah, what the Bible (the distorted version created by the Christian Emperor Constantine in Istanbul in the third century AD ......and by the Church in the years that followed) has to answer for.

I was a seething mass of resentment that he was so much loved by everyone and I was not. His cruelty was invisible to everyone else. I was later told this is common. And I felt invisible myself, overlooked. To the point where so many people thought he did the cooking. 'What a wonderful chef your husband is!' I could not understand why my hard work, skills, my caring and loving were not recognised, let alone appreciated or rewarded. This rewarding of bad behaviour puzzled me for years.

I now see that life simply reflected what I was doing.....rewarding bad behaviour. I finally understood, and stopped doing it with John in 2006. I found a sermon of Dad's on this theme. It has been fascinating that as I finally finish this book, with my father's sermons retrieved from Spain where I left them, some of them jump out at me with links to my words.

By 1983, after eight years of it all, the boys were growing up and things shifted a little.

It was a time of Breakthroughs and Breakdowns.

Sennacherib comes in many ways… Chronicles 2, Chapter 31 v.20-1, Ch 32, v.1

'Hezekiah wrought that which was good and right and faithful before the Lord his God …he did it with all his heart and he prospered. After these things and this faithfulness, Sennacherib King of Assyria came and thought to win them for himself.'

What a dreadful tragedy it seemed - Sennacherib of Assyria was one of the most vain, cruel men of his time, his sole ambition was self-aggrandizement. To satisfy his boastfulness, his armies swept the Eastern world at that time, burning cities, deporting and bludgeoning men.

Hezekiah.King of Judah, was one of the best men of his day. He began his reign handicapped by his father's follies, follies that had almost brought the Kingdom to ruin.

With his heart and soul he threw himself into the work of reform, and he restored prosperity to his people. His people believed he would be rewarded. Yet the story tells us that as soon as his work was done, the rapacious Sennacherib descended on Jerusalem to try to undo the life's work of a good king.

Here is one of the puzzles in life. It happens so very often.

In this twentieth century the character Sennacherib wears many masks or faces. Sometimes he appears as an unscrupulous syndicate intent on destroying small businesses built with a lifetime of effort. Sometimes as a personal misfortune bringing bitter struggle, worry, poverty. Sometimes as a bereavement, perhaps the loss of a child, to a Godly family.

Sennacherib comes in so many ways.

We can understand him coming to some men and women, they invite him into their lives, no mystery about the collapse of a rotten business or disease raiding those who defy the laws of health, no mystery when despair seizes those who have crossed God and his eternal Law from their lives.

But WHY should those who love God with all their heart be so attacked?

The problem is an old one. Sennacherib seems to get away with so much. What shall we say about it?

Religion is NOT a charm against misfortune. Hezekiah's people thought it was, but they had to learn, as o many of us do, that it is not. 'why should I suffer thus ,' they say. Its true that religion makes for health and peace, but it is not a charm against evil. If virtue paid and evil did not, what worth would it have? Everybody would become virtuous.. religion would become an investment with the promise of high interest. We are a world of free men and women, goodness must be chosen… even Jesus could not escape his Cross.

Religion rallies itself against misfortune. Hezekiah doesn't take the challenge lying down. He cannot fight his enemy in the field but he puts up a fine resistance. He stopped the water supply to his enemy, and he built a wall. He rallied his people. The challenge of evil can bring out the best in us. If Hezekiah goes down he will go down with his flags flying.

Piety rallies itself to God. To rally to oneself is good, to rally to God is better.

Sennacherib drove the King to God. His army was attacked by plague and he was glad to go home. But it doesn't always end like this. Jesus was NOT delivered from his cross. Sennacherib seemed to win on Good Friday, but it was God's day on Easter Day.

As with Jesus, so it will be with us. A disgrace has become our symbol of redemption.

Not always in this life does our Easter Day come. But when evil hits us, we can always say

'Father, into Thy Hands I commit my spirit'.   AMEN

my instructor said to me ' you only have to do the next bit, just deal with that, forget the rest. And if you make supremely helpful and I passed despite making a mistake. I

Learning to drive was the first path out of my hell for me. It took ages and truly felt like Everest but I did it and it was the beginning of reclaiming my self. When I was taking my driving test at the advanced age of 37, I was so terrified and anxious, and my instructor said to me ' you only have to do the next bit, just deal with that, forget the rest. And if you make a mistake, let it go, just do the next bit'. I found that supremely helpful and I passed despite making a mistake. I said to the examiner when he told me 'but I didn't turn off my indicator after that roundabout' and he said 'Do you WANT to pass or not?'

It was JUST in time.

This part coming is hard to write so I will write it quickly and succinctly. Please forgive this. It is not casual, just too painful to dwell on. Soon after that Miro's violence when drunk escalated and finally he kicked Daniel as he came up the stairs to help me, Dan had often tried to protect me from it all. Ben was never witness to it. I think Miro made sure of this, he wanted Ben's allegiance. Next day when I returned from a neighbour's with the boys I said, 'If you don't stop drinking, I am leaving'. _I was serious and he knew it. No mixed messages, no smiles. And he stopped. (It took so long and so much to get me to finally do what I should have done right at the beginning. Say 'I will not accept this' and mean it.)

Yes, he stopped, but he was unable to cope without alcohol and his mind deteriorated fast. It was frightening in a different way because it was not just when he got drunk, it was totally unpredictable. The physical cruelty stopped but the mental cruelty grew.

It came to a head as things often do, around summer solstice, when he sent me and the boys off on holiday and closed the restaurant in busy early summer and collapsed. I don't know what happened really, there were no witnesses. But my mother took him in, and tried to help. She took him into Exeter one day, (how? she never drove) and they had coffee on a roof terrace, only one storey high. He suddenly ran and jumped off the roof and broke his foot badly, which never really healed. He was conscious throughout. It seems he did not want to die, just be unable to do anything. But I don't know. I never will.

My poor mother.

I returned from holiday to Heathrow, to an announcement that I must go to Information, and there were our loyal customers Ros and Jack, who drove us back home, and were under my mother's instructions not to tell me why. When I called her she still could not tell me for many minutes. Torture.

I went to the hospital. He was gone. Quite gone. Utterly weak. Blank. He lay and stared at me. There was no light in his eyes, no fight, manipulation or any of his usual mocking cruelty. Or his humour and charm.

I could not eat. I went down to seven and a half stone. I bought Complan but couldn't swallow that either...... I could not 'swallow' what was happening.

He was transferred to a psychiatric hospital.

I could not contemplate trying to look after him as well as run the restaurants single handedly. In honesty I was petrified. So Miro's brother came and took him back to Yugoslavia, and I set to work, ably aided by Liz and Carrie, two wonderful students who we had arranged to come and help for the summer. Together we ran everything efficiently and harmoniously for the whole summer. Thank God I could drive.

I remember seeing John Gordon, a homeopath/counsellor – I went because my nose wouldn't stop running, had always been so but was much worse. 'You are weeping inside' he said. He listened to me talking about being unwanted all my life then said, 'so you've been fending people off all your life have you'. I said, 'oh, no, not at all, quite the opposite', but in later years I remembered and I wondered....I saw him a lot, and I went to exercise classes.

I read Norman Vincent Peale's 'Positive Thinking' (Much much later my mother said I took that book from her and never returned it. She felt I cornered the positive for myself and left the negative for her. I monopolised the positive in all my family. We polarised. But what was I to do? I felt until very recently that this kept me alone.) I learned from a yoga teacher that confidence is being free of fear. This was a bit of an eye-opener. I had always felt so lacking in confidence, and always felt that all my fear was Miro's fault. I would stupidly tell him how afraid I was, hoping it would make him realise how it was for me, and help him start to care for me. But caring wasn't something he could do, when he was so tortured and depressed. And my confession was a wonderful way of giving away my power to him, he fed off my fear and the power it gave him. I never dreamt anyone could want to hurt others deliberately, I was still so innocent.

So I learned to take responsibility for my fear. And paved the way to finding my power.

Slowly slowly I began to care for myself...... faint glimmerings of a return to self from the deep submergence in children and overwork, in someone else's torment.

Horrifyingly, it seems, looking back, that my tentative breakthroughs were accompanied by Miro's breakdown.

He returned much later in the year, still heavy and pretty broken, but better; I was very fearful, but met it all head on with a short haircut and earrings. I didn't know until much later that he was fearful himself of how he would be received. I had no idea of my own power. He was never the same again, never had the same power or charisma. We soon got a new long lease and successfully sold up the next year. I remember he had hoped I would have already done all that for him, and was disappointed. He always had such a faith in me and my abilities.

My whole sorry story of my overwork came to an end at the end of 1984 with the sale of the restaurant and me having abnormal cervical smears and a hysterectomy. I lay there drugged to the gills with morphine, seeing vivid hallucinations, in agony despite the drugs especially when I was being sick as I endlessly was. I thought I would die. One hallucination was of what I saw as the Wheel of Life. A vast wheel, slowly slowly turning, rimmed with myriads of points of light, each with its dim way into the centre.

My friend Lucinda brought a colossal armful of garden flowers and plonked them down in a big vase on the table across the bed, right in front of my eyes. I felt like those flowers saved me, brought me back somehow. She had (has) a great old vicarage in Drewsteignton with a wonderful garden, and I used to take our scraps over for her chickens and pick flowers for the restaurant in return.

Recently, with my beloved Swithin I revisited Lucinda and Stephen in Drewsteignton , to attend an Inaugural Lunch at The Old Inn which is coming back to life in the care of Charlotte, after so many years of offering little to the community. S and I stood on the stairs in the Old Inn, and he held me while I painfully and silently remembered the happenings there. It was a healing moment. A release of something. Forgiveness for us all and letting go. S was a great instrument in my life and I was in his.

It was wonderful to hear how well Miro and I and our work are remembered, how much my food was loved. And painful to remember how many people had thought for so long that he did all the cooking; I was almost invisible, well I felt I was. I was so terrified of criticism I kept hidden in the kitchen. Oh thank God for my progress from all that, for my independence, relatively, from approval. Miro took all the credit but all the CRITICISM too..... he was not affected by criticism. He was in many ways wiser than me, an egotist who also had a magical quality, a tremendous power. But he could not be open about his pains and fears and take responsibility for them.

My family were silenced by what happened to me. They stood there terrified, transfixed by their hyperactive ever- capable and over-responsible mother stricken down for so long. My mother was not able to bear hospitals so did not visit me. I was deeply resentful of that.

I don't know why it was all so bad, but it was. After a week I began to surface. And as usual began to write, and related a little to the others I found around me. I remember one old lady looking at me and saying respectfully to her husband, they were deaf so I could hear, 'have you seen her eyes, they knock me back' and 'she's a thinker'. I was pleased. I rarely had recognition and I felt recognised. Starved of approval, and still so much trapped in ego, it meant too much to me. But, it was a gift.

The restaurant was just that month sold and I could rest and so my body said 'aha, now lets ground her for half a year...' My womb was ripped out and my life was a disaster. I tried to leave him again but still I couldn't. Ah the weakness. Such weakness.

But I eventually bounced back, as always..

...... and I had already been Dreaming up new futures. This time involving travelling.

Phew. All that pain has just flashed through me in a moment, as I sit in my new life, savouring so much. So happy to be a whole person - not needing a man in my life, or indeed company, to be whole. And the reward is ironically such pleasure in company because there is no neediness!!!

Right now, France, its delectable pleasures all around....endless pleasures, in this divine playground. Wonderful friends, loving support. So much laughter.

We drive home to Devon singing.

.

Our Motorhome in the wilds of Yugoslavia

Chapter 5
Silves, Portugal…… Exploration

July 7   On the Trail of Henry the Navigator

My oldest friend – from my girls' grammar school days. Her mountainside paradise has become, over the last five years, my punctuation point. My still place between worlds. My turning point. I am so grateful for it, have been three times now, …I am almost in tears with the sun soaked flowery heaven of it. I am always in motion, always amid drama and happenings and journeys both inner and outer, she is simply here maybe twenty years, caring for one place.

I am also almost in tears feeling so sad that I did not contact them last year about Daniel- they clearly can't understand why. Like I didn't contact Anna who was so fond of him, or his university. Shame and guilt, mine and his, and it needs feeling and knowing. It needs to be laid out in the sun.

And I do this, around the table in the deep shade of their veranda, I bring out all the feelings. And finally, many tears later, I say 'Someone said to me…. "it's sad, it's really really sad, but it's part of life. It's up to you to make sure it's not all of your life"…..and this makes sense to me. I have to move on and be happy without guilt over where I went wrong, or anger over where he went wrong. I have to accept it all as how it is and was.'

The first time I came here, I arranged it not knowing it would be the very week of moving out of the family home into my first home of my own. Completion (simultaneous with exchange) was due while I was away, so I went nor knowing for certain what was happening. I had packed up before coming away, and booked a van and man for the day I returned. This time, I arranged my holiday not knowing it would be happening a few weeks before I set off around the world. Again, I can pause here and take stock before a major development in my life.

I lie by the pool, which deliciously has no parapet and you can lie in it or by it and the scented valley and mountains stretch below and before you…

I am remembering my Ben's triumph a few days ago. After his brother died he decided to learn how to grow things, and got himself a place at Bicton College of Agriculture, studying Horticulture. He struggled with it all, affected still by the family trauma, but he came out of it with a credit, and was told it would have been a distinction if he had not been so stressed. I remember him walking up though the sea of parents in hats and suits, in his new jacket and trousers, to receive his certificate. I felt overwhelmed with pride and respect.

We will both move on now.

This visit, I am finding myself drawn to the story of Prince Henry the Navigator, who was responsible for the beginning of the European worldwide explorations. I am off around the world myself in three weeks time, so this is pretty understandable. Prince Henry has become a legendary figure who is thought to have invented light and manoeuverable ships called caravels, and he sent scores of them off on ever longer voyages, organising and financing it all himself.

Henry gathered at his Vila on the Sagres peninsula something approaching a school of navigators and map-makers. This place, a promontory on the edge of the open ocean, had an otherworldly reputation, and had been called the Sacred Promontory by Marinus and Ptolomy (from which the name Sagres derives). The only building still surviving is the starkly simple little church within the fortress. The school of navigation was like a magnet to the best brains in Europe concerned with the nautical sciences. Henry was a learned man at the very leading edge of navigational science. He is described as a person with no luxuries, not avaricious, speaking with soft words and calm gestures, a man of many virtues that never allowed any poor person to leave his presence empty handed. A Prince indeed. I am entranced by his statue in the port of Lagos – from where he dispatched all the ships - by his far seeing eyes and stature.

It is clear he was a most remarkable man. He was a prince, politician, warrior and grand master of the Order of Christ, but his fame endures mainly because of his monumental contribution to geographical discovery and the opening up of trade and cultural links between Europe and the East. He was also a very devout man, and became an ascetic and a celibate…..he was Governor of the Order of Christ from 1420 until his death in 1460. The Order of Christ was a Portuguese Military Order originating with the Templars. A powerful man.

At Sagres, I felt a tremendous sense of this power as I stood on the great Compass on the headland. This massive windrose's purpose is not known, but it feels amazing and inspiring for me as I approach my own explorations into the unknown.

July 14

When I return to England, summer is full and rampant at Old Meadow. The land feels feminine, and I am reminded that I am on the Mary Line, a great energy current or ley line crossing England, intertwined with the Michael Line like a huge serpent. I lie in the grass and write

On the Mary Line in Summer

In tune
Here in the eternal Feminine
warm grass
nourishing

I stop and slow
and breathe
and long to lie naked in the green
to reach naked for the stars
to run naked in the wind

I wear pink and warm colours
pick flowers
sleep

my feet draw the energy
pink gold soft red
my legs strengthen
I am soft and firm
I glow
and grow

ripening in the sun and rain

lying on the grass I write
absorbing all the gifts
of earth to every cell
through every breath
open
receiving
so receiving is giving
and giving receiving

soft moving and murmuring
wind and summer rain
clouds and leaves and air
sun for a moment

the cat passes by
the grasses sway

75

the air smells warm
I expand

The cat sits and washes
I sip my tea
A chink of blue sky
Light gleams on my hand
And warms my face

Shadows cross my paper
And fade
Trees rustle strongly and are still
A dog barks in the distance
Up by the moor
Where the buzzards swoop
In the wind

The cat stretches in the
Glancing sun
Squinting in the brightness
Of the moment

I remember many Earth Mysteries Group trips to churches and other sacred sites along the Mary and Michael ley lines, which cross the country from west to east, from Cornwall to Norfolk. The astonishing difference between them…. 'male' lines are strong and thrusting, fast and straight, female are sensuous, winding, slower. Dowsing rods show this directly and clearly and it is amazing to feel.

As I prepare to leave the Centre for four months, and set off on my travels, I am remembering the travelling years of my marriage, after the sale of the Old Inn. From 1985 to 1991 we drifted around Europe every summer in our motorhome for at least two months, often three. I knew nothing then of ley lines and little of sacred sites, but did have a tremendous sense of place and of holiness.

The second Dream. A Home on Wheels

After listening to my schoolfriend Arna and Dave waxing lyrical about motor-caravans, we had formed a dream of travelling around Europe in one, and before too long we had used the cash proceeds of the busy Whitsun of 1984 in the restaurant to buy a glorious old Commer Highwayman, which we of course named Whitsun. And off we went every Sunday after the riotous open-fire cooking lunch in the barn to practice. The only casualty was our own wall. It was a very great pleasure (not driving into the wall) and Ben and I have wonderful memories of camping at Exmouth beach and on Dartmoor overnight. That was possible in those days.

LEY LINES

Are the energy meridians of the planetary body, like those of the body on a larger scale. They flow out from the planetary chakras, transmitting chi or subtle energy. This energy is not measurable in the usual sense, it is not electromagnetic. Some are strong powerful motorways of energy, others narrow lanes. Some are sensed as 'masculine', some are 'feminine'. We can feel this flow with dowsing rods, or our hands...

The Mary line has many churches and local placenames dedicated to the Virgin Mary along it, and similarly the Michael Line

DOWSING

Dowsing, or **divining,** detects water, earth energy lines, auras, metals, gems or other such objects without the use of scientific apparatus. This is an ancient art. Dowsers use Y- or L-shaped twig or rod or a pendulum to, however some dowsers can use just their hands. 'Ask' the rods where the water is. They can also tell you how deep, fast, at at what depth the water is.

You can also use a pendant as a pendulum to ask questions. Hold it still, tell it 'show me a yes'. Wait and it will spin one way. Then 'tell me a no' and it will spin the other. Then ask a question with a yes or no answer.

Some people get into doing this too much, it becomes a kind of cop out. We need to use our brains, get in touch with our intuition and make our own choices. But it is a great way to feel the connection to 'magic' for yourself and it is very empowering...

I must have really loved cooking because even in this 'time-out' I would cook...one pot meals which were easy on space and washing up, and quick.

When we sold the restaurant in 1985 we sold Whitsun for a profit and bought a luxurious one-off conversion with burnt-orange velvet upholstery – not the best reason to buy really and we certainly didn't sell that one for a profit.

With me just six weeks out of hospital, we took off for Yugoslavia in the dark early hours of deep February, waved off by our friend the local doctor out on a call. The van was laden to the gunwales so that the wheel arches scraped. .....crazy. We wondered aloud as we lumbered off if we could possibly get to Portsmouth let alone Yugoslavia, especially as we aimed to go right across the Alps...
I had articles about all our motorhome travels published, so I've copied bits of the one about this journey here.

'Ben was sick all the way across, but wouldn't let it cramp his style so was followed around by a steward with a bucket. And when we tentatively drove off the boat, we hopefully followed another van who turned out to be equally at a loss and we and a long trail of vehicles following us went round and round...

But then suddenly we were out and we realised headily that we were in France and exhilaration seized us and in that moment our year off began. We stopped by a police station in Bolbec, and sat in a tiny crowded restaurant ecstatically breathing in the rich atmosphere. Then of course the morning French rituals of boulangerie, charcuterie...

After getting lost in Paris, terrified on the Peripherique, and savouring some exquisite towns, just stopping for the night where we fancied, we began to consider our route. Directly across the Alps or not/ Motorway or cut across the Jura? Foolishly we

headed for the Jura via Poligny, and soon were driving blissfully among ski slopes, and then zigzagging down the endless Col de Faucille with the great blaze of Geneva far far below. It was like coming into land.

In Geneva we wandered awestruck amongst the banks and drank beautiful coffee by the lake, then drove on towards Mont Blanc through more ski villages on the spellbinding heated motorway. We stopped for the night in a restaurant carpark, waking in early morning hush to spectacular views and frosty air.

We descended triumphantly into Italy, what a trouble free crossing in February! As we congratulated ourselves, saying it pays to be foolish, what were we worried about, we dropped into a thick grey fog , and we were abruptly silenced, ploughing slowly through it for hours as we crossed northern Italy. Looming road signs read Venice and we looked hopefully for some sign of Mediterranean warmth. Suddenly I said in curious innocence 'what's that white stuff?'. Miro said, equally undisturbed, 'I don't know' and continued peering through the fog. Then well past Venice, we both said 'Good God it's SNOW' and within moments we were battling with a raging blizzard.

PAN HAGGERTY

A great and sustaining one-pot dish for van travelling. You need a big straight sided stainless steel frypan with a glass lid really. Fry sliced onion and some garlic in butter and oil, (so it doesn't burn) then layer in sliced potatoes, seasonings, more sliced onions, and grated cheddar cheese. Repeat layers till pan is full. Finish with cheese. Seasonings could be salt, back pepper, cayenne, dry mustard.

Cook on a medium, then low heat until cooked through, about 30-40 minutes. A knife should go easily though.

Grill the top to brown it if you can. You can just put it in to a hot oven in a nice earthenware dish if you prefer.

Play with it...

Add choooed bacon into the layers, or mushrooms or charred red peppers, or chunks of Chorizo sausage, or arrange sliced tomatoes on top.

Ring the changes with the cheese too, use stilton , or goats cheese...

Whatever you fancy...

life's's all about knowing that...knowing what you fancy, what you want.

QUICK 'STEWS'

In just half an hour on a cold night travelling you can have something really warming, cooked in one pot...

Fry chopped onion and garlic, add and brown chopped meat ...use either grilling meat of any kind (NOT stewing) or small chicken pieces or chopped cooked chicken or meat. Or skip the meat if you are veggie and make a flavourful veggie stew.

Stir in some flour and cook a moment, then stir in liquid: stock cube and boiling water, some left over wine, or cider if its pork, or tinned tomatoes. Add potatoes, small whole ones or chunks, sliced root vegetables, chunks of leeks, maybe button mushrooms, herbs, seasonings. Its whatever you have that feels good together. Simmer it all for half an hour, taste and correct seasoning .

Try combining meats, or adding chunks of bacon or sausage or chorizo sausage to pork or chicken. Or use white wine and cream, or red wine, with chicken bacon and mushrooms...mmmm. Try adding beans with bacon and sausage to make a 'cassoulet'. Or minced beef and chili and peppers...

The wind blasted the van, the snow filled the screen. There was nowhere to stop except the drift-piled shoulder. Desperately investigated our position on the map and saw we should be near a Services. Never had a short time seemed so long. There wasn't much traffic and we crept along, isolated in the maelstrom, lights feebly stabbing at it.

Our wipers stopped, and the van began to jump along like a frog, and lifted in the hurricane. We were frightened. I opened the window to see and let the blizzard in, but I could see a little, I kept saying yes, keep going straight, Then, just as we really despaired a faint blue light appeared in the white screen then we could distinguish letters, then the word Servizio. We limped blindly into the glorious light, with me hanging out of the window fighting the blasts to try to see our way.

We stopped, breathed out, then in again as the van lifted horribly in the wind and everything rattled and swayed. But unbelievably providence did its stuff and there was a motel at the Services, and we joined the trickle of battered motorists negotiating the drifts and wind to the quiet warm still reception. We got the last room. The van we left to the mercy of the elements, glad for once it was overladen.

Next morning was wild but clear blue, and as the motorway was still blocked we took the cleared coast road to Trieste, gaping all the while at the snow covered beaches and the sea attacking the drifts.

Trieste was a frozen city, iced to a standstill. They still speak of that unprecedented winter with awe. Trust us to be here!..... with no way out of the city, the steep roads were like skating rinks and one horrific slide was enough to turn us back. I don't remember much of that frozen time except for a wondrous pizza cooked in a huge brick oven with a wood fire in it.

Eventually Miro put Ben and I on the long slow warm train to Knin, and went off to deal with the situation. He had to go a long way round, and then wait hours while the customs emptied the van (they must have been amazed.) ('Don't worry', I said to my readers in the article, 'they only do that to Yugoslavs'.) He then had to drive the van along the perilously icy and wind-lashed Dalmatian coast road, which is a thousand feet up, with no barriers. He had redistributed the load low and hoped that and the 6 wheels would keep him from joining the other caravans frequently to be seen far below on the rocky shoreline. No doubt it was easier without me squeaking with nerves.

When he finally arrived in triumph, I was tucked up in blankets on the balcony enjoying the sun and snow. After so many years inundated with pressure, we were just enormously happy to STOP.'

And so we did, until Spring sent us off to explore Yugoslavia , wandering south down the coast we had travelled by boat in 65, this time in a gorgeous motorhome...

It was just as beautiful, no devastation here by unplanned tourism. Developments were tucked out of sight of the exquisite little walled towns and harbours. Everything was uncrowded, romantic and peaceful as ever.

To Yugoslavia in February

Sandra Popavac and her husband ran a successful restaurant in Devon, sold it, and bought a motor caravan on impulse one Wednesday and were off to roam Europe by Sunday. This is the first article in a series Sandra is writing exclusively for MCW about their extensive travels in Europe.

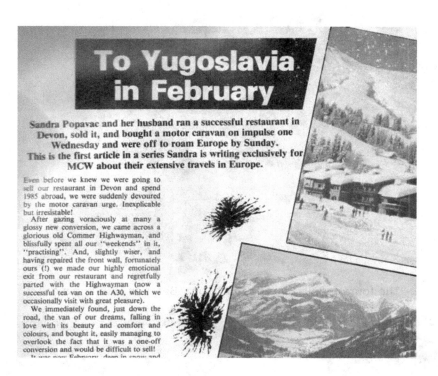

Even before we knew we were going to sell our restaurant in Devon and spend 1985 abroad, we were suddenly devoured by the motor caravan urge. Inexplicable but irresistable!

After gazing voraciously at many a glossy new conversion, we came across a glorious old Commer Highwayman, and blissfully spent all our "weekends" in it, "practising". And, slightly wiser, and having repaired the front wall, fortunately ours (!) we made our highly emotional exit from our restaurant and regretfully parted with the Highwayman (now a successful tea van on the A30, which we occasionally visit with great pleasure).

We immediately found, just down the road, the van of our dreams, falling in love with its beauty and comfort and colours, and bought it, easily managing to overlook the fact that it was a one-off conversion and would be difficult to sell!

It was now February, deep in snow and

When you begin to have a niggling feeling that maybe the family can't live indefinitely on croissants, dubious barbecues and french bread, but you want to avoid an overheated juggling of pans, pots and plates in your square metre of kitchen – and after all baked beans aren't the stuff memories are made of . . . ??

All in the Pot
by Sandra Popavac

PART I OF A RESTAURATEUR'S APPROACH TO MOTORCARAVAN COOKING

Just follow this system and in half a very pleasurable hour you can put out your steaming aromatic panful, light a candle, open a bottle or two, and settle down to watch the sunset....!

If you take a suitable stock cupboard with you, you can summon up your Pot at a moment's notice. And when you've spent a glorious morning overspending in the local market or charcuterie etc., you can incorporate all sorts of delightful goodies!

Also take with you one large straight-sided lidded frying pan and one large lidded saucepan (I like stainless steel –it's Brilloable! – and those new clear lids – to avoid running out of Brillos!) Plus a sensibly sized chopping board, not one of those silly little ones which mean you end up knee deep in onion skins. Add your favourite knife and youre all set.

The four of us in Elmside, Miro, me, Ben and Dan in his hat.

Marjolein and I in Bali

Our huts are the building centre left.
Between the Sacred lagoon (shown) and the
Indian Ocean

Chapter 6
Singapore and Bali …… Harvest

1 August   My harvest begins. It is the Celtic Lammas – Festival of First Fruits of Harvest.

I am somewhere above the Middle East, flying Singapore Airlines, squashed between two large sleeping men, scribbling by the light of another wakeful woman in front. I am afflicted with restless legs, then restless arm. I am remembering Ben seeing me off, we went up on the roof to enjoy the planes and left it too late for me to get a window seat or an aisle seat. I'll get a lot of practice during the months ahead…. He stood watching me go down the slope into Departures, I kept looking back, I was sick with trepidation. 'What AM I doing?' I said to him. 'You'll be fine' he said, used to my histrionics. I sit in my seat and feel terror.

After a while I stop worrying about disturbing the sleeping men and I turn on my screen. There is one on the back of each seat with a remote which pulls out of the arm on a lead, and one channel shows where you are on the journey. I am enchanted by this. Difficult to believe now I know. Finally I put a film on and I sleep.

Next morning I step out of the doors of Singapore Airport and I am knocked right back by the steamy heat. I've taught about it for so long but the experience is still a gorgeous shock. And the people are so graceful, so beautiful. The dazzling streets race past the taxi window.

That night I cant stay in, it is impossible to just go to sleep, with all that outside. I ask reception if it is safe for me to walk alone. 'Oh yes, 100%' they say happily, so I set off to wander Singapore at night, huge hot drops of rain sploshing heavily on my face. The shops are all open and the streets are thronged. It is midnight. At 1am I sit in a Borders Bookshop dipping into books, drinking coffee. It is packed with people doing the same thing, sitting in armchairs, on the floor or leaning against the shelves. I buy a book called 'A Woman's World' – stories of women on the road. I walk for hours, hot, wet, exhilarated.

This is the garden city, everything is bedded in vegetation. Monumental shops, shops as temples. The hotel coffee shop is in a glass atrium 15 storeys high, hung with exotic trailing plants with colossal hot flowers and I am sitting here giving myself a stiff neck from gazing upwards. Then my Prawn Mee soup arrives in a massive vase-like dish, all corners and pedestal, blue and white ornate china. A tureen just for me. The soup is so beautiful, with large prawns in the shell, chicken and wafer-thin pork and slices of something white and quite exquisite. It is all so delicate and aromatic, I sit and savour it and the scene around me, trying to take in the fact that I am in Singapore.

Back at the airport, I am for now feeling calm, still, poised ready to travel for the sake of it, not to get anywhere. Travelling in the moment. No tyranny of time, no lists. Just the necessity, when moving, of taking great care of myself and my few possessions. I am wearing the leather money belt I bought on impulse at Heathrow, with all my documents, cards and money. I tell myself I have time to focus on me, on practising walking tall, straight, connecting with people or not as I wish. I've had so much company, so many challenges, to be alone is a balm.

I've been feeling terrified, I've done so little preparation for this, all of the work I've done was to leave things OK at the Centre. But now I have so blessedly little to do after the last months. Once I returned from Colorado and knew what I had to do, it was a marathon. But I know I'm doing the right thing: it feels necessary to go around the world, and the signs have confirmed that this is the time. On the sole of my new sandals is - a sunburst spiral.

I will leave those prints everywhere. I am not looking FOR anything. I am JUST LOOKING. Rebecca's bon voyage card of Wandering William sitting very upright in a small boat looking around him is perfect for my trip.

Soon I cross the equator. To a different sky and a different spiral.

3 August   Bali

The sunset coming down into Bali – my first tropical sunset (and proved to be the best ever) – scarlet, leaf green, violet, magenta, orange. All the Indonesian islands below, dark in the crinkly pale blue sea. I have extra bad earache and am torn between ecstasy and agony simultaneously.

Bali airport, aaargh. A maelstrom of clamour, colour, noise and crush. Oh such confusion, fear and uncertainty. I am very uncentred, better to say swamped, and do not stop to get bearings and make choices. Despite total mishandling I land a wonderful taxi-driver called Ida, who sorts me out. (My whole journey was made so much easier by a succession of heroic taxi drivers). He tells me Chandi Dasa is over 2 hours away and a journey I should undertake in the light because it is beautiful. It will not cost a lot. He delivers me to a hotel, probably quite a normal one but a great culture shock for me, and arranges to collect me in the morning. He is reluctant that I should leave the bright lights of Kuta; he says sadly 'but everything is here for you!'

Dreadful night, tossing and turning in dank sweaty heat, everything a grimy brown and the bathroom an indescribable hole. Everything feels very dark and damp and nasty. Yet outside under the trees in the lamplight sit tourists happily drinking cocktails who must be in similar hell-holes. I am full of fear and inadequacy. Finally I am brought to my senses by my ear twinging sharply and I say aloud to my self, 'For God's sake Sandra, you are not in any pain, that's all that matters, there's nothing wrong. The night will pass and the light will come again, and you can always just go straight to Australia to Mary's.' and I fall asleep.

4 August   Chandi Dasa, Bali

Ida faithfully collects me in the morning and brings me through all the iridescent green terraces of Bali to the office of the Ashram Dawn has told me about. He comes in with me to make sure I am alright. I am nervous. I have no confirmation of my reservation. 'I wrote to you' I said, 'Sandra Hartley'. 'Ah yes' says a tiny and very old but very dynamic lady. Ida smiles, relieved, and goes on his way. And in a moment or two a very beautiful young woman with a long black plait is leading me across bright green lawns between thatched huts under stupendously tall coconut palms, and along the Indian Ocean shore and onto the little terrace of a pair of thatched bamboo huts with their backs to a lagoon and their fronts to the ocean. On the terrace stands a lovely woman in a blue dress. 'Hello' she says, smiling, 'I am Marjolein, I am Dutch, I am staying in this hut here'. 'Ah' I said, breathing out in the impossible bliss of it all. All this and a friend too. On the terrace are two very comfortable looking cane armchairs with a table between them. 'I will bring you some tea' says the beautiful young girl. A little later she walks gracefully up my steps with the tray balanced effortlessly on her head, and Marjolein removes the teacosy(!) and pours tea and hands me sweetmeats…..

Aaaaah.

I am in the Ghandian Ashram of Canti Dasa in the village of Chandi Dasa. Canti Dasa means 'Servant of Peace, Chandi Dasa means Servant of God. Servant of Peace in Servant of God. It is a small place on the east coast of Bali run by Ibu Godong, who is 77 and was the wife of the deputy governor of Indonesia and is still very actively involved in Indonesian politics and the United Nations.

When dusk drops suddenly, I drop in to the ocean, melting straight into it. It is a warm bath, silky soft. I float, looking up at the Southern Cross.

Dinner is in an open-sided cane-roofed dining platform. The large table is covered with a crisp white damask cloth and a silver candelabra. Simple local organic vegetarian food of high quality is served, and bats fly overhead. Some of their droppings spot the cloth. The company is good, the conversation wide-ranging and in English, Dutch, Indonesian. Afterwards we are all out on a wide terrace near the ocean, and there is meditation and music and singing. Then Marjolein and I walk back to our huts with a torch.

In the morning a teapot sits in a padded nest in a teacosy on the terrace, with spiral-patterned glass cups and a plate of biscuits. I sit in the armchair and watch the fishing boats, which are colourful insects with long legs skimming the sea, like this.

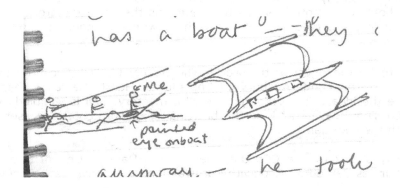

5 August

We ride one of these insects- with a lovely young man from the ashram- to a deserted beach, white sand with palms of course, and crashing surf. The landing is a feat. He catches fish as we sail, with a line, and cooks it on a grid of banana bark over a fire of coconut shells. We have picnics too, wrapped in banana leaves. The fine white sand is patched with black volcanic sand, soft dark grey like smoky ashy satin with a glimmering patina. The surf is so white on the dark sand, set against all the lush foliage. A study in black and white and greens.

We return to a pot of golden tea and sit watching the coral gatherers. An old lady in a conical hat and a sarong wades in the lagoon, bending down in the water. A girl sways along with a basket on her head. A man loads a boat. The ocean, the white line of the reef, the diminutive islands, rising vertically out of the sea with their curly trailing jungly tops, like this

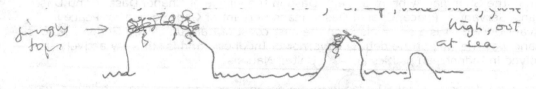

And to my right, the mountains, in shades of blue and grey, very faint and hazy, hover over the sea.

7 August

Sailing out beyond the crashing reef, over flat seas of blue –white milk, to watch the sunrise. Ethereal shape of the mountainous island of Lombok rising out of the haze. The sacred mountain of Mount Agung towers over Chandi Dasa, her foothills like robed hands holding this palmy village safe and her sacred spring feeding the lotus lagoon. Agung erupted in 1963, in serious displeasure at the Sukarno regime.

This mountain holds my eye so strongly that I cannot easily let it go. I am speaking with it. Our boat rests motionless on the water, as the great equatorial sun lifts over the white sea into the pale sky. We sit with it, with the mountain and its held but terrible power.

This is said to be the navel of the world. The Sexual Centre. Crestone is seen as a Crown Chakra, Stonehenge/Avebury in England as Heart. Hawaii is base chakra I believe. I like the idea of this, though it is all a mystery. Bali is a fabled and mystical island symbolising heaven and earth, bringing sexuality, creativity, sensuality into harmony with the spiritual.

I am suddenly struck by the CCs this year. Canti Dasa in Chandi Dasa, Crestone Colorado, Chartres Cathedral, Cadgwith Cornwall, and the Convergence Centre.

This afternoon we are squashed in a 'bemo', Bali's public transport system, about 16 people with chickens and boxes of fruit and veg crammed into a very small, very battered minibus, its doors permanently open, heaving itself up hills in clouds of smoke and blasts of horn and roar of talk. It's like being in a travel book.

Ubud is Bali's capital of style and culture, full of artists, reminiscent of Sante Fe. Cosmopolitan, sophisticated, green, rich with temples, galleries, markets, designer shops, elegant cafes. Marjolein and I lunched at a vegetarian cafe full of corners and galleries, she had an appointment and I stayed on watching everything with great

SACRED SENSUALITY

This beautiful world, our senses, our bodies, have been given to us to relish and cherish and savour by God, by its creator, its Source.

It is a divine playground given to us. We have forgotten this, forgotten the delights of sensuality, of really SEEING, really HEARING, really TOUCHING, really SMELLING, really TASTING

If we come into the present moment with full awareness, not contaminated by past or future, we can return the erotic to our everyday lives. Return to the joys of sacred sensuality and sacred sexuality. The erotic has been feared, discredited, distorted, but it is time to find the respect and gratitude for its beauty again

appetite. Then I hunted out the Lotus cafe, where apparently one can lounge on cushions and listen to jazz by a Lotus pond, but I was out of luck this time, the pond was being cleaned out. This was a tourist haunt. Tourists look so white and glum. The contrast with the local vitality is striking and sad. Poised graceful bodies in glowing silk sarongs and whitest of white tunics, bright sashes. Happy brown faces.

I enjoyed the monkeys at Monkey Forest Road as they played with my skirt and stroked my feet….. until they drank my water and stole my camera!!!!

Then we are back in the bemo, very hot and tired, blessedly less crowded for the return trip through the forests and rice terraces and villages in the gathering dark.

After supper we sing again and Ibu insists that I sing a piece of my own. I am utterly appalled but I sing 'the River is Flowing' in my own style, slowly.

The River is Flowing
Flowing and Growing
The River is flowing
Down to the Sea

Mother Earth carry me
Child I will always be
Back to the Sea

Everyone joins in, and I am told I have a very good voice. This is a great pleasure for me. My first time ever singing alone in public. Having always been told I can't sing. What is it with this thing of telling people they can't sing??!! Marjolein is teaching us 'Annie's Song' and every night we get better and better. I love it and still sing it

You fill up my senses, Like a night in the forest
Like a mountain in springtime, Like a walk in the rain
Like storm in the desert, like a sleepy blue ocean,
You fill up my senses
Come fill me again

What better song for this magical place where spirit and sex meet? It can be sung for God or for a lover.

8 August

We swim in the sacred spring at Tirta Gangga for full moon- a glorious maze of terraced gardens and ponds. And at night we sit in a beachside bar with Terry and Angana from the Ashram. The full moon eyeing us between the coconut palms. The night sea is warm sheeny black satin draping itself at our feet, drawing us in, and I slip into it later when I am alone.

9 August

This morning the tide is very high again with the full moon, but a wind has blown up and the waves are smashing over the wall. Just now there was a wave which came higher than the hut. Like this

All I see from my terrace is a wall of dark green and white water and now the thatch is dripping and the sand at the foot of the steps is a foot deep with water.

Marjolein has gone now. She is truly good. I am missing her. Travelling friends: such a depth of togetherness in just a few days. She gave me so much. Now it is cloudy and windy and the sea is wild and I am lonely. I have a day of loss.

I go to collect my air-tickets which I have had changed so I have longer here. A little man on an upright wooden chair outside a tiny wooden shack at the roadside does this!! There is a handwritten sign 'Transport Shop'. And here are all my tickets, beautifully changed since this morning, at a cost of £6. I am enchanted.

Walking back, I am also enchanted to see what I can only call a crocodile walking a few metres from me, in the mangroves. Wow. It is over a metre long and looks like this.

The crocodile has for some years been my symbol of 'receiving what I want'. So I feel no fear at first, but find the enchantment worn off when I go swimming and remember it is right there.... am I still resisting receiving what I want?! I am told it is a rare privilege to see it, that it does indeed live right there, and is a relative of the Komodo 'dragon'. I am also told the trees are full of snakes. Aaaargh.

10 August

Ibu takes pity on my loneliness and arranges for one of the young men to take me to a temple on a hill and to his family home on the back of his motorbike. 'I think you will like this,' she says, looking at me knowingly. Indeed I do.

I adore motorbikes. (Dan once took me on the back of his....such pleasure to roar off with him. His family home is a raised complex of buildings round a flowery courtyard, with open pillared living areas. The floor is very shiny tiles with rugs. I sit on cushions and am served tea and sweetmeats. Everyone is interested to see me.

11 August

Then next day Amasdi takes me to the Mother Temple at Besakhili. The car crosses all the iridescent green terraced hills, climbs and sweeps round a high bend into a new world. Before me rearing in a vast ravaged landscape is the volcano: Batur. Black rivers of petrified lava snake down its gigantic flanks. The crater smokes, and I can sense the sulphurous gases and the sharp crumbling edges of hot rocks. Smoking gashes dot the slopes.

Then yet another world appears before me, the most sacred place on the island. We climb and climb to The Mother Temple, with all the Balinese in their ceremonial dress, up many sets of wide flowery steps, through many pairs of ornate gates, guarded by pairs of ferocious colourful dragons and lions. At the top shrine, at the top of 1000's of steps it seems, they all place offerings of bamboo baskets of flowers, and flower petals, which you can buy at a stall below. Amasdi has done this and we make our offerings and bow. I am part of the ceremony... I can scarcely believe it. I am part of the line of people high in the Upper Temple, being blessed by the priests. I can see no other white face. Incense drifts, bells ring, and a complicated ritual begins, incense smoke is scooped into hands and passed over the face, and hands come into Namaste. The priests place petals in the hands, and say prayers, and pour holy water into palms. I drink it and then dab my face. Holy water is thrown over me. The priest sticks rice to my third eye. Asmadi sticks petals to my face. Namaste. Blessed. We bless each other.

We walk down, and I feel strongly aware of Asmadi and I together, brown and white, in this holy place.

At one point in our conversation she said 'In peace there is no room for despair'. I must be more transparent than I know.

This was my first meeting with the Mother God, but I was scarcely aware. I still spoke to my 'Lord'. But what a way to meet Her. Two years later I began to really acknowledge Her in my daily life, to live with the Divine Feminine.

THE DIVINE FEMININE

Mother God. The Great Mother. Goddess. The Feminine Face of God. . From about 25,000 BC perhaps far longer, the image of the Goddess as the Great Mother was worshipped as the fertile womb which gave birth to everything. With the Iron Age, which begins about 1200 BC, and the development of patriarchal religion we have lost this, and in the Christian Church only the Virgin Mary, pure and sexless, remains to us. God is remote, male, wrathful, strong and demanding and punishing.

We are encouraged to be in fear of Him. Women are sinful and our bodies shameful and to be hidden. Sex is only for procreation and pleasure is a sin. Women are there to be mastered, like Mother earth.

But Taoist tradition never lost the shamanic understanding that relationship with Nature **was** the key to staying in touch with the source of life. Goddess is the warm, loving, nurturing, soft and accepting Source of All.

She speaks of Sacred Pleasure and of Joy and Play.

Books now, even mainstream ones, are speaking of the suppression of the Divine Feminine. All is changing.

At last, after millennia of patriarchy, we are moving to an age of balance, and of mutual enjoyment and respect.

12 August

I wake to sound of singing and look out of my back window. A long line of people is stretched across the lagoon singing and rhythmically hauling out weeds and passing them along to great baskets at the end. Harmony. Community.

Friday 13 August

I've been thinking about my new-found freedom and about how good my mum has been about it. I am in the Telephone Shop calling Mary to arrange my visit to her in Sydney, when I look at my 'things to do while away' list and realise the date – mum's birthday- she was actually born on Fri 13th and all her life complained it meant she was unlucky. I told her it was actually lucky. Anyway I call her straight away and she is just so thrilled. Amazing system, you sit in a quiet booth in an armchair, and just call and then you go up to the desk and pay!!!! No cards, coins, fuss, anxiety, delays.

I find it hard to leave Bali. I can only do so by thinking I will return. I have met an American called Chandra who sees the ashram differently, sees the employment of the young people as negative, keeping them from finding a life for themselves.

But I think the principles and atmosphere here are a good preparation. I have been very fortunate to stay here and I say a mental thankyou yet again to Dawn at the Convergence centre who told me about it.

Bali has been a miracle, a personal harvest time. Just as happened when we sold the restaurant and took off, and then came back from seven months in Yugoslavia in the van. No home, no income, but….

Elmside - a Miracle

When we came back from our seven months in Yugoslavia in 1985, we had of course no home to come to. Our possessions were all in a friend's cellar.

So we parked our motorhome on Exeter quay and put Ben into the nearest school. I can't imagine how we did that. They must have needed an address, but I guess we said we were about to buy in the area. He has memories of bringing friends home to the van!!! They were entranced.

We looked for a house, and I cant remember how we got a mortgage when we had no income and not much capital, but I think it was something to do with the bank feeling guilty about having advised us badly over investing the proceeds of the sale: it was something of a miracle I know. We were looking at places which were either big or small until Miro sensibly suggested a middle way and we found 56 Elmside – four double bedrooms in three storeys right in the heart of bedsitland. We needed to let to pay the mortgage.

Elmside was clearly the one because it was fully and perfectly furnished down to the hoover, the linen and the teaspoons....... including a wonderful L-shaped Bauhaus creamy-white sofa. (We always said we bought the house for the sofa, though I grew to hate it later, as Miro seemed superglued to it..) As we had sold the restaurant equally fully furnished, we had nothing to speak of so the whole thing was ridiculously perfect......

We moved in, and were immediately perfectly comfortable. There was even tea in the cupboard. It had been a rental property. We registered with the university and within just a few days four delightful Americans were occupying all our three spare rooms. Ben came in with us, having been used to that while in the van. I loved the Americans – perhaps this was the beginning of my love affair with America. I soon learned to say 'hi' and 'you guys'. It was also the beginning of many happy years of taking lodgers, and I totally adored income you didn't have to work for.

We had lots of people to see after so long away and I enjoyed cooking for just a few at a time, all the pleasure of it with no pressure.

This was our harvest time, after so long working so hard. We had a comfortable spacious home of our own, good company, a whole expanding and beautiful city right on our doorstep, Miro seemed better – and I guess I felt protected by the lodgers! - and we had a future to create....

CRAB IN TARRAGON CREAM ON AVOCADO
A very quick and different starter

Use white crab meat. Blend double cream, yogurt, and mayonnaise, with a dash of tarragon vinegar, a touch of Tabasco sauce, and some finely chopped fresh tarragon. Slice the peeled avocado into fans, and pile the crabmeat at the centre of the fan, and spoon over the cream. A good sprig of tarragon to finish and there you are. You could of course pile the crab and cream into the avocado halves. Alternatively, use watercress, spinach or rocket salad in place of avocado. A few tiny crisp garlicky croutons are rather a nice addition. Or serve with garlic bread.

NOISETTES OF LAMB WITH DUXELLES TOPPING

Tie boned lamb loin chops into little medallions with string -or ask the butcher – and fry in oil and butter. While they cook, fry very finely chopped onion, mushrooms and mixed fresh herbs – parsley, chervil, thyme, rosemary - in butter till soft. Season with salt and fresh ground black pepper and taste. When the noisettes are nearly done through (stick in a knife to see if the juices are pink not red and nearly clear) add some alcohol to the juices ...white wine is good for a spring dinner, but could be marsala or sherry, whatever you have or fancy, then arrange on a platter or plates, top with the duxelles mixture, pour the jus around and if it is spring serve with baby new potatoes, whole fine beans, and whole baby carrots with the stumps of their green tops on..

You can turn the duxelles into a crust with more herbs and breadcrumbs...grill it to brown the crust. Or cook the noisettes in the oven till the meat is cooked and the crust is crispy. I have also used peeled and fine chopped aubergines in this topping.

You can do something like it with veal or pork steaks too, or try a topping with apricot and a little fresh ginger and breadcrumbs for pork. (but don't serve ginger syllabub after!!)

GRAPE AND GINGER SYLLABUB
A pudding from way back. Rich and wicked.

Whisk 2 egg whites till stiff, fold in 100g caster sugar, then delicately add a 284ml chilled carton of double cream and 150ml chilled white wine,. Add some halved white grapes and a little ground ginger and syrup from stem ginger. Taste and adjust till you like it.. Spoon into elegant glass dishes or champagne goblets.....on top of more of the halved grapes and some stem ginger in syrup.

Serve immediately with sponge fingers or ginger biscuits (or even those extra good pricey chocolate ginger biscuits). You can chill it, in which case it will separate, but Its still delicious.

You can make it plain with wine and a little lemon juice, and top it with crystallised lemon slices. O r you can use brandy and sweet sherry.

The Queen St properties (after selling)

Our van behind 44 Queen St

Dan and I – on a travelling summer

Chapter 7
Australia...... Challenge

14 August   Singapore Airport en route to Sydney

I'm reclining in an easy chair in the Great World Plaza, there's a huge world map in floor tiles, and on the wall, clocks for all the major cities. The world at my feet literally. A glossy grand piano, and a cello are being played by dinner-jacketed musicians. Polite waitress service. I'm tired out from walking up and down this very swish but also very long airport. Don't seem to have achieved a lot but the time has flown. I've done my emails, just love the instantaneousess, posted cards, bought a pen -from WH Smith(!)- been out onto the terrace to feel that steamy air again. Fought temptation unsuccessfully and now have a red silk kimono with a dragon. Also a keyring with a shark whose mouth lights up when you press a button.

I left one of my bags at the ashram and my jacket on the plane. Oh dear. Where's all that poise and taking care of myself gone?????.....will need to visit an Australian chemist as I know my sponge bag is in the lovely new rainbow holdall sitting waiting disconsolately in the dining hall....

16 August   Sydney

Mary is my friend Ann's friend. She lives in a nest in a courtyard in a gorgeous area of Sydney full of elegant houses with lacy balconies. It is full and overspilling with all her things; she is an antiques and bric-a-brac dealer and she has a jewel of a shop called the Frolicking Frog. It is filled with treasures from the 50s and 70s mostly, and she supplies movie-makers.. Delicious. She overspills herself, with kindness and generosity. She even wanted to give me my bus fare and wouldn't give up. 'Thanks mum!' I eventually said.   A dear soul who loves her very large diabetic cat called McPherson. We bonded instantly and had a lovely companiable time.

But Australia is very masculine and shows itself with bravado almost as soon as I arrive. Mary and I are walking down George Street. I have bought a leather hat in the spectacular Chinese Market. Two men whip it off my head and run off with it. Mary runs after them and gets it back with a lot of shouting. Then suddenly they come from behind and they push me, nearly knocking me over. Mary is ashamed for her country. 'She's only just got here' she shouts after them 'what must she think?'

Very different to Bali.

It is a shock.

The weather joins in the attack. Record breaking bizarre torrential rain, daily. And lightning. They have had a year's rain in a month: it will they say be a beautiful spring in a few weeks. Spring!!! It feels very weird.

But I brave the deluge and see what I can of this magnificent city. Then it's off into the bush.

August 20   The Blue Mountains

They ARE blue. It's the eucalyptus apparently, a haze of blue resinous aromatic oil in the air. The pass into these mountains is spectacular: the train chunters heavily up, winding through the gorges.

When I reach Katoomba, I find a bus which takes me to the main attractions. I go on the Skyway twice: a cable car crossing the Katoomba Falls, looking down the 250metre drop. Then there is the old vertical railway, which used to haul up minerals and is now cleverly a 'ride' which drops you straight down

the escarpment . It is supposed to be the steepest in the world. You are almost 'standing' up in very slopey seats, not caged or strapped, and you are plunged down.....hanging on for your life.
They'd never get away with it in nannying England.

21 August

Sitting on a bench at Echo point, Katoomba. It is early morning, bright clear air. A very chilling cold. I am glad of Mary's donated wrappings. I am almost alone with this stupendous view, this grandeur.

Cloud fills the miles-wide Jamison valley, sunlit strata of piled escarpments glow above the white lapping cloud. Folds of trees, dense, appear below in ephemeral rifts of cloud. The Three Sisters on their precipices in silhouette against the white seas.
A photographer tells me that this a quite a rare sight. Apparently they want to make the Jamison valley a World Heritage Site; I can't believe it isn't already. She has serious equipment, and I admire it. She says she had a major accident two years ago and is just getting back into professional photography. She says she is so grateful for all the help she has had from her family, it has quite healed their difficulties. She has struggled to receive it all and keep a measure of independence, quite a balancing act. As she was going, she said, desperately hunting, 'I've lost my keys!' 'They'll be there' I said. A minute of jiggling, 'you're right!' and she was off. I think we both felt better for the exchange.I sit on, drawing. Tourists start to appear. They only stop a moment to photograph each other against the view and then they are gone.

Then I walk along the escarpment edge to the Three Sisters and I climb very tentatively down the steep metal steps fixed onto the precipice to the narrow bridge to the Sisters. Sometimes I am in cloud, but mainly I can unfortunately see straight down to the tops of the forest in deep shadow far far below.

Ibu Godong in Bali has given me an introduction to her friend and healer extraordinaire Isabel Bellamy, who lives near here in Wentworth- coincidentally the name of my mum's home area in Surrey. There is a huge green valley here called Hartley too! AND a place called Bennett (Dad's old family name!) I go to lunch with Isobel. She is another very old, wise and dynamic lady.

I watched her work, healing by dowsing with a pendulum and WRITING, using an incredible array of charts she has made herself. Someone phones about her daughter. Isabel takes me through to her workroom, and uses a Mager (colourwheel) Rosette. Her pendulum points to a psychological problem. Then, using a 'Treatment Wheel' she has prepared herself, the pendulum points to homeopathy as the appropriate treatment, and then to cactus as the treatment. She writes the remedies on a tiny piece of paper and places them with the girl's name, in the centre of a decahedron within 3 circles drawn on a larger piece of paper. The circles are necessary to contain the need and to stop the healer being drained. She holds her pendulum over this. At first it is still, then gradually speeds, anticlockwise as negativity clears. Then it positively whirls clockwise. When it stops, Isabel folds the edges of the paper up and places it on a shelf with hundreds of others. The large room

is lined with narrow shelves full of these, and of charts and notes, remedies and all sorts. I am staggered by the intricacy, the detail, the comprehensiveness of her approach. And by the power of just WRITING the remedies – vibrational healing of a different kind.

She tells me that every line drawn must be left to right and every circle clockwise. Negative to positive.

She 'does' me, and diagnoses a psychological problem again. The treatment wheel reveals the remedy to be VENOM!!! She talks about buried anger and bitterness. I am not surprised. That might be a long job, I think with a rueful grin. She worked with me to begin to clear it.

Her husband was a doctor. She has been maimed by two separate operations: one hip operation which left her with one leg shorter than the other, and a cataract operation which left her blind in one eye. She said ruefully 'doctors! Maybe no more doctors in my next life!' She was so calm and accepting, humorous.

I have just seen that in 2005 Isobel published a book about her work called Radiant Healing. I feel privileged to have met her, realise how old she must be now, and still working. I would like to do that, keep working on what I have to say to the world 'until I drop...'!

21 August   5.30pm

Sitting on a seat in Bell railway station- two tiny platforms with a flimsy shelter incongruous in the middle of nowhere. For hundreds of miles around, just empty bush. Getting darker by the minute, and colder. Waiting. To get off here I had to knock on the guard's door and request a stop. I only knew this because I was staring meditatively at the timetable on the wall and it had this symbol by 'Bell' – 'request only'. Aaaargh. Near miss. But saved as usual.

I foolishly arrived here meaning to telephone from here for my lift to a New Age Centre called Glastonbell (recommended by Caroline), and to buy my supper in the village. I didn't know there WAS no village. I've been having a losing battle with a rusty payphone with a loose dial but I've finally talked with the operator. She finally agreed to put me through and I am told Philip is out and will fetch me when he returns. 'No we don't know when'. But, thank God for the phone! Saved from my own foolishness again.

So I sit here on this lonely platform in the emptiness of the Australian bush and wait. Ah, a light has come on by some beautiful magic.

I wait on. This MAY teach me not too leave things too late?

It is very dark now and my fingers and toes are cold. I sit in my little puddle of light with the dark desolate immensity around me, and various strange noises begin.

I write pages and pages of diary to avoid being afraid.

At 7pm, after what seemed hours a truck pulls impatiently in and an ill-tempered voice summons me. Philip says nothing whatsoever until we reach his centre. He then briskly abandons me, saying abruptly, 'Sean is here, he will get you tea'. Sean is in fact meditating and I sit in the cold dark kitchen for 15 minutes, uncertain of what to do. Sean eventually appears, tall and graceful and incredibly handsome, in a black meditation robe and cap. His face is extraordinary. He is Canadian. He lit candles, put on glorious soft music and the kettle, produced slippers, made a fire, produced soup with pasta and spinach, and proceeded to give me an evening of wide deep fireside conversation I will never forget. He said to me, 'people have caused you much anguish'.

He also explained to me the situation there. Philip has been, a month ago, diagnosed with bone marrow cancer. So it is a time of transition here. He is apparently having to face up to a lot of issues he has been denying. There is enormous tension and a lot of anger is surfacing. No-one is sure how he will work with all of it or how things will work out for him. I couldn't have arrived at a worse time. I am mystified as to why I was not told it wasn't a good time when I rang to ask if I could visit. I guess it's all part of the denial. I don't know.

Everyone is contaminated with the tension, a Japanese girl called Mako comes in not to say hello but to tell us not to waste electricity, there is not much sun at the moment. Seans tells me she is angry and is leaving to return to Japan. Someone called Cherie is lovely he says but not here, she will be back by breakfast.

My sleeping quarters are completely bare, with a stripped double mattress, a pile of blankets (thank God) a candle and matches. I make a cave of blankets and curl up in it, head inside, warming myself with my breath and trying to stop shivering. It takes quite a time. I wake to see I am in a gable room with a stained glass window and door panel. Sean slept on a mattress outside my door like a guardian. I found him there when I ventured sleepily out. I nearly tripped over him. It was all quite surreal. I have no idea why he slept there. But looking back, he must have been keeping me safe from something.

I go nervously down to a tense and confrontational breakfast. I cannot remember and did not record what was said. I am made to feel very unwelcome, foolish and small. Eventually Philip walks out and I find myself crying. I am deeply ashamed and retreat. Feeling unwelcome always triggers me off. Sean said, 'What an interesting breakfast'. Cherie, who is indeed lovely, takes me all the way to Katoomba and has lunch with me. She is interested in my reaction. 'You are very sensitive' she said. 'Overso, I am a chicken' ' I said sadly, and tell her about Isabel. We had a long talk and we enjoyed ourselves. My favourite thing is really getting down to the nitty-gritty in one-to -ones.

23 August   Plane to Auckland

Australia proved to have a violent theme for me: the initial hat episode; Isabel's prescription of Venom, (interesting that the Bell episode followed this- and I really saw my reaction of TEARS instead of ANGER....!); the reception or lack of it by Philip; the photographer's accident; Isabel's operations; Mary's cancer a few years back; her shattered foot; my violent dreams; all the car smash repair places everywhere; and the WEATHER.

I concluded that it is indeed A VERY MASCULINE COUNTRY AND THAT IT 'HOLDS' OR REPRESENTS MY BURIED ANGER.

RESISTANCE

What we resist persists. Resistance is the root cause of unnecessary suffering. When we resist we energise exactly what we are resisting. Let be.

When we fight something, it gets more attention and grows. That's why all publicity is good publicity!!

It may well be better to focus on the beauty and balance of the Earth than on fighting environmental evils! Better to focus that indeed 'Love Actually is all around' (complete movie title) than on hatred.

THE DIVINE MASCULINE

The masculine …… strong thrusting, direct, intellectual, 'knowing about', outward directed energy, as opposed to the receiving, soft, heart based, inward taking feminine. We need a balance of these within, in their true - undistorted by fears - form. The divine Inner Marriage.

The distorted masculine is angry, competitive, cruel, seeking domination over others and over nature. The distorted feminine uses manipulation, assumed weakness, and 'wiles' to deal with the distorted masculine.

The male anger is the result of suppressed and unacknowledged fears and emotions. Males are not allowed to be weak. Anger is a protection, attack as defence, defence against showing fear. Fear could not be shown when hunting way back at the beginning….! So fear often got buried under anger in men, and they now are trying to find their vulnerability, whereas in women anger is buried under fear….and we have to find that.

To find the TRUE genders again and make that inner marriage….

My Aussie friend Lora's remarks about its history come to mind: a friend of hers told her that it was settled in 'Newtonian times', that it is to a large extent a 'spiritual desert.' I felt this. I resisted it and my resistance made it all worse..

But such sweetness in amongst it all. The evening when Mary showed me proudly a sunlit Sydney- the bridges, the Heads, the Downtown lights against the sunset- and Mary's very special kindness and generosity, Sean and Cherie, faces at the party Mary took me to and where I felt very welcome.

But I am glad to be on the plane to Auckland.

Australia challenged me and I sat on the plane remembering the challenges of Queen St, which was our next project when we returned to the UK and bought Elmside. The project had tested me to my limits and was to do so again in years to come

---

44-45 The third Dream- 44 Queen Street.

We set about looking for a new project the next spring, 1986, something we could renovate and turn into a restaurant. We had no capital of course, it had all gone into the deposit for the house, so why we thought we could do this remains a mystery.

After much fruitless searching I was in yet another agent's office, being insistent that there must be SOMETHING forgotten gathering dust in a file... and he looked up as if I had triggered a memory and fished about for a while. 'There's this, its been on the market for two years. Its wrecked inside'.

Harvests bring challenges...they keep moving you on. Later that day we stood looking up at the gorgeous cream Regency terrace in Exeter's Queen Street. No 44 was at the town end, with a beautiful balcony. The terrace was newly decorated outside but No 44 had been the builders base. Before that some squatters had torn out banisters, ceilings, floors and it was seven storeys of decrepitude and squalor. Externally perfect, internally rotten. We gingerly made our way around, growing increasingly more excited.

It was on a lease from the Church of England. No terms were listed. I wrote a letter, offering to do it up inside in return for nine months rent free, a low initial ren for four years, a 20 yr lease, with rent reviews not less than every four years.

We got it. To our astonishment. (that should have warned us......)

I was nervous of the scale of the undertaking and wanted to keep myself out of it, but Miro insisted I was on the lease. I resisted it all actually, despite having secured it, I must have sensed what pain this project was to lead to- but eventually I gave in. We borrowed twelve

thousand to open a restaurant over three or four floors and then planned to use profits to do up the rest, slowly, letting each floor for offices as we did it. We hoped to sell the underlease of the restaurant fairly soon so we could focus on renovation and also take it easier ourselves.

So Miro started the work. He loved it, spending money, overseeing builders, doing it all with great style and originality. I stayed at the education office where I had a boring job as assistant to the eccentric Community Education Officer (sounds better than it was...) and became a clockwatcher. I had never experienced boredom before and did not cope well with it. I did a lot of head scratching.

I was deeply involved with the battle to do up the buildings too, especially all the paperwork and red tape. Someone said, 'what a nightmare, doesn't it get you down?' and I said 'You just keep on going, focussing on the vision, step by step, knowing its all on course. You don't waste energy reacting. You just do the NEXT THING.'

Of course I joined in the restaurant project after a while, I couldn't resist it.... and people were missing my cooking

This was when I came into my own, I think. I had been practising Zen.

I no longer had downcast eyes or fear of getting it wrong. I walked tall as I entered the restaurant. I was receiving much more attention.

I remember an old friend talking to me one night, saying very seriously that he felt I had been very good with Miro....(!!!!) that I had allowed him to be himself. And had also helped him give up smoking and then drinking. I knew it wasn't like that but I was pleased with the observation. I liked that man a lot actually, and I know how he felt about me. But interestingly Miro told me he was gay, and so I never saw him as a man really. But much later Miro told me he had just married, and he laughed at me knowingly, and I realised I had been deliberately misled.

Another great friend, talking with me one night, said, bemused, 'Were you brought up by the Jesuits?' and 'why are you so serious?'. I said 'Now I'll get serious about not being so serious....!!!!!!' . It was only after my divorce that I really began to laugh, and I don't think those friends would recognise me now.

I was revelling in being able to do in the restaurant what Miro had always done, and get to know our customers and enjoy them all. I was interested in people now, not worried about how I seemed to them or what they thought. I didn't mind mistakes. This was major progress in a short time.

We had done this exercise in Sati, where we all stood in a circle throwing a long pole around it, one to another. The aim was to do this without screwing up our faces or exclaiming when we dropped it.... faster and faster, more and more complex, until we achieved our aim....and of course by then no one was dropping it...a .clever way to teach

WATERCRESS STILTON AND MUSHROOM PATE
WITH MELBA TOAST

For summer garden lunches...Blend (not too much) 12 lightly fried button mushrooms, half a bunch of watercress, a quarterpound of stilton, two cloves of garlic, two tbsps of quality mayonnaise, 3 oz butter, a few spoons of cream or yogurt, cayenne pepper, salt and fresh ground black pepper. Chill the mixture, which should still show texture and the nature of the ingredients.

For Melba toast ...just slice horizontally THIN sliced bread, and toast under the grill until it curls up. Watch carefully, its very quick. Pile loosely in a basket.

BEEF STROGONOF

My version...I love it, it's fast, gorgeous and a bit addictive I have found...Melt oil and butter, saute some chopped onion till soft, then add thin strips of fillet steak, and sliced mushrooms. Flame in a generous splash of brandy and stir in a lot of tomato puree, black pepper, and about a small cup of sour cream per steak (sour your own double cream with lemon juice). Bubble it for a minute or two till it's reduced to a sort of deep rich salmon pink colour, taste and adjust cream, puree, seasonings till you go aaah...stir in butter to thicken and gloss it and eat it straightaway with lots of hot white crusty bread. Dip the bread in the sauce and just taste that...

SOLE FOR ANGELS

Our guests called this and variations on it 'angel's food'. Roll fillets of sole with smoked salmon, prawns cream cheese and asparagus, microwave briefly till done, (or poach but it falls apart easily). Put carefully in a shallow au gratin dish, cover with a white wine and cream béchamel to which prawns have been added., and grate some cheese over the top and brown. Serve bubbling.

I won a weekend in London.. We set off very early to get the most out of the time, and wondered at the quietness of the train..... then when we arrived at Paddington we thought a war had started. No tube, long long queue for taxis. Finally we were driving through a tree strewn capital, wending our way, turning round again and again as the road was again blocked. It was October 87. We got to the hotel, to find they had tried to call us to postpone the final, but we'd already left. But we were treated to our weekend anyway, plus dinner on the house. When the final actually came around, we'd had a function that night and I had had too much of a punch which Miro had made stronger than usual(!) so I was somewhat ill when we boarded the sleeper train. I got through somehow, making a big beautiful platter of little parcels of tangy prawn and cream cheese mousse, some wrapped in smoked salmon, some in wilted spinach. I didn't win, but that was better because the restaurant was almost sold and they needed a practising professional chef. It was my accolade after so long cooking for our restaurants. Prue Leith sat next to Miro at dinner of course and really seemed to enjoy him....even in his depleted state women fell for him. One of our regulars, in her seventies, said to me 'If I were younger I could really fall in love with your husband, my dear.'

And just as planned we sold the underlease to Pizza Piazza for a brilliant premium and rent at the end of 1987.. Simultaneously we took on the head lease of Number 45, so we now had 44 and 45, and sold the underlease of the lower floors to Pizza piazza. This was a huge legal process, and nearly foundered many a time. The last day, I had severe flu and was panicking at the last hurdle – so much rested on this deal, and I remember clearly it was the first time I put into practice what I was being taught in the Zen practice... 'Everything is perfect right now' and let go of the future. ...next day the phone rang 'It is done'. Big outbreaths....

We packed up our personal stuff from the restaurant, including all the gorgeous collection of unusual china and sacks of vegetables, and brought it to the house, which filled rapidly. The builders moved straight in to extend the kitchen, and we abandoned the chaos and all four of us set off to Mayrhofen in Austria to learn to ski as a celebration...

*The experience became an article... **'Innocents on Piste'**...*

'It didn't augur well for our initiation into the world of skiing when I realised on the way to the airport that my passport had expired.

As it was the realisation scarcely penetrated because a) Completion on our massively complex restaurant business deal had stretched itself out weeks till a few days before...b) I was still woozy from flu c) home was either semi-demolished by builders extending the kitchen or stacked with contents of said restaurant d) it was blowing a gale and hailing and last but not least e) it was three oclock in the morning...

So as I doubtfully contributed my inadequate passport at Bristol airport I scarcely cared. A lot of phone calls by staff generated a bit of paper 'you can fly with this but they might field you straight back...'

I still didn't care.

But when the Alps glittered into my window my spirits lifted and I began to have painful visions of an ignominious return to Luton or something. By the time I stepped out into the diamond bright air I was panicking. Miro took one look at me, grabbed my passport, put it under his, and suddenly we were borne in a heaving mass of skis and skiers, all colour and cacophony, and we were through and all the fears and agonies of the last 5 months negotiations were quite gone.

Most of that glorious week saw me in a mountain restaurant terrace deckchair with gluhvein and ecstatic – probably insane - smile. I did manage the beginners slope a few tentative times, but being as unfit as you can get while mobile I was happy to leave the swooping to my sons. I wasn't encouraged by my inability to master the draglift either.

Miro should have done the same but he got uncharacteristically possessed by excitement and went off down the intermediate slope with no clear idea of how to stop. Next thing I knew he was being carted off to casualty to have his foot put into plaster, and was destined to spend the rest of the week in bed being avidly attended by chambermaids. He didn't seem too distraught...

Meanwhile Dan and Ben whizzed about the mountains in clouds of powder only appearing to down vast quantities of gulaschsuppe. Unfortunately on our last day, while I was ill-advisedly venturing up to 13000ft, (more on that later) their enthusiasm led them astray.. Onto the blackest of the black runs in runs, dropping dizzily down the valley, despite strict instructions to come straight down after skischool.

5pm. 6pm. 7pm. With the courier (who was getting to know us poor girl) we searched and waited. The gnawing fear was like nothing I could remember. 8pm and the Rescue Helicopters were called. It put all agitations about our financial future into perspective.

Then they walked in.

They had taken so long struggling down the precipitous ice that that they had missed the last skibus and decided to walk three and a half miles in the dark and the snow in their heavy skiboots, avoiding the road so they could ski more.

We were a foolish family. I'd also overstretched my limits in my determination to reach the top of the mountain beyond the glacier. I took a cable car, a gondola, another gondola, and four long chair lifts. It was at first stunning, magnificent in the extreme, breathtaking. But on the last lift it was too breathtaking as I found my little chair dangling thousands of feet above the glacier, which was just visible through the clouds below me, the skiers there mere dots. Alongside the creaking chairlift was sheer icy rock wall plunging into swirling snow and cloud. I shared the last lap with an intrepid skier who 50 yards from the top suddenly flung up the crossbar to which I was desperately clinging with frostbitten fingers. I sat there terrified I was going to jump off. I learned that day that I am not cut out for life at the top.

I had originally had an idea of a mountaintop restaurant, how I can't imagine. I really was at the very top, in a howling blast of icy blizzard, with nowhere to go but get back on the terrifying chairlift ... I never knew I could be so afraid. The wind was blowing the chairs about and they kept stopping. There was no one to be seen, on any other chairs. Just me, swinging about in the maelstrom unable to feel my hands gripping the bar. I frantically pictured another sort of bar, one with hot wine and weinerschnitzel, and eventually the struggling lift reached the bottom. It was immediately closed down, I was the last person up there....

I returned via the myriad lifts, ill equipped to face the worse traumas of the evening.'

All I can say now is, thank God I finally stopped being a drama queen. But it was to take years yet...

We began to renovate all the offices of both buildings, and let them out. Then started a period of great abundance, with fabulous long travelling summers, which would take another book to describe. Every summer we'd load up the van and head for the ferry, wandering around Europe. Ben was popular in every place we stopped, he always had either his BMX bike, or skateboard, or remote control car, and was immediately at the centre of a group of kids.

Dan didn't come, he had his own life, though I still was concerned about him, he was angry and touchy. I still thought it was just his age, but he was getting older and it showed no signs of abating. But he did one summer get the boat to Santander and travel back home slowly with us. I loved it, and we had such a good time.

These were mostly good times, Miro was less jealous when I was there all the time with him, and he was happier without responsibilities, they had always got to him, and I just adored being in the sun, living the gipsy life, our only work to keep tidy and keep topped up with petrol, water, gas, food and emptied of waste...the simple life.

Perhaps it was about then that Miro wrote this poem for me. I type it now from his original one typed on a typewriter, and I smile at his accent coming through, and how he was, this man of mine.

To Sandra

When wisdom pierces my knowledge
All barriers of pettiness will be gone
I'll come in naked naivety
And present you futuristic happiness

I'll cross boundaries of simplicity
And give extravagance a spin
You will be centre of all femininity
And we shall we seekers of sun

We'll curb and understand expectations
And drive to an imaginative land
Presenting new reality to men
And his castles made of sand
Our aim will be a future
Stationed in an interstellary land

This is the original, but I felt he should change the 'sun' to 'sin' so that it rhymed. A highly, highly significant request, wasn't it? I have to humbly take my share of responsibility for our downfall. I'm sorry Miro.

But the extravagance bit was prophetic, the wisdom and emotional nakedness was what he wanted from himself and the curbing expectations bit what he wanted from me.......and the presenting new reality was his wish that we work together to inspire...but we could achieve none of these.

I weep. We loved each other. I love you Miro. Here are some lines from something else he wrote, one summer as we travelled:

Summer

The limestone rock is burning under the heat of the sun, only the pine trees provide respite in their shadows, and everlasting monotonous music of cicadas reaches to the mountain peaks. The summer nights, the long hot days encourage the imagination to dominate reality..... Sandy beach and sea are united in a permanent loving embrace...
An orgasm of living is felt...with the pulsating sea...the bird cried out in the distance, two figures on a motionless sailing boat look up at the sky, loneliness and peace surround them, while they seduce nymphs of eroticism, bathe and suck with youthful thirst the burning emotions of love....
The earth is naked to the sun.
The huge glowing red mass comes in all his nakedness to touch the edge of the sea, overwhelmed by his power the whole beach falls silent, while unashamedly the hot mass enters the depths of the warm womb of the sea....
Dusk cuddles the sky. Billions of stars appear, surrounded by mystical hope. In the illusion of the night they present us with the illuminated wonder of the universe.
If you ever asked whether we are an inescapable part of the universe, its impeccable harmony can be felt on lonely beaches of the Adriatic sea, during the early summer night. ....the ecstasy felt transforms itself into a protective clothing of
love and living.

Oh those summers.

Images, so many images. T shirts and shorts, sun -faded and roughly handwashed, flapping in the sun on a makeshift line. Watching shooting stars by a fire by the Dordogne, floating down the river in the current, stopping with a few other vans for the night, quite free, under pines near the bay of Archachon or on lake Brienz, or high on a mountain pass. Floating in the middle of lake Annecy in our little yellow rubber boat and then turning on the motor and whizzing to some little bar for coffee or wine... stopping on some deserted beach, and cooking supper in the sunset ... crossing what you could only call a desert south of Zaragoza. Ben skateboarding under the Eifel Tower, and all of us gasping at the Grand Nuit de Spectacle at Versailles. The burnished green-gold of Burgundy, the amazing Brigerbad with its exciting artificial pools breathtaking rapids and waterfalls, and the limestone gorges and pools of the Dronne. Taking our boat into the Gorges du Verdon after inching the 22ft American motorhome along the Corniche Sublime hewn like a notch into the top of the 700metre cliffs. Drifting in the glories of Lake Garda. An electrician in his beret coming to a vast camp site high on the Auvergne to fix our fridge, and charging almost nothing, but stopping of course for a glass around the fire we used to make in our barbecue…. I could carry on forever.

And it was all only a little more expensive than staying at home…mostly wild-camping, moving slowly, spending little. And I always saved up part of my wages for it.

But at home the situation insidiously metamorphosed into nightmare. For four years Miro sat on the sofa and got steadily more paranoid and more extravagant. I worked but he refused to, he really didn't know what to do, and before long, when suddenly our rent went sky high, and the fire precautions cost a fortune, and the rates rocketed and so on and on, and it all turned around and became debt, I really don't know how.. It was a spiral, of madness and helplessness. Of sabotaging success…and I did not have a clue how to deal with it all.

I realise now how hard for him it was to know what to do. Procrastination comes when we are unsure how to do whatever it is... and we have to ask for help. Whether for a massive problem or some little thing. At Chard Festival of Women in Music, we used to have sticky bun sessions – if one of us had been putting something off, we would say 'sticky buns I think!' and someone would go and get them and we'd all gather with coffee and thrash out how the difficult task could be done. The task could be handed over to someone who found it easier if necessary…..that's teamwork, and authentic living. Not the best for the waistline though...

I let it all go on, trying either to shame him into action or to encourage and help him.

MOTORHOME ONE POT COOKING

Soon there's a niggling feeling that you can't live indefinitely on pain au chocolat and charcuterie and bagettes....then you can get cooking....
And remember these dishes are not just for vans...they are a great way of minimising washing up!

Based on pasta......boil your pasta (fresh is great) in water with a stock cube for flavour. You may not need salt in that case. When it's nearly cooked, add things in combinations that appeal or are what you have....like sliced mushrooms, peas, tinned corn, chopped peppers, avocado, broccoli florets, tinned asparagus, herbs, leftover cooked meats or charcuterie, strips of bacon, tuna or salmon, prawns, mussels, cheeses.
Its fine just so, but you can stir in a good dressing, or cream, or cream cheese, or all of that...!!!. I love the cream cheese with herbs. Or add a tin of chopped tomatoes and some tomato puree, or a touch of harissa (chili and garlic paste). Grind some black pepper over...and serve hot ...it needs nothing else if it includes protein and veggies.

Based on rice......I mostly used basmati when in the van, it's so quick, and I now know its got a low GI....!!! But have included two really nice combinations using brown. Use that big lidded frying pan. First fry a chopped onion, in butter and olive oil, soften on a lowish heat, then add the rice for a moment, stir till transparent, then add water (boiling or cold) and stock cube, boil and simmer till nearly cooked. Then add things just as you did for the pasta.
Try a 'paella', stirring turmeric into the rice at the frying stage to make it yellow, use plenty, then add cooked chicken, then a bit later for a moment cooked prawns and mussels and peas. Check they are all hot through. Add chopped herbs, pepper....and stir in some butter or extra olive oil to gloss it up a bit.
Or try currying it, stirring curry paste (or powder) into the frying rice. Add chopped apple, sultanas, chopped peach or apricot at the same stage, maybe some mango chutney or marmalade. Add hard veggies and /or cooked meat or prawns etc near the end, give them just enough time to cook or heat through.. hard boiled eggs are really nice in this. You could also use some canned coconut milk as part of the liquid.
For Oriental rice....with strips of pork, bamboo shoots, palm hearts, all those oriental goodies you can get now, and soy sauce at end, or I love beaten egg stirred in until it's cooked. Or try strips of omelette, but that's another pot!

'Hash' meals. Fry Onions, garlic, leftover potatoes or rice, leftover cooked veg, cubes of salami or garlic sausage, or tinned corned beef. Season very well indeed. Try covering your glorious mixture with grated cheese or cubes of mozzarella and browning under the grill. You can do this with mince and kidney beans and chilli powder or paste or sauce too....dip your bread into hot chilli.
Cheese melts I adore to fry a load of chopped veggies, like peppers, aubergines, onions, mushrooms, tomatoes, courgettes, then distribute through it all lumps of cheese – feta, mozzarella, goat, stilton, and let them heat and partially melt.

Main thing is....what have you got...and how can you put it together to make something great...? Bit like life....yes????

I had come a long way but I was still very judgmental, and in the grip of fear and was no help at all. He had never recovered from stopping drinking and his breakdown really. He had strong defences of the attacking kind if anything was said directly, he knew how to keep me quiet.

An old friend once met us in the street, we hadn't seen him for ages, and after a bit of a chat he said to Miro 'you aren't sending her out to work and slobbing around are you?' My face must have been his answer. He looked at me with a mixture of pity and exasperation.

Behind the bar in the restaurant in Queen St,
watching speeches during a function

Chapter 8
New Zealand...... To a Place of Power

22 August Auckland

Flew Air New Zealand for the first time. I'm sad to lose the exquisite service of Singapore Airlines but pleased to note that the wallpaper symbols match the design on the sole of my sandals (bought for the trip). I am leaving sunny spiral footprints all around the world. And I didn't even notice the sole (soul?) design until I 'd bought them. The colours of the airline are turquoise so what with that and the spirals I'm feeling nicely on course.

Read the Spirals 'Ingredient' and you will see why I was so pleased to find it unexpectedly on the soles of sandals bought for my four-month global journey, and to find it cropping up everywhere I went....
As the plane came across the Tasman Sea from Sydney there was a circle of rainbow on the clouds within a fainter one and outside that a bright circle of white light. It stayed with us. As we descended the shadow of the plane was in this circle, which brightened. The shadow
got larger and larger and eventually outgrew the circle just as we dived into the cloud.

SACRED SPIRAL

is one of the oldest known symbols of personal power
(by which is meant mastery of self and connection to the divine,
not mastery of others)
is one of Nature's basic patterns - DNA, galaxies, whirlpools,
vortexes, and just the water flowing from the bath....
it has always been worn and used by initiates on Native American
Vision Quests
and is the basis of the Sufi Dervishes dance
it represents the journey to the Centre of one's being
to find the divine core
always draw the spiral clockwise, from left to right, for positive
power
I like to trace it in sand on a wet beach, in snow, in the wind,
or place stones or flowerheads in a spiral pattern .....
use it with awareness of its ancient power with humility and love

THE POWER OF WRITING

Just writing out an intention with ceremony and awareness
can begin to change how we see ourselves on a deep level.
It is those deep beliefs that shape our future.
Write to clarify and to affirm.
leave white space around the words
write clearly with beautiful letters
Make lists of things you really want to do
(not out of ego but really - ie even if no-one would know you 'd done
them...) but just writing at the end of the intention "If it be thy
will" helps us TAKE IT ALL AS IT COMES
while still putting all our passion into visions.
It keeps us flexible and relatively imperturbable
Leave your Writing in your Sacred Space
with flowers or crystals on it.
Look at it. Read it aloud.

I like New Zealand. It all feels good. Easy, pleasant, helpful. There is a big upside down map of the world which says in huge letters

THE WORLD IS YOURS
GO FOR IT

"Indeed I am" I say tearfully .
I find myself noticing the "Zeal" as in South Zeal on Dartmoor, where I have been so happy. New Zealand in my book is the New Land of Enthusiasm. I pick up a brochure about Gisborne on the East Coast of North Island. It says:

"FIRST TO SEE THE LIGHT"
This is because it is the first city to see in the new millennium. It is universally accepted that
it is the first city to see the dawn each day. Huge projects are underway under the banner of FIRST LIGHT TOURISM. GISBORNE 2000 - THE EVENT.
They expect more than 25000 people here.

Looking out of the window I see another huge sign saying

NEW ZEALAND _ HUB OF THE SOUTH PACIFIC
I am in the South Pacific!

I shake myself. The South Pacific has been drawing me for two years and now I am here.

It was when I had a windfall from the unexpected sale of a barn in France. I remember looking at brochures of tall ship sailing here, and realising that just 3 *weeks* would cost me a few thousand when all was said and done. Far more than I had. I will have had this four *months* for far less than twice the amount, travelling independently.

Have just noticed how many stamps I am gathering in my passport. What a pleasure. It doesn't happen in Europe any more. I am writing "writer" in all my immigration forms because there's no room to put "Director of Arts and Therapy Centre" It actually feels very powerful. It reminds me of my day with Isabel Bellamy in the Blue Mountains in Australia. And it is what I want to do. What I *am* doing as I write in this journal. Travelling and writing. Being **"Wandering William"** as on Rebecca's Bon Voyage card. **Just Looking**. Not looking FOR anything.

I am walking out into the sunshine to the tiny plane that will take me to Rotorua to see all the thermal reserves. So good to walk out to a plane and climb the rickety steps instead of going down those tentacles straight in to the plane. This way you know you are flying.

I am so thrilled to be going on such a little plane. Someone gives the propellers an experimental turn. The pilot shuts the door, tells us a few safety things, then rolls up his sleeves, and goes into the cockpit which is all of a piece with the cabin. If I lean into the aisle (one seat each side of it) I can see his view.

We trundle along and then heave ourselves up into the blue. New Zealand spreads its green self below us. Before too long a blue lake
appears and we dive down to it. The yellow and white shores of the lake are gently steaming.

I am travelling unbriefed, with no guide books or bookings. It gives an edge to the whole thing somehow. Serendipitous. A sense of openness and exploration. It feeds curiosity. It allows the Universe to provide exactly the right learning experience for me if I do not protect myself with certainties, bookings, plans. Diving down into the unknown and seeing what happens.

Rotorua is such a tiny airport that there is nothing there to guide me, but there are always taxis. God bless taxis and their ever-helpful drivers. But I am feeling a strong urge to drive. Especially after not after all hiring a car in Australia because of all the deluging rain. The hire car desks seem closed but a very young girl appears at one of them. She appears completely thrown that I want to hire a car, but makes a phone call and says someone will come. Meanwhile I go and get a cup of coffee. Fortunately they take Aussie dollars.

My car is purple and very large and curvy. They didn't have a small one so I got this for the same price. I know it's an expense to hire a car but it feels right. The car takes me to a hotel on the lake. Steam and hot water erupt from a primrose and white encrusted artificial geyser. There is a hot mineral pool with more of them.

PS. The Lake Plaza proved to win my BEST HOTEL AWARD (See full listing at end of book).

It is pure heaven. I haven't sunk into a hotel room since Singapore, a lifetime ago. The bathroom is my perfect bathroom. (Well at the moment) Pristine. Streamlined stylish sophistication. (Gosh) White and palest beige, very plain clean lines. and simple curving shapes. One wall is mirror. Fluffy white towels, white bottles of goodies. The bath has no overflow so I can lie in water right up to the lip of the bath.

this felt great

Surprisingly for such a suite there is no plug gadget, I had to get a teaspoon to lever out a soggy rubber one.

There is a guest laundry so all my travel-weary clothes go in the machine, and there is a pull out clothes line over the bath to hang hand washing on. There is an iron and board in my closet. I will be all sorted by the time I go!

I walk out and brave the sulphurous fumes to hunt down some supper. A Korean takeaway provides Tempura - huge prawns and vegetables deep-fried in a fine light feathery batter. It proves to be enough for a family. I manage to eat nearly all of it., but am prostrated on the bed, where I discover the Discovery Channel for the first time and watch a timely programme about volcanoes.

August 23 Rotorua NZ

I set off early in my purple car with a bunch of brochures to explore the thermal reserves. I have done well to hire a car as there doesn't seem to be any other way of seeing it all. I'd thought it would be around the lake but it isn't. So my instinct was right .

And now, as I walk through tree ferns in Waimangu glad of my red wool cloak and woolly hat, I am suddenly confronted with Frying Pan Lake. Hissing, bubbling, steaming; opaque pale turquoise and powder blue, with the soaring Steaming Spires of Cathedral Rocks above., which are needle like and serrated and apparently constantly changing shape. I walk for two and a half hours through this very alive landscape, past hot streams, Inferno Crater, Path of the Tree of Knowledge, and Mother Earth Spring, which is appropriately No 13 on the map.

You can see why I told my mother that 13 was a great day to be born.

I walk meditatively, feeling the active presence of the Earth Goddess 'Gaia' (I recall her statue in Tresco), without considering time. There is a boat to catch at the trail end to sail on the huge crater lake, but I have no watch. I forget about it and, interestingly, I arrive dot on its departure time. Except it seems I am the only passenger.

Thus I find myself being Wandering William again with a cruise boat all to myself, drifting on this very tranquil lake. The captain, who is called
Len, offers me some of his coffee, which after my hike is definitely the **winner of** my BEST CUP OF COFFEE AWARD. I am given a Mars bar too. I am out on the bow deck, leaning against the 'bridge' with my legs stretched out before me, and Len describes everything to me through his microphone. All just for me!

This lake is part of The Volcanic Valley, formed in 1886 when the volcano exploded along a fault line 17 km long. We purr almost silently into remote and ethereal Star Crater. The energy here is almost tangible and I tingle with it. It is interesting that Len slows the boat so much and does not say anything until we are leaving it.

Then we cross the lake again to the Steaming Cliffs. Now I am kneeling in the bow peering down as the boat inches in to the geysers. The largest shoots steaming hot water every 4 minutes exactly and we time our approach to arrive as the jet subsides so that I can look down into the vent.

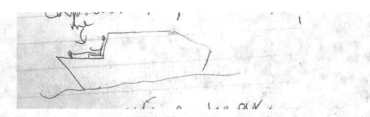

Seemingly silently the boat slides back towards the tiny wooden jetty. Then there is a figure waving from a steaming rock, and it is the bus driver who has been fishing. "Shall we stop for this Maori" says Len. Back at the jetty the bus driver drives me back to the Visitor Centre car park in the rickety shuttle minibus. It has a fresh flower in a narrow vase of water fixed to the windscreen.

I am so pleased my visit was in off-season. The morning had a surreal quality which would have definitely been lost amid the crowds.

This feeling was even none the worse for a mustardy hot dog at the cafe at my next port of call **Wai-O- Tapo**, which means **Sacred Waters**. I would like to spend time in this country one day and really look at the Maori Tradition.

There is a **Sacred Path** at Wai-O-Tapu with a very noticeable presence. Very hushed. It led through trees and shrubs and grass all liberally dusted with what looked like fluorescent orange powder paint - a kind of lichen adapted to the heat of the vulcanicity. Note that orange is the colour of the Creativity chakra. There was a small bright turquoise round pool to the left, which was particularly strong energy, then an archway of the orange smothered trees, then the path led up onto a hilltop with a circular grove of tall thin (and green!) trees. I sat in the grove for a while, eyes closed, sensing an enfoldment in warm safe green arms above all the fire.

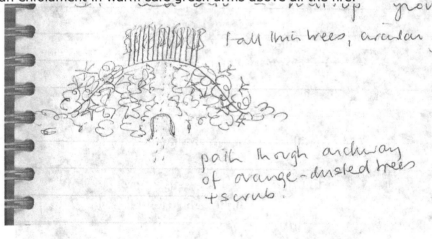

117

NUMBER THIRTEEN

13 is the feminine number.
There are 13 lunar months in the year.
The patriarchal Gregorian Calendar adjusted the months
to 12
which is why we have odd numbers of days in each, and
need a leap year:
this latter being a kind of concession to the feminine -
giving women to chance to propose marriage then!
The fear of the female made the number an unlucky one!
All connected with the Christian church's regarding of
women as the source of sin.
(the Church's doing not the teaching of Christ.)
Before Christianity in Britain the Goddess was revered
and all truths tolerated and respected.

SOLITUDE

Making trips alone has a very different quality
an intensity of pleasure and sensation
It is communion
with Nature (or Art) , which is the manifestation of
Source or Spirit
It's a way of "plugging in" to the loving power of the
Universe
showing itself to us as Beauty
Walk tall and slowly, breathing from the belly, and relaxing
with every outbreath.
Letting go all that has been and is to come.
Coming into the moment. Looking about us with awareness
of the holiness of everything.
Breathing in beauty and love.
The Shamanic Walk.

Hidden in the reserve up a narrow steep tortuous path is **Grandfather Lake**. I found this without design, and I was completely alone still. I never knew either of my Grandfathers, and I have had a lot of trouble with men generally(!) At this lake, I felt I met my grandfathers. I sat on a rock above a waterfall, talking to them aloud. It was totally spontaneous, there was no decision to do this. I felt sad and also pleased at the unsought connection. I must have been there half an hour. I had a lot to say. I left feeling blessed.

My father's father and grandfather were Master Masons in freemasonry. Dad never said. Nor did Mum. When dad died, I was given a certificate. I was rather entranced. And very recently I unexpectedly met a Mason, a modern day Knight Templar, who gave me a day in London which I will never forget. We lunched at the Masonic Club in St James, and saw Phantom of the Opera from the best seats. In the Club I touched the stone brought from the Temple of Solomon in Jerusalem. I felt connected to my grandfather as never before.

He bought me beautiful perfume for day and for night, and offered me any trip I wanted. I was being tempted, but sadly for many reasons I knew it must go no further. I felt a great gratitude, and compassion for him. I think this was a 'gift from my grandfather' in a mystical sense, a sign that healing had happened right through the angry male line of my family. My genuine compassion, when I held his hand in the theatre and when I kissed his cheek goodbye, felt powerful, as indeed it was in the story being enacted on stage....when she kissed the Phantom in compassion, she won her freedom and that of her lover.

I also, as I sat by Grandfather Lake silently after my 'conversation', felt the growing up within me of a newfound respect for what men have achieved on this planet. I have always focussed on their aggressiveness, destructiveness and weakness, and felt bitterness at their refusal to recognise the feminine and its importance in keeping a Balance in the world. They have so often exploited, possessed, tormented and tortured. All out of fear, and greed. Now it feels as if the two worlds - the simple, nurturing and loving matriarchal and the complex competitive, technological patriarchal, are coming together in mutual respect and support internally and externally. I find myself thinking that what they have achieved is extraordinary, marvellous - would, could women have done it? I know we have supported them. And indeed many of us in many ways have *colluded* in the whole sorry tale of oppression and colonisation of the feminine.

119

So what seems to be happening to me here is a fundamental change of attitude to the male. Inner and outer. Which is probably due to my increasing ability to protect myself from male aggression, and to express my *own* anger and maleness. Which brings me to my feelings about all this vulcanicity.

It is safe because it is being continually released. Mother Earth's anger is here not suppressed but gently expressed all the time. Rhythmically. If we can find the same ability to not suppress rage or disagreement but feel it and know it and express it appropriately with out being thrown off balance by it we can remain in a safe equilibrium. There is metaphor in everything. This style vulcanicity is enormously beneficial to the community. It is used for electrical power, for healing, and sport; it is a valuable tourist attraction and provides minerals...and so on.

All without dangerous side effects. I ask, as I watch the spectacle, that I might find the skill to form of my angers a valuable resource to myself and others. I also remind myself that I can also accept myself just as I am, buried anger and all! (Isabel Bellamy's speedy diagnosis) This could help me deal with my addiction to 'becoming', to change....

I am asking to reclaim my own full power, the process which began when I learned to drive in 1983, and continued and grew fast in 1987.

September 1987 Reclaiming my own Power

On Wed 3/11/04, newly in Andalucia to continue this book I wrote 'Have just spent the afternoon reading old journals from 20 years ago. My God. What a distance I have travelled in 20 years. I cant believe what a mess I was in. Ruled totally by fear, and locked in cycles of thinking and emotion that went nowhere but suffering.. My God. How grateful I am to be 58 and wiser.

When did it all really change? It was when I met Mala, and John Garrie - The Sati Society (Satipatthana is Mindfulness), I think, in 1986 when we'd just settled in Elmside and acquired the lease of Queen St. I was working in the Education Office as assistant to the Community Education Officer and saw the reference Roshi had written for Mala's 'Health and Self Healing' course. What a jigsaw life is, how beautifully it is cut.

I began to work with meditation and mindfulness, with the outbreath and posture, gesture and facial expression. Our meditations began 'May all beings be well and happy and free

120

from fear'. Mala told me to breathe out fear and breathe in love, to walk tall and lengthen my stride. 'It makes me feel arrogant' I said worriedly. 'You need some arrogance' said Mala. The dawning of social skills, of confidence followed, as I learned how to walk, to breathe, to 'backward circle'.. That's when the balance of power shifted. After that the college came along and I began to be independent. I have a lot to thank Mala for. She introduced me to her teacher Roshi John Garrie, a Zen master who had founded The Sati Society. .Satipatthana is mindfulness, and was the path the Buddha took.

I began to realise I NEEDED some egotism,   individuality. I was kind of the other way round to most people. I had always had a sense of Oneness of All, and had no boundaries to speak of. Huge vulnerability. Huge joy. Great connection with God.   But I took on all guilt, appeared guilty when I wasn't. I still do that sometimes.   This must have been VERY confusing. It was for me, let alone others. But Mala and John Garrie seemed to understand all this and   slowly I began to find a way to be me and be safe. I began to find much pride within me, which had been well buried, and I found the way to deal with prideful thoughts was to substitute gratitude. And love.

I learned to walk, to stand, to take every action on the outbreath, to breathe out ALL my breath. I began to feel myself in my body, rather than a head trailing one. I began to let go of fear and anxiety and found what confidence feels like. I was meditating to John Garrie's Peace to all Beings and it was very powerful

I would come up the stairs from the kitchen, in my white coat (which I still had from days temping in the hospital!) moving from the belly on a backward circle. And emerge into the restaurant tall, poised, balanced, feeling myself pulling gazes towards me. It was magic. It was what my husband had been doing forever. He was sarcastic (obviously threatened, and I had moved on enough to see through the sarcasm to this) 'Someone been teaching you how to walk, have they?' I smiled, undisturbed. He would rave but I didn't respond. The trouble was the quickest way to get him to stop was to pretend I was hurt, then he was Ok for a bit. But that was a dangerous game and I had no intention of doing that a lot. Just when I had to. From then he began to deflate. He needed my power channelled through him. I was getting ready to take on being a whole person, fighting my own battles.

45-46 Magdalen Road

After travelling all summer in Europe in 1988 following the sale of the underlease of Bennetts restaurant, I looked for work. And there in the Express and Echo classifieds was a tiny ad: 'A-level geography tutor required, 12 hours per week.' I was a qualified teacher by virtue of my harrowing probationary year at Deer Park in Cirencester. (At church, someone said 'we hear you have a Geography degree, could you help out while someone is off for year…?' Four years of struggling with discipline followed.) I had never taught A-level and indeed had not taught at all for 15 years, but nevertheless I was sure this ad was for me. Ken Jack, the Principal, gave me coffee and said cheerily, without preamble, 'Can you start on Friday?'

MINDFULNESS

Mindfulness means to bring the whole attention to what you are doing NOW. The mind and body keeps moving away from the now, into past and future. Both bring agitation. The past often brings pain, the future fear. We seek identity in past and future....achievements, and plans and strivings to be better....But the only important thing is being with what you are doing now, with awareness....being With It. rather than all over the place. Mindfulness means full attention to what we do...with acceptance of What Is, just as it is. Not wanting things to be Other. This brings, by itself, grace.

BACKWARD CIRCLE

Stand or sit straight. Calm. Relax. Let go. Breathe out slowly, circling shoulders backwards. Drop them, relaxing even more. Feel the inbreath (or the attention)rise from below the belly, up the front of the body to the nose, then breathe out feeling the breath or attention going down the back. Making a circle. Feel the whole circle, up the front and down the back. Visualise it turning within. Feel that when you do this you are stable. Walk or run or relate from a backward circle, not a forward circle. You will not fall, you will see further not down wards, you will pull attention towards you rather than repel it. This is powerful and I still use it habitually with gratitude to Roshi John Garrie.

PEACE TO ALL BEINGS

Peace to all beings
may all beings be well and happy
and free from fear
peace to all beings
whether near or far
whether known or unknown
visible or invisible
real or imaginary
born or yet to be born
may all beings be well and happy
and free from fear
peace to all beings
within and beyond the imagination
in the world of ideas
in the world of memories
and in the world of dreams
may all beings be well and happy
and free from fear
peace in all elements
of earth and air and fire and water
fulfilled in space
peace
peace in all universes
from the smallest cells in the body
to the greatest galaxies in space
peace and light rising
peace and love and comfort and ease
to all in need
may they be well and happy
and free from fear

by John Garrie Roshi

Later I noticed the address of the little tutorial college – 45-46 Magdalen Road . A good follow-up to 44-45! Now, I realise, Magdalen is symbolic of abused disempowered feminine, and of true female power, and indeed the college gave me back my own power and enabled me to get a divorce and support myself. Until then I had NEVER supported myself and simply didn't believe I could. But I was earning proper money for the first time and when the time came in 1991 I was able to survive alone on my own wages.

I mulled over how to start without displaying my ignorance. I bought the Revision Guide from Smiths and drew up a 50 question test. Rapid-fire short-answers. It worked like a dream. I worked hard for the next year or two to keep a step ahead of my students, but I slotted into what became a home-from-home, a second family, a safe haven from Miro's escalating mental illness, with the greatest of ease and enjoyment. I have such memories of those 9 years.

I was also working hard with the Zen practice, attending a week long Basic Workshop with Roshi, and another more advanced one, plus Mala's classes. I remember Roshi standing on the stage before hundreds of us at Lickey Grange School near Birmingham, in his white robe, every inch the magician and actor, relishing theatricality. He wrote 100% hugely, right across the flipchart. 'You are 100% responsible for your lives, for everything that happens to you' he said. Many questions and protests. Someone said 'So if I'm murdered its my fault?' ' You are responsible for it happening to you, YES, but don't get into blame.'

I was transfixed, I had always known this somehow, and now here I was hearing this amazing man tell me all the things I'd always sensed but never spoken of because I knew no one would agree. It was thrilling, awe-inspiring, satisfying. I came to know that yes, as I suspected, I WAS responsible for everything that had happened to me but now I saw that meant I could change what was happening. If I had the power to attract/create all that, I could use that power to attract a healthier happier (EASIER!) life.

It was during those years that I experienced something that I now see as pivotal. There had been a row and Miro had gone off into town in anger.

I stood by the big bay window watching him walk off. Normally, I would be in a state, full of fear and nausea and my whole being dominated by a churning in my stomach, clutching in my throat and pain in my head. It is hard to remember these feelings now. I stood there quite still and I don't know why but I became aware of my awareness, of my consciousness. I had a sense, not in words, that I was complete, needed nothing and no-one to have this awareness. It is hard to put it into words. 'It's not so bad, I can do this, I can be just this, just this consciousness. I am not dependent on him for that'- something like that. But basically I believe I touched my higher self, independent of, to use Eckhart Tolle's words ' external conditions and not coming from reaction or resistance'.

*It was brief, that moment, and definitely UNspectacular, and a long long time before I realised how important it was, but it was probably looking back THE shift of my life. The shift to conscious living. I became my **own witness and felt the 'security' of the soul. I have no idea why it came at that moment, but I had taken steps towards change and the universe was helping me.***

I was becoming as Miro himself put it, 'my own person'. I said to him one day 'I don't need you to punish me in advance any more'. 'I know' he said. I was at last stopping being so hard on myself. The end of my marriage was approaching, because it was becoming clear that he still needed to be hard on himself, and therefore to punish, to push pain outside himself instead of looking at it. The new me did not choose that in my life, and the boys were grown. It was time to move on. He found the new me even more unbearable than the old.

I found it was me always fuelling the car, and thought, yes, its me putting the power in now.

I remember Roshi telling me to leave, to trust the magic, to use the magic, that the world was full of it. It took a while after that: 18 months until I actually did leave the security of coupledom and the Known behind and step into the Unknown with just one friend, my lovingly remembered Krys, to support me emotionally.

I think I gave him more than he could bear. I took his abuse and his depressions both too seriously and not seriously enough. Too seriously in that I took it personally and went down with him. Not enough in that I allowed him to abuse me, didn't stand up for myself. As an only child and a sheltered one, I had no training at all in dealing with other people's stuff, or with depression or anger. Anger was not permitted. I was way out of my depth. It had never occurred to me that people wanted to hurt other people – that it made them feel better.

He said he had always feared I would go, but also was himself torn between staying and going (like me) and had wished I would have an affair so he could know he should go. I told him I had been far too afraid of him to do such a thing, he went berserk if I so much a smiled at a man. But he was all bravado. What a muddle we both were. We didn't know what to do, either of us. And then it all got of out of control anyway, and at the twelfth hour I managed to go, when it was really difficult, when the business mess was at its worst due to his years of illness, and it was also really terrible for him personally. He felt so abandoned.

Now, I feel compassion for us both. All I can do – and it's a powerful thing to do- is say over and over again the words of the Hawaiian healer written of by Joe Vitale in ' Zero Limits'. ' I am sorry. I love you. I forgive you.

Thankyou. I love you' and address them (as the Hawaiian healer does) to the part of me that created my marriage. This works. Try it.

I feel it is very appropriate that I am here in this place of natural power. So I take my time to breathe in - and more importantly out -and absorb the energies of this land, as I walk through the rich riot of brilliant colours of the Artists Palette and the Champagne Pool and the Bridal Veils and Devil's Bath ....Strong metaphors respectively for creativity, material abundance, sexuality and the cleansing of "sin". It was still to take me some years before I became comfortable with my sexuality. First I had to become comfortable with my own power.

On my back to the delights of the Lake Plaza, I felt drawn to turn left, and after climbing over a hill saw below me a floodlit mineral pool like a jewel in the blue dark. Needless to say I stopped and basked in the steaming water, watching the local people having family supper on the wooden deck.
New Zealand will call me back, I suspect. I barely began to taste this land, which is sprinkled with signs saying:

CLEAN UP
THE SPIRIT IS SWEEPING THE GLOBE

and so on to Fiji....

WHAT will I find there?

HO'OPONOPONO HEALING

Joe Vitale, an American teacher of personal development, heard about a therapist in Hawaii, Dr. Ihaleakala Hew Len, who cured a complete ward of criminally insane patients without seeing any of them

"'I was simply healing the part of me that created them,' Dr Len said. Joe didn't understand. Dr. Len explained that total responsibility for your life means that everything in your life-

simply because it is in your life. is your responsibility. In a literal sense the entire world. -- is your creation and everything in it is a part of you. Heal that and you heal the world.

In his new book Zero Limits, Joe Vitale gives this 'healing via self-healing' process as

'I love you. I'm sorry. I forgive you. Thankyou. I love you' ie love, humility and acceptance, forgiveness, gratitude, and back to love

METAPHOR
In reading the road of life

we interpret what we encounter as we would the elements of a dream. Some metaphors are archetypal or 'communal' and well known; others are very personal and the meaning is only known to ourselves.

Noting them when they present themselves is fascinating, and fun

It adds a new dimension and meaning to living each day

It is best to keep light hearted about it all

as well as honouring the timeliness of their appearance

and the orchestration of the whole

Deep Magic indeed

For our *Use*

My hut on Leleuvia Island   Arrival on Leleuvia

Chapter 9 Fiji...... Confrontation

24 August   By coach across Fiji

I am sitting in the front seat looking through the big front window. It's not a bad coach at all, even if the windscreen is cracked across. I am feeling *enormously relieved*.

When I landed I had of course no bookings, no guide book or knowledge of the place. I actually felt very very frightened and lonely. Everyone was in pairs of course. The big board of resort vacancies was all pricey, like 100 pounds a night.... and anyway I didn't know one from the other. I thought, between clutches of fear and the old shame of being alone that I have long battled with, "I've got it wrong this time. I should have got a book or something."

So I told myself, get the money first, and in the long queue at the Exchange I had time to quieten my turmoil. Of course as soon as I did, what did I see but a neon sign saying ACCOMMODATION AND TOUR AGENCY. I clarified in my mind what I wanted.

I had been thinking about this, and writing it down in my diary, on the flight. I straightened my shoulders, told myself I could be very proud of myself for undertaking this journey alone and walked in to the very swish little office.

Behind the desks were two *very* black smiling women with lots of very frizzy hair with flowers in it. Their English was perfect. I said, trying to sound confident, "I want to stay on a tiny island, very quiet, with good white beaches". I paused, and added hopefully but without much hope -if you see what I mean, "I want a hut on the beach, but it mustn't be too expensive". They sent me to Leleuvia. They arranged the bus across the island, cheap accommodation in Suva the capital, another bus and a boat to the island, the week at the island, and a good hotel in Suva on my return because the other was full. (How *grateful* I was to be for that .....!!!) I paid for it all - in total only £100!, and they hung a shell necklace around me and took me out to the waiting coach. How about that?

I thought I had to do it all myself and its all been done for me. I am so curious. I'll probably get apprehensive later but right now it feels great.

So that's why I am so happy sitting on the coach being carried across all of Fiji's main island. In the middle of the Pacific Ocean as far from England as I can possibly be. I'm wearing three necklaces,the shell one, my Santa Fe turquoise, and Mary's one of all different coloured stones. I remember Mary and Macpherson in their Sydney nest of treasures with affection.

Notices along the way:

- above a bar -

    "LICENSED TO SELL FERMENTED AND   SPIRITUOUS LIQUORS"

- road signs -
  WE LOVE YOU
  LEARN WITH US
  GOD BLESS
   DO THE RIGHT THING -KEEP FIJI CLEAN AND BEAUTIFUL

- hoardings with big picture of palm trees etc –
  WELCOME TO   SEVENTH HEAVEN
  WHERE YOUR DREAMS COME TRUE

I'm so pleased to see coconut palms again, so tall and thin and wavy.

The bus is bouncing along the switchback road at a fair old rate. We stop endlessly to pick up tourists, locals, children, parcels and mail, and shopping and luggage. We pass

RECIPE FOR DEALING WITH FEAR
"ON THE HOOF"

Stop or slow if possible

Feel the fear fully and say "just fear -it will pass"

Breathe out very fully and feel body relax

Bring the attention to the belly, away from the solar plexus emotional centre

On next outbreath straighten shoulders by circling them up and back

and dropping them down very relaxed at the back of the circle.

Lift head and look straight ahead. Clear forehead, relax jaw and hands -add a slight smile!

Keep breathing out - It cuts through fear

Remember you're OK

and whatever happens is going to be right and it always has been so far

Visualise plugging yourself in again to that support

be clear about what you choose to happen next

move off alertly, keeping as centred in the belly as possible

IT TAKES NO MORE THAN A MINUTE OR TWO....

Panic comes when we get disconnected, that's all

smoking or flaming bare mountainsides (burning cane stubble), endless hummocky fields of sugar cane, burnt orange earth, shacks of painted or rusty corrugated iron, acacia trees, rain forested ridges fading into the distance, endless churches of every imaginable variety, bright orange trumpet flowers on trees, very rackety dishevelled buses packed with people and with no glass in the windows. It starts to rain and they lower tarpaulins. I hope Fiji isn't in the grip of El Nina too like Australia.

Now there are villages of little wooden or iron shacks cosily set around green open space. There is often a chapel and school. The people are tall and strong and straight and very black, and the women billow with colour and frills and ribbons and bows.

Now we drop off two small boys in skull masks, giggling, at the gates of a boys' club. The crinkly black face of the driver dissolves into a fond grin and we catch each other's eyes in humour.

Now and again we drop tourists off at swish resorts. I don't like the feel of them at all. Most of the people there look pale and elderly and not overfull of vitality. What will Leleuvia be like?

25 August   Suva

After **four hours** (I'm still feeling good amazingly) we are all of a sudden into the urban buzz of Suva and I am whisked away by a taxi driver (the bus driver must have told him...??) and for about 50 pence am delivered to my "hotel". I stand in the hot damp dark and look at the strange structure of my abode for the night.

It's an extraordinary place, quite narrow and deep and yet hollow in the middle. So its a sort of U shape, the front (top of the U) open to the street. As you climb the concrete painted steps to the opening you see a wide concrete staircase leading straight up to the upper floor, which has a concrete gallery with metal railings all around the inside of the U. The bare, shabby but reasonably clean rooms lead off this.

This is a backpackers place really. Confident young slim things are giggling and chattering around the place. I am feeling nervous all over again, struggling with feelings of out-of-placeness, shame of aloneness and fear of being laughed at and all sorts of "stuff", mostly totally irrational and rooted in the long distant past if not a previous life. I have to remind myself always it seems, that when I get into all this sticky stuff it's just Ego... and also that I have a right to be wherever I choose to be. It is getting easier. And I wanted to experience this sort of travelling having missed out in my youth. And, it's where I've been sent. And, it is extremely cheap.

I stand looking out of my window at the gleaming rows of puddles and glossy rain-heavy flora and do some internal rummaging soothing and disciplining and finally feel something approaching grown up again. I go and explore the kitchen and say hello to some folk. And of course there is absolutely **no** reason at all for me to have been so screwed up....and even if there was there wasn't if you see what I mean.....?

Each pair of rooms has a sort of kitchen - no stove- and a 'bathroom', just a large streaky concrete shower stall and a stained lavatory. I think it must have been a building of 'apartments' for the local people now used for lodgings. There is a *very* shabby and antiquated common kitchen and sitting room. I put the big blackened kettle on the encrusted stove and find there is no china or cutlery or pans, so I go down to the cramped and grille-ed little office to ask and am allotted my ration.

The man in the office confuses me; I am not sure whether he *is* a man as he is wearing a beautifully tailored grey skirt and has elegant brown legs and shapely ankles.... he has a detached and nonchalant manner, with an aura of decadence around him. But he always calls me by name and is very courteous in his faintly superior way.

People are friendly and helpful, and I relax some more and try not to feel pathetic. I walk out in the dark into town to buy supper and tea bags and coffee (which I'm still using now as I type my diary in Crestone Colorado. Every cup of Nescafe labelled Papua New Guinea takes me back to my first nervous night in Fiji). I feel vulnerable out walking past the seedy ramshackle shops and seedy lounging staring men so I do a lot of walking tall and brisk and breathing out, and am glad to reach my room.

26 August

All dawns bright and the roads are full of flowers and tropical greenery. The bus for the island doesn't come for me until midday, so, my spirits rising in curiosity, I walk into the town centre. Here the mystery of the hotel man is explained. Everywhere are elegant men wearing tailored, wrap-round, knee-length, grey, navy or brown skirts. Black men and brown men, carrying briefcases, and with sandals on their feet.

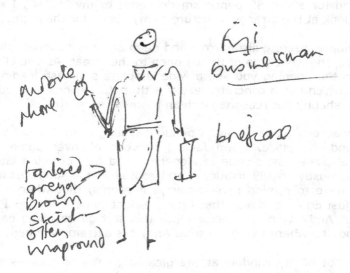

I am entranced and sit watching the scene at a table outside McDonalds (everything else feels a bit suspect -like dungeons . This is the capital, it is not a tourist area, and the seafront has no cafes or gardens. I guess I never dreamt I'd be pleased to find a McDonalds!). The town centre is standard stuff apart from the men, but I get some essentials bought and when I reach Leleuvia I am very glad I did.

The policemen wear white skirts with zigzag hems. With red shirts. I am certainly in a different world.

EGO - STICKY STUFF

I know when I get into all this stuff about how
people are seeing me
it's just ego.
when we start feeling inferior superior inadequate
self deprecating humiliated pretentious
complacent...... or irrationally anything...... it's ego
defences are ego
when we want to impress its ego
when we cant accept compliments its ego
if we have clear boundaries and speak our truth
skilfully we don't need defences
"transparency is our best protection" (channelled
by Anrahyah in Crestone)
Ego is the self that is fashioned by fear
and by all the false beliefs about ourselves that
we collect in bucketfuls in our early lives.
It's not our real self - that's out of sight at the
bottom of the bucket
and needs to be fished out and given a good wash and brush
up

so it shines again
and we "come from" a clear place
which is what changes lives ours and others'

133

smart
red
shirt

white
zigzag
hem
skirt

Fiji
policeman

Now I am on the island bus, which proves to be only just about still on its wheels. We lurch along. I am the only tourist. It seems I am going to the end of the world. Four hours yesterday and how long today? Well, I'm seeing Fiji. I bounce up and down on the chipped and scratched metal seats, thinking that never have I felt more suspended in the unknown. I have no idea what I am headed for. The "brochure" for Leleuvia is minimal, without pictures. I am pleased when we stop to collect two tourists. It makes a big difference.

Over a very long hour later (we stopped at the fruit market) we bump down a dirt road and there before us is a mangrove lined wide green river and endless dense rainforest on all sides. At a tiny wooden landing stage waits a small launch, a black man in yellow oilskins and dark glasses, and a very sun-scarred and browned young blond Englishman, and a load of empty water barrels. Vast quantities of boxes etc are extracted through the glassless bus window and stashed in the small wooden boat.

Standing dazed in the sun in this place straight out of "The Mosquito Coast" I meet my companions, who are young student doctors. A very slight, pretty girl called Jo and an Asian boy called Han with an exceptionally sweet face and a tendency to look about him in wonder much as I know I do. They are English, amazingly.

The launch proves to be a speedboat and we hurtle away. It is very invigorating and I am thrilled to bits and suddenly feeling that this is all going to be OK. There is a great swell, it has apparently been raining and windy for a week, and the tarpaulins are down, so we can't see where we are going. But here I am in a small boat being 'Wandering William' again.

tarpaulin down

large engine

luggage

me. Wandering William again.

An hour later, the boat begins to slow, and Sean crawls over to raise the tarpaulins, and there in the sunshine is Leleuvia.

few tiny huts, thatched

hammock

white sand

still water of lagoon within coral reef

white sand spit

My desert isle.

Coconut palms and tropical lushness atop a miniscule island fringed with blinding white sand. A handful of ramshackle thatched huts. All set in glowing turquoise blue and green sea that glints pale gold in the coral shallows.

A hammock or two strung between palms. On the distant horizon the rugged peaks of a larger island.

It is unforgettable. One of the winners of my BEST MOMENT AWARDS. We land on a spit of white gold sand. In a wheelbarrow sits a fat black baby. (See photo).Four dogs splash into the sea to greet us. We climb out and paddle in. The wheelbarrow tips over and the baby falls out, quite happily. The barrow (labelled TAXI) is righted, and piled with luggage. Boxes are shouldered and dogs are jumping and slowly we walk up the hot sand to the huts.

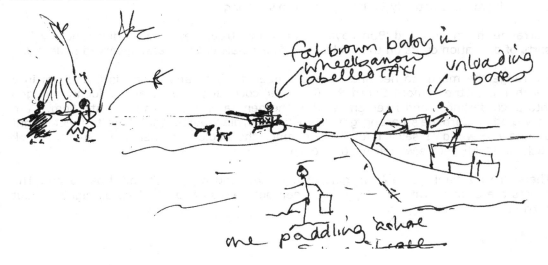

fat brown baby in wheelbarrow labelled TAXI

unloading boxes

one paddling ashore

135

My hut is blue painted corrugated iron and is called Fishers Lodge. (also see photo).It has a tiny sandy verandah on the beach. And a large netted double bed. There is a lean-to with a coldwater showerhead and almost entirely brown lavatory. "It's lovely" I say gratefully to the smiley Fijian lady beside me. She looks well pleased and we look happily at each other.

I lie flat on my beach in deep bliss and try to take in where I am. Two of the dogs come and join me.

I walk around the island, still deep in bliss. I sun myself some more at the furthest point, then move into the shade of the fringing palms. I am motionless, eyes half open sometimes closed. Absorbing. Next day I am to remember this.

Later there is supper in the thatched open-sided 'restaurant' . A mountain of vegetable fried rice preceded by 'long' soup. (that's what it says on the blackboard menu, I never found out why). Which turns out to be a 'fruit bowl' (it was that large) of what is probably just stock cube soup with minute noodles and vegetables. How come it's so **good**?

There are only a few people here. I have lost most of the feelings that harried me in Suva. The accommodation may be similarly primitive but urban surroundings make it SO much worse. I actually ENJOY them in this setting.

I arrange my much loved 'Bon Voyage' cards, my 'treasures,' my candles, and my four sorts of divination cards on the shelves which are part of the massive carved bedhead.

I arrange the mosquito net and clamber under it. Lying and taking in that I am in a beach hut in the remote South Pacific under coconut palms, I am suddenly plunged into pitch darkness and I remember that the generator gets turned off at 11pm. I am very glad of Caroline's parting gift of a lovely purple Maglite. ("I'll take the violet light around the world" I said) I fondly remember the eagle's feather smudging she took such care with before we left for the coach.

There are no blankets so I am glad of my cloak and my beach towel as covers. The sheets are clammy with humidity so I sleep between sarongs. I sleep all night without stirring.

27 August – 1 September   At the End of the World

On the 2nd September, sunk once more in safety in a Suva hotel room, I look back at my diary of those days of the apex of my journey at the end of the world. There is a feeling of "It is done". I make myself tea (oh, electric kettles!) and with huge oo-uu-tt-br-ea-ea-ths of relief and no small measure of pride, I write:

"I have survived 5 nights (6 days) on a very tiny snake infested island in a shark ridden ocean. Alone in a hut with no electric light at night.

I have spent 5 nights (6 days) in Paradise.

Both are true."

This is exactly what I wrote, and even now in 2008 in a different kind of end of the world place I feel a deep satisfaction as I edit these words, as I did when I typed them in yet another end of the world place in Andalucia. I realise how much detail I would have forgotten without my journal. And there is pride in that too: a year lived as if it were my last MUST be recorded and in such living, dense with experience, with living on the edge, to record that experience is yet another challenge.

Also, I think about that pitch darkness every night, with only a tiny Maglite for light. I remember how the shack had a foot high gap all around the base of the 'walls', and the sea snakes and god knows what else so close. I think about darkness. There is I think now, darkness and darkness...

I have dreamed of all these places, and I am discovering that my being contains them. That the world is very small and infinitely large, and that I am much bigger than I knew. That I am the world, that each of us is the world. That we are all one. (I typed this first as allone) That everyone I meet, everywhere, is an aspect of myself. That we have only to love ourselves in all our aspects as we are, to love everyone for who they are. Or vice versa. On my desert isle, my greatest joys and fears came together and I met myself as a whole. It is said that when one reaches "the end" of a quest one sees oneself.

But to go back to my diary. I type it just as I wrote it.

Here I am on Paradise Island. 17 hectares of coral cay, in my blue "beach bungalow" (read 'shack') called Fishers Lodge. I recall the fish around my "Wandering William" card (from Rebecca), and my fishy ring that Ann made. What will I catch here?

It is fraught with dangers. Paddling along, I saw a Crown of Thorns. This is about a foot wide like a sunburst, covered all over in two inch long spiky spikes. It is very

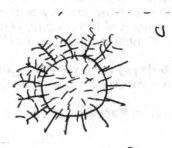

venomous - fatal. Apt name.

Not what you want to find underfoot. Good job the water is so clear. There are so many of them they are destroying the coral and even culling isn't keeping them down. Recently they took 4000 off the reefs around Leleuvia and still they come back. It is a good name for something which is consuming so much beauty.

It seems that where I lay so relaxed, in all innocence, only yesterday,

"loads" of sea snakes sleep in the shade under the trees, just as I did.

(The *computer did that itself*, believe it or not. So I must clearly leave it be. When I looked up at the screen I jumped. Just as I did when the dogs barked and I saw the snake coiled at the top of the beach in some dead palm fronds.)

When I saw the snake I was just so angry that I could never again relax on the beach or swim in peace. The dog picked it up and played with it and I was *terrified* that it would bring it to me.

DARKNESS

There is the beautiful
original natural darkness from which all springs.
Light comes from it. It feels very soft, feminine,
velvety; it wraps us gently.
Then there is the darkness we have come to
associate with evil, and to fear. It is seen as the
terrifying unknown.
It seems to me that just as there is distortion
of pain to become unnecessary suffering, there
is distortion of the dark, dark has been given a
bad name, associated with the vilification of the
feminine.
We will not fear the unknown or the future if we
trust spirit, we will not fear the world if we are
honest about ourselves. What we do not want to
see in ourselves will be seen externally, and we
call it darkness.

But it put it down and I walked rather speedily back to the huts. Where I met Kate for the first time. How fortunate I am that the few people who are here are English. I was so pleased to meet Kate and tell her about the snake. I really needed to tell someone. She told me that they more or less never bite humans or dogs, but that they are more deadly than most snakes put together. You are dead in 3 seconds if you *are* bitten. They have no fangs and their venom is so far back in their throats it is very difficult for them to bite.

(Here I have scribbled in the margin.... "is this ME? or what I FEAR I am? Hence the fear?" I still dont have the answers, but this fear is a very strong and apparently irrational one.)

Later walking more watchfully I saw another one, moving slowly up the beach from the sea. It was in the same place and I sensed that they like that shady western side of the island, that they did not come up on the beach on "my" side of the island.

I expected my challenge here to be the nothingness of it, the aloneness and just being-ness. Always after a while revelling in bliss my old demons of loneliness and abandonment come crawling up , but the sea snakes rather dominate the challenge scene here......I must try drawing one:

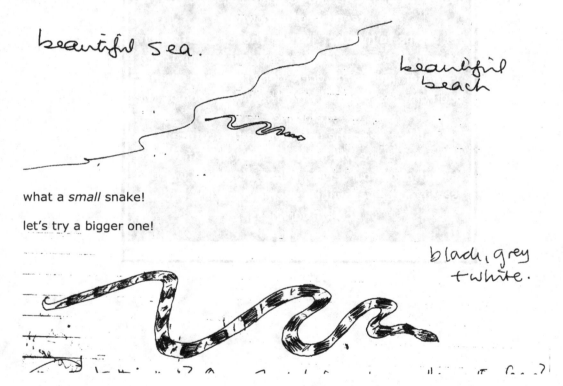

what a *small* snake!

let's try a bigger one!

(Every time I look at this drawing it alarms me. I think when I return I'll have to try some hypnosis?!?!)

I pluck up courage and go wading in the lagoon at low tide. I feel so nervous of everything there - millions of long thin spiny tentacled starfish, gross sea slugs, and one sea snake asleep in a pool. Everything dozing until the tide comes in. I am very glad to get back onto the dry sand. Where I happily find the shore to be starry with starfish and their imprints.

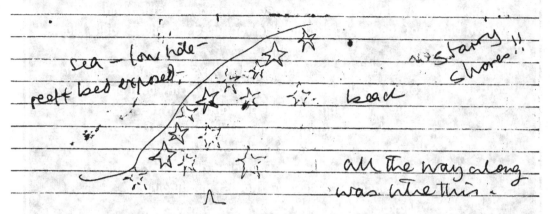

The Tropics make me nervous. But I'm so glad I've experienced them. I was in innocence swimming all the time in Bali........but I dont think there was so much there....except the dragon!...... this is *teeming* with life. And it's too much for me.

But I am here and I am surviving so far, and I am loving it nearly all of the time. And welcoming the painful feelings that are being triggered. But I am happily aware of the good hotel in Suva.... thank God the backpackers was full. Oh how I am looked after....

The night is cold and cloudy, and I am sitting in the "restaurant" with a dog at my feet (these lovely dogs have been such a blessing) drinking a cup of tea and eating my way through a packet of cherry cookies that Leon found for me. We are all wearing jumpers and trousers. It's El Nina again. I'm just so glad I'm here this week not last, when it rained nonstop.

I am really confronting my stuff, having nightmares about my marriage.

(Yes the computer did it again)

For three nights I dreamt of the violence and cruelty of my marriage. And woke agonised and despairing of the continuing presence in my dreams of my ex-husband.

PROJECTION

Subconsciously I chose my husband
to act out for me parts of myself I did not want to own.
Being with him allowed me to "project" my masochistic tendencies,
my own brand of insanity onto him. He tortured me and I could blame
him
instead of myself. He did to me what I did to myself – showed me what I
did. He mirrored me, I never needed to look at my own problems
while I was fully occupied dealing with his.
He punished me in advance for infidelities he feared.
Guilt invites punishment and I could blame him
instead of looking at the guilt I carried about my sexuality
ever since my strict Methodist upbringing.
Maybe this is where the snakes come in.
Being with him allowed me to project my inability
to break rules, be wild, risk disapproval, and cause trouble....
I could experience these close to me and not have to take the blame.
I could play holier than thou, the righteous one.....forgiving him
clearing up and reassuring him, trying to "help" him.
When something in someone terrifies, angers, bothers or irritates us,
then we can be sure that there is a message for us there.
Either we are projecting ,or envying but not daring to have, that quality
or we are being asked to set limits or boundaries about what we will
tolerate – to take care of ourselves.
My staying 25 years in my marriage was collusion.
I "agreed" in an unspoken unrecognised bargain that he could behave
badly if I could have the payoff of letting him take responsibility for my
wild side. Collusion is destructive to all parties.
I knew this from years of therapy but "dregs" remained
and my travels brought them up to the surface with a vengeance.
Once fully seen they dissolve away.....
unless there's still more, and really all we want is that they
come up and show themselves .
BECAUSE UNTIL THEY DO WE LIVE IN FEAR OF THEM IN OTHERS
This is where the weight comes from.
If we own our whole selves with love and compassion and responsibility
We live free of fear......   ....we live lightly

142

After nearly seven years. When will it end? I gave into this wretchedness for about an hour. What the hell do I have to do to be free of it all? I am aching all over as if I have been battered.

 And my pillows say "SWEET DREAMS" and "SWEET FRAGRANCE"........!!

Then it occurred to me that HE REPRESENTS MY TORTURING MYSELF. He is after all just an aspect of me. Whenever things were really good he used to turn on me and torment me. Whenever *I* have some space for me after a while I start to indulge in the old stuff. He isn't in my world any longer but I still do for myself what he did .....just as I am now here in Paradise. When his image appears in dreams then I am being reminded of this. So.... I can practise being kind to myself, as well as disciplining my masochistic mind. It's holding the balance of these that is the tricky bit.

(The diary changes then.....becomes buoyant)

I brave the cold "shower", which is tied onto a nail with a piece of string, and emerge exhilarated and smelling like a Bounty Bar. It is all the Fijian coconut oil toiletries that I got in Suva to replace what got left in my "Bali bag". I'm sitting in the motheaten old tan velvet armchair, which I have dragged out onto the verandah. I feel very nice, in my bright yellow Bali sarong. It is hot but there is a wisp of breeze, and the birds are chirping in the stirring palms.

A large white bird with a long neck and long wings each with separate feathers like a bird of prey takes off from the waters edge.

Later I lie on my beach. Languorous. Empty white sand. It is Sunday morning. A pearl of a morning.

 Exquisite. Sometimes I roll down into the liquid opal of the lagoon's edge, and lie there

I am on my island
long dreamed of
island
dreaming in the morning sun

I will remember this
it will be part of me
now

a still clear silence
transparent
at the heart of me

white gold and turquoise
palest greens and blues
hover
in the sun

143

motionless mother of pearl
sea
threaded with gold
tracery

the only sound a grain of sand
toppling
and the ocean murmuring on the far off reef

in the clarity
new islands appear beyond the horizon
faintest grey
like soft angora heaps

I am the sand
I am the sea

I lie in the sea
as it stirs the sand
it moves me
slightly

I am the sea
as it strokes the sand
I am the sun as it strokes the land
and lights the gold threads
weaving the water

the golden water spreads my hair
takes my limbs
in, and out,
I am lost in gold
and opal and pearl

touched by tiny transparent fish
and sunwhitened coral and shell

my limbs and my hair, a billion cells
flow in and out

lost in the pulsation of eternity

The remainder of my time on Leleuvia is a kaleidoscopic blur of memories. I watch the happy Fijians sweeping the sand, wading the vast coral shallows in long rows with nets, chanting as they close in the nets, singing as they chop in the kitchen, and daily carrying everything to and from the boat as it left or arrived. Babies sit on shady tables eating lunch with podgy black hands, a toddler sits under the table in the sand, putting sand in a cardboard tube, and emptying it, over and over again.

I eat "flower" soup, "combination" soup, and the best chips in the world. They win my BEST CHIPS AWARD. I swing idly in a purple hammock with "my" spiral symbol all over it.

I watch a yacht which suddenly appeared, I fantasise about being aboard. My fantasies are blown when the real occupants come ashore for supper, and prove to be rather like the sick looking occupants of the expensive resorts on the mainland....I paint the sea, experimenting with my watercolours to try to catch the transparency and the light and the layering of colour. I sunbathe with three dogs, one at each corner,

and draw one of them. I read, but am conscious that when I do I enter another world and really I want to be in this one. I am holding my book 'A Woman's World: Travellers Tales from Women on the Road', which I bought in the middle of the Singapore night, when I go for my tea to the hatch. One of the Fijian women looks at it, touches it, and reads the title slowly to herself. She smiles broadly and gets my tea.

In the evening a slender, pale brown, wise-looking little man called Vincent comes to talk to us about the Island. It is very special, he says. It is teardrop shaped, not round. There is a legend.....as he begins I know this is going to mean something to me....

lying on sand next to

A king had a favourite daughter whom he adored. But she came home with child, and he sent her with her servants to sail far away, so that she would not disgrace him. As they sailed she gave birth to a daughter. They had not enough water for the child as well as themselves, so she abandoned her on a little island that they came to. Leaving a pot to collect rainwater for her to give her a chance. The girl survived and grew, and to this day her footsteps can be seen coming in and out of the water, and her lonely cry can be heard. The snakes do not go to the side of the island where she walks to swim. And the island became the shape of a teardrop.

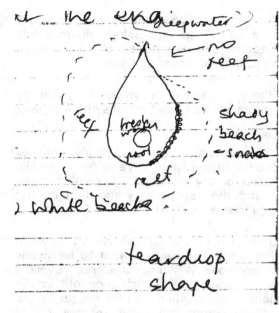

at ... the end deepwater
no reef
shady beach — snake
reef fresh root
reef
white beach
teardrop shape

And to this day the pot of water is there in the centre of the island and there are never any mosquito larvae there ....

unless there is need for a a warning to those living on the island. In that case mosquitoes appear, and the snakes go right across the island. This has happened if there is too much noise and partying it seems!

My life long themes of shame, and abandonment. It serves to show me yet again that I am on course. And my sense about the snakes not sleeping on "my" side was right. I don't think I could have borne it if they did. We are challenged but only as far as we can take. I am learning to coexist with the snakes now. And to accept my fear of them.

I ask Vincent the meaning of the name Leleuvia: he has his own idea, "a way to cross over". This feels right and I like it. I have done some crossing over. He thinks it is appropriate because you can nearly cross to the big island at low tide - the reef is miles out.

After this we sit in a circle for the Kava Ritual. Kava is an a root-based natural tranquilliser which is drunk regularly on Fiji with great solemnity. Disputes and issues are brought to the Kava Circle for solving. "I should have had some when I nearly trod on the snake" I say. The liquid looks like dirty washing up water in half a coconut shell, and too much of it numbs you. Vincent tells of how men can sometimes not walk after a long ceremony. I soon feel my tongue go numb. It may be partly because of this that Fiji is such a peaceful and happy place with no shouting apparently..., though Vincent adds that it also means that Fijians are not very successful in business. But as he says, when men have their land, and their families, in a rich and fertile country like his, there is no poverty. The contentment is the true richness.

Kate and Dave have T shirts handpainted by a very graceful young girl also called Sandra who is living on the island for a while. They got her to paint "KATE AND DAVE'S BANKRUPTCY TOUR on them. I said "I know the feeling".

I go out with the Dive Boat, and enjoy passing Honeymoon Island. I've been gazing at it for days. It is miles out on its own, a heap of sand with one palm tree. I watch Kate and Jo and Han and the Divemaster and assistant get kitted up and drop backwards off the flat bottomed boat. I know the ocean is teeming with sharks but I long to at least snorkel for a moment. At last my longing overbalances my fears and I jump in in a very ungainly fashion, wearing Jo's snorkelling gear. I am utterly thrilled by this new world, and manage all of five minutes before suddenly wondering whether a shark is anywhere around. Getting back is no picnic unfit as I am, and Dave finally hauls me unceremoniously up through the engine space. I fret that I was too heavy for him, which is pretty symbolic of my fears in relationship generally.....but I am well pleased at my small adventure.

146

The last morning is Kate's Last Dive. Dave is staying behind to pack, and Jo and Han left the day before. The morning is glowing iridescent exquisite pearllike glory. The boat knifes cleanly through golden glimmering turquoise silence into the sun, and then suddenly there are dolphins leaping in the bow wave. And then again later, surrounding the boat, and we are sailing in a frothing sea of leaping diving spinning dolphins. The boat stills.

It is a moment of grace.

We feel blessed. "I've never known them come so close" said the Divemaster. "there must have been 30 of them"

And then they are gone and the boat lifts and speeds, flying into the wind towards our little island in an aura of glorious ecstasy mingled with the bittersweetness of leavetaking. The air is alive and tingling. Kate is in the bow, head flung back, legs dangling overboard, arms outspread Titanic style, hair flying . I am standing behind her, very straight, very rooted to the deck, feeling very tall, as if I encompass all of this and more. We are right in the moment. There is nothing else.

I share a cigarette with Kate and Dave to celebrate the dolphins. It reminds me of my last ceremonial cigarette in France at Solstice when four of us went to walk the Labyrinth in Chartres Cathedral. 'It takes a lot of bottle, what you're doing' said Kate. They gave me their Rough Guide to the USA, for which I was to be profoundly grateful. (The States proved to be one place, surprisingly, where travelling unbriefed does not work so well....and I was of course in possession of a guidebook!!!) They'd driven all the way across the States before coming to Fiji. Seeing all their photos and listening to them I feel so excited that I am going to have nearly three months there.

The boat is being loaded and it is nearly time to go but I have one further small initiation that I have set myself. I have to walk to the Pot that Vincent told us about. The water pot left for the abandoned maiden. It means walking through an almost invisible deeply leaf- strewn path to the centre of the island, all too aware of Vincent's talking about 'loads of snakes'. I walk very slowly and gingerly. It seems a long way, but at last I reach it and I sort of know it's OK now and walk back much faster as if my test was already passed. I am quite jubilant and run to the boat.

The Fijian woman who liked my book also comes running arms outstretched and gives me a huge hug. It was like she found some other part of herself in what I am doing. She waves as I jump into the boat and we speed away.

'Where are you staying in Hawaii?' asked Kate, 'in a hotel?' 'No, in a private house on the beach where people go to swim with the dolphins' I said, suddenly realising how wonderful that is 'It's supposed to be quite swish though.'

'I could do with a bit of swishness!' I added.

Kate does her Titanic bit again until the swell gets too much. The green river is just the same, and the ramshackle bus. A huge outboard motor is being extracted through the window. I notice that the people waiting to go out to the island mean nothing to me. Kate and Dave and Jo and Han did.

Dave says, 'Let us know when your book comes out'. 'I will' I said, 'and it will'.

Sean unloads my case. 'I think you've got a man in here' he says. 'I wouldn't like to take it round the world.' I said 'Books paper and paints....'

But then I think. **EXACTLY. A MAN IN MY CASE. HEAVY.**

But I'm on a journey to learning to travel light. And not carry my past with me.

2 September   Mission accomplished

I am sitting VERY comfortably propped up on pillows in this beautiful bed in this beautiful room in the Peninsula Hotel in Suva, with a tray of breakfast. (I note I have come from *island* to *peninsula*....some connection has been made.)

The windows are wide open: they slide back leaving a big open space so that it feels like a balcony. The room is big and newly renovated (more metaphor) with the same clean lines, pale plain neutral colours and simplicity of the Lake Plaza in NZ. And the same pristine bathroom. **Never** has a hotel room felt so good. **Never** has a bath been so blissful.

Well I've sent the bus away. It came to collect me. How's that for service? I'll have to get a taxi across the Island!!!- but I've been told they're quite cheap. Four hours bus journey and leaving all this **now** (9am) is *not* what I want. I ring reception and they look in to things. It seems that for less than a taxi (which are relatively cheap by our standards) I can *FLY*!!!!! and for 26 pounds!!!!! (no pound sign on an American computer) and taking 25 minutes!!!!

IT IS IN THE TINY AIRPORT OF NAUSORI THAT I AM ALL OF A SUDDEN *SWAMPED* WITH EXCITEMENT, GRATITUDE, JOY, PRIDE, *REALISATION* OF WHERE I AM.

It sweeps through me as a quite large Royal Tongan plane roars in in its rainbow colours. It is clearly an event. All the colourful Fijian crowd flock to the windows to watch. Holding children and pointing. Tears are in my eyes: *I know where I am and what I am doing.*

148

From the perspective of time I now see that this was my 'Mission Accomplished' moment. I was flying out of the Southern Hemisphere, destination swishness in Hawaii USA. I had graduated from tackling alone the dangers of the tropical unknown .

I am so grateful. So grateful too to be almost the only white person here. Only two pale unsmiling white ladies primly reading amid all the hubbub. Otherwise thronging Fijians. Women like galleons, sailing proudly in full colour, flowing with frills and ribbons and flowers. Wide haloes of black frizz and big white smiles. A tiny girl with so many frills bows and flowers as to render her almost invisible.

Oh, a misjudgment. One reading lady has got up to look and there is almost a smile on her face.

In rolls an Air Fiji plane with -yes - the spiral symbol on - it's following me. It's also wildly decorated with fluorescent goldfish, flowers, palm trees, sea, starfish, shells and birds. Large black men wheel out large blue wheelbarrows to bring in the luggage.
PS. I had to stand on scales for the check-in.........I didnt look....back to food combining in Crestone I think.....

Now another Air Fiji island shuttle has flown in: this one is blue and has dolphins all over it.

Watching the crush of little planes is a lady wearing a long blue skirt with a large printed image of Princess Diana on it saying 'QUEEN OF HEARTS' ENGLAND and her dates.

There are only a few metres between the standing and queuing planes. A new arrival bears the legend 'THERE'S A NEW SPIRIT IN THE AIR'. Another plane taxis off and it immediately whisks into its place. More wheelbarrows converge. Its all very fast and furious. Air Fiji alone apparently takes 70 planes out of here daily. Little red tractors tow little red fuel tanks.

Men, elegant in their business skirts tote briefcase with one hand and talk into mobile phones with the other. Their vast befrilled and beribboned ladies incongruous at their sides.

Now it's my turn, and I am guided out to 'New Spirit in the Air'.

Up we go, over the rampant green of the forests and the endless empty savagery of the mountains, tentacles of which seem to reach to almost touch the airport at Nadi.

It has been a terrific £26 worth.

The plane to Honolulu is delayed so I check my case in (No. 13 desk...I had 'chosen' it and that was indeed the one I was directed to) and go in search of a taxi to go into the town to hunt an Internet Cafe. Result several rather confused taxi drivers. But my instincts are_getting honed, because I immediately see one who looks right but he sends me to the one ahead. But neither he nor his fulsome mates have any idea of what I am on about. By which time someone has hopped in his taxi and he sends me back to my preferred driver.......

He says, 'No Internet Cafe, but how long do you have? I could show you the coast and countryside? How much currency have you left?' 'not much' I say, and tell him,

'Plenty!!!' he smiles, and he proceeds to drive around giving me *masses* of information, and answering all my questions. Because I liked his face I had got into the front seat and could really see. And I had been thinking 'there's still so much I want to know'.....

He is an Indian, very smart, with a kind clever face. He tells me about the sugar cane, the drought, the Sleeping Giants Mountains, the appalling cost of education, the freshwater mussel collecting, the hydroponics farm, the pig battery, tourism, and the Fijian character. We see sugar cane 'trains' with dozens of trucks, on tracks a couple of feet wide if that, going to the cane factory which belches smoke in the distance.

We see stubble burning to the edge of the road, flames and black smoke billowing over the road. They can't put fires out due to lack of water. The cane grows again after burning, without replanting, for five years. The plants are short this year, only 3 feet instead of 9 due to this drought. Fiji usually produces over 400million tons of sugar, but this year only 100. Small farmers can usually live on their sugar sales, but not this year......

We see the schoolchildren in beautiful uniforms of apricot or orange or yellow dresses, or shirts with white trousers for the boys - spotlessly clean of course. We see groups of chattering women in roadside clearings cleaning the mussels and selling them to passers by. We seethe dusky peaks of the Yasawas Islands where such films as the Blue Lagoon were made. We see the raised pipe network of the Hydroponics Farm which is feeding Fiji this difficult year: so weird to see fat cabbages and lettuces sitting on narrow pipes a metre off the ground. Clever really, endlessly recycling the nutrient filled water, which isn't lost to earth or air, and the height allowing less backbreaking harvesting. Fields and fields of it all....

All in all it is a useful flight delay....it also means less time in Honolulu Airport at the dead of night waiting to fly to Big Island. Same thing happened flying from Singapore to Sydney.

I feel good. It's been a confrontational, dark and enlightening apex to my journey, it's a kind of ending, its all downhill from here, relatively. It also been staggeringly lovely.

The Fourth Dream... in France, a Crossroads, another Confrontation, another Ending.

Like the dishevelled barn I found in Semur-en-Auxois in our last travelling summer 1990, I was at a crossroads, and like the name we gave it -'Maison des Tournesols'- House of Sunflowers - I was turning my face to the sunshine of living independently, to my own inner male perhaps, without the endless agony and misery of living with mental illness. I knew that the life my husband was choosing did not resonate with who I was. I knew it was not good for him to be with me. I had work to do on myself.

That spring 1991, when Miro went off to France with Ben in motorhome number 3 – a swish spacious American Midas - to start the renovation and avoid dealing with the mounting problems of Queen St and debt, I started therapy.

I knew I wanted to get a divorce and I wanted to look at the whole thing with a professional to be sure I was making the best choice for us all.

I asked Miro's psychiatrist to recommend someone as I guessed he would know what my problems were. He sent me to Patricia Dyehouse, who lived and worked in a gorgeous house above Soar Mill Cove near Salcombe. 'I can't go all the way down there' I said. 'Why not' he said 'she's the one for you'. And for four and a half years I drove the hour and a half twice and later on once a week. When I first went I wailed that I couldn't afford it all. She said 'can you afford not to?' (and she was a busy therapist with no need to entice) and I just went for it in trust. Somehow I managed it, don't know how. For a while I couldn't find the money and she said, 'pay me later' and I did.

Thursdays became my own time, my time out from the mess. My blissful days of solitary freedom. I packed a picnic for the beach or fields or ate fish and chips on Salcombe,

harbour. I had the journeys to mull over the therapy process undisturbed. I took my journal and wrote it all up as I went. Determinedly Pat and I unravelled it all, and, along with my Zen and Dance teachers, built me up again.

*I learned a lot about **Projection** very quickly in the first sessions with her. I learned how I had projected my wild side onto Miro, not daring to own it. He could in the old days on Dartmoor smash up the restaurant and I could be good girl and clean it all up, yet I felt the excitement of it somewhere deep deep down, without having to take responsibility for bad behaviour. .*

I read Herman Hesse at the same time. 'When we hate someone we are hating something that is within ourselves. We are never stirred up by something which does not already exist within us. There is no reality beyond what we have inside us.' 'It was not my lot to breathe freely in fullness and comfort, I needed the spur of torment.' I wanted to move past this now and accept whatever I found inside me.

I went out to France for the summer, driving our Mazda badly in great trepidation, with two sleeping teenager friends of Ben's. I set about giving my marriage all I'd got, giving it the last chance I knew I'd regret not giving it, with all the newly learned tools at my disposal.

'In twelve weeks', said Miro to his family, 'she's done for Sandra what I've been trying to do for 25 years'. He also said I'd brought a package with me – all the problems of home of course, that he had fled. It was intense, sexy, hot, and we talked a lot, and I listened a lot. But I think we knew it was the last tango.

151

THERAPY

'the unexamined life is not worth living'…. Plato
Therapy is about getting deep, getting real, getting authentic. So you get to say 'I get it! wow, I get what my life is about.'
Therapy connects you with your true self, which has got pretty immured in a load of conditioned stuff.
Combine it with stillness and silence on a regular basis, and with some fast movement too. So you also get connected to the Sacred.
Then you can move forward exploring not as a frightened little lonely ego but as a soul, an aware spark of the Divine, secure in that, full of love and wonder.
There are a million kinds. I feel the right one crosses your path if you are genuinely wanting to get sorted. The only pre requisite is being prepared to own your problems, take responsibility for them.
Then you can get somewhere. The therapist will listen non judgmentally, will accept and allow, as you uncover all the shitty stuff you have hidden from, have buried, have turned your eyes from. You learn not to blame anyone, not even yourself. Just SEE.
You find out you don't have to be perfect, just be what you are…BUT what you are under all those conitionings. This is what confused me for so long people saying 'just be yourself' – but who was I? –was I all those insecurities and hurts and prides?
I didn't think so.
The danger of therapy is getting stuck in past pain, and this happens a lot, so watch for it. If you are learning, and discovering, going 'ah right, yes, I see what has been going on', you're doing well.
When that process stops, quit, but quit well. Achieve a good closure, with respect.
Don't get into blaming the therapist. If he /she is not working out, see what has been gained, be grateful for that, say so, then leave.
I found therapy invaluable. Thanks Pat!

152

He said one day 'You found all our places. I just saw that. You found the Muzle Patch, the Old Inn, Queen Street and this barn, you decided to have motorhomes and travel.'
Another day in a temper 'I'm fed up trailing around after you' and 'I' m fed up with all your endless discoveries'

Yes I can see now how it must have been. Poor man. It was the other side of the coin. I saw myself as a helpless victim of the madman. He saw me as a judgmental and dissatisfied control freak obsessed by her spiritual path and addicted to change and development and making dreams come true and drama. He had to live with my unspoken criticism, condemnation, and disappointment, and my passion for my own spiritual journey. He said he could not compete with God. That I felt no one was good enough for me. He tried to teach me to accept not expect. I avoided my own stuff by my preoccupation with his. He distracted me from myself and he made me feel better about myself in comparison. I see the past with an objectivity now which is humbling but healing. I also just began, faintly, to acknowledge my innate goodness and openness, my joy, and how hard that must have been to live with for someone so tormented. Certainly I projected my own torment, but his was of a different league, one that reflected the horrors of his background.

I see now he also showed me my worth....my joy, my innocence, my love, my generosity, kindness, my goodness and caring, my response-ability, my strength ...so much...how would I ever have seen it without the context of my wise but tortured husband? It was years later that I came to see all this. I had to travel through the more negative stuff of my Shadow before finally I could see the 'Light shadow' hiding in the darkest corners. I see also how seductive is the negative, how 'cool'. We have to dare to be uncool. Wonder is not cool. Amazement and enthusiasm are not cool. Poetry is the communication of amazement, it is said, well one kind is. There is the other sort, the 'cool' sort, which is the communication of anger and despair.

Those horrors, brought to renewed life by the war in Yugoslavia, caught up with us there in our French idyll and so did the huge and escalating problems of Queen St, and we had to return, and it soon became clear that Miro was not going to be able to deal with any of it.

We went out to France for half term. I wasn't going to go, I'd come to the end of my road, but Miro's brother let him down and he said I had to go, he couldn't be there alone. I stupidly went, then spent the whole time ill with sinusitis (irritation with someone close according to Louise Hay's little blue book 'Heal Your Body') after clearing out the dusty hay loft.

I do remember the excitement of seeing the lorry come to take all that old hay away, and the liveliness of it all. It seems that was the moment the Dream was stopped mid-reel, all the cast in mid movement, frozen for ever.

Until the moment in Spain in late 2004 when the lorry came up to John's House of Dreams (Cortijo de Ensuenos) bringing the first load of building materials...I gasped with déjà vu....the Dream was re-starting...

Then one night just after we returned, after days of inactivity in the face of the onslaught from the Banks, the Inland Revenue, the Head landlord (the Church of England), the tenant(the Rank Organisation) and the Fire Authority, he stood in the shower and said 'I've got great faith that you'll be able to sort it all out'.

And I thought, 'yes, maybe I could, but not while I'm coping with endless unpredictable abuse from you'.

On one of the last days, just after a most beautiful lovemaking time on the sitting room rug by the fire, when I was feeling warm and relaxed for a wonderful moment, he suddenly said something cruelly and out of the blue about my fancying a man we had met on our trip a year ago. (I hadn't). It stabbed at me, in my relaxed state, and I said 'I will never make love with you again. Never. If you can speak to me like that moments after such a time, I will never relax with you again'. He seemed shocked into silence, amazingly. We stopped talking and started to watch Inspector Morse. It was, aptly, about obsession. He said sadly 'oh, my God, obsessive, possessive love'. He had a certain awareness of himself and his frailties. It was one of the things that kept me with him.

Another day he said, 'but you know what you are worth don't you?' and I said 'no that's the trouble, I don't. I kind of did, but not now. You have trodden me into the ground. I have to pick myself up with Pat's help, find my shape again, learn myself again'. Tears rose to his eyes.

'You nearly destroyed my joy' I said, 'and I let you. but I am going to put myself first and I will find it again'.

It was moving into the unknown, into the darkness.

Breaking the egg

'The bird is struggling out of the egg. The egg is the world. Whoever wants to be born must destroy a world. The bird is flying to God' - Herman Hesse's 'Damian'. I wrote notes on this book. It reassured me that my rebirth needs must be destructive. The later you leave it, the more destructive it becomes.

I said to Miro, 'We are in a river, flowing fast, where the flow will take us I don't know, but I feel when it throws us ashore we will be in different places.' On one level I had cried wolf so often he did not believe me. On another level he had waited all our lives together for me to leave him.

Finally I realised – a powerful and huge realisation - that he thought I was only staying because of my own problems; I saw his mockery. He laughed at me because I stayed to be insulted and abused. I was sacrificing myself for him, protecting him from his weaknesses,....I preferred things to be my fault because then I could do something...it was the only way to have any power in a helpless situation....yet another aspect of a need to be in control. Weird. If I took too much responsibility I felt better. If I accepted he had to take responsibility himself the whole situation was out of my control and I was afraid because I knew he would not be capable.

One day soon after this realisation I suddenly knew I must not go on a day more. Ben was away, and I wanted to spare him the toughest stuff. I remember I was ironing at the time and he was as always on the sofa watching TV. I could not wait until the time was right. I told him, very seriously and quietly, that I could not live with him any more. I suggested he go and live at Queen St in the flat. I would stay in the house until it was sold to pay off a few of the huge debts. That would quieten a lot of the problems and give him a chance. I had no real idea how it would all work, there

didn't seem to be a way out, but I knew it was right. I didn't know how Ben and I would manage. But I just took the bull by the horns and did it and he actually knew I was serious and he agreed to do what I suggested. Something went out of him.

Next morning I left for college. We had agreed he would start to move that day and sleep at the flat from then on. He was sitting heavily in the blue armchair in the bedroom window and tears were in his eyes. A flock of birds flew past. I kissed his forehead. 'I'm going now.' I said. And I went, leaving him sitting there.

Later that day he appeared staring-eyed at college, clearly in a state of total psychotic breakdown. I don't remember what happened or what was done. I only remember the fear. It was the start of a terrible time.

I carried my school Gideon New Testament with me and repeated the 23rd psalm endlessly. I recall sitting with it at the round family table while the social worker, psychiatrist and my GP talked with Miro to decide whether to section him. He was very wild by then but I don't want to describe it. It was so harrowing. I just read the psalm and imagined Jesus sitting with me: I felt protected even as I trembled, clenching my fists and shoulders. I remember after they took him away sitting on the edge of my bed, howling and sobbing, and my GP sat there next to me holding me and saying gently 'The right thing happened here tonight' over and over.

I went to see him in the mental hospital and he said from what seemed like deep under dark swirling waters, 'You wont leave me now will you?' I said, 'If I don't I will go under as well. If I stay, you will only do this again when I leave next time.' I was branded callous and cruel by the staff. Perhaps I was, or perhaps I was just very fearful – or very brave, or all three. But it was all I could do at the time. I had reached the end of my tether – and it was a tether part of him needed to keep me on. A few days later he turned up blankfaced at Elmside and I gently walked him back to hospital. We stood at the junction of Magdalen Road and Barracks Road and he said, 'You have been beautiful to me Sandra'. It was I think the end.

Thinking about it now, the significance of those road names strikes me. The old male dominator world of Barracks, where the hospital was and the divine feminine, so long suppressed and vilified, of the Magdalen , where the Tutorial College was. And, our home for eight years, the years of the decay and rotting of a diseased marriage and the increasingly severe mental illness in Miro and its onset in Daniel, was in Elmside....!!

Miro went back to Yugoslavia, and I set about sorting out all the mess and with a lot of honest communication and the unbelievably supportive help of two solicitors and a surveyor, all those huge hostile organisations turned their resources in support of a solution. I did eventually pay off all the head rent owed, get the fire certificate, did up both the buildings, and pay half the bank debts – 'my' half. I am very proud of what I achieved. It was a monumental tangle and apparently insoluble. Step by step I went on in trust, putting my mind to juggling my way through all the maze of financial demand.

Something was working with me, no disasters befell the properties, I never had to do more than I could, I always sensed at the last minute something I had to do. Walking to the bank for a meeting it would come to me what I had to say , what plan I could propose. Yes, I am proud. Yes, how else would I have known what I was capable of, how resourceful I was.

Years later Miro said during one of the intermittent calls persuading me to go back to him 'I'm sorry I lost all that money'. But it takes two, and I should have put my foot down long long ago. I recall again Mrs Drew of Castle Drogo saying to me in the early 80s 'I don't know why you don't go on strike dear'. And another customer saying 'it's not good to allow yourself to be walked over'. I was so afraid of him I never saw his fear of me, never knew my own power. I left my strike too late and the consequences were far worse as a result. It was over 10 years AFTER the divorce before I was free of Miro, who came and went, periodically invading space with no compunction, ignoring court orders, and left a trail of havoc everywhere.

On Christmas Eve I went alone to the cathedral in Exeter for the Bishop Grandisson service, and queued patiently and numbly for two hours. I was shown to a seat right at the very front. It was a blessing so I knew I had done the right thing.

Daniel, Ben and I spent a quiet and nervous Christmas, it was hard to reassure them it was for the best. How dreadful it must have been for them and what guilt I carry.

But I dreamed that my father was walking towards me and gave me this huge hug, and so again I knew I had done the right thing.

GETTING HELP

If you have to 'break eggs', get help.
DON'T try to go it alone if you are trying to escape from someone or something dangerous, whether it is a violent husband or your own addiction or both.
These days there is LOADS of help, be grateful for it and use it.
When I was at the end of my tether there was nothing really.
Talk about it, let it out, let fresh air wash through it.

The Vision of Joshua 'Into the Unknown'　　　　　　**Joshua Chapter 5 v**
13-15

Sometimes in the very early hours of the morning when the world is still, perhaps at a crisis in our lives, it seems as if a veil is torn and a flash of lightning lights the darkness.

It seems that now and then an inward eye opens and we suddenly stand in the presence of God, seeing what was invisible before.

Sometimes when the vision dies and the brief awe and elevation of the spirit vanishes, no mark is left, but sometimes a permanent effect is felt and we are never quite the same again.

Joshua, we know, pupil and assistant to Moses, had succeeded his chief when Moses had died, and had led the Hebrew nation across the desert and the river to the country they are to conquer for an inheritance. Here they are, just over the border, looking back at much suffering and much joy. Before them lies the unexplored, the unknown. Joshua goes on ahead alone, and stands quietly waiting for his God to speak. If he had not been tuned in, he would not have received his vision.

He lifted up his eyes and above him towers a vast figure, with drawn sword. He trembles.

'Art thou for us or against us?'
'As captain of the Host of the Lord am I now come'.

And Joshua fell on his face and did worship. 'what saith my Lord to His servant?'

And the captain of the Lord's host said to Joshua. 'Put off thy shoe from off thy foot, for the place whereon thou standest is holy'. And Joshua did so.

And Joshua knew his people were divinely overlooked and attended, as they moved into the unknown of this new land.

He knew they had only to go with respect for this holy place, , to move with Gratitude and Reverence for the sacredness of the time and the place….of the moment. No declaring of wondrous Things did God say to Joshua.. just to cherish the right spirit within them.

And so it is for us, whenever we stand at the edge of the unknown. We can go forward in his strength. Taking care to honour wherever we stand as a holy place.

AMEN

River Meadows...... My clean-slate home

Chapter 10
Hawaii...... Stepping into Magic

2 September

On plane to Honolulu, just noticed the engines. They are HUGE. 4 metres long at least and 2 metres wide. Especially amazing after the propellers on the little plane from Suva, which they turned by hand.....

The plane is entirely full of stiff-suited Japanese businessmen, because it goes on to Tokyo. I will never ever forget them all laughing uncontrollably at the unexpected showing of the 'Alice's Wedding' episode of 'The Vicar of Dibley'. Our TV gets everywhere. Breakfast was noodles.

Now, we are coming down into Honolulu, it has taken me by surprise, it looks like I imagine Hong Kong to look. So many skyscrapers, and houses flowing up the mountains.

Big Island, Hawaii

America I just love you.

I could cry. The USA again, and something about it touches and feeds me and sends my spirits soaring. YES!!! OH YES!!! I am swamped by joy, gratitude and love. Reminds me of when I landed at Boston, and when we first saw the valley in the Rockies. What is it all about, this America thing? ('Your future' said Rose when I said it to her back home) It's about expansion, I think.

I am sitting eating a 'small stack' of pancakes –anything but small – in the Aloha Performing Arts Centre. On the till is a silvery angel whose wings flap when a button is pressed. Hiring a car was just so easy, all of 5 minutes. I am driving a dark green Mustang convertible (for the price of a small car) across fields of black lava and between huge hedges of vivid magenta bougainvillaea. Black and magenta and greens seem to be the colour of Big Island. Hawaii is the South Pacific crossed with the States. Bliss.

It is HOT. VERY. And it is only 8.30am.

And now here I am in this unbelievable place - Napoopoo Captain Cook. What is appearing before my senses may well be the best life on earth can offer. This most beautiful of houses, shapely curves, one storey spreading itself voluptuously by the sea, all glass and wood, huge glass or mirrored walls, expansive spaces, set on the black lava shore. A curvy blue pool is set on an oval white terrace built out over a black lava promontory. The house is surrounded by a vast wooden deck of a pale almost colourless green, and which snakily entwines with the white pool terrace.

I lie on a sumptuous lounger and take in the stupendous jagged black and green volcanic cliffs across the bay, the Pacific crashing dark blue and white on the black, the dog Anella sleeping at my feet. This is a conservation area for Spinner Dolphins. I hope to swim with them. I only came to this house because I didn't get round to calling Joan Ocean and so she didn't have room for me and called Lorayne, who caretakes this house. The surprising rewards of procrastination.

Hawaii (am I really here?) has a lot in common with Rotorua. Active but 'safe' vulcanicity. 'Big Island is an active volcano' said the plane mag. It is I know from all my years teaching Tectonics a 'Hot Spot' with 'basic' lava. The earth's crust is moving over a point where a plume of lava upwells, due to convection currents deep within, from the molten interior. The crust keeps moving and a chain of volcanic islands forms, with the most recent one the active volcano. The lava is thin, because it is very hot from so deep deep down, and when it erupts it forms new land, as it does in Iceland'. It does not gum up the works and explode and throw boulders and ash everywhere like thick cooler 'acid' lava. That is formed when the earth's crust melts when pushed down during collision of tectonic plates. Here the lava does not explode under pressure but flows, at varying speeds but relatively steadily. This speaks to me again about anger and rage. Don't let it stay still, thicken and set, causing explosions!

Lorayne has left out an Osho Zen Tarot (what a combination!) card for the day. It is 'New Vision' 'In the end, you just accept who you are, you let go of the struggle'. The image is a figure holding a sword in the right hand, a snake in the left and a phoenix on the head. Shed the skin, be born again from the ashes, take on our power – my own masculine power perhaps. I am reminded of the snakes on Leleuvia and the Centre back home in the buildings I named Phoenix House.

I am still surprising myself in mirrors. After a week of the mirrorless desert isle.

I look very young, lean, very blonde, and very brown. The taxi driver thought I was 40, and I know it was genuine. He too looked young for his age. And I remember too waiting in reception in the Suva hotel, seeing the TV just that moment showing Shirley Valentine asking for her table and chair to be set by the sea. And there she was sitting with her pitcher of wine and her glass, looking. Just as I am looking. Falling in love over and over again with the world. Recalls Joanna Macy's 'World as Lover, World as Self'.

But I am also remembering that I am carrying all that buried anger that Isabel Bellamy saw, and the 'man in the suitcase' that Sean in Leleuvia joked about. Work to do still. I have no idea how this is to be done. I do shiver sometimes when it crosses my mind. But not now, this is not the time, and I will know when it is. So until then, relax and enjoy.

I drive my dark green Mustang up the gently sloping flanks of the volcano, the road getting increasingly cracked and the lava more vicious. Vegetation drops away and the land is black knotted ropes of lava, with an occasional stunted tree. All savagely sculpted against the solid blue of the sky.

At the top, I climb down the path into the crater, and I find myself walking across the hot lava crust, with occasional smoking cracks, and in roped off areas, I can actually see down to the red glare below. I am amazed. I 'ask' that I am alone, and after a little while the other tourists do go, and I am able to raise my arms and shout to Pele, the Goddess of the Volcano. I call Her and ask for Her help when the time comes to address my own red and molten angry depths. I kneel, with difficulty - it is hot - and surrender myself to her. I ask also for her help with my base chakra, that I can feel strong and confident in my physical and financial base in the world. I am so grateful for my solitude in this tourist (and geological!) hotspot.

After perhaps half an hour, people arrive, and I make my way up towards the restaurant terrace and sit eating and looking down at the gigantic smoking crater where I walked. Extraordinary. This crater is on its way to being inactive, as the hotspot 'moves' to the south east: really the island moves with the tectonic plate, and the hotspot beneath stays the same and produces a new island.

Another day, I drive to the more active vents on the southern coast, where molten lava emerges from fissures and flows into the ocean, in a tremendous cloud of steam. Here you can't walk close, but I walk as far as I am allowed, the heat burning my feet through my shoes. I can't see the red lava because of the steam, but I know it is there, just perhaps a quarter mile away.

All the fire energy makes me long for a man, for passion, company and touch, ...oh touch, and flesh, skin.... I find myself, for my penultimate day here, in a very depressed and lonely mood for a whole day, and I droop around in that stupendous place.....marvelling at how I can be depressed staying in that house on that island. What a waste. And how often life is wasted like that.

161

PELE – HAWAIIAN GODDESS OF FIRE

'Described as "She-Who-Shapes-The-Sacred-Land" in ancient Hawaiian chants, the volcano goddess, Pele, is passionate, volatile, and capricious. To this day, tales of Pele's power continue. Whispered encounters with Pele include those of drivers who pick up an old woman dressed all in white accompanied by a little dog on roads in Kilauea National Park, only to look in the mirror to find the back seat empty. Pele's face has mysteriously appeared in photographs of fiery eruptions, and most people who live in the islands-whether Christian, Buddhist, Shinto, or other-speak respectfully of the ancient goddess. After all, she has destroyed more than 100 structures on the Big Island since 1983, and perhaps even more awesome than that, she has added more than 70 acres of land to the island's southeastern coastline.'
Words by Betty Fullard Leo

We can in all Goddesses find aspects of ourselves, and Pele can show us our ferocity, and the creativity and beauty of that ferocity. She can show us what lies unseen below the twisted ugly masks we create to hide our depths...

I guess I'm coming nearer to the end of my solitary travels and will soon be in Crestone again. Company. I have been a long time travelling alone now. A sad and mystified part of me says, 'why do men never approach me????'

My last day, I am to swim with the dolphins with Doug and another travelling woman. I stand on the edge of the sea, or I try to, the shore is massive jagged black boulders. HOW am I supposed to get into the sea? I shake my head but Doug takes my hand and somehow it is achieved, we launch ourselves from a rock, don't ask me how. We swim out to the boat and head out into the bay. Then suddenly, I am being effectively pushed off the boat and I am swimming on the surface with my snorkel looking down on a whole stream of dolphins swimming below me. These are wild and free, wary - not like Fungi in Ireland, who is used to people touching him all the time for healing, to the extent that he feels almost tame.

Doug again takes my hand and we swim along with them just below us– and he points to a mother with her baby sort of stuck to her back. We swim along just using the flippers, and feel a part of the great shoal.

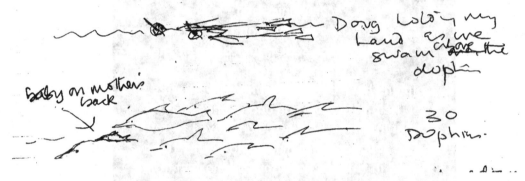

Doug dives down and blows bubble rings looking up at me they grow to be a metre or so across, silver tubes in the water.

It is wonderful that he only has me to look after, the other traveller is used to it all. What a way to leave Hawaii.

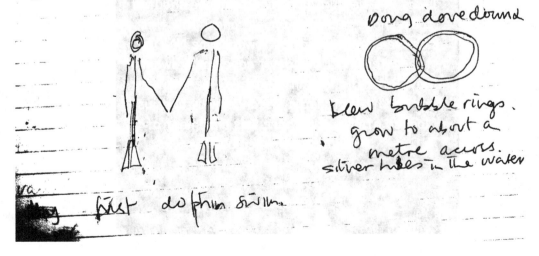

163

DOLPHINS

It seems that the encounter with wild dolphins if it is free, honourable and respectful, brings a sense of unconditional love to wounded hearts.
They bring this gift to us.
They show us how to play, how to live lightly and playfully and lovingly, with high levels of communication.
Eye contact with a dolphin can feel very moving.
Touch even more so. Or just being in their energy field.
Dolphins have been shown in many studies to help with isolation and depression.
Funghi in Dingle Bay in Ireland loves to touch and be touched by humans, and seems to have stayed in this one location so long just to be there for all the people who come to see him.
When I met Funghi it was not long after my divorce, and I was very fearful. My first trip away with new friends.
I was in a wetsuit alone and someone shouted from shore, 'here he comes', and I felt this massive creature moving towards me UNDER the water and I could not cope and I swam away. But I did look into his eye... he knew my fear and he surfaced a distance away and just looked at me....and there was a moment of stillness between us.

Awe.
And Grace

Afterwards the other traveller whose name I forget, comes back with me while I throw everything into a case and then we go for lunch (in the two hours I have set aside for sorting my stuff !)....I was to regret the hasty packing at LA airport, when the security guy opened my case, winced, and hastily shut it again.

I drive to the airport, and as I do, flowers fall into the open topped car, blown by the hot breeze, and settle on and around me.

At Honolulu again, after a day savouring Waikiki beach, I am booked into a cheap hotel without 24 hr reception, and the door unexpectedly locks firmly behind me as I struggle out with my baggage at 3am, to await my cab to the airport - I have asked the hotel to book one, and which they confirmed done. It doesn't come.

I am standing in a dark empty narrow street, way off main roads, in the middle of the night, with no way of getting back in or phoning. No mobiles then … … and I have a plane to catch.

'Ok' I say. 'I need a cab to pass'.

And, do you know, believe it or not, a cab rounded the corner and I ran out into the street waving desperately.

He said to me, shaking his head, 'I don't know *why* I came this way. Cabs don't'. I offer up yet again my seemingly most frequent prayer 'Thankyou God for saving me from my own foolishness'.

Miracles, always miracles.

It was like that when I was looking for a home after all the challenges which followed my stepping into the unknown with the divorce. So many miracles, and so like the glorious arrival in the safety and luxury of Hawaii after stepping into the challenges of the unknown tropics. I sit on the plane to Los Angeles and remember.

It strikes me now, sitting here at my snowy window in Vermont, gazing at the spectacular view, how, as I slot the next flashbacks into the diary, that they always seem to have a link with that bit of diary. It's as if on my journey I did indeed remember my life chronologically as I went. Themes emerge. As they do in life.

And now, the luxury and beauty of Hawaii and that of River Meadows.... Interesting. I am so enjoying the juxtaposition of my past life with the then present of 1998, and with the NOW of 2008.

July 93 To River Meadows

I think the time I most used the technique of affirmation was when I was trying to move from Elmside and find the right new home. After a year of sorting the mess, I felt it was now the right time to sell. Ben had had a year of continuity in our family home to adjust to everything somewhat, and I guess that was true for me too. We loved living just the two of us together, it was so easy. I remember with great pleasure the neat stacks of skateboards and rows of trainers at the foot of the stairs, the pounding feet going up to the attic, and his friend Emma saying 'we should be paying you rent'.

The house sold the first day on the market, and I had been trying to buy or rent a home for Ben, (now nearly 19) and I ever since. Sarah had made an offer for Elmside of the asking price to the agent right then using my phone! But after weeks of trying I realised I was too close to the mess and had too low an income and I was met with pity and rejection. One day after a particularly harsh verdict I sat under a tree in Southernhay Gardens, put my head in my hands and wept, not able to care who saw me. I was hunched over in deep despair. I could see grotty bedsits. Dirt, squalor, ugliness, the pit. Sarah was wanting to complete and Ben and I had nowhere to go.

Some days later I had a call, totally out of the blue. 'I hear you need a mortgage' 'yes but its not possible' 'let me try' 'you'll be wasting your time' 'that's my problem'. It was not some chancer but a young man from the Black Horse Estate Agents. I still don't know how or why. But not long afterwards, I came home one day, and as I approached the house, I seemed to hear his voice say 'Good news!' and indeed the phone rang and his voice did say that. Yes. That's how it was. I was bemused, didn't dare hope. But, where could I afford to buy? I was not daring yet to look out of my pit of bedsit darkness.

As I was looking in the Express and Echo that week I suddenly saw leaping from the page a large advertisement for a new block of apartments on the canal called River Meadows, priced very low. (It turned out to be that the builders had gone bankrupt). There and then, unseen, I said, if there is one, that's what I want. It was a clear, unequivocal decision, sight unseen. I went to see them and arranged to buy a two bedroom one. I could not believe it. Then the Black Horse young man said he couldn't raise that amount. Back down again, glad I never really believed it possible. Went to look at tiny mean terraces in the wrong bits of town, which after dreams of canal-side brand new flats was appalling.

Then one sunny blowy flowery April day I had another call out of the blue, this time it was the girl from the River Meadows Sales Office. 'A one bedroom flat has just come back on the market and I think it has your name on it' she said exuberantly. Ben and I went down at lunchtime. I shall never forget opening the door into that little flat. My mouth dropped open and my hand went to my heart. Sun poured through the skylights and windows, it was all spanking new with a pink glow to it. Soft pinky beige carpet and subtle pink walls. A delicious bathroom and luxurious little open plan kitchen. The sloping-ceilinged sitting room had arched windows to the west looking over to the hills and big windows to the east looking across the big courtyard and through a gap with a communal terrace to the canal and river. I was entranced, delirious, and utterly captivated.

AFFIRMATIONS

Are brief powerful positive and highly charged statements we can repeat to ourselves, which can change the mindset, attitude, feelings and inner beliefs which create our lives moment by moment.

We can pull one out every time we find ourselves in an unhelpful thought pattern.

This is a good way to begin to master our thoughts... becoming aware of each out-of date and sabotaging reaction and replacing it with one which makes us smile.

Affirmations help us free ourselves from the over-dependence on other's opinions and to write a new script for the play of our lives. Write them and post them all over the place. Say them out loud, sing them .....

SING THEM

'I deserve a fresh start'

'I am loved'

'I am free'

'I am walking proudly into my future'

'Abundance and love are all around'

'All my needs are met with ease' (my friend Carol's)

'I am held in the arms of the Universe'

I gazed at the bathroom with its skylight and sloping ceiling and I remembered in some awe a similar waterside eyrie in Falmouth that I took mum to on holiday in 1992: I had fallen in love with it, so squeaky clean and stylish, jewel-like and sunlit. I thought strongly then that I could and indeed I would love to live in something like that, even though it was so small - not realising that I was creating my future with that thought......for within a year I was living in just such an apartment.... And yet I had never heard about creating our own reality then: it was just after I moved there that I found Gill Edwards book 'Stepping into the Magic' and immediately recognised it all.....

Then another miracle happened and my worry about where Ben could live was solved, because Miro suddenly left the flat in Queen Street (which he had moved into without my knowledge some months ago), and gone to Belgrade. So I cleaned up the squalor and Ben and his friend Phil moved in there and had a whale of a time. Probably more of a whale of a time than I want to know about.

I had some time ago arranged to visit my friends in Portugal for the first time and it just so happened to turn out to be the week leading up to Contracts & Completion, which were planned for the same day. Just before leaving I stood looking across the river and the canal to River Meadows. I was with two friend s- at that time I only had three (apart from my college colleagues) - Krys, Ros and Mara. 'Can I really be going to live there?' I said in wonder, thrilled and also terrified both that it wouldn't actually happen and that it would and I would have to face the challenge of living alone for the first time in my life.... Could I really live in my 'clean slate' brand new delicious little eyrie? Could I really be so independent, paying a mortgage and all the bills by myself? I knew money was very very tight. I'd been driving around those waiting months saying to myself 'I deserve a new fresh beautiful home – my clean-slate home'. I must have said it thousands of times. I had to trust.

I took off not knowing if River Meadows was mine or not, but feeling an intense sense of being at a punctuation point in my life, with a whole new chapter about to begin. I took off in the plane, aware that I was taking off from the family home into my own future, my own empowerment. The take-off in a flight is a fantastic place for affirmations and really FEELING them. But its also great to feel and say them when walking through a door, looking at a great view, stretching up high, in a circle of friends, at a sacred place, when walking the hills or lying in a bath!!!....

I stepped out of Arna and Dave's car into a magical billowing of colours, scents, sounds, to a world of drinks in the deep shade of the cane veranda and floating in the blue pool hanging on the edge of the view of the sunbaked Algarvian valley. I was transported to paradise. I sat silently drinking it all into my body and soul. I barely read a thing, just received all the beauty into my traumatised body mind and spirit. At the end of the two weeks I stood up to leave, spread my arms to the landscape and said, 'I feel free'. And I flew back to my apartment.

......And so it was that I moved out of the dark memories of Elmside into the fresh new clean-slate home of my affirmations. To big skies, still reflective canal waters, rushing

river, swans, ducks, quayside walks to town, and paths along the Riverside Valley Park toward the coast. I was truly blessed.

I had of course taken this on in faith. I didn't know how I would pay the mortgage through the summer holidays, and I could not sign on for unemployment benefit as I did not want to risk jeopardising my mortgage at such an early stage. But as usual the miraculous happened and Ken at college offered me a student, dear Georgina, who came to my home all summer for lessons!!

I was beginning to learn to trust. Though it took another four years of hard inner work, until 1998, to really know the power of faith and surrender, and until 2000 for what was a kind of last click into place of total trust that happened in the Study at Cricket Court (a secret War Room for Churchill)....

I pinned this on my notice board:
'When you come out of fear you create what you fear. When you come out of love, you create what you love.'

Waking every morning to my views and my perfect home, I would think, do I dare to love it? What if I lose it? But I decided to risk feeling the love and gratitude, not knowing at the time that feeling those creates more of the same.... Now, I know that is one of the great keys. I look back and I see how the manifestation process happens all the time, even when we are not conscious of it. Consciousness just makes the living process so much easier, so much more exciting. I remember mum's minister asking how we were coping and mum said to him that we had our faith, and I said 'I tell myself to Trust in the Process of Life'. It was early days but I was getting there.

That was the start of a whole new 'magical' life, that move. I knew I was looked after by God after that. That we can co-create with God. And so I dived into a summer of space and rest beside the water, with the swans and the ducks and Gill Edwards' book for company and inspiration. My father talked of co–creation in several sermons, without using the term.

I cooked just for me on the clean new worktops, at the clean new built in cooker and hob. Comfort food, and simple one bowl salads, fast pasta or vegetable meals, a chicken roasted one day would give me the pleasure of 'roast' and last a week cooked each day in different ways and made soup too. I usually had a box of cooked potatoes or rice in my fridge to make quick meals with. I ate looking at my view, quietly, SUCH a new way of living. I had never lived putting my own needs and desires first.

I had indeed stepped into the magic that summer of 93, and in the autumn I stepped into a whole new world of friends and fun when I started to 'Dance to the Heart' with Dilys Morgan Scott – Gabrielle Roth's 5 Rhythms. With that and Patricia Dyehouse plus the plus the rediscovery of Sati - (walked into what I thought was a lecture on Buddhism and found people on the floor doing armdrops! It was Roshi's student Sensei Paul Taylor's group) - I started determinedly to sort out the mess inside my head.

'Because the Lord hath need of him'　　　　　St Luke Chapter 19 v 31
(extracts only)

The Lord hath need of him, and the Lord hath need of US.

The independence of God is a great truth, it helps to check our vanity and bring us to know our place in life – yet it is only a half truth. The other half is that He is dependent upon US for the fulfilling of His human plans for the world.

Men and women stand in special relation to God, made for sonship and partnership with God.

God and man are bound together for cooperation. To man God has given one world to manage, to understand and develop, as a partner with God.

He has need of us.

He will not force goodness upon us, he has given us free will, but he needs us for the good of this world. Man is saved by God's grace, but through man. God feels our attitude toward Him. The most perfect feel most perfectly. The Cross means just this. That pain sorrow and suffering, that agony, are what God feels on account of human sin. Once we feel that, things begin to happen. All sin becomes sin against Him. The sway of Christ is over conscience, mind and heart.

He hath need of all our talents and gifts for His work in the world. God wants us to love, he wants a world of true loving children and a true world for his children.

He hath need of us. What is our answer?

AMEN

ONE BOWL SALADS

These can contain anything, whatever you have around. I love them. . They can be quite celebratory for lunches with friends if you put lots of things in them and have hot bread in a basket and local yellow butter....

As well as the standard lettuce, tomatoes, cucumbers and peppers (TEAR the lettuce, chop the rest) , add sliced raw mushrooms, chopped avocado, fresh herbs-torn, watercress sprigs, mango, pineapple, or cooked beans, olives. You can include chopped cooked potatoes, rice, pasta, cubes or crumbly bits of cheese of any sort, left over cooked meat, shredded deli meats, even bits of pate, hard boiled egg, tuna, prawns or smoked fish, nuts, toasted seeds. The new jars of chargrilled peppers or artichoke hearts are great. As are croutons (just fry cubes of bread). Mix meats cheeses and fish if you like.

Toss it all in a dressing of your fancy. My friend lora's is the best:
Olive oil, lemon juice, LOTS of Dijon mustard, garlic, salt and pepper.

Play with combinations, but really its whatever you have or fancy.

REALLY COMFORTING POTATOES

When you need nurturing, this will sort you out. In a nice terracotta dish layer sliced potatoes (not the sort that go fluffy) seasoned with salt and black pepper and plenty of nutmeg, a little cayenne. Cover with double cream and knobs of yellow butter. Bake for about 45 mins until potatoes are tender and its all bubbling and thick and glossy.

You can add things of course....cheese on top, or layer with something...bacon, mushrooms, sweet potatoes, butternut squash.

It's a good guest dish too, served perhaps with 'dry' meat or chicken. I like it with chicken roast or fried covered with lots of seasonings and paprika and mixed dried herbs. As you eat, the red of the paprika marbles deciciously into the cream...

MORE COMFORT WITH POTATOES – Yugoslav Style

In Yugoslavia I learned how to cook Swiss Chard, and when I was on my own I cooked it a lot, it fries up well as a sort of bubble and squeak next day. They fry onions and LOTS of garlic in good olive oil, till soft, then add large chunks of peeled old potato and cut up chard stems. Add boiling water, salt, and cook it all down until tender and most of the water should have gone. Then add torn chard leaves, add more olive oil, fresh ground black pepper, and simmer a bit longer till the leaves are cooked but still green. Stir it all up. It should be wet but with no liquid.

Under the Redwoods, San Francisco   Ben (18) in Mum's garden

Chapter 11
Los Angeles and San Francisco……
Last laps

9 September   LA

I am deeply grateful for my Rough Guide, courtesy of Kate and Dave in Fiji, because at LAX arrivals there is no info to be seen anywhere. As it is I look up a suitable motel in walking distance of the train station for next day.

My cab is darting around over a 14-lane freeway. This is the city of the car. I remember when I was teaching, showing a video about how some ridiculous % of LA surface area was devoted to the car. Was it 70% ? - cant remember.

I have no feeling of wanting to stay here, even though my motel has a Buddha in the entrance, and head for the train station, to take a train up the coast (mmmm!) to San Francisco and then to Denver.

On LA Union station a tiny dark wrinkled man with a long pony-tail and a very large grey top hat is driving a sort of tractor pulling a long snake of trolleys.

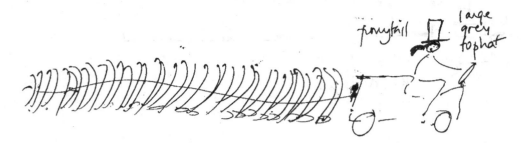

Amtrak to San Francisco

The Amtrak train has 12 huge double-decker silver carriages. It is wonderful to be travelling on the GROUND. The usual over-the-top-happy American welcome and service lifts me, as it does every time. I'm in the high glass observation car, with a flock of old ladies perching and chattering and giggling. It seems to me that old ladies either go for it with great humour and travel and have quite raucous fun, or they stay home. I know which kind I'll be all being well.

As soon as we come alongside the ocean, there are a pod of dolphins, larger ones, just offshore, moving parallel to us. The train STOPS for us to watch them …..yes really!!!!

Then there are fields of sunflowers, oh happy sight. Great beaches, great surf, gold cliffs cracked open by chasms and slips. Vineyards in stripes to the hills in the distance. There is a whole string of oil rigs a mile offshore. And houses like sugar confections along the beach.

The train crawls along, I wait for it to get going, but it never does. Apparently all US trains crawl. I wonder why.

A gold miner from Perth tells me you often only get 3 or 4 grams of gold per ton of rock and it's still worth it. A girl from Seattle invites me to her home.

And, eventually, the glories of San Francisco appear, and there is Pauline, my old friend from River Meadows who emigrated, waiting for me. Her house hangs off the mountain in the forest in Mill Valley. I am stunned by it. She feeds hummingbirds pink syrup on her wooden balcony.

We eat at a Thai restaurant called The Angel of Grace. It is a completely perfect meal. Exquisite everything. To eat, you take off your shoes, climb onto a polished pale wooden platform, and sit on cushions on the platform with your legs in a well beneath the low table. Our waitress is tall and slim and wears a green and gold sarong. The others are tiny but they all seem so tall above us.

Pauline drives me across the Golden Gate Bridge, and shows me her city, it is of course fantastic. I remember the steep streets. 'You're not going to drive down that!!!' as the car tipped forward and hurtled down….But all too soon, I am on another Amtrak train, to Denver.

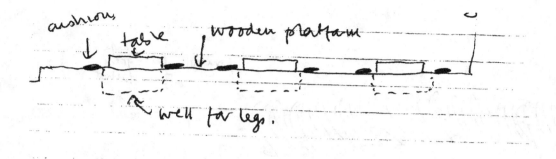

11 September   Amtrak to Denver

As consolation for leaving beautiful SF I have a fabulous miniscule sleeping compartment on the upper storey, it is a womb with a window, lengthwise to the train, with coat-hangers, tissues, towels, shelves, and a foldout washbasin, and I can if I want lie there watching out of the big window.

I know I have been remiss at not contacting Joan in Crestone before, and in SF I couldn't reach her, oh worry. Pauline remarked that her number being 'not in service' might mean she never moved out there from Virginia after all. This puts the fear of God in me. I have to TRUST. After all, I got to Joan Ocean's in Hawaii and couldn't stay there and actually got somewhere better. Still.... wobbles.

At Reno there is a long stop and the platform is full of smokers. There are yellow plastic stools by each door to get out with. Everything is yellow with sunset – gold uplighting behind smoke grey mountains. Glimpses of the neon streets of the city make my mouth drop open.

I look at the VERY large tight-trousered-and-belted wobbling lady conductress and have to make an effort not to stare. My gaze drops diplomatically to her feet, which give me a different surprise. Such neat well shod shapely little feet and ankles. Like one of those paper games where you fold paper and draw body parts one after another.

The train, which is very very long, is now trundling heavily through Utah, with pauses every now and again to get its breath. This is mesa country, classic 'slope retreat' where steep angular slopes retreat back to form tablelands and flat topped stacks rather than sort of wearing down all over in a curvy way. It takes me back to teaching and my classroom. Suddenly, in the midst of this Leap, this Unknown, everything familiar and known seems so sweet and dear. Part of me just wants to return to safety. I am suspended in space and time, with no idea of what lies ahead, watching America roll past.. ...America is mainly wilderness. Emptiness. The power of America lies in its spaces, I think, and its self- sufficiency. But there is danger in self sufficiency – no need to reach out, no interdependence and it is frighteningly easy to project and to lose touch....

A bright green field appears for no reason I can fathom in the distance in the middle of the cracked khaki vastness. There is of course no building to be seen, no animals, no road, and no possible mechanism for watering, but there it sits, brilliant green.

174

We're really hitting the spaces now. Ochre and khaki, wadis of crenellated mud, bizarre horizon of sculpted rocks. And… wow… a road. Hours since Salt Lake City in Nevada and here is the only settlement since that, a few houses and a gas station. This is uranium country I am told.

Now we are into canyon country, and the red and yellow Glenwood Canyon towers above us, filling the glass roof.

13 September   Denver

Worst time of trip, maybe. Arrived 6 hours late in middle of night and got a cab to a hotel the driver said was open. It felt like birth pangs leaving the womb of my compartment. Joan's number still Not In Service, oh panic. Phone to UK blocked. Bill and Joan's number has answerphone on, Marsha's blocked. Motel no help. Blocked everywhere. I try all morning. Nothing and no one. Aaargh. I am cut off. Desperate. Paralysed with fear. Right in my stuff, unwanted, trapped, alone, fears because money nearly all gone, and I have no real home in England and anyway I don't want to go back, I want to go to Crestone, but Crestone is, I feel shakily, blocking me out..

Rejection looms.

Then Anrahyah saves me. 'We'll get you here, don't worry'. She told me to trust the intuition that brought me here, and to be fully present in Denver. ' Bless you, bless you!' I almost weep. The block has dissolved and I know all is well. Connection! Breathe out….and I find myself seeing how it will all be, all of a sudden. I visualise being collected, being driven to Crestone, don't yet know how or where to, but it will all happen. I see myself unpacking my box that I sent ahead. Opening mail. Getting on email and phoning home, walking, having coffee in the Desert Sage, driving to Alamosa to open a bank account, going to the Mountain Zen centre to meditate, soaking in the Hotsprings, climbing the mountains…… I feel the pleasure of it all…

And of course it is EXACTLY that feeling of gratitude in advance that creates our reality….

It happens quickly now, that process, but I remember those years at River Meadows when I was learning how it all worked, and learning about me, and delving into the mess inside me. It took years, but I was so grateful just to have the chance to focus on just myself and look after just myself, and I loved my new home so much, and all that love and gratitude bore me along beautifully if painfully at times into an ever more beautiful life…..

Working it all out at last – with Zen, Dance and Therapy

Sorting the mess inside my head took some doing. But I was alone, undisturbed by anyone else's stuff, nothing to distract me from finally looking at ME. And I was in my beautiful home and Miro was in Belgrade.

175

I was surrounded by supportive metaphor. The flood relief channels were there to safely channel all my excess emotion, the still canal waters were there to reflect perfectly what going on in me, the swans were graceful, the ducks humorous, and the glue factory kept me from falling to bits as I took myself apart!!!!! It was all very watery – appropriate to this time of diving deep into my emotions.

There was a moment when I was teetering terrified on an edge - I guess now it was a panic attack, but I went to the doctor and got some tranquillisers for emergency use and I started meditating regularly. I would 'drop into a sit' here there and everywhere. It worked. So so slowly though, and accompanied by loads of sinusitis, a non-stop running nose, and full blown days-long migraines complete with vomiting and nosebleeds..... very messy years. But I never felt that appalling edge again and somehow I kept working and somehow I always paid the bills. And the friends and the fun, the disciplines and the therapy supported me as I faced into myself and tried to work it all out.

It was a kind of second adolescence, the hippie years I never really had because I was always studying as a teenager, and was so isolated. A kaleidoscope of parties with dancing and guitars and group hugging and singing and lying around in heaps stroking each other, of camping on Dartmoor with fires and more guitars and swimming naked in tumbling rivers, of lying naked again on hidden beaches eating picnics and talking talking talking round fires of driftwood......of wonderful words to me in lovely handmade birthday cards.

And all so SAFE......The men in the circle were gentle creatures, non-threatening, great to dance with. They were just lovely to me. I felt admired and enjoyed but I battled with feeling unattractive. But I was just setting out away from entanglement on to a path of ease, and I had a long road to travel before it was right to 'merge auras' with a man again, so I was 'protected' from this. It was to take much work to heal my battered energy field.

I was thrilled and astonished with what life was offering me all of a sudden after so many lonely years - a whole host of like-minded friends. And one of them lived in the next apartment block: Pauline, who was later to respond so magnificently to breast cancer by moving to California. I met her at a New Year's Eve party. I noticed her straightaway: she was so stylish, so eccentric in short skirt, hat and boa and all in black, always in black. We quickly discovered with delight that we were neighbours. Her flat had big black string spiderwebs and a huge hammock and fairy lights. Towards the end of my time there her workplace moved next to mine too.....

*One day.... ' I can't be Sandra Hedley any more' I said to my friend the writer ('Riding the dragon') Roselle Angwin. 'I get called Mrs Hedley and that's my mum'. I thought a bit. 'I've always lived in my head. I changed my life in my head and I'm dragging my body behind me' 'You could be Legley, or Handley' said Roselle, 'or Bottomley'. much laughter. 'Or you could be Hartley' she said in a different tone of voice. 'Ah' I said. **'Sandra Hartley'**. 'Yes, YES' I knew it was right.*

So I went to my solicitors and became Sandra Hartley. I am still.

WATER

Represents the flow of emotions. We can look into clear water for reflections, be energised by rushing water and crashing waves, let the current take us.
We can honour its mystery…. The Water of Life.
We can float on the current of life…. surrender and not resist.
Water is so strong because it does not resist, it flows around obstacles, and it wouldn't dream of trying to flow uphill!!
We can keep clear water on a personal altar, refresh it daily, float petals in it, honour it. We can sit in ceremony beside water and honour clarity and flow and non resistance….and power.

EMOTIONS

Are our energy in motion. E-motion. They move us forward but if we get stuck in them and don't keep them moving we are in trouble. When taken into excess or distorted by negativity healthy emotions become unhealthy. Protective fear becomes anxiety and panic, protective anger becomes hatred resentment and malice. Love becomes obsession. We can drown in them all too easily – so we need to learn to swim!…to master them rather than have them master us and run our lives for us. We can also drown others in our emotions.
We need to become aware and watchful of our emotions, the thoughts they bring, and the further emotions the thoughts bring…the spiral of thoughts and emotions that can take us down every time….this is fine when investigating ourselves but not when we have identified the patterns. Then it is time to take care with how we think and feel.. .
and have the spiral take us up not down

And indeed, suddenly the communication blockages are cleared. Anrahyah calls to say a teacher called Jennifer from Crestone is in Denver and is driving down the very next day, oh what miracles!!!!! And thank God JOAN calls, welcoming and warm – Anrahyah has called her. She is waiting for me. And ….MARION is THERE already. I am amazed. My colleague from the Convergence Centre is travelling and we planned she would come and spend some time with me. And she too had trouble contacting Joan. Don't know what happened with that. Fear fulfilling itself as usual I guess, but I don't know what released it.

But, no matter, I'm now energised and off to explore. Denver is waiting. Mile high city…….

14 September

Am now sitting beneath a 55 story skyscraper (yes I counted) shaded from brilliant sun by an umbrella, on a roof terrace restaurant eating Double J Limousin New York steak and fries. Skyscrapers have enthralled me ever since I first met one in Boston in April and they've continued to excite me in Singapore, Syney, Honolulu, LA, San Francisco and now Denver.

Trams are ringing below. Free buses shunt people up and down a mile long tree-lined fountain-and-seat-filled pedestrian mall. Mile high, mile long. Clean wide town, airy and sparkly. Empty this morning at 10.30am, as shops don't open till 10am, but now at lunchtime it's buzzing. It feels a very male city. Its to do with the crisp airiness, the height and the straight lines everywhere, and the fact that it is full of extraordinarily handsome men too!!!!!…… Lovely to sit and watch!!!! It is buoyant, glittery, alive and pristine. Cleaner and fresher than San Francisco, which seemed more female somehow, curvier and more beautiful and flowery. God, is there no end to the gorgeous men passing below me?

And, oh glorious connection, there are messages on the phone when I come in!

Later

As Jennifer drives us, in her car called 'Wind' in Native American, over Kenosha Pass into the ancient battlefields of South Park Valley, I see where we stopped in April, the place that had such an effect on me. Someone has placed a pipe and artificial flowers there. I get out and we stand in the great silence of this place and I bow and honour the old pain, and I let it go.

And now…….on to what I have come all this way for.

View of the mountains from Joan's house in Crestone

Top Deck of Joan's House in Crestone

The Rose Room, Meditation Room at The Convergence Centre, Exeter

Chapter 12
Crestone Colorado...... Destination

My heart swells with excitement. Here I am again. I came around the world alone to get here.

And just as we crest the Poncha Pass into the San Luis Valley, the sunset turns the Sangre de Cristo Mountain peaks red. 'What a welcome' says Jennifer 'It doesn't happen often'. (and indeed I haven't seen it since...) As we round the corner into the

Crestone road Jupiter appears in the sky, and as we near the village, an eagle passes low in front of us, flying ahead....

This Valley, like the Great Secrets of Life, is relatively unsought. As I said at the beginning of this book, look at even the smallest relief map of the USA and there it is, a high flat area clearly visible in the middle of the Southern Colorado Rockies, a vast and empty space on the population map. A remote alpine desert valley, the highest, I hear, in the world – though I don't think that can be so.

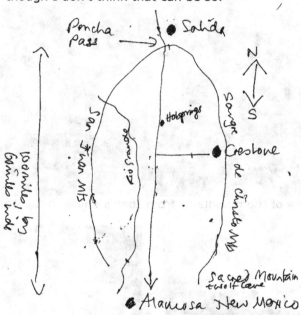

It is for centuries a Sacred Valley to the Tribes; they called it 'The Bloodless Valley' because it is their place of ceremonial Vision Quest and hunting and fighting are forbidden here. This valley holds secrets, and these secrets were honoured, sought and valued above all. The Pipe Carriers were the secret carriers, and they were the most honoured members of the communities.

How different it is in our societies.

The San Luis Valley is flat khaki and ochre desert, 100 miles long, 60 miles wide, though because it is so clear and featureless you can see from end to end....and it seems less but also more... It is an ancient rift valley 30,000 ft deep, deeper than Everest is high, filled now with layers of sediment and aquifers. It is almost completely ringed by walls of mountain 14000 ft high. It has 360 days of sun. It is a place of the utmost purity, the air is the cleanest in the USA, and the atmosphere is all immensity and infinity and utter beauty. It is awe-inspiring and I am going to live here for nearly three months.

Something about it, perhaps its clarity, protects it. It seems to me to insist upon relentless honesty and it is too much for some to take, and they are more comfortable in murkier lands. I don't know. But that is what I feel. I am honoured to be here, and who knows how I will respond.

Well, here I am, I tell the spirits of this place.

180

Wherever I have been in the States, when I am asked where I am headed, the response to my answer is the same: 'where???'

Only one person has heard of this place and he regarded it with fear. 'Now? And in November? It'll be way below freezing. You're mad'.

Well….what did I do in November? I lay on the sunbed in the sun on the top deck albeit in a jumper, I sat outside cafes with coffee in the sun, I lay in hotsprings, I drove to ski country, I climbed through crystalline air to 10000 ft and saw tracks of bear, mountain lion and lynx.

'There's no one there….' he added….. Only a community of people from all over the world, and centres of all the world's major religions and philosophies, that's all….

A secret spiritual feast in the desert.

15 September   Marion's visit

Travelling with company...tentatively but proudly driving Vince and Mary's huge red car... all over Colorado, and socialising together a little in Crestone.
.
What different pleasures and challenges.

The difficulties of her soft voice and my deafness, of my slipping into inadequacy when faced with nervousness, her being 'courted' and my being ignored...my stuff in fact….

And, interestingly, her responses….. she says it is her responsibility to be heard, hers to calm her nerves, and mine to realise I am so quiet in company I appeared uninterested. What a revelation to me. I thought people weren't interested in me and it is seen as the reverse. Bit painful but very revelatory. That is, the ignoring reflects my apparently ignoring.

Marion gave me the same - true - answer that John Gordon did, and still I didn't fully take it on board. When friends are honest it is the greatest gift.

She also sees the 'cold power' that Rachel talks of in me (Caroline saw it too), but reminds me it is just a part of me. She sees the deafness in my right ear as my male side not hearing because I can't deal with my own anger. Possibly true, bearing in mind Isobel's diagnosis! I later came to see it as also my refusal to listen to the male voice, which gave me so much pain. She said healing is possible, she healed her sight for a while, so it is possible.

We drive through the clouds and snow and Arctic Tundra up along Trail Ridge Road. We stay at Dripping Springs and in Boulder, and there I buy my big red fleece blanket.

And then I drive home alone to the stillness and big silences and vistas of Crestone, and Joan has the chance to go to India for a month and I unexpectedly have the big white house and its three decks all to myself…..hmmmm….is this good news or not….it is going to be a challenge…

Alone in Crestone

My task is to STOP, and to stop ALONE, and for a protracted time. Can I do this? Phew.

Always when I stop, in come the demons, I get fearful, depressed, lonely, all sorts of stuff.

Whatever is, is whatever is right at that time. I know this. But. There is still a but. Can I actually stay in this state of connection through a long time alone? Where I know so few people? Can I tolerate perfection? Paradise. I am in paradise, in a paradise house, in a paradise place (in my view). There is no pressure at all. No work. No plans or preparations to make. Nothing at all I HAVE to do. This is challenging. Space.

I expected these demons on Fiji but I got the snakes instead, fear of external snakes and memories of my marriage nicely distracting me from those writhing inside myself. They visited me in the perfections of Bali and of Lorayne's in Hawaii and I lost three days of paradise to them .

I have been round the planet Just Looking. I am in one of the planet's most awesome places Just Being. I am proud and grateful, humble and satisfied, AT THE MOMENT. But how long will it last? I have my chance to rest and write, in a place so close to God, after a life of so much effort.

Well, I didn't do badly actually. Here's what my journal, written to be part of this book, has to say, I've just typed it straight in.

October 5

I'm sitting on the top deck with a beer. But what I'm really drinking in is the view.

How can I convey to you this sublime sunlit Rocky Mountain valley, the vastness of it all, the power of these Sangre de Cristo Mountains ranged along the immense desert plain, like indescribably ancient beings cloaked in smoky blue as dusk falls. The mountains to the west streaming the scarlet and gold sunset fire……..the whole vast sky is glowing with sunset. Truly this place is another world, so long traditionally held sacred, suffused with grace. It expands the being. Once it has been experienced, nothing is ever the same again. Or so it was for me.

And how can I convey to you the place *inside* of my being which I have come to after all the pain, and after the journeyings, external and internal?   Like my new surroundings, I can only describe it as being (most of the time) suffused with grace. And I can only feel gratitude.. I feel, at one with -and in- a loving universe, trusting it all. You have read some of my story now and you might see *why* I now trust it all. It would be *churlish* not to after so many signs that I can.

All this may seem crazy when I tell you the facts as the world might see them.....
I sold my flat 15 months ago, even though I knew I could neither get another mortgage or afford to rent, and after a year used the proceeds for this travelling

sabbatical. I have no home or much furniture etc of my own but I have been able to share the loveliest home I have ever lived in with some friends, and I can go back there. I gave up two teaching jobs to run my beloved and beautiful Convergence Centre -a Centre for the Creative and Healing Arts, which I set up with no money at all and which refuses to make a proper income (so far...).

So I have at the moment no income, and my capital is gone and my credit card maxed out as they say here. (But always there is enough somehow). There is no way of knowing whether the Centre will produce me any income when I return. At the moment I have no husband, lover or rich friends! These are the 'facts' in the 'worldly' sense and yet *I have never felt better. And the future excites me.*

I am living here now, for two and a half months, lodging in a most beautiful brand new house full of exquisite things and fabulous views, with a car and a computer to use. In a 8000' high village which is probably unique in the world. It is an hour from the nearest small town, four hours from a city. The variety of original homes is incredible: earthships, domes, straw bale homes, old car tyre homes, adobe homes, A Frames, log cabins. .... A few minutes walk away are the Carmelite Monastery and the Sri Aurobindo Centre; ten minutes drive away are the Mountain Zen Centre and the Haidakandi Universal Ashram, the Eagles Nest Hawaiian Huna Centre, and Sanctuary House, which is a Sufi Centre and where shrines to all major spiritual paths are being built around a Chartres style labyrinth....... And this is just some of what is available here.

It is a place out of this world, yet it is profoundly challenging in that here, hidden from the world, you cannot hide from yourself. Many people cannot take it. It is said to be the Crown Chakra of the planet, and to be on a higher vibration than the rest of the world. I do experience that as being the case here despite the fact that I often get a bit dubious about some of the New Age stuff. There is a fine, pure, clear feeling here. Nothing is ever locked and all is peaceful collectively (though not on personal levels – people suffer here as they confront themselves). When I arrived I said to Joan, 'where did Vince and Mary put the car keys?' (three months ago!) 'Oh, they're in the car, its open, they're probably under the mat' she said. This is where I have come to a halt after travelling for two months all around the world. I have been **Just Looking** and now I am **Just Being**.

And so, despite the 'facts', I regret nothing and I know I'm 'on course'. Synchronicities and signs pour in daily. There is always a reason for everything and I feel that everything will unfold and become clear, so long as I keep MYSELF clear, and listen. (And, even if I am totally up the creek and mad as a hatter, well, I've had the time of my life, and I can always get a job....... !!!!!)

Because **whatever** happens I know it is for the **highest good**. If I don't like it I still trust it though I certainly wobble alarmingly at times. But then I just feel the wobble fully, but also step back from my wobbling self and watch what's going on. Compassionately. So a part of me is in that secure place always no matter what. Getting to know myself better and better by being ruthlessly AND kindly honest with myself. Watching for the message. Everything is a message. It becomes absolutely fascinating to watch how God/ Goddess/ Spirit/ Universe/ Source/ Higher Self/ the Angels communicates. It all adds another dimension to living, makes it all make sense, and is highly entertaining as well as profoundly inspiring.

I go into the house, which is very bright and light and white, very swish, and very full of treats and toys like a dishwasher and filtered water and an oxygenating machine, an exercise ball, videos and music and books, and binoculars to watch the mountains with. I go into the gorgeous bathroom for a bit of a lick and a polish and then pick up my keys, which are on a key-ring with a shark whose fierce mouth opens and reveals a flashing red light. I bought it in Singapore Airport. I'm off to the Zen Center for evening meditation.

The car grinds up the steep dirt roads, negotiates the twisty rutted hairpins. It bucks and lurches; it's like a rodeo ride. There is a stag, mesmerised for a long moment, in the headlights. I walk up in the pale blue light from the full moon, through the juniper and pinon forest. I can hear the Bok, a wooden gong calling the residents to sit. They are in silence from supper until breakfast and the Center is hushed. Quietly I leave my cloak and shoes on a covered shelf on the deck which surrounds the Zendo and I enter.

It is dim, and glowing, serene, and utterly silent.

It is a Japanese style Meditation Hall with raised platforms around the edge for sitting. There is a wooden Buddha surrounded by fat white candles. A few dark robed, still and very straight figures are already sitting, their backs to me. I bow and take my place, on a black mat and cushion, facing the pale wooden wall.

I hear others come in, a faint rustling, and then the Singing Bowl is struck, and there is total stillness and silence.

Half an hour later, the bell rings and we slide off the platform and stand in silence a moment. We walk until we are in a line and then the pace slows until we are barely moving. We walk slowly round and round the wooden outside deck.

I have been meditating (NOT regularly but "continuously on and off"....) for twelve years, ever since Mala's class. I used to suffer from such guilt about not practising enough, but I found that rather defeats the object of the whole exercise so I gave up the guilt (it took a while ....) and so long as I went to a group each week I accepted my otherwise erratic pattern. I was learning not to give myself a hard time.

I found that if I said I didn't have to, I often did. It's like food. I am very much too fond of it. When I am giving my digestive system a holiday, but I pass a fish and chip shop and am smitten with desire, I say, 'Well, I can have it'. It just means that today is my treat day and I can be extra careful tomorrow. So I think 'Well then I'll leave it to tomorrow'. And I walk on. So far it has worked quite well really. It is a good technique for contrary souls like me.

Tonight my meditation is far too busy, thoughts and feelings whirling and I spend far too much of it waiting for the bell. But I know that is because of the full moon....

Next morning it is actually Full Moon Fire Ceremony at the Hindu Ashram. Brilliant sunshine. This is easier than quietening the mind, the full moon always pulls me out of myself and magnifies everything going on in me. The ceremony is all bells and drums and harmonium, and singing and dancing, garlanded imagery of Babaji, with fruit and flowers and spices and incense and salt and rice to throw on the fire as the hundreds of mantras are chanted. The sound of the big white conch shell echoes out into the wilderness. I know I'm going to have to go to India one day. That's something I'd really regret not doing.

After the ceremony there is brunch and good company in the solar heated earthship. It is one of the Ashram members' birthday but he can't be here. A pumpkin is placed ceremonially on the table and decked with cowboy hat, scarf and sunglasses. A cake with candles appears and we all sing Happy Birthday to the pumpkin.

It feels like family and reminds me of my Centre in England.

Driving home I stop to look out over the Valley. The 'mighty Rio Grande' runs into its centre from the west, bringing irrigation to the ranches within it's reach - huge circles watered by quarter mile long rotating metal arms. To the east is the unbroken towering wall of the Sangre de Cristo. No roads cross the 50 mile long northern half of this range, it presides over the ochre and old gold and khaki of the sagebrush vastnesses so flat the forty miles I am looking across to the mountains in the west seems like ten. And yet it is also infinity.....distance both shrunken by lack of feature and expanded by the same..... It is all surreal, otherwordly. Out of time.

Every day, I think, speak, call out, whisper and sing my boundless gratitude for the privilege of being here. I bow to the land and its spirits.

Next stop is downtown - Wild West meets the New Age. This was a thriving gold mining town for a couple of decades last century, wild and lawless, with seven saloons, a heaving gaol and one extremely tiny church. The women of Crestone (clearly a formidable bunch) got fed up with it all and together they burned all the bars down. Maybe they tapped into the 'energy' here without knowing it....

Now it is a tree-shaded, dirt-roaded collection of log cabins, and a makeshift store or two, plus a new age shop opposite the genuine wild west Liquor Store complete with hitching post ..... and a llama wandering about. I head for The Post Office which is spacious and brand new, with the Stars and Stripes outside and hundreds of PO boxes inside. It is the high point of many a person's day, to come collect the mail each day - a seriously social event. I've got a letter full of anecdote from a friend in England and sit at the Burrito Wagon transported temporarily to a very different world. It has apparently rained more or less all the time since I left.

7 October

Next morning at 6.55am, the still full moon in my sign of Aries is hanging in the reflected sunrise, still, proud and whole. The frosty plain spreads below, the air is crystalline, the sky flawless and the sun is washing palest rose pink across the snow caps of the west....I go in and lie wrapped in turquoise duvet drinking tea writing this.

As I have breakfast on the top deck in the sun, my mother rings and confirms the rain story. I am instructed to put the sun in my pocket when I set off for home.

Later I trek up to the Meadow way way up the mountain. My lungs managed the climb, and we sang a lot to keep bears at bay. I cannot believe what I am doing. It's beyond postcard. Like the lake Josh and Judy took me to on Saturday. I am speechless really.

10 October

I sit, feet up, before the big glass doors, watching the light changing, from the warm indoors. Light is pouring over me, my robe, the bone of my legs, the edges of my hands, the white pen, the hair in my eyes, my nose, all suspended in light.

The pen is stopped. There is only the light in the comfort and stillness and silence. A faint whirr from the wind outside. Just light on my body, warmth, my breath. An awareness of vibration. Of consciousness.

The shape of my knee, my left thumb holding the notebook, my right hand's thumb and forefinger holding the poised pen. The network of lines crisscrossing the skin. The stripes on my left thumb nail. The rise and fall of my belly, beneath my warm robe. The fine hair on my knee catching the light.

The wind blows a little more, and the sun dips behind smoky streaks of charcoal cloud, gilding their edges, sending rays above and below, where they are pooling in an elipse on the plain. The mountains are black behind me. My breath continues, my life, my awareness. The fullness of emptiness, of simplicity. What more do I want but to breathe, aware of the miracle that is.

Now the sun is deep yellow light lying tenderly on all it touches, stroking the plain with gold. Soft golden air, dark grey clouds with soft vulnerable underbellies and bleeding grey into the clear heart-stopping turquoise above, sculpted gold leaf edges, angora and smoke heaps of mountains….

Flute music drifts up the stairs, and a small cloud in the south for a moment is shaped exactly like a dove carrying an olive branch, and I feel it as a gift to me, because I saw it and it was so fleeting.

11 October Carmelite Monastery Mass

Such grace. The presence of God in yet another tradition. The last time I attended a Catholic mass was with Mum in Chagford on Dartmoor on Easter Sunday, when her friend had asked that a mass be said for Daniel. I feel tears rising. I am so touched by it all, the nuns and the monks, the ethereal singing without any instruments, the stained glass, the bowing to Christ. I can't hear much of what the priest says, but phrases jump out. We sang 'We are building a city of God'.

'Brand new life' 'new world, new life' 'gratitude is the key' 'accept the understanding and the love of a man – the Christ'. I do not think I 'should' take communion, but I want to, and I do, and it feels right. I honour the tradition and that is I feel what counts.

The same feeling as at the Ashram at the full moon ceremony, when I took turn to wave the lamp and bow to the Mother, to Babaji, to the mountains around and the plain below, to the moon.

Universality. This has been my preoccupation since a young girl, when I argued with the Methodist Minister that all spiritual paths are divine and lead though different ways to the same Source.

And now, in the white north of Vermont USA, I walk across snow and through tall trees to the spectacular new 'All Souls Interfaith Gathering' Church here on Bostwick Farm on Lake Champlain. Around the walls are symbols of Buddhism, Judaism, Islam, Hinduism, Christianity. The hymnal holds songs and response readings from all these faiths. I remember when I was 11, in Jersey, and was chosen for our Church float in the Battle of Flowers, which had a huge globe made of flowers, British, American and Soviet flags in flowers, me – blonde, in pale blue, and a dark girl covered in blacking in a grass skirt .... and the message 'the Hope of the World'. I was to marry someone from the Eastern bloc and become so intimate with that culture, and I built such a strong relationship with America, and my next partner was to be American. The theme of my life in flowers at age 11...maybe....

12 October Mesa Verde

I am on my way to the Grand Canyon. Naomi (a shamanic teacher from Crestone) says this will be a special trip, and she has lent me her hexagonal tent and her lamp. This is the first time I have camped alone and it is out in the middle of 'Indian' country of SW USA. Why does it feel so normal? Once you DO something you immediately expand to include it in your consciousness and it is part of you. I get quite a thrill looking at the little tent, which went up easily considering I didn't ask how, and the big red car, and beyond the horses under the yellow aspens and the mesas fiery in the sunset. The tent billows with bedding: lounger cushion and duvet and pillows. I have filled my hot water bottle at the showers.

13 October Crossing the Desert
10am –7pm

I meet the desert within of course: boredom. I meet guilt too as a result of that. I meet the part of me that does not want to live. I am totally un-in-awe-of Monument Valley and the whole vast landscape. I am overheated, frustrated, exasperated, yes, but mainly, just uninterested. 'Is that all?'

Driving from Cortez with no signs or mileages, nothing, no towns. Just long empty road ahead. I am in the desert with no signs and all I can do is keep going. The loneliness and the emptiness at the bottom of my being curdles and claws within me.

I decide eventually that I might as well get to the Grand canyon that day. It is much much further than I thought. But once there are signs and mileages that helped. Little goals are the way through....and knowing where you are.

When I finally get to the Rim, at Desert View (no thankyou) it is indeed no, the campsite is closed and I have to drive another 28 miles. It is late and will be getting dark soon. I look out at the Grand Canyon with fury and disinterest. Can you believe that? Me? The original 'Ooh Aah wow' person utterly uminmpressed by one of the world's biggest tourist attractions.

And with that here ends this notebook. I wonder what if anything the next will hold.

Now, I think, my God, I had no mobile phone, no means of communication...there I was out in that desert all alone for a whole day in an old car....

14 October Grand Canyon (new notebook)

Hotfooting along the East Rim towards the Campsite in Grand Canyon Village, I am still in exasperation at first, but then, suddenly, there are TREES, lots of them, conifers and aspens in gold and *I have never been so happy to see trees in my life.*

Note: totally unimpressed with some of the worlds most famous scenery and thrilled beyond measure by TREES. Maybe this journey has finally un-enamoured me from landscape as primary passion. It is LIFE that I need.

And then, driving along in the COOL evening forest, having passed several lookouts because I want to get to the site before pitch dark, I suddenly for NO REASON pull into one, and lo and behold as I go up to the Rim happily shivering in the cold, there are Michael Orchard and Lynn Bartholomew (now Guardians of Chalice Well in Glastonbury). They too had pulled in for no reason. Can you believe that? Friends. The real richness. We arrange to meet later.

The Campsite is definitely 'Best Campsite of the Trip' award winner. Tents can literally get lost in the forest. My pitch (just a large area of forest cleared and with a number, not allotted, you can choose) has two sacred circles of stones with small altars around junipers. Plus a firepit and grill. A raven feather lying waiting bluely for me. I picked this pitch by instinct and it turns out to have all this.

I pitch Naomi's tent, spread my red fleece from Boulder, and make a fire with sage and juniper for a much needed cleansing.

15 October

I get up very early and find myself walking for hours. The canyon is deserted. I am at peace. Still not so thrilled with it as I am with the unexpected meeting, the campsite, raven feather and Naomi's tent. How many people get to use a shaman's tent for their vision quest? Then, ravenous, I find what has to be the 'Best Breakfast of the Trip' and I sit feeling the magic sparking around and through me.
Later: Sitting in Bright Angel Lodge with hot tea and large cookie, waiting and warming, for sunset, inside a huge stone fireplace under an equally huge spread eagle

– coloured and feathered... The world is going by my wooden inglenook seat. . Dishy Frenchmen, not so dishy Germans, exuberant Americans, poker-faced Japanese.

For some reason I am remembering the terrible fearful morning in Denver. If I hadn't had that delay there through blocked communications I wouldn't have experienced the glorious clear sparkling energy of the Downtown, and nor would I have had that magical journey down with Jennifer, and seen the Sangre de Cristo turn red in welcome at sunset as we crested the Poncha Pass into the San Luis Valley. If I had just trusted that it was all for a reason I would have spared myself all the old-being fears that overwhelmed me at the Days Inn. I am also remembering how my train got into Denver six hours late, and at 1am....and how I stepped out into the middle of the night with nowhere to go. It was fine. A taxi appeared (just the one, and no one else wanted it), and took me to a hotel. Like in Honolulu. I am always looked after.

Just today, as I thought I had to type out the a large chunk of the Crestone journal, from where I set off on this trip..... as I turned to the pages, the electricity went off. So, I thought I would conserve battery for emails in case it lasted a while, and I began to look through the version of this book printed out in Spain over a year ago. And there was that whole section already typed and printed. At that moment the power came back on and I hunted out and found the missing section on the computer....power failures are rare here, and this one lasted just long enough for me to find I didn't need to type pages and pages of journal again....

16 October

Wake up full of dreams of levitating with a man and of a large red and orange butterfly! I lie there still enjoying them, idly noticing that the tent seems very wet and dark and heavy. Put my head out and gasp. SNOW.

Go scooting up to the Rim but of course the canyon drops 5000' almost vertically so no snow in it. White Rim surrounds the red, orange, grey desert chasm within. It is cold, windy, snowing fitfully then thickly. 36 hours ago I was baked and broiled in the desert in temperatures in the 90s, fixed in the sun's glare through the car window for a day. Now I am hurrying shivering through a blizzard to the Bright Angel and a large hot chocolate.

I decide to stay on a night. Can't pack a wet tent really. The café fills my hot water bottle and I wrap up in the tent with it. I have some food, a book, my notebook, incense, I have an altar with the raven feather and a natural wood spiral, and some purple flowers. The sun shines through the tent walls.

Later I walk or hours, and manage to hop on a rim bus back. At night there is rain and thunder and lightning but I feel safe. Deer are around- I peek out at them. Sometimes the wind gusts and blows the tent walls but it doesn't reach me.

17 October   Canyon de Chelly

After the obvious and populous Grand Canyon, here I find the ancient magic. Strong energy, numinous, full of spirits. At sunset I stand alone on an overlook, in the reddening rocks. I honour the spirits, bowing deeply and then standing tall and straight, and I say aloud, 'I thank the Spirits of this Place and I ask that they help make my way clear to me as this Time closes'.

This dramatic and beautiful labyrinth of canyons has I read 'been inhabited for 6000 years, its occupants have included the Anasazi civilisation which saw itself transform from nomadic huntergathers in prehistory to settled agricultural and artisan communities building stunning cliff palaces (like The White House in this canyon) in the 12th century. The Anasazi would prove be resourceful, adaptable and, ultimately, the most enduring of the Pueblo cultural traditions. They occupied a large area of the Southwest before suddenly disappearing. The Navajo have lived here for the last 300 years. They still rear sheep and goats in the canyon, and plant crops on the brilliantly green valley floor.'

It all makes me want to find out more. But mainly I just am so privileged to soak up the spirit here. I pitch my tent in the free site provided and open myself to a night in this amazing energy.

18 October Silverton

Am having breakfast in a café after a night warm amid rampant Victoriana. I intended to camp up here in the mountains but at 9500' its too cold – my water bottle in the car is frozen this morning. Yesterday evening I looked out over the snow with the lights coming on as the sky pinked and dusked.

Now, I watch a Greyhound bus unload its disparate load of stiff and yawning passengers; cowboy types with hats and bowed legs, native Americans with long black hair, young men in woolly hats, two very fat men. I feel grateful for my car.

Four Corners

I stood in the centre of the bronze inlaid plaque. It says, 'Four states, come together in freedom under God'. I have the sense of groundedness, of foursquareness, stability, and also of possibilities, of many directions open to me, and indeed of 'my' number 4. ….number 4 follows me around… Clockwise from top right, the four states are Colorado, New Mexico, Arizona and Utah.

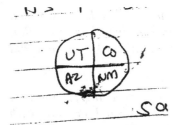

A woman came up and said 'It takes a lot of woman to cover four states. Aren't we powerful'

November

Yes. We are powerful.

And...the great power of AGE.

I feel it. I am back in Crestone, the sun still shines on this deck. I still can hike in the mountains, singing to warn the bears and mountain lion and lynx....

My journey has brought me around the world to the Sacred Valley, I am full of the energies of all the Holy places my path took me to, and I feel immensely strong. Soon the Year will end and I will fly home and put that strength to use.

How I don't know. What will I decide to do about the Centre, and how will it be? How have the community been without me? Can I now step away and leave it to others, follow my heart out of the city? Where will I live? What will I do? My money is gone now.

I have no idea where my path will lead me, but I will follow it into the darkness, my hand reaching out ahead of me in faith.

New Freedom, New Creations....

The Wheel of the Year Group

On November 5th 1994 Pamela (new friend from dancing) and I sat watching the huge bonfire at Ottery St Mary. We were getting our breath back after running around the streets evading the flaming tar barrels. Medieval scene, quite surreal. The men of the town charge into the crowds with great barrels of blazing tar hefted on to their sacking-clad shoulders: believe it or not the responsibility is with the crowd to keep themselves safe. A wonderful event clinging on to life in the nanny-state that Britain has become. The smoke and flames are carried triumphantly through the streets, a great ritual cleansing of the town dating back to God knows when.

'Ritual is so important' we said. 'I miss the ritual group I had in Nottingham' said Pamela. 'Then let's start one' I offered excitedly as is my wont.

We ran the Wheel of the Year group for one year, winter solstice to winter solstice. It was a great experience and lots of people came along. We started with just five of us in my flat, and at summer solstice 25 of us were creating a spiral on a beach and making a fire, and floating in a moonlit sea…

On Winter Solstice Pamela, Maya and I spent a blissful afternoon preparing for the first ritual. We made a Wassail Cup and ceremonial Bread, and decorated my flat with evergreens and fairy lights and ribbons. We spread a cloth and made an altar to the four directions and elements and to celebrate the Festival of Winter Solstice. It is all new to me and I am learning avidly. Our group is to be called 'The Wheel' – a circle celebrating the Wheel of the Year. This natural Celtic cycle has been the basis of my calendar, the structure of my life ever since, along with the moon calendar.

It was during this ceremony that the idea for the Convergence Centre came to me, almost fully formed and including the name. It was to be a centre celebrating the coming together of mainstream and alternative, of the healing and the creative arts. Pamela said 'I'll help' and we set about it all together, as playmates. Soon Lu joined in, and he had ideas, and as I was very busy teaching they took over the decor and running of it. It became a truly beautiful space thanks to them. They invested money in it, and I paid them back later.

The Convergence Centre

So, I took a newly empty space in the Queen Street properties and turned it into my beloved Centre. It was the best creation of my life. Every time a space became available I expanded the Centre. It grew and thrived and was full of people, a real community, bringing together the healing, creative, spiritual and technological arts……we expanded together and laughed and discussed and wondered together. Many of us remain the very best of friends.

These quotes lived on the crowded main noticeboard…..

'Whatever you can do, or dream you can, begin it. Boldness has genius, power, and magic in it.'
'As soon as you commit yourself, all sorts of things occur to help one that would never otherwise have occurred. A whole stream of events issues from the decision raising in one's favor all manner of unforeseen events, meetings and material assistance which no one could have dreamed would have come their way'.

Johann Wolfgang von Goethe and WH Murray

'Our deepest fear is not that we are inadequate. Our deepest fear is that we are powerful beyond measure. It is our light, not our darkness that most frightens us. We ask ourselves, Who am I to be brilliant, gorgeous, talented, fabulous? Actually, who are you not to be? You are a child of God. Your playing small does not serve the world. There is nothing enlightened about shrinking so that other people won't feel insecure around you. We are all meant to shine, as children do. We were born to make manifest the glory of God that is within us. It's not just in

some of us; it's in everyone. And as we let our own light shine, we unconsciously give other people permission to do the same. As we are liberated from our own fear, our presence automatically liberates others.'

Marianne Williamson, quote used by Nelson Mandela.

'The Invitation

It doesnt interest me what you do for a living.
I want to know what you ache for, and if you dare to dream of meeting your heart's longing.

It doesnt interest me how old you are. I want to know if you will risk looking like a fool for love, for your dream, for the adventure of being alive.

It doesnt interest me what planets are squaring your moon. I want to know if you have touched the centre of your own sorrow, if you have been opened by life's betrayals or have become shrivelled and closed from fear of further pain. I want to know if you can sit with pain, mine or your own, without moving to hide it or fade it or fix it.

I want to know if you can be with joy, mine or your own, if you can dance with wildness and let the ecstasy fill you to the tips of your fingers and toes without cautioning us to be careful, to be realistic, to remember the limitations of being human.

It doesn't interest me if the story you are telling me is true. I want to know if you can disappoint another to be true to yourself; if you can bear the accusation of betrayal and not betray your own soul.

I want to know if you can see beauty, even when its not pretty, every day , and if you can source your own life from its presence.

I want to know if you can live with failure, yours and mine, and still stand on the edge of the lake and shout to the silver of the full moon, 'YES!'.

It doesnt interest me to know where you live or how much money you have. I want to know if you can get up sfter the night of grief and despair, weary and bruised to the bone, and do what needs to be done for the children.

It doesnt interest me who you know or with whom you have studied. I want to know what sustains you from the inside when all else falls away.

I want to know if you can be alone with yourself and if you truly like the company you keep in the empty moments'.

From 'the Invitation' by Oriah Mountain Dreamer.

193

FIRE

Represents the passionate creative spirit, the wild free risk- taking adventurous aspect of ourselves. It is enthusiasm (which means 'God within'), it is passion, it is sensuality and sexuality.

It burns away the dross, it purges and cleanses and transmutes.

It is important to find our own fire if we are by nature placid, or to learn to manage a very fiery nature so we don't burn out or burn up, or hurt others.

At ceremonies... or at home ...we can write what we want to let go of and throw it onto the fire with awareness.

Ancient fire ceremonies remain here in the West Country.....at Ottery st Mary every Nov 5th the men shoulder blazing tar barrels and race through the crowded streets. The responsibility lies with the crowd to get out of the way. Wonderful. This is a ceremony of purification of the streets. It also brings a huge energy.

Fire demands respect and care and honouring.

Fire dances....

Fire purifies.....

Fire forges.....

And Fire is alchemist

So these principles guide our community. Many people have come and have contributed, been helped and have savoured the atmosphere.

When I left on my trip rooms were permanently let to a homeopath, garden designer, an artist and graphic designer, a group therapy practice, an earth energy researcher, two counsellors, two psychosynthesis practitioners, a webmaster, a masseuse, a rag wallhanging and rugmaker, and a plethora of therapists and courses and groups rented space by the session. We had two beautiful attic spaces for groups. I took a meditation and spiritual development group weekly in one of them.

Reiki

I trained in Reiki, with Tanmaya Honervogt, and began a small healing practice at the centre after a while. As was my nature I received more pleasure from giving the energy than receiving it, and Tanmaya pointed this out as something to remedy. I was pretty staggered by the energy flowing through me, and I took myself a bit too seriously as usual, and found I put too much of me in instead of just channelling, so I got ill sometimes after treatments, and felt I had better stop since I couldn't correct that.

When I first was attuned, I got seriously overheated. No idea why. Paul said 'It's switched something on in you'. I could not touch my body without the hand and the area touched flaring with heat. It was difficult. I gave my mother a treatment and was knocked off my feet, fortunately against a wall. She enjoyed it though. I can still feel it now as I type, the energy if I focus on it.

One day, driving a group of us back from Paul's Centre near Shaftesbury, I noticed smoke from the engine and stopped the car, got everyone out and away. Fortunately there was a phone box right there...and the Fire engine was just round the corner!!!! Usual miracle!!! The firemen congratulated me on not opening the bonnet because as soon as they did flames burst forth...

It seems even my car was overheating. I could not afford a new one so was grounded for the summer, and that was I think for the best, to be grounded when I was so fiery. I walked everywhere. I went to a talk by Ffyona Campbell the walker and was very inspired. I had a backpack and got very fit and brown.

When autumn came I thought whatever am I going to do now I have to go to work again. I walked between colleges and centre and home and got exhausted. Then amazingly Mum heard that Aunty Phyl had left her money, and asked that Mum give me some, so I was able to buy a car!!!! This time I was wiser and I bought a reliable Polo from a very nice garage. They sold me my next Polo too.

COMMUNITY

The nuclear family replaced the extended family, and relationships became far more unsupported and claustrophobic. People also started moving so much. The tribe was lost. Now even the nuclear family is fragmenting and loneliness is at its greatest ever.

We need community. Groups of like-minded people coming together by choice in a healthier way, in honest but loving and respectful ways. This doesn't happen overnight, and harmony takes a lot of practice, but its great work. The Buddhists call it Sangha. We all need a spiritual community or sangha.

I think in future lots of living by both individual and families will be in community. The community will have respected elders, who will hold the vision and wisdom of the group and help with conflicts..
Children will be brought up by the group, and the elders will teach them about life. In the meantime we can gather a few friends and meet regularly to share our journeys.

TOUCH

Touch is so so essential to us all, but we have been rather starved of it in the west. Of all the senses this one has been least relished and honoured in ordinary life, as sensuality has been increasingly given a bad press. It has collected unwholesome connotations and we have lost its beauty and healthiness.

It is important to arrange regular touch in our lives, through massage and Reiki etc and as it becomes more familiar we start to touch people, family, friends, our babies and children, to hug and kiss and hold, to stroke and massage, as a matter of course. Lovers bring fresh loving attention to every part of the body. Eyes need to touch too. Eye contact, held softly, can change a lot. A new closeness springs up. Relationships start to heal and communication flows. We need to find the erotic in everyday life not just in our lovemaking, to heighten all the senses and cherish the beauty around us.

Roshi John Garrie's Last Workshop in Taliaris in Wales.

'Walk the length of your mat' (2 metres) said Roshi, looking evil. 'In half an hour. No standing still and moving occasionally. Move very very slowly, with fine awareness of the feet and toes and the contact with the mat.'

I had come to John Garrie's last workshop before he retired, partly as a tribute to his magnificent teaching ten years previously when he was in Devon, partly because his organisation 'The Sati Society' - teaching his own brand of Mindfulness and Zen - was moving from their stately home Taliaris in Wales, and partly because the workshop was called 'SLOWING DOWN. BEING GENTLE WITH OURSELVES'

My life was ridiculous. I had been racing, hurtling. Two teaching jobs - at The tutorial College and at Exeter College - who had asked me to introduce Environmental Science there, running the Centre, and the management of the properties, plus numerous activities and an ever growing group of friends. I would slow down and then find things piling up again. I hated to miss anything. I had a little book by my bed 'Meditations for women who do too much'. There is a horribly true bit about such women needing to overwork in order to feel included.

No wonder that I was seriously nauseous attempting the Kin hin exercise. The setting was very formal and I was terrified I was going to throw up or have to leave the room. I was just preparing to do the latter (unheard of) when the bell rang. Roshi looked straight at me with horrible glee. 'Saved by the bell' he said.

Early on the last morning, considerably wound down, I walked with my roommate through the forest to find the Lake, which I had not managed to find on other trips, or the day previously. It is a hidden, secret lake which allows itself to be found when the time is right. The other day I had raced around hunting. This time, slowly pacing, with no expectation, we went straight to it.

It was like an Arthurian Legend. Still and mirror-like, wreathed in the early morning mist, surrounded by trees with no path to the edge. In silence we gazed. Expecting to see the hand bearing the sword rise slowly from the waters.

I went home and prepared to reduce my life to manageable proportions.

Except I didn't really (!) and it took a couple of severe falls before I got the message and gave up Exeter College. I think my work in life is not to work too hard.

Breakthroughs

The falls came with a time of highs and lows which I watched carefully, and which presaged a new calm. The storm before the calm!!!!

It was December. There was a moment in the attic one night in meditation. A not particularly good meditation, with many thoughts. BUT I suddenly KNEW that everything is perfect. PERFECT JUST AS IT IS. Such a joy in the moment. Wordless knowing. This was a big moment, looking back. A simple quiet recognition, but now I see just what a big realisation it is. It changes everything.

And in a one-to-one with my teacher Paul, another wordless moment. A moment of utter oneness with him as our eyes linked and features seemed to shift and the world blurred and there was Communion. That is the word. Communication shifted beyond words to communion. He said 'Enjoy the power'.

He had said to me there is no separation between inner and outer. I was talking about symbolism and mirroring. He said that will fade and I am needing it for security. I couldn't yet take that on board. He said, 'It's like loving. You there, me here, no separation. All one.

So why did I in the early spring decide to leave the practice?

Dan was ill. He had left college when everything was going right for him, returned to Exeter and was sharing the flat with Ben, and suddenly admitted himself to the mental hospital. I was visiting and trying to help but of course I could not. He kept saying the right side of his (very handsome) face was so ugly it was repellent. It was terrible to listen to. I could only hold his hand and say I loved him.

I still had trouble not going down with my loved ones, and I was sensing myself in a very messy place, feeling a slide into the abyss imminent. I spoke about it to Paul and he just kept telling me I was fine, my life was fine. (Mine was, but Dan's wasn't and I couldn't understand why he couldn't see that meant mine wasn't either). I needed creature comfort, I needed my mess acknowledged, seen and heard and witnessed. I needed compassion. I was very frightened, confused and helpless. Someone said I had been bypassing the emotional journey, in the austere path of the observer and Paul's reaction confirmed this to me. So I left. I called him and he was very shocked.

In the spring I began to (unconsciously really) allow myself to dive deeper into my emotional being. Dan had left the hospital and was back at college. I could allow my focus to shift back to me.

Had I been neglecting my creaturehood? Had I, with the Zen work and with Gill Edwards 'Growth through Joy' work, been up-levelling too fast and bypassing the emotional level? Seeing the interpretation on a higher level too fast? Gill warns about this. Not letting my 'creature' have a chance to rage, grieve, burn, and wail.

On an April Friday morning I watched myself sink into my wound, reach the bottom of it, see, feel, describe, acknowledge it in utter despair. My separation, isolation, unlovableness, madness, dangerousness. I feared I was dangerous to love. I feared the madness reflected my own. All the old accusations of being repulsive and foul that I had grown used to replayed themselves in my head. I wallowed. My head began to ache and I felt sick. My nose bled. I was sick. Blood and vomit mixed. Some part of me, small but there, watched all this.

Then I watched the point when an 'oh well' rose to the surface of all the thick black viscosity. With it came a steely strength like none I had known before. It filled me, just as I was, JUST AS I WAS, spreading through every part of me and out into the world. It was a moment of reconnection, reconnection to the power supply. I think the more fearless the appraisal of fear in the cut-off place the stronger the flow of power when plugged in again. And then, wrapping the strength, softening it, came the compassion. Pure compassion pouring love into the open wounds bathing a bruised and battered heart and mind and body in warm pink and gold light.

This awesome combination of strength and compassion is God within us. Our diamond point buried in the layers of our selves. The God within us charges us to overflowing with Radiance, ready for service. We are called to be midwives of the new age, agents of the evolution of human consciousness. We only have to follow our passions and our bliss, we only have to love and enjoy. We can allow ourselves to be as we are, and love ourselves just like that, in HUMILITY and PRIDE. Humility in our pain, pride in the God within.

Power comes directly from pain, I discovered many times, from getting in touch with it. So the wound is the most valuable experience of all. As the power flowed into me, stronger and stronger, I was ablaze. Pulsing, vibrating, transfigured. I strove to keep grounded by remembering my pain. Such a clarity came, total certainty alongside total uncertainty. The direct experience of and acceptance of paradox.

It felt a good way to meet my half century.

18.4.96

'I am 50' I said to the mirror.

Wow. 50. Last year I struggled a lot with 49, knowing 50 was coming. 'But, here it is.'

My party was to be later by the river on May Day under the full moon. I had friends to dinner, a magical concoction of candlelight, loving faces, gifts, wonderful words of appreciation and so much fun. It all supports me as I work to find stability.

One day, I came across magnification techniques, building the feeling up to maximum intensity. 'I don't deserve prosperity' 'I DON'T DESERVE PROSPERITY' building and building until I am yelling at myself and until 'YES I DO' comes storming, authentic, strong and sure from deep deep within......and there wass a cellular shift, a belief is changing.

I noticed when I am receiving lots of flattering attention (as I was then)I start thinking I should have more, and when I am being ignored or rejected I start thinking I don't deserve what I have, I am dangerous. I know that Stability will only come once I remain undisturbed by any of it. 'Though the sun sets in the east the Buddha sits'. When I can keep my value of myself steady through rejection and praise. Ongoing practice.

I trust the Universe so much of the time now. But I haven't trusted myself with other people. It's increasing though, erratically.

May day, my second party.....

The clarity and stillness of the night. The huge red then orange moon lifting from the deep blue horizon. The river flowing gently and wide, the ring of protective nightlights, the circle of glowing faces within it, the poems read in the firelight. Diane 'attending' me. She said she felt she had done it before, dressing my hair with flowers, being my 'handmaiden', in another life. She felt we had been sisters, and she was preparing me for my initiation as a Priestess.

I said to myself again 'Beware, Sandra, beware of ego trips'...there had been all that acclaim when filming earlier in the day for Tanmaya's Reiki TV programme, then all the wonderful birthday words and cards. People asking my advice. I am not ready to deal with it all with equanimity.

At one oclock the few of us remaining sat by the fire and listened to Mara (a Yugoslav friend) singing sad Russian songs as soft white mist rose from the river and settled in the valley. Then, slowly, we walked through the mist in awestruck silence and climbed up through it into the moonlit night again.

I LOVE THIS DIARY. It is new. The huge pages, the hard back, the clear wide lines. I feel I have space to express myself as never before. Remember the little diaries? All SQUASHED AND TANGLED. I was like that, congested. I am unravelling it all.

And it is manifesting externally in a Centre to express myself in - writing the newsletters and talking and running my little group. I gave a talk called 'Trust the Magic', which was very well received: I had prepared several huge blue sheets of card to focus the group's attention and to structure myself. Ultimately, we only have to relax and enjoy, I said. I was getting there.

By the end of May I realise am only dangerous to love because my loving supports too much and feeds egos - without the necessary expression of the negative or the protection of anger. I give more than can be borne. The fear of abandonment if I criticise or if I express my own needs. Stems from Mum early on. I say something and she is ill...

It is where the earth breaks under pressure – faults – that the energy flows through. Our energy flows from our stress points or wounds. In the body healing for wounds is provided BY the wounds. From our faults we are healed....if we protect people from their stress-points they never have the chance to access the power. We disempower them by taking on too much responsibility, by 'loving too much'. If we allow ourselves to be abused we abuse the abusers. This is what I have been doing.

MAGIC

The Connecting Force or energy that is in everything and everyone and is there for us all to use. The Oneness and Mystery that defies explanation but can be experienced and Known. This Knowing becomes Trust, which brings an openness to Magic, and an ability to live in uncertainty, and the whole Glory escalates....

OLD WORLD

Fear...conflict...unawareness...blame...competition codependency...addiction...loneliness...need for approval andto impress...institutions with power over...domination...victimhood...pain. Patriarchy...male-female polarisation and distortion Science and the intellect separate from spirit..loss of spiritual connectionresistance...confusion...karma.. war..judgment...sadism...'realism'...disallowing of mystery...fear of Magic.. burying of personal and planetary rubbish ...pollution personally and of planet...exhaustion... depression

NEW WORLD

Love...Awareness...appreciation and honouring of life...acceptance and joy in difference and diversity....celebration...wonder....joy and delight...trust during the tough times ...holism..oneness...personal responsibility....co-operation...partnership... idealism...creating our own reality....co creation...kindness....compassion....male-female differences less...opposite sex found within oneself...sensuality and sexuality become sacred again...magic and mystery honoured...groups of people come together in a healthy way...peace and bliss

Through 1996 I held my small group weekly – 'Trust the Magic' and at one point I gave a talk with the same title. I talked about Paths to Magic...I see them as Meditation, Healing, Movement, Therapy and Creativity, leading to inner space, energy, understanding, trust, and unlocking of potential.... through to what I called Dynamic Contentment. I had asked a question endlessly when young: 'should we be contented or should we be disatisfied and aspire?' I had answered it at last. We do both. We hold both. We aspire from a place of contentment. Change can only happen from a place of acceptance. I also talked about the Old World and The New World, the world that evolving as human beings will bring us into, a world based not on fear but on love......

We saw the planet for the first time from space in the 60s as we explored outer space and we began to see ourselves and our world from the outside. We began to value the planet and ourselves as a whole. The world began to change, with all the Flower Power of the 60s, but people were not ready...it is a slow long path to taking the responsibility needed to safely reclaim personal power from the institutions (church, state, and men!). Science and the Sacred begin to come together at last.

Fragmentation of society occurred as people worked on themselves and separated from unhealthy 'dominator' relationships. Slowly the Eco-Spiritual Revolution began, Silently and in each individual, at a soul level....It grows apace, and events in the Old World escalate in horror as the World Ego kicks out against its demise. So parallel to each other, at the same time, the human race moves Quietly towards evolution, and Noisily , its roar fanned by the media, the Old world fights for its life....

Things get clearer for me, but I am on a personal level still suffering terribly about my Daniel, who is now suddenly in a Cambridge mental hospital and is actually staying put. I thought this might be good, that he might open up and get better, but no, he is apparently psychotic and on medication. I have been wanting to see him but he refuses. He wants me out of carer role, Ben says. When it was Earth Healing Day at Wembley I went up in a coach in tears with my friend and spent the whole day amid 10,000 people crying to God to heal my son.

But I had to keep going, keep to my own path too.

Towards the end of 1996, don't know quite when, I stood up in front of my class and realised I didn't want to teach any more. After 9 years, it was enough, because I realised I had stopped learning, I knew the syllabus inside out, and it meant my teaching had lost something. It was my education into our world and what we have done to it. It supported me through my divorce, but now I felt I wanted just to be at the Centre and give it all I had. Slow down further. And, interestingly, a young woman called Clare Bridges came in and said she would like to teach Environmental Science. I said 'Would you like my classes?' Ken the Principal was shocked and unhappy but accepting. I carried on teaching my brilliant Geography class, determined that they get high grades, and they do. I remember consciously sitting there knowing these were my last lessons. Finally after years in a mould and fungus infested room I have a beautiful room overlooking the garden...everything is better than when I began. But I know it's time to go.

Life is suddenly slowing right down, But....in my journal I have written 'I am so worried about Dan. He has been in Fulbourne Mental Hospital in Cambridge for 5 months. I am so helpless. I spoke with mum. She doesn't know what to do either. Ben says Dan still does not want me to go there. When he was in the Mental Hospital in Exeter I went all the time but felt so helpless, nothing I could say or do could help and Dan said he did not want me to have to be carer again. He got better then and moved. Maybe he moved so far away so I would be spared. But I feel so confused, so helpless, so guilty. He is ringing sometimes.

As for myself, my experience of empty times is shifting. Instead of fears of abandonment and loads of serpents within, I feel pleasure at my space and sanctuary. AT LAST.'

One of these blessed quiet days, I found myself writing out a list of all I had come to Know as true guidelines. Here it is, just as I wrote it, in no particular order..

- *Keep clear....breathe OUT, relaxing every muscle and cell*
- *Love...breathe in love to every cell.....breathe out love to the world*
- *Keep the attention in the PRESENT, out of past and future*
- *Keep a clear vision of the intention for the future*
- *Have no attachment to its coming to pas*
- *Remember Hope is an affirmation of lack*
- *Have no need or wish to impress*
- *Take joy in and honour what IS, as it is*
- *What we focus on expands*
- *Have no need for things to be OTHER than they are*
- *Know that what is deep within will surely be reflected in circumstances and events and other people's treatment of you*
- *Nothing is safe, nothing is sure, there is nothing to fear*
- *Do my best possible without overwork or martyrhood*
- *Accept slips and mistakes – note them with honesty and let them go*
- *Allow and savour the flow of giving and receiving*
- *Keep boundaries clear and consistent*
- *Know that truly loving intent protects completely*
- *Know we are all one at depth*
- *Look after self first with love and care*
- *Everything passes*
- *Witness feelings and be aware of the witness*
- *We are100% responsible for everything in our lives*
- *Others' reactions are their responsibility.*
- *If we are disturbed by others they are mirroring us in some way*
- *Neediness is fear of a need we perceived is or will be unmet*
- *Every event is a message, a signal from our soul – there are no accidents*
- *Be clear as to real wants, not wants of ego*
- *Preserve times of stillness and silence*
- *Wonder at the world*
- *Keep a light touch*

- *A pure intent and heart means knowing our impurities*
- *Honour the dark for its essential contribution*
- *Whatever happens happens for the highest good*
- *Feel rich NOW*
- *Remember…3 H's …humility, humour and honour*
- *Love and allow*

Also I was beginning to see that my guidance was not external, but my own inner higher self, my inner teacher. 'Signals from the Soul', and when we let these guide us, I call it 'Soul Control'.

Had a coffee with Mo, the homeopath at the Centre. A deranged man stopped and looked at us and I felt the old fears of madness. THAT fear is still to be dealt with. The work goes on….but, I feel I am sustaining a clarity I have not felt before.

I accept myself just as I am. I go on 'practising living' ….learning how to engage with life in all its trials and triumphs from a peaceful point deep within that keeps me safe.

Yes that's it….practising living….fully engaged with it all, no hiding, right there in the moment face to face with it

Dan

My diary, my beautiful big diary ends suddenly just after coming to this peaceful place, on February 17th 1997. The rest of it is blank.

Mum and Ben and I were so helpless, so frightened, had become so sick at heart for him. But for me this was contained to a saving extent within this peace….

On the 15th, I wrote a small poem about my evening:

So much space

Time spreads unfolds

its wings

the evening lies   soft

around   me

faintly purring

a   train   passes

mumbles   at   the   edges

of   the   stillness

I read it to Dan on the phone. He thanks me for the stillness but I hear the wistfulness and I long to able to really give him this peace.....

But I can't. Oh God, I can't.

On the 18th he took his own life and on the 19th he died.

There is no diary until 1998 began. Nearly a year blank with pain and incomprehension. But I do know that the peaceful place I had so recently come to was to bring me through it all. I was given what I needed to survive.

And Ben too, had come to a place where he knew it was the best thing for his brother, terrible though that seemed.

Summer 87 to the Hills

After Dan died my mother and I and sometimes Ben too huddled together every weekend for months. We felt so strongly that something big had to happen now between us, left in a gaping bloody wound bewildered and hurting, guilty and angry. So we planned together as we sat in her little sitting room, and we decided to sell our properties and buy together something big enough to give mum an independent space and me rooms to let out to pay a mortgage.

My exquisite riverside flat sold the first day it was on the market, and I started to hunt for our dream. But it wasn't to be. There was nothing suitable for both of us. We were not meant to dream together - or live together. Or we both held a buried resistance to this. My mother's flat would not sell.

I knew I wanted to spend the summer up on the high moor in a caravan. I think I knew underneath that if I could walk and sit in the wilderness I could do my weeping with the bleak rocks and bogs and windswept rain to cry with me.

A small caravan materialised fast - and one hot afternoon dear Glenn helped me move my essentials out to the moor up above Throwleigh. All my furniture and stored things went to Queen Street where it was very useful.

I remember the migraines, the nausea, all back with a vengeance, and the condensation pouring down the windows, and pipes leaking and flooding the van; one day I came back to inches of water pouring out when I opened the door. All summer I was damp and struggling with water, my world so precisely reflecting my inner state. Drowning in the emotion. It was a very wet summer. HOW is it that nature always reflects what is going on???? I sat on wet rocks in the rain up on the moor and I talked with Daniel and I shouted and wailed and screamed. There was no answer. The dark red pain burnt and stabbed through me, bringing me to my knees on the wet ground, and I prostrated myself before the elements storming without and within.

But the Centre held me. I was surrounded by and helped by a loving community including nearly 30 therapists!!!!! I had given up the teaching just in time, because I couldn't have done it, nor would I have found it easy to let go in my fragile state. My instincts had protected me again.

Soon after I moved I heard from Ben that Miro had been allocated a flat by the Council: and it was just round the corner from River Meadows. I had been looked after yet again. If I hadn't moved when I did, I would have had to sell with the feeling of running away. My instinct to sell was spot-on.

I remember slowly realising I could not live with mum. The distress came to a head and I had a migraine for days. Then in the midst of it there was her anxious face at the streaming window, her friend Angela behind her. This was astonishing, she did not visit me, ever. She came in, with a bagful of invalid food and sat down and looked at me, lying racked with pain, and said that someone was actually interested in her flat. I gasped and blurted something incoherently about not being able to go on with our dream.

She was silent, then she spoke as I had never heard her speak to me before. She looked me in the eyes and said uncharacteristically firmly,

'Now listen to me. This is your mother speaking. You are not to feel pressured. That plan is over now. It's a new stage.'

She was really speaking from her soul and I heard. Some higher part of her came through. She was setting me free. She drank tea and left. I got up, pain free, went out to buy a newspaper for some reason and there was Nelson Mandela on the front page. 'FREEDOM DAY'.

Soon I went to Old Meadow to housesit for the autumn, planted parsley, and ate all the runner beans Caroline and Marcus had planted. When they came back from South America, I found a room in a shared house …where the dark caught me in it's web again , but not for long.

And then 1998 dawned and the worst of the pain had receded, and I took off on the wings of the universe and I began to fly…..

What I see most in writing all these flashbacks to my past story is this....

We live, through so much. We get things so wrong. BUT there is ALWAYS the thread of support that keeps up going. There is always that something miraculous which saves us from going right under.

As these miracles keep on happening we begin to know we are looked after. We are being offered the opportunity to trust life. The faith turns into experience so now I say it would be churlish not to trust when I have been looked after so many many times.

It is no longer faith that sustains, it is sheer weight of experience. I can only be grateful and praise.

And once we have that trust, then fear is no monster any more, and so our lives can get better every day free of fear and the negative outcomes it creates..

So, even when it's hard to know why, we begin to trust in the grander, the invisible, picture. The splendour, the grandeur, beyond our comprehension

'Only praise'

said Rainer Maria Rilke.

And of course the praise and the gratitude and the love just keep on creating more of what we love……

W. H. Murray said

The more the soul knows....
the more she loves.....

and loving much....

She tastes much.

End of Rememberings
End of my Year's Pilgrimages
and End of Part One

RIGHT AND WRONG

We all have our own truth.

Being right has nothing to do with it, is only an ego game, played to give a feeling of superiority and security.

There is only love and compassion.

Neale Donald Walsch says 'The idea that you call "right" is the idea that someone else calls "wrong." The solution that you call "perfect" is the solution that another calls "unworkable
What will solve all of this? Not attack, that's for sure. And not defense, either. So what is left? Simple human love. The kind of love that says, "It doesn't matter who is right or wrong. It only matters that you are not hurt. And that we both can benefit. All true benefits are mutual."

Once we can relate in this way, once we know that wanting the best for ourselves means wanting the best for everyone, we move from the stress of 'win-lose' to the ease of 'win-win'
and we breathe out in a great and glorious sigh of relief.
When we want the best for everyone the best comes to us. And....vice versa....

PART TWO

......AFTERWARDS

Higher Sea House

The big communal sitting room –
We had no furniture until Carol joined us
but we loved all the space....

Chapter 1   Into the Void

From my window in Vermont   February 2008

I began working on this book again in November 2004, exactly six years after the end of the 'Year Lived as if it was my Last'. I was in Andalucia, in the Alpujarras, a remote valley between the majestic Sierra Nevada and the coastal range. I was off on my adventures again after a long period of stability. I needed to write about what came after that Year.....so I had packed all my journals and favourite things into my beloved Dragon-green Polo and driven to Spain to write...I had friends there, I was excited by it all and had rented a delicious casita , very serendipitously as always.

I had come to such a good place before Dan died in early 1997, and again as the Year drew to a close at the end of 1998. I came back to the UK in full strength and faith. But then the theories got put to the test all over again....I had to really work on walking he talk of all the books and the teachings...

The first week in Spain I read all my journals from the past twenty years as I lay in the sun on the roof terrace, under the steady gaze of the mountains, and it had been a deeply humbling experience. Also deeply shocking to remember what a life of negative thinking, suffering and seeking had been like. How hard and heavy I had been on myself and therefore on all those around me. So much going round in circles, so much mess.

I picked all the freshly- ordered notebooks and bits of paper up off the floor, selected the journal from November 1998, and I started to extract and type. I was cast back into the last days of Crestone, Colorado and my return to England.. It was not easy, and I wanted to get it typed as quickly as I could.

But, I was so reluctant to start. So, I started from the POSITIVE place I had come to..

Crestone, Colorado - the last days.
Signs and Decisions.

November 1998

It is some days before I leave.

The music is swelling and swelling, I lie wrapped in rugs in the clear serene dome that is the Lindisfarne Chapel at the Zen Mountain Centre and let David White Dove's improvised sounds lift my soul.

I have circled the Planet. The Planet is now within me. My consciousness contains it. I suspected as much, from all my years of studies and teaching of Geography and Environmental Science. I guessed I didn't NEED to travel. I travel because I want to look around me. To be a witness, for the Divine.

Next day, lying still and quiet in the hot sun on the top deck, snow in the blue shadows under the pinyons, a deer, motionless, looks up at me. I look back. Eye to eye.

I have been reading 'The Mists of Avalon' and it is drawing me back. I draw a big egg shape and fill it with spirals of words, about England.

Soft rain... wet roses... cathedrals... stained glass..... barefoot on dewy lawns....good newspapers...... mists over soft green hills.... vegetables

213

growing..... horses at the fence..... eggs and honey on the farm stall.... stone circles.... pubs....cream teas..... fish and chips at Lyme.... lights coming on in the valley.... grey seas.... castles and towers.... libraries.... BBC.... soft voices.... mystery and magic... and most important of all, my friends.

Later Josh shows me photos of their time in Fiji. 'It's so far away' he says sadly ', 'No its not' I say, 'it's right here. Everything is right here, is everywhere. Like all of us is in every cell'. It is after the blessing of their land. A circle of some thirty people, linking hands in the crisp sunlight. A drumbeat. A Native American calls the four directions and scatters cornmeal and tobacco. A fat 'cigar' of tobacco is passed around and smoked. A cairn of stones is built. I promise English soil and rose petals to bury there. Prayers are sung.

This space now, this whole glorious Planet, will be carried within me as I take my steps into the Void, into the Unknown, very soon now.

I know it is a void because I have had signs. I dream dreams to try to avoid knowing it. It works sometimes.

The Centre was full and thriving when I left, but I earned very little from it, and leavings were imminent. So despite my confusions I think I knew on a deep level that it might simply not be ever financially viable. I also knew on that level that it was a strong connection to my marriage. It was also 24 hour responsibility, with people using it every evening and weekend, and everything had to be just so all the time, which all tired me out. I also knew I was very very attached to it.

So, looking back now, I see that this global journey to the Native Americans' Valley of Vision Quest, which fell so readily into place, was provided for me to give me some detachment. And now I have, in this remote place, asked for signs and received them. It has been painful and I have had difficulty writing them down.

The first was that a few of my beloved community began to need to move on and income dropped. But rooms can fill again just like that I thought. But they didn't.

The second was that not long before I was to leave I heard that my car had died, and could not be resuscitated. I was dismayed. I could feel events closing in on me. I sensed real challenge was coming, in what form I didn't know. The end of my Year was not looking or feeling as I had imagined. Not that I had imagined any 'next stage' at all... just some kind of triumphant return, maybe a revitalised centre flying under its own steam, my role reduced, but GOOD and POSITIVE. I had faith....

10 November

The third was a fax received out of the blue from my solicitor, with a letter, threatening and psychotic, from my ex-husband. Followed by increasing reports of very unpleasant harassment of the Centre and of other tenants in the Queen Street buildings. More faxes came, wanting action to deter him.

Why is he pursuing me, still torturing me, what do I have to do, I am asking God in the deepest seriousness, what do I have to do to be free of all this madness? I have worked with it all for so long on such deep levels. How much longer??? Do I have to let go of the buildings or do I fight for them I don't know. But there is no good news at all coming from there.

I draw an Animal Medicine card: Grouse (Sacred Spiral) in contrary position. This indicates: dissipation of energy, lack of discipline, lost connection to Source, lack of clear intent behind outpouring of energy, in a tailspin, going down the drain, spinning in the head. Too right!!!! But what to do? I work to connect again, to ground and centre. Not easy. I draw up tables for and against. I create all sorts of drawings and spider diagrams. I look at finances, my motivations, imbalances in the centre. A decision has to be taken on the basis of How Things Are Now, I write. Not How They Might Be. Too late for that. No more time to See How It Goes.

I hear that Miro has burst in on one of the centre homeopath's sessions with a client and yelled abuse. The spiral plunges. **Oh God WHY??? WHY????**

I am back with all those despairing questions again.

Then one evening I watch Greg Braden's video about the 'Zero Point Field'. He says something which grabs my attention.

He was himself pondering why he had attracted such tough stuff into his life – my mouth drops open and I turn up the volume - and he says that yes we attract events that mirror how we treat others, but he knew he wasn't treating others in such as a way as to attract such terrible events…. By then I was sitting forward riveted.

Then he says, it dawned on him that we also attract events that mirror how we JUDGE people. That the negative charge of judgment and criticism attracts the same vibration….

This is my answer. Now I know what I have been doing to attract all this.

I had had no idea of the creative power of our judgments, and I can be very judgemental. It was time to stop. Time to replace judgment with discernment and compassion. Discernment sees clearly but has no negative charge.

And I think **'NOW I can go home. NOW I know why all this is happening to me.' It may take awhile but it will all stop. What a gift.**

17 November

Breakfast meditation at the Zen centre. I am delighted to be going to meet my fellow meditators at last. But the sit is an extraordinary one and I am granted a clear vision of myself in regard to the centre (though I can't really put it into words). My drive for perfection so I cannot be criticised, my believed need for popularity, approval, identity and a strong belief that I have to 'pay' for company and community, and much that can't be put into words, but I SEE.

And I see that all this also kept me in my marriage – the pattern continues. And so, no breakfast for me, I am struggling not to weep or be sick, the vision is churning me up and stabbing at me, and I drive out as I so often do to the end of the track into the desert. Dead End, it says, when you get there. Yes. I sit and weep for a long time because now I know I have to let the whole property go somehow. How I can't imagine, there are still such debts and its said to be worthless – leases with such high rent they do not command a premium on transfer. I don't know, I never understood it all.

19 November

Yesterday I went hiking up the mountain with new friend Yvonne, a beautiful black girl. We reached about 10000ft. We stood still for a while and I felt we were two trees in the forest. I told her about the number fours that 'follow' me. She said, 'Ask Bill about the number four, it's about preparing the angels'. Of course I was, I'm ashamed to say, pleased by this. I also talked about the centre and found myself swept up by her being so impressed. Oh dear. Swiftly followed that night by a horribly vivid nightmare of Miro walking belligerently into Joan's family room. I see once I have calmed down that I was so easily tempted back into it all. Oh pride.

22 November

I had breakfast today with Lucille. She talked for two hours... 'and that's just the tip of the iceberg' she said, finally. I tried to speak but she seemed not to listen. But she said, as a part of her story, but very strongly and pointing at me and looking me in the eyes, **'Get out. Get out now. While you still have a skin'**. And I shivered. I knew it was a message coming through her for me. I will do it. I will get out.

Sun is pouring in as I write. It always helps me.

23 November

At Anrahyah's Synergy group, I said, 'I wont be very popular when I return'. She looked at me penetratingly and said, 'popularity isn't the most important thing any more – you don't need it any more'. If that is true it is a major step forward. In the visualisation I saw swans swimming amongst lotuses with golden centres, jewels in a lake, gold coins spilled beside it, and I felt such peace. I was swept along a gold tunnel into white light with a white draped altar streaming white light, and a golden chalice stood on the altar. Then seeing the whole planet streaming with rivers of gold light and feeling the Christing of consciousness. Then a church with a Christmas tree and a rose window. 'Grail consciousness' said Bill.

It was another gift to help me.

24 November

I go home in two days. Today I went to Naomi's new home. Naomi is a shaman. She sees things.

Her new home is out near the end of the road where I have been drawn so often to feel the remoteness and see the stars. 'Dead End'.

I told Naomi this. I saw her face and I knew what she was going to say. She said, 'I don't know if I should tell you this'.

216

It is hard to write this because it felt so personal. Last year a man murdered his wife there and then killed himself. At that place where I was so drawn, time and time again. I would drive there automatically.

Naomi has her own tragic story, a lot of which parallels mine, and she is going to be living there working with that energy.

'You have big work to do' she told me. I shivered. We agreed to support each other. I had yet again been thinking of keeping on Queen St, and yet again I was reminded in a very clear way to cut all ties.

I saw what may be my karma, or at the very least the result of one path I could take – the continuing path, and I shivered in horror. But then I saw we have a choice, and I can break though it, change direction. I will see Caroline Ives when I get home and I will do the 'Cutting the Ties that Bind' work, and I will cut loose one way or another from the whole of Queen St, and I will meditate on breaking through the 'membrane' that connects me to it and to my marriage, it is flesh-coloured, rubbery, tough, but I will pierce it and it will fall to shreds and disappear and I will be through.

And then I went to have my hair cut and Kevin said, entirely unprompted, 'we do not need to be consumed by karma. It can be dissolved in a flash'. I said 'I needed to hear that'. And he gave me a book about the number 44 to take home.

I am pretty much broke now, but in my post forwarded by Dawn is a new credit card offer, so I take it up and with luck it will be waiting when I get back. Joan wonderfully asks if I need to borrow some cash. 'I know you'll pay me back dear' she says. (I did) Bless her. More gifts.
.
Then Gabrielle gave me a healing session. I was holding her two power staffs, one in each hand, they are for Releasing Patterns. I held them high, and wide, and then I shook them strongly outwards, several times, and as I did Gabrielle made this incredible noise. After that I just shook and shook uncontrollably for a long time, holding this feather, 18 inches long, turquoise and gold.

Now it is my last Crestone sunset. The mountains are pink and the western sky is fiery. The weather forecast says that the temperature will drop next week. The sun has stayed out for me and kept his heat for me until now.

A very bright moon comes up over the snowy peaks later to bid me goodbye. I have grown accustomed to them, to the scale of it all, the simplicity, their bulk and glow in the darkness, their pink and purple in the magic hours.

26 November

I have just watched my last Crestone sunrise from beginning to end, about one and a half hours I think, wrapped in a blanket, outside. This is of course whole sky sunrise.

217

SIGNS

Signs come from Spirit, from the Divine or from the divine part of us - some higher more Knowing part of us - our soul or Higher Self.

They come in a million ways, and once we get used to them some little or big jerk at the insides of us will tell us 'yes, that's a sign'.

Things people say, things overheard, things on the radio when you switch it on, visions, dreams, strong feelings, premonitions, thoughts welling from silence, events themselves, themes of movies, bits of novels, weather, animals, divination cards, horoscopes(!), numbers and symbols...the list is endless.

They guide us and help us.
We just have to tune in, to the frequency...
The frequency is love

They say in Crestone that here you watch sunrise in the west and sunset in the east. Reminds me of the Buddhist saying: 'though the sun rises in the west the Buddha sits'. Maybe if Greg Braden's Zero Point Theory comes about and the earth starts spinning the other way this might happen??!!

First wisps of pale pink and violet flare out into orange fire over Mt Blanca, the whole bulk of the sacred mountain silhouetted against it, gold, yellow, apricot, brighter and brighter, then pink-gold clouds raying out to touch the ranged peaks, shaped at first like a prone body, arms outstretched over its head. Arms are growing into wings, glowing, a vast angel appears before me, and the whole sky and the snowy peaks are alight with a pale violet and pink. The mountains to the north take up the refrain and are rosy, ethereal, surreal, angelic, against a sky of white fire, and a celestial vision is all around me.

Crestone is bidding me goodbye in style and I am moved beyond measure. I give formal thanks, bowing deeply to each of the four directions as the glow fades, and go in, in gratitude for yet more signs that I am on course.

I am going home to wind up the past. God help me.

Soon Will Porter (who does airport runs) comes to fetch me and we drive away, I'm in tears, he's trying not to notice that.

The Journey Home

Except there's no real home to go to.

I will miss this. Ochres, khakis and putty of the harsh land. The road ruler straight to the far horizon. The meditative driving across vast spaces. The cloaked mountains always on the horizon, their faces lighting up in sun, the shadows of weather moving across the plain.

27 November   Will's parents' ranch in Golden, Denver.

I can scarcely take in that I've left the vast spaces behind. Here I am with wide highways, skyscrapers on the horizon swathed in pollution haze, newspapers and news, lawns, traffic roar.

I'm sitting watching Will's father mend a fence the horses dismantled. I was feeding them apples and as I walked away they walked one on each side of me, very close up, I could feel the strength and warmth of them. I put my hands up over their shoulders, walking with them kind of tucked under my arms. What a feeling. I am timid but courageous. I am being given some horsepower!!

One of the horses turns his head and nuzzles me. I have a sudden vision of what it would be like to work with the land, of how fit and strong I could get. Who knows?

On the drive up, I said to Will, unpremeditated and very clear. **'Those properties are a millstone he hung around my neck to keep me tied to him, to keep me in prison'.** As I left Crestone I accidentally broke the chain of a necklace worn the whole journey; I dropped it in the bin, saying 'I hereby break all chains holding me back and I step free'.

At least I know what I have to do now – HOW is another matter.

Thanksgiving with Will's family – such a gift. They didn't want me to be in a hotel alone. So many people round the big table. Lots of shrimp, a huge turkey, and such warmth. Oh, warmth. Will and I talked into the night. Great conversation. He read bits of books to me, and when I said 'yes, that's right' and 'ah that's lovely' he said 'you actually know all this don't you?' I rather fancied him but he made it clear that that was not right, but that that was because he was not right for me, he did not feel worthy.

So Will gave me something else too. He made me see me through his eyes, my quality, stature, warmth… my power. It is something else to take home to give me strength as I go into battle!

28 November   A dorm in a Denver hostel

I decide to save $50 by staying in a hostel. Reminds me of Fiji but this time I am unafraid, interested, even though it turns out to be a dark hole squatting in a seedy street; the dorm has no light, colourless too - short rotting curtains, dusty piled up bunks. The carpet is stained ragged and brown. I feel the feelings of living beings trapped in this, cut off from beauty and light. The heating roars all night, or something does. 6 metal bunks in a room 4 m x5m. Someone has put a wet sweater to dry on the only empty bunk and I have to cover the wet sheet with the thick blanket and wrap myself in my own fleece blanket. Amazingly I sleep. One girl is dark, bent and scarred. One is tiny, oriental and sad. They have no home but here. I can't believe it. They are surprisingly tolerant of my presence: I must seem a strange visitor. 'There's coffee on' they say, and they tell me their dreams as we drink it. The sink is spotless. I try to find the right words and must have done because the girl called Joan touches my arm, and says thankyou.

On my way now, heading home. But… the plane suddenly, sickeningly, shockingly, dives right down and the snowy wastes of the Rockies rear unbelievably close. We level off just clear of the peaks and the pilot tells us we are returning to Denver.

I thought in that few seconds, do I want to die and be spared what is coming? No. No, I'll see it through. Oh but if I do have to die, I'll see my Dan!!

But when we do finally leave for LA (the fast descent was due to a dog having been discovered in the way sub zero hold!) I am, with no warning, foully and thoroughly sick. Just like that. No time even to get to the loo, or get out a bag. I am never airsick, and I have never been so shocked and horror struck. But I cope somehow and survive and thank God no-one was in the seat right alongside though the man in the aisle seat is averting his gaze and engrossing himself in his book.

I know I simply cant 'stomach' what is coming…even though I am choosing it.

30 November

At LAX I sit stone still through the long wait, and I sleep the entire long flight to London, without moving, under my red fleece. Numb. I have no interest, energy, appetite, or emotion. And at London when Ben wasn't there – flight was early- I just wait, sitting on my cases with a blank face, mind, and heart.

But then, **there he is, my beloved Ben**, after 4 months, and his tall thin body is hugging me and then we are on the coach and there is England, ethereal watercolour, glimmering mist, vibrant green. I kept thinking I had some special sunglasses on and went to take them off but no this is the colour of England.

HOME

Old Meadow to Higher Seas?

I am not at Old Meadow with Caroline a day before Glenn calls me. 'How would you like to come and live in Somerset?' I recall my envy when I read of their move to Higher Sea House and I say 'I may very well like that….' And at 11.11pm on 11th December we drive into Ilminster and to what might be my new home. I leave my shampoo in the shower by accident, but am glad I have marked my new territory. The knowledge of Higher Sea House makes all the difference to the coming weeks.

Early December: Meeting of all those involved in the Convergence Centre

40 people are crowded into the Rose Room attic. There is silence as I walk in. Everyone is waiting to hear what I have to say. I sense curiosity and hostility and support….. It has taken some time as I have had to get a car sorted out …. on top of everything else and severe jet lag I came back of course to no car. But now I am here again in this peaceful sanctuary.

I said, looking around at all the dear faces, something like this.

'I walked into the centre today and I felt such pride and joy in it. I began it 4 years ago, with no money, no ability to borrow, and scarcely enough income to live on. Just a vision. I remember well the first fire Pamela and I lit in what became Richard's room, and how we wrote 'The Convergence Centre' in big red letters on a whiteboard. It grew with the help of my friends Pamela and Lu and of all of you. I have loved it so much.

BUT I have always had to subsidise it with money, work, time and energy, and increasingly I have felt this was not right, and that Exeter didn't really want it. I was tired by the time Sarah came along earlier this year, and was glad of her fresh energy. But she was soon disheartened too and amazed at how long I had struggled.

The chance that Crestone, and Dawn, gave me to disengage and recharge seemed heaven-sent. The months of my absence would show which way the Centre itself wanted to go – whether to fly as a fully fledged bird without my being 'mother', whether to shrink to a manageable size, or to shrivel and die. It is now clear to me that my vision is not shared, and that I cannot sustain it alone.

So like Lucy Grant and Yon and Michael before me earlier this year, I have decided to close the Centre on 31st December, 4 years to the day.

Quality serviced Centres are simply not viable in this city at the moment. I am attempting to sell the leases of the properties to the purchasers of the restaurant, and will arrange for any of you interested in renting from them to be able to do so.

My ex-husband left me these properties to manage when he became unable to do so himself due to his failing mental health. I realise now they were the ball and chain he left for me….. He left several apparently insurmountable crises, which I resolved, working with the Fire Authority, the Head Landlord (The Church of England), and the main tenant (the Rank Organisation!!), the Inland Revenue and the Banks. He also left a great deal of debt, but I have succeeded in paying off half of it – 'my' half so to speak. I have completed the rent arrears payments to the Head Landlord, and only bank debt remains. I am proud of what I have done, the responsibility I have carried and the Centre created in what I have called 'Phoenix' House.

Since my son died last year my ex-husband has become much more severely mentally ill and I return to the news that he is becoming a serious danger. The police have advised me not to be in the buildings. His family have written to me from Yugoslavia to tell me he is making severe threats of violence against me, our son, and the properties, and they advise me to take their letter to the police. But the police and the mental health authorities are unable to do anything at all due to the way the law stands now. Hard to believe but true. This only affirms my decision.

So I have come, with the aid of many signs, to a point of Surrender. I do this in faith. I will always remember Gervaise Hallen (one of the therapists) saying to me 'I never cease to be amazed at the power of faith and surrender'.

I am moving to Somerset in the New Year, and because this was arranged the minute I got back and before I became aware of the full challenge of the situation I know I am not 'running from' but rather 'moving to' out of my own choice. I have been looked after yet again.

I still have faith that everything that is happening is for the highest good of all. But that doesn't help with the fact that this is all very very painful and I am going to miss you all and this place very very much.'

It was very quiet. I know I wasn't understood by many, but I felt I had expressed myself and the situation to the best of my ability.

Mid- December

A few days later, I saw my ex-husband in town and I was so angry at that moment, at something else 'coincidentally', that I spontaneously poured it out at him and felt it protect me. I felt safe within it, and I saw why so many people feel vulnerable without it. It was interesting for me, I've never really *used* anger before in a personal situation – though I've used 'righteous anger' purposefully to useful effect once or twice in business. It's fear of anger, in others and of the possible effects of my own, that I've had to deal with. He backed off as I shouted at him.

I am still afraid of him, but it is interesting that **I have not been the one to suffer his madness this time. He is acting out other people's demons**. What a role he plays. I also notice that the fear itself is much much worse than the actuality, and that reduces the fear!

222

I said to a therapist at the Centre 'How much of my fear is projection and how much is keeping me safe?' Like most therapists he didn't answer (!!!) but I have a feeling that I've dealt with a fair bit of the projection and now I'm just keeping safe. Sometimes I have a glimpse of what is happening, amid all my fears and pain.

*I wondered later, **'Is he playing a role to help us all move on?'*** Getting me out of Queen St and Exeter, away from him at last, Ben out of his rut here in Exeter, and I was to discover, my mum was affected too. We were all 3 stuck. One day maybe I will be able to thank him.

Its rather like Daniel's death catalysed so much last year. One day we'll all be in another dimension together and will look back at it all.

But right now I am still in the Dark, and indeed it is the Dark of the Year.

On Winter Solstice 2007, after reading Osho's 'Book of Secrets' on the subject of Darkness:

Entering the Dark. The Dark of the Year, the Deep time, the Turning Point.... ...at Winter Solstice the sun is farthest from us, at its lowest point in the southern sky, casting long shadows across the palely lit land, a land drained of colour. The days are short and dark and cold and we turn within into our own dark, our own unknown. Shapes and structures emerge, become clear, the rampant and vivid flesh of summer's growth vanished into the hard cold earth to nourish the seeds of next year....

The Dark of the long winter night and the harshness and spacious clarity of the winter day, give us the tools to prepare for the next year. This is the time to go deep deep within, to see what we find there in our inner space and inner darkness. We need to be brutal but compassionate, loving but not sparing, honest but accepting. This is authenticity. It will nurture the seeds of next year and bring rewards beyond our dreams.

The oceanic, undefined, boundary-less, infinite, POSITIVE, feminine, DARK is the womb of life and light. Light always has a source, contained in the great Dark. Darkness is unlimited. Only the Essenes, the School Jesus was taught by, see God as Darkness. We need to enter the Dark before we can carry the flame and the light. We are as a culture deeply afraid of the dark, of the undefined, the unknown, of losing our sense of self, of facing our demons.

We need at this time of the Year to walk unafraid into the pitch dark, and sit with it in love and trust. Open our eyes to the dark and stare into it, let it touch us, let it enter our eyes, let it ease and soothe and relax us. Take time. Nothing is required of us by it, no action or thought is necessary. Just to sit in the dark, undisturbed, in stillness and silence, let go, and be aware. Dissolve into it.

To be with the dark can dissolve all human torments and fears. Surely they can come strongly to us at first, but if we persevere, witness them consciously from our souls and soon they will slide away..... and in their place comes, calmly and lovingly, bliss.....

Interestingly the Japanese successfully treat mental illness this way: they leave patients alone, in the dark. Many Native American vision quests and Buddhist meditations involve this practice too.

So for Winter Solstice meditations, find or arrange, pitch darkness....not so easy in this light polluted world....alone is essential at some point, but groupwork of this kind has its own power. When we have come to love the Dark we are strong within, to walk our path in the light with pride and humility, and love and gratitude.....

Out of Queen Street: end of an era

Full moon last night, bright skies, sun today. In Okehampton with Ben, having coffee, before he comes with me to help with the move, from both Old Meadow and Queen St to Higher Sea House. Caroline is unhappy I am going but I know it's best because she was anxious about Miro's behaviour.

I think:

224

I've made my choice, I've acted. I'll continue to take the steps... I am choosing freedom. I'll know and accept whatever happens next as being for my Highest Good. If all proceeds as I choose and I can sell the head leases my gratitude will know no bounds. If it doesn't so be it and I trust one day I will look back and feel equally unbounded gratitude for the outcome!!! ....when I know why. AND I wont act out of fear... if I do want to visit the centre I will. I will follow my intuition and trust.

A new journal has been given me for my new life by Marcus called 'The Leap' by Jane Evershed from Minneapolis. It has wonderful annotations and illustrations.

I recall the last lines of an Anita Brookner novel:

'And I walked out into the bright dark dangerous and infinitely beautiful street'

And Ben and I paid for our coffee and set off.

Sun shone.   Queen Street was deep in Christmas stupor and the streets were empty. Ben and the same man and van (third time lucky) moved everything of mine out of the Centre and up to Somerset to Higher Sea House. After 13 years of this particular challenge, I am trying to let go. No disturbance – I imagined angels all around, large glowing male angels, some dressed as policemen perched on the van....

Ben and I drove up in my new little red car, (paid for wonderfully by my mother, who is just so relieved I am back at last) stopping to have full breakfast at the Little Chef: I am out of there.

Higher Sea House is my new sanctuary. Glenn says to mum, 'We are so glad to have her here'. It is so so beautiful, this L-shaped pink thatched farmhouse in a hamlet called Sea, which, fabulously in my present situation, isn't even on the map.

It's a frosty morning and I sit drinking cappuccino and eating teacake in a sunny café in Chard. My new home sits beautifully amid the fields and sky waiting for my return. The veggie plots lie under their mulch, the greenhouse shelves sit waiting for pots of seedlings. Perhaps there will be a cat one day, to sit on my lap. And chickens too. I want to GET STRONG PHYSICALLY. I want physical work, simple work, use my body not my head, earn enough to live.

It's a new place again, fears and panics threaten too. I remember River Meadows, how afraid I was I wouldn't be able to support myself. It's just the same, but this time I know I was OK then I was looked after and it will be the same again. And just like then I'm in such a beautiful place.

A good place to be at Sea with no compass but the inner one.

But I haven't even begun to feel the losses yet.

New Year

A full year has passed now since the beginning of this year lived as if I only had a year to live.

Not the ending to 'The Year' I had envisaged, I think ruefully, as I sit in my void and wait.

Ben and I spend it together at Mum's, and he teaches me to play poker. It is a fascinating exercise for someone as transparent as me.

On New Years' day I experience a sudden release from the fear of 'Miro at the window'. It may return but it went for a while.

And on New Moon, I worked with Caroline Ives to 'Cut the Ties That Bind' me to Miro. This is a powerful practice when done well. We took hours to do it and were both exhausted, and the imagery that came to me, and which I described out loud with my eyes closed was incredibly strong.

At the end I said, following Caroline's words, shaking as I did so.

'I bless you and release you. You are free. I no longer collude in your torment. I am free.

I set us both free, blessing the past, in gratitude for the learning and the experience'

My journal (that one with little sayings at the top) says today 'the shadow below now a memory...'

I said to Glenn and Nancy, 'I seem to have been in mid-leap for so long. Certainly a year, probably two - since I sold my flat. How much longer must I be in this unsupported place'

'Well' Glenn said slowly, 'If you've been in midair that long, I think you must be flying, Sandra'

17 February   Saved by a Dream

The rollercoaster of the last 2 months has been a jigsaw as usual, a challenging symphony. I daily wrestled with my age-old fear of bankruptcy, and I was condemned and battered on many fronts. But the proposed sale to John Mitchell, who was buying the restaurant underlease from the existing owners, enabled my initial 'exit' from the centre, and gave me time and hope over Christmas. Miro's harassment in fact helped as it quickly and effectively emptied the Centre!!! And as I could not safely be there that too helped my exit. His actions actually *served* my decision to close the Centre.

Interesting how things work.

The lack of a definite refusal by John meant that I could honestly keep the idea of the sale going for the banks. I really thought I would sell, and cover the debts, I had such faith.

But then I had a dream, a very powerful one, in which I was told clearly that they would buy the Restaurant, but they would NOT buy the head lease from me..

CUTTING THE TIES THAT BIND

This exercise by Phyllis Krystal removes the energy of unhealthy relationships from your auric field. Visualize an infinity sign with white inner circles and the outer circles violet – violet is transformation and white is new beginning. Imagine you are standing in one side of the figure eight and the person you want to let go of is standing in the other side. Then imagine you are having a conversation and you are telling this person how much he or she has helped you in your life, how much you appreciate the experience. See the cords that connect you to the person, ask for the cords that need to be cut to light up. Feel the feelings that come up.

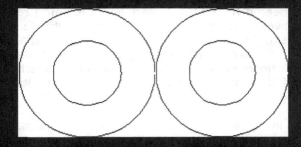

Then using whatever comes to you- sword, golden scissors, knife, cut the energy cords you have built between you. See the cord fall away, see the ends absorbed by yours and the other persons being, making sure that the cords are healed and sealed. When you have finished thank the person and then cut the circles in half allowing each half to become a complete circle. Say good-bye and see them in their circle floating into the distance. Do this daily until you feel they have been released .

In the nick of time I held back the considerable advance rent about to go out and withdrew the cash, to support me for a while, as otherwise I had only credit. This was a worrying thing to do but the fact that the dream was given me just before the payment was due to go out told me it was right to do this.

Soon after I heard that they were indeed not going to buy. I said my prayers of gratitude for the dream many times. Then at the twelfth hour I heard that the office tenant – the only other user of the upper floors, was interested in buying and so the hope went on....

Letting go Responsibility

I was called angrily by this tenant often during that time– they, almost the only remaining people there now, are being harassed and abused and frightened, they have resorted to working behind locked doors. Miro keeps turning up waving a copy of the Lease and a tape measure, saying the buildings are his and he is in charge, then ranting and threatening at anyone in the way. I have worked so hard with the Mental Health Authorities and the Police, and my lawyers, but all agree a Court Injunction would be useless. He has ignored them before, and I have had to deal with him myself.

After much thought I am writing formally to all the Authorities to put on record the events of the past months and their admitted ridiculous powerlessness to help, and to report my Intention to now 'sign off' from what I have seen as my responsibility for his behaviour. We have been divorced for 7 years and it is time I recognised he is NOT my responsibility. I received a letter from the Mental Health Team, acknowledging the situation and apologising for the fact that the law did not at the moment allow them to do anything at all. It seems unbelievable, and reminds me of when there were squatters in the lower floors of no 45 and the Police and I watched through the window as they lit a fire and the policemen said, 'sorry love, know its crazy, but as the law stands cant do a thing'.

Helplessness. Always in my life, helpless in the face of blatant madness.

I am under attack from centre practitioners too. I wrote back in anger to a man who had been a dear colleague and friend for 3 years: 'I cant believe that knowing me as you do, you can't see that I would never walk out on responsibilities, that I am under such huge pressure and I need support, and that I am literally afraid for my life. One day I'll have the strength to say 'Fuck off' when it is needed.' I am finding out who my friends are. I am so afraid, but still know I am doing the right thing. When I made my decision in Crestone, I knew it would be hard: 'Mother' has withdrawn support and is asking for it instead.....'

I am surviving all this unpopularity and attack. I had some face- to-face confrontations earlier this year to give me some practice. My practice of watching myself is fundamental to my survival, as is that of living in the moment as far as I can. My central fear is of not being able to hold my own boundaries, that I will give too much. My fear is of my over-fast and empathetic responses – my response-ability, my openness. I need clear boundaries to my response-ability: I need to learn not take on guilt or responsibility that is not mine. I need to trust myself to respond to the presence of anger and hatred from a calm undisturbed place.

But in the midst of all the battles I ALSO have this sense of casting off my chains. Freedom, but not a shred of security anywhere. I am just 'staying with' Glenn and Nancy at the moment, I am not a legal tenant yet. I have no money, job, resources, so I would not be acceptable. I am being stripped.

I have cut my hair short.

I visit Glastonbury. To everyone's disbelief in the States I had never been there. The last few weeks in Crestone I was reading the book 'The Mists of Avalon' that Glenn and Nancy gave me for my journey and it helped to draw me back to soft and mystical England..

So this is my first visit to this sacred place, a sense it would be in my life now much more - it is only 45 minutes away. It was, as it should be, wreathed in mists: the Mists of Avalon are before me. We stood on the Tor and we could see nothing at all. Surreal. An island in a sea of fog. I said a prayer that my journey be less fierce now.

Not to be. The fires are just beginning.

My birthday tea, April 18, 1999. Ben holding baby John

Chapter 2.   Into The Fire

1-8 March   Hospital

Drips, needles, curtained beds, rattling trolleys. Back amongst it all after so long. Memories of my hysterectomy in 1984.

In excruciating abdominal pain, as I put my bag together to come here on strict instructions from the doctor, the phone rang, and I heard that my tenant will NOT buy the lease.

So I sit here on a hospital bed, waiting, doubled up with pain, knowing that bankruptcy is now my only option.

All afternoon I wait. They won't give me painkillers until they know what's what. I am just left there clutching my stomach.

But funnily enough if I had heard the news without all this pain, it would have been even worse. It kind of puts it in perspective. I write 'I am going to trust. I will get well'.

Suddenly I remember that I am going to be walking to Culbone Church on Sunday: and I somehow KNOW I am going to be going. So, it can't be appendix, if it was I'd have to have an operation and be unable to go. I really do wonder at my thought processes- being so sure of that(!), when the universe is making me declare bankruptcy as soon as I get out of here. It was almost like a choice.

But I am still battling with 'what if????'s.

Suspected appendix is in fact only a urine infection. (Pain on letting go of unwanted waste material - as usual the physical reflects the metaphysical!!!)The doctor should have known, but as I said this period in hospital is saving me in a strange way from the shock of inevitable and immediate bankruptcy. But I am exhausted too.

Later:
I have been removed into a side ward because, they say awkwardly, they have to do this in case its hepatitis A. Shame, self pity rise up my gut. The nurse found it hard to explain to me, she looked at me with pity and discomfort. I have more scans and horrible tests and there is a shadow they don't like, it could be bowel cancer. I look at the doctor with disbelief.

I am feeling suddenly at the end of the road of suffering. Cant do it any more. Had enough. Despair. I find myself asking myself ' Do you want to take this opportunity to leave the planet' – the same question I asked as the plane to LA seemed to tumble.

This time I don't really know how to answer.

I am beginning to drown in my shame and my losses. An insane and vengeful ex-husband, a so beloved first born son who committed suicide, a father who could not stand up for me, and left me with a mother who's in many ways about 5 years old and wants to be queen, a chronic inability to make a proper living, and now, this. Hospital, tests. Total insecurity. Loss of the Centre. No income. Bankruptcy. Unloved. Never cared for. Endless cruelty. Life has been too cruel to me.

I am crying for my total abandonment here in a place of so much suffering. I feel forgotten, drowning in a lifelong disbelief and disappointment that I - and my pain - am unnoticed, unsupported. A wall of numbness I didn't know was there has crumbled. Help me, God, the River of Life has dried up again and I really cant see how it can flow again….

When I start to look at the negatives and the pain, my life is appalling. And no-one has come along to love me and be loved by me. No one is there to care for me. I want that to happen before I die. To know real, tender, caring, love between a man and a woman.

Contentment and gentle warmth. Oh, warmth. Never for me.

After a childhood so 'nice' I was unable to ask to go the toilet I have certainly immersed myself in 'not niceness'. I ran away to the wilds of Yugoslavia to explore a world of pain, colour, touch, fear, torture and torment, loving and weeping.

Whatever I thought I was doing all these years I have totally failed.

Failed all round, for everyone, for me. I failed to help Miro, Dan, Mum. I fear I fail to help Ben.

Note squashed into the margin here – 'here I go taking responsibility again for other people's choices. I didn't fail them, they failed themselves. God that is hard to say. It sounds so cruel. I am so afraid to be cruel. I guess I need to learn to be cruel to be kind. I have pandered to them.'

I have never dared be cruel, not since I was a young wife and I once roared at them all. I felt I used to make mum ill. Miro got ill. Dan got ill. But they made their own choices, all along. Oh its been so safe being alone. I am so afraid of my own cruelty. I remember a restaurant customer saying 'you don't need knives here do you, you've got your tongue, Sandra'. I remember mum saying Aunty Phyl had an acid tongue. I loved my Aunty Phyl.

Here nine pages of my journal are filled with roarings. Huge capitals. I sat up in the hospital bed in my little room and I screamed and roared silently all day.

'I IDONT DESERVE THIS FUCK YOU ALL FUCK YOU ALL I ROAR AT THE WORLD AND AT GOD AND MY ROARS CIRCLE THE PLANET AND BLAST THE ATMOSPHERE NOTICE ME DAMN YOU ALL I AM A BEAUTIFUL SOUL AND I AM INNOCENT AND I DO NOT DESERVE THIS DO YOU HEAR.'

'I STAND ON THE MOUNTAINTOP AND I ROAR MY PAIN
I HAVE HAD ENOUGH DO YOU HEAR'

I have drawn myself on the mountaintop, and on the top of the planet, with huge red zigzags of rage bellowing out from my huge open mouth, and I hold unsheathed swords in my hands.

They come in to tell me that there are new strange 'things' in my bowel on the latest scan and I see they are concerned, and I must have more tests.

I write: 'Dark dark pain fills my eyes chokes my throat and my heart. My belly is like lead and knives, heavy sharp hot. Yet numb all over between the knives. Numbed dead finished.'

'A the end of the Year there is only disaster. At the end of the Leap there is only despair. Unwanted. Abandoned by my God.

What is the point?

There is only loneliness. Forgottenness. Hopelessness. Helplessness. Am I come to destitution? I have £30. I understand my son's despair and his action.

It's not what I expected. I trusted so. I cant start all over again.'

And the rage grows **AND GROWS and I lay here Pouring out rage**

RAGE

and I am on top of a mountain again with vast vistas and the earth is shaking , and great winds howl, and thunder crashes and lightning splits the trees, and my screams pierce the clouds, and waves drown the earth, and the seas rise and I am bellowing at my God

NO MORE I DO NOT DESERVE THIS. DO YOU HEAR ME??????

Afterwards, calming a little, I notice that the journal annotation for the day is 'the atom has been split, the challenge is to put the planet back together'. And on another day filled with my roars, 'like the clouded leopard who does not roar, and hunts by night to survive'.

And for the page I am just starting: *'High Drama on Planet Earth....though I walk seemingly alone, Bouncing back from Brutalities, Reeling from wars and destruction.......my stride is lengthened, my soul is strengthened to know that your goal also is that sunlit glade of sanity where visions of clarity and healing abound'*

Waves of new energy shake me

'I Blast out of my body and energy field all poisons and 'things' unwanted, all held griefs and angers and agonies and resentfulnesses. And I Blast that MAN OUT OF MY SYSTEM I THROW HIM AS FAR AS I CAN OUT OF SIGHT GONE OVER THE FAR HORIZON. I ROAR MY BIGGEST ROAR AS I THROW HIM. Hundreds of angels male and female lend their strength and he is GONE. I am flying in fury all around my planet be gone be gone from my world flying to all corners, pushing the winds and the waters ......'

I have just had to compose my face and body - the doctor (very dishy I notice even in this state), just came in to say 'you'll be relieved to hear that there is no hepatitis A, and the bowel test has been fixed up for this afternoon'. I said 'Whatever it says, can I go home tomorrow morning and come in as an outpatient for any other tests' very firmly. 'Yes' he says. I nod. He smiles at me, touches my arm.

I look at the annotations on the journal again, my BE GONE's all over it: 'Contamination of dreams, volcanic eruption or total nuclear destruction/ give me candlelight at night, music, and a garden to grow.'

I begin to write pages of hundreds of wavy **CLEAN, I AM CLEAN, SQUEAKY CLEAN**

'Step by step by step, I reach out and in and all around for freedom from guilt and shame .

I SING MY INNOCENCE FROM THE MOUNTAINTOPS.

Journal annotation reads…. 'women change the world….in so doing we hold the key to universal peace'

Looking back, that private room was a gift, as was the shame, the humiliation, the fear, the everything. It was not clear to me for quite a while. In my time of trial then and later I was given opportunities for release and sustenance. I know now that I had to go through all these losses and shames. I recall Paulo Coelho's 'Fifth Mountain', the story of Elijah:

'life is made of our attitudes, but there are certain things the gods oblige us to live through'.

March 9   Culbone

I emerge from hospital naked, stripped to the bone, and the next day a large group of us walk to the very special Culbone church on Exmoor.

How strange that this place is where I am brought today, and it *was all arranged so long ago*.

I sit on the healing seat, and they all chant over me.

I pray. God help me stop doing everything the hard way.

Nanny takes a picture and when I see it later I gasp, I look about 75, I am not the vibrant woman in the pictures taken in Crestone. I am empty, exhausted, finished, at the end.

March 10   Exeter Bankruptcy Court

Out of hospital, into here. I take the necessary steps, numbly but effectively, and I continue to rail at God.

Great kindness here from everyone. Judge White(!) took about 3 minutes to grant the petition. Sent to me a Receiver Mrs White(!!!), who was so kind I was almost in tears. She came with me to the Centre and told me to sit down, while she did her thing, and she said 'take the plants, and anything else you need'.

The Head landlord on the phone, spontaneously remarking with energy 'Best thing for you Sandra'. Bank managers wishing me well, despite their losing money.

Going through forms with another Receiver, Mr Thresher(!) I commented ruefully on my inability to make money and said how ironic it would be if I did now. He said 'This will be the making of you'. He was strangely respectful. What an amazing thing to say!

I write: '*there is a strange power in all of this. In failure. In being in the abyss in awareness.'*

I am aware, from a distance, of healing happening. Mum said apologetically, 'I've only been half a mum'. I said 'well you're being a whole mum now, mum'. She's given me

CULBONE CHURCH

Culbone derives its name from a Welsh saint, St. Beuno, or Kil Beun, who was a healer, and his church sits on an ancient Celtic religious site. It is at most 35' long "the smallest complete parish church in this country." It is mentioned in the Guinness Book of Records and also the Domesday Book.

It began as a small monastery in 430, and there has been a church here since 635.

It has been over its long history a place of banishment or refuge, for lepers, offenders, refugees, charcoal burners, practitioners of magic, the insane, outcasts of all kinds over the years.

It has also been a very productive and harmonious community for long spells of time.

Over thousands of years this place has been offering a healing and a cleansing to victims of the darkest that life brings...

£1000 in cash so I don't have to work for a couple of months, and that after paying for a car for me! I feel so ashamed that she has to do these things for me.

Spring Equinox

Our Earth Mysteries group ceremony for the Equinox is gentle and lovely in the garden at Higher sea House, but I feel the heartrending fragility of spring this year, and I watch the unfurling world still numb and untouched by hope and without singing my praises to its creator.

But I do feel the warmth of the friends holding my hands in the circle..

28 March

It's a Sunday morning, the sun is shining through the french windows, the sky is clean and blue. Early frost has melted. I sit here quietly. I am absorbing silence, solitude, stillness, calm. Can't waste this moment worrying about hospital barium meal test results or what Mrs White will say about my paperwork.

Journal annotation 'peace moves like quiet Sunday morning sunshine'. I bet you don't believe all these stunningly appropriate sayings so eerily printed on the right page...??

I think perhaps I am waiting for the losses to hit me.

Glenn Nancy and Nick are in the States and that is giving me this time of space to sit with them.

31 March

I have space. Space is dangerous.

THIS is the divorce. THIS is the end. THIS is the death of my son. And the premature death of my father. THIS is the end of my resources. Now comes blackly the space for all the grieving. All the pain has rushed in to the dark spaces and I will have to endure it. Pain in my throat, behind my eyes, burns. I wail alone in the empty house.

Easter Sunday Morning

Sitting at Mum's kitchen table. Suddenly tears are running down my face as I look at her. She gets up, comes round and hugs me, stands there holding me while my body shakes and I sob and sob.

Later she brought me tea in the best cup and saucer 'thought you'd like the silver spoon'.

Is this for my rebirth? It doesn't touch the despair but it is there for when it can.

It will one day? Will it?

Cadgwith Cornwall. Vine Cottage is at the top,
centre right

Chapter 3   Cleaning Up

14 April   Discharged

I go to the hospital to see the doctor for my results. At long last. Uncertainty from the first week of March - do I have bowel cancer?? - though as time went on I guessed not, but couldn't be sure. I remember the doctor from hospital - the dishy one. 'It is nice' he remarks, 'to see you again'. Strange when I think how I must have appeared during that week.

'Complete discharge' he says, smiling. Huge gratitude surfaces through layers of griefs. And I had taken an angel card for the trip and it was gratitude! Is all the pent-up anger discharged now too?

The healing seat at Culbone comes suddenly to mind, a picture of the group – some 20 people- toning over me. Nanny said I would be healed there and then. That picture of

237

me was perhaps the first taken of me without even a hint of a smile, naked. My incurable optimism stripped away. I am real, unmasked, sad, old, disappointed. Abandoned by God, faithless. Can I step out from behind my smile? Will there be anyone there? Inside me, for me??

When I look now at that picture and at the ones taken of me as I left Crestone, I cannot believe it is the same woman, or one the same age.

So much I am and have done has its roots in loneliness, in not being chosen, or sought. All these years trying to find out why. *'Other people do so much wrong and receive so much from others' I cry silently to myself in confusion.* Hatred, envy, incomprehension. All this tangle of inferiority and superiority, excess humility, hidden pride, excess warmth, hidden cruelty. Its all ego stuff, all of it. A self perpetuating spiral of suffering. I give up now. This mess of motivation has to come to an end.

I am suddenly, energetically, *bored* with all the circles and tangles. And equally suddenly I remember Roshi saying 'One day you will get bored with suffering'. It only lasts a moment, this energy and this insight, but it was a strong shaft of light for that moment.

18 April My birthday

My birthday a year on from our fantastic party in Crestone. I am still quiet, subdued, living in an interior world, roaming in dark empty spaces, but holding tight to my friends and family. Ben is here, Glenn and Nancy and Nick just back from the States in time, Philippa, Jenny, Mike and Millie, Lucy, Andrew & Lisa with the new member of the 'family' born in the midst of all my trials: John Matthew. He was born on the anniversary of Dan's death and he means a lot to me. I had picked an angel card for him and it was Birth. They brought him into hospital to see me and I held him. It was just before the move to the private room and the anger. In the place of my worst pain I held a new baby who will always be connected to me, and I knew that he is a very special child.

Wake to bright clear sunshine, the first swallow of summer wheeling in soft air. Apple blossom on the trees. There are so many exquisite gifts and such warmth surrounds my chilled soul. I see it but cannot feel it. Andrew and Lisa's card is their own divination card for strength. Lucy arrives with cake and champagne and I Ching cards she had made.

Her cake has a musical candle which refuses to be blown out. It would not stop singing, and in the end we put it in the fridge and it sang away in there as we ate our lunch. The freezer stopped it, but every time we took it out it started singing again. But then when we wanted it to play for tea, it wouldn't. Looking back now, it was bit like my story. I finally stopped singing too.

But in the evening the New Moon and Venus are hanging brilliant in the electric sky. Just like New Year's Eve last year. I regard the sky from my dark night of the soul.

Somewhere in me I glimpse a fact. I am naked, powerless, giving nothing, quietly overwhelmed by helplessness and there are people loving me and supporting me in that place. I am not buying this. It is freely given.

238

I perceive for the first time in my life that those people are the most important thing in my life. Not the spring morning or the evening sky, not God's landscapes and beauty, but God's people. It is sad that it has taken me until I am 53 to know this.

I have just finished the Leap journal, where the girl on the cover strides across the abyss. I have finally let go of the need to arrive on the other side of the chasm. I am still there above – sometimes in - the abyss, suspended, but I sense, very very tentatively, that perhaps I *have* arrived somewhere after all.

19 August Cleaning up

'Spiritual advancements follow a fall'….
We have been listening to Wayne Dyer's tapes. Brilliant. I receive this information from place of sad humility and quiet. I can see it may well be true.

I am sitting on the shore by Chard reservoir watching ducks and reflections. Reminds me of River Meadows. I walked here cross-country, field by field.

This morning I paid my rent and bills with money I have earned from cleaning and clutterbusting, and I still have £100 on the building society account I prudently set up before the bankruptcy. I have more work 'clutterbusting' tomorrow, and I am cooking in the pub on Sunday and Monday, so another £100 to come. Such wealth. It truly feels like riches.

I am learning to live simply with cash. I earn it and allocate it, carefully. I luckily have the Halifax account, which has remained in place, but no cheque book of course. I had opened two new accounts before the crash, hoping at least one would remain usable. I had no credit of course. We live very cheaply, growing our veggies, cooking, sharing all the bills between 4 adults. (Carol has joined us there too). My rent is therefore only a quarter of £700!!!! It all worked so well, living in a fabulous house with minimal costs.

I laughed again one day. I have always laughed too much, but the last months not at all. Even Glenn couldn't really make me laugh, and he always does….a real gift to people. It feels strange when I feel it bubble up again, and it makes me smile.

Coming back to life. Someone said 'Its not love that will save the world, its laughter'.

And Glenn and Nancy have asked me to be ceremonialist at their wedding on St Michael's Hill. Rachel bought me a card about Stone, about the need at times to be like a stone and simply endure. I find this very helpful.

The neediness for recognition and admiration seems to have gone out of me. The humiliation, destitution, grief, anger, rejection, fear and pain of the last six months brought with them a growing discovery that friends and family were there for me just as I *was*. Unconditionally. My needs were met and could be spoken. I feel loved. Gosh, did I write that?

LAUGHTER

Who knows what it is, but what an invention.
What a fabulous mysterious funny thing.
Laughter is letting go.
Letting go control. Letting go seriousness and
seeing the delicious absurdity of it all. It's the
best antidote to gloom and heavy stuff. It cuts
through all the crap. If we can laugh at
ourselves, at how seriously we take ourselves.....it
can all change.
I remember lying in a circle heads to centre,
hands on bellies, and someone started laughing.
And soon the whole circle was roaring with
uncontrollable laughter at absolutely nothing.
Laughter coming from deep in the belly. Till it
hurts...
Fabulous.

There is a dawning realisation that, if I hadn't sold my flat, it would have gone in the bankruptcy. And that if I hadn't gone round the world that bit of capital from the sale would have gone too. And that if I hadn't been ill, the bankruptcy would have felt much worse, because when ill, health seems the ONLY important thing. Also the combination of illness with financial ruin finally got my anger out of me. (Whether it was all of it remains to be seen.) How things do fit in. What a jigsaw, what a symphony.

Simple work, I do now.   I call it M&M – 'Mature and Multitalented' -cleaning /organising/decorating but getting paid well for it this time, and appreciated. I am metaphorically 'cleaning up' my life I guess. My favourite customer is Jules. We have these wonderful conversations. She is a writer and Jungian psychotherapist. She is the author of a serious tome on the Goddess, and I cannot believe that she is in my life.

In 2005 on Midsummer Day in the garden here at Barley Hill, Lora and I started M&M Mark Two. She listened to my story of it, and said 'that should be a website' and promptly went in to register the domain name. And matureandmultitalented.com came into being, an e-directory showcasing the skills of the over 50s. We said:

'**Do you think it is time that the value of age and experience is recognised? We do. At matureandmultitalented.com we are** reinventing retirement, putting the wisdom **and expertise so often wasted, to work and enjoying it. If not now then when? Matureandmultitalented.com makes lifetimes of experience available to a world that needs them and totally supports its members in choosing as well as earning from the work they really want to do.'**

It didn't succeed, but we gave it our very best, learned so much, met so many people, and had a fabulous time. And I believe many people benefited from all our work on it.

Nearly getting the Chard Festival of Women in Music publicist job was a blessing, the long conversation with Angela the director gave me such confidence, but I knew I wasn't ready yet for stress. The house is great and we're enjoying Carol being with us. We all went to the beach one day; suddenly we were in this wholly other world of sun-oil, sandcastles, sea, ice-creams, children playing, it was so shockingly delicious, so alien to where I had been I stood staring, blinking in disbelief.

Wayne Dyer talks about the process of creating our own reality. About how showing off, fear, and resentment block the flow. Coming out of love and gratitude for what we have chosen to create puts us in the flow. Keeping the process private, between us and God, keeps the ego stuff out and the flow going. So, gently, slowly, privately, I begin to think of working towards a new life.

Am very much supported by our Higher Sea House Community, by the meals every day around the big farmhouse kitchen table. We cook in turns, sometimes together. I love being cooked for, cooking for, belonging…. We live on very little money too. It is a beautiful beautiful house, Nancy is brilliant at finding the very best! Glenn always makes me laugh, Nancy listens endlessly, and Carol brings her special brand of emotional honesty and wisdom. Yes I have to cope with all the losses, but I am given this wonderful house and community to do that in. Looked after again. It takes time for us to grieve fully, and I had perhaps been protected from the worst of my grief for Daniel until now, when I had no responsibilities, and time to enter it.

The 'fall' process lasted about nine months (!)–I call it my 'Terrible Time – the Queen would call it her Annus Horribilis. It is pretty blank really. No diary. I recovered and then I cleaned…. and cleaned…… It lasted from just before the journey home in November to the eclipse of the sun late that summer. I will never forget that….

We camped in a circle, perhaps 20 of us, close to the cliffs of East Prawle near Salcombe. My friend Jenny has family with a farm there.

We waited on the grass on the cliff edge in silence, watching the dark grow, the air chill, the hush fall as the shadow of the sun filled the sky. The cliffs as far as the eye could see lined with people huddled together in blankets, arms around each other as day turned to night. The enormity, the profundity, were truly awesome… . for a moment there was a glimpse of the shuttered sun through the massed dark clouds. It was dark for an age.

Then, from the WEST, the gold streak of 'sunrise'. My heart leapt. I remembered my thoughts that last morning in Crestone as we watched the light grow from the western horizon, encroaching steadily and slowly on the dark. A bird sang for the 'dawn' and suddenly the light was blazingly upon us, and the sun warmed us and brought all the cold still figures to life. Shadows were released, collective and individual, gone east with the shadow of the sun. A cleansing had passed over the land. We ran down to the beach and into the sea shouting and laughing.

For the first time, I felt I had emerged from the time of Endurance

4 September   Glenn and Nancy's Wedding

I am still not fully restored but I'm coming on.

I will never forget being celebrant at G&N's 'alternative' wedding. Millie (a wonderful artist) being my handmaiden and making me a great and beautiful garland to wear. I used the coach microphone – (could get a taste for microphones – a part of beginning to make myself heard I guess.)

I asked everyone (50 of us) to walk in silence up the hill - St Michael's Hill near Yeovil. The beauty, simplicity, sincerity of the vows - they used those from Neale Donald Walsch's 'Conversations with God'. The setting high on the hill in the sun, the glowing faces of Glenn and Nancy, and she was so beautiful that day with flowers in her hair. Ben was there and when it was over I could go to him for a hug and sit with him. Such a privilege and such a pleasure.

22 September   Confirmation

definitely playing the part of my ex-husband. Amazing how this happens. I have the chance to deal with the fears finally but safely: we have been working through it all all year really.

GLENN'S TUNA PIE

While they are still hot, mash about 4 large old potatoes (for 2), the fluffy sort if you can, mix in a little milk, a knob or two of butter, a tin of tuna (per 2 people), some grated cheddar, chopped parsley, salt and pepper, dry mustard. Put it all into a flameproof dish, top with more grated cheddar and sliced tomato too if you like, and put it into a hot oven until hot through...not too long. Then brown under a grill. Fast, filling, cheap, and gorgeous. You can add mushrooms, red peppers or sweetcorn ....

RABBIT STEW OR PIE

One day we ate a still warm undamaged road-kill rabbit. Glenn skinned it, gutted it, cleaned it up, I butchered it, and we made a stew. It felt a bit strange, we resisted at first, but it was delicious and we came to no harm. I don't recommend it though, it was a risk I guess.

Anyway, roll the rabbit pieces in seasoned flour, fry a chopped onion, then brown it all in oil and butter. Put it in a big stew pot or a pie dish, add chunks of bacon (or rashers), leeks and carrots, mixed fresh or dried herbs and a bay leaf, seasonings, and cover with stock. For a stew add chunks of potatoes, stir well, boil up, and simmer for an hour. For a pie, leave out the potatoes and after half an hour simmering, put the mixture in a pie dish and cover with shortcrust pastry (with a hole in the centre) and bake until the pastry is golden.

BEEF STEW WITH DUMPLINGS OR COBBLER

We ate so well, only having to cook a couple of times a week if that. We all loved these old fashioned warming dishes. I did put weight on though....!

Fry chopped onion till soft and a bit caramelised, remove, then roll cubed stewing beef in plenty of well seasoned flour, fry in batches to brown, in a flameproof a casserole dish. Put all of the onion and beef back, heat up again, stirring in a little more oil and then when its all hot a bit more flour, then add beef stock gradually, and bring up to the boil, stirring. It will thicken because of the flour. Add a bay leaf, some sprigs of parsley, thyme, rosemary, and some sliced carrots, whole potatoes, any other root veg you have, maybe leeks too, plus a glass of red wine or of brown ale or Guinness. Let it all simmer aromatically in a medium oven for nearly a couple of hours. Then make either herby egg-brushed scones to top it with for a cobbler and cook for another 15 minutes till they are risen and brown. Or make herby dumplings and add to the stew for about 20 mins – they will rise and go fluffy. A knife should come out clean. (Dumplings: twice as much SR flour as suet, plus herbs and salt and pepper, mix with water and shape into balls. Scones: four times as much flour as margarine or butter plus herbs and salt, mix with water till firm but soft, then roll out, brush with egg and cut into circles..)

When its all browned put the dish on the table and go for it....

This sense of emergence is confirmed in my therapy group, where one of our circle is definitely playing the part of my ex-husband. Amazing how this happens. I have the chance to deal with the fears finally but safely: we have been working through it all year really.

Wonderfully, the group, which I joined some time after Daniel's death as a support structure, allowed me back after my travels. Today, I spoke my truth about how he was being with me, and he actually answered from his heart, and I saw in his face some of what Miro had suffered from; I saw NOTHING TO FEAR. I did not lose my power. I just felt compassion for him, and gratitude for my full of life feeling. It was like a replay of Miro and me but with witnesses and I learned I am OK and he is only sad and lost.

I learned much much later that he knew of and actually had met Miro once!

It isn't that simple or fast of course. My journal is often full of the usual masochistic ramblings, but in between those times life is often very good again, and the worst of the pain and numb emptiness does not reappear.

I am listening to music a lot these days. More and more. In the bath, as I fall asleep, driving, with the others by candlelight in our big sitting room. Magical times. A new dimension to my life. Music was not really in my life at all. A new harmony?

8 November

Down in Cadgwith again with Ros, lying in my bed – drawn up to the window as usual so I can look down on the village, so adorably crooked, and the two coves. The sea in the swimming cove is an astonishing turquoise under a dark grey sky. Extraordinary.

I love this comfy padded headboard even though it's so naff. Eating bread and honey and sipping tea. Yesterday we walked to Kennack Sands and coming back as darkness fell we rounded the point at the Huer's Hut and there was Cadgwith in its cove with all the lights coming on and chimneys smoking and smells of suppers cooking. I sat for a while quite still on a bench, absorbing it. It could be a century ago, two. It is timeless.

9 November

Thinking a lot about control, talking it through with Ros. How threatened I have always been by the helplessness of my intimates, how I try so hard to make them happy and they get worse and worse, until I get frightened and want to abandon them, and then they slip completely under. Did I choose Miro because I sensed he would not abandon me because he needed me, so did I feel I could 'control' him? And ironically ended up with the uncontrollable. With the can't win/can't please thing. Because of the need to please, to win.

I had been in Exeter the week before to do an M&M clutterbust for a friend of a friend. I still avoided Exeter on the whole, but felt 8am should be safe enough! As I walked through the centre, suddenly I heard my name called and there in front of me totally unrecognisable but for the voice was the man my husband had become. I gasped, my mouth dropped open in shock. I knew he had been in trouble for assaulting women and for trashing his council flat, and looking at him this was easily imaginable. He was a drop-out, a vagrant, dirty, ragged, stooped, walking with a stick, with very long bushy curly dark hair and a bushy beard, and he was fat. His face was a mask of madness.

I acknowledged him without a smile, walked on fast but confidently, but he followed, all the way to my destination, shouting abuse and once clutching at me. But no more that that. No more than that. I was not afraid, and I told him that, strongly. 'You have become what you have chosen to be' I said. But I was churning inside. When I reached the house, I felt his desperation escalate and felt suddenly vulnerable, and I saw two men working with a skip opposite. I called them 'can you help...this gentleman is bothering me'. They sped across to me, tow large burly builders, and the awful figure my husband has become melted away....

I never saw him again.

Oh the pity of it. The waste of it.

If I am not to end up like my mother, alone and terrified of partnering anyone because they won't be perfect, and in case they need looking after, or cause pain or trouble, I have to make the shift inside to be willing to not be in control, in charge of....to trust in fact. Extend my trust to an intimate relationship. If I don't, the fear of the uncontrollable will be a self-fulfilling prophecy; it will make it all worse. If I can act NOT from fear of the uncontrollable, ie let go and trust even in intimacy, then those situations won't be created and anyway I actually will become free of the fear. It begins to make sense.

I also have this big fear that I feed my ego by showing people up, on a very camouflaged level. I remember Mala saying 'You are such an example to us all Sandra'. Ugh. On the surface in those days I was afraid, controlled and abused, Loving Him Unconditionally Despite His Awfulness. The Good One. Underneath I was (?) controlling, aware of his inadequacy and showing it up by my competence. Living alone or with a 'controlled' man, I can control my life so that I am admired. All pretty Yuk. There are pages of self-castigating diary here. Can I risk getting it wrong/being disapproved of/ being rejected.

The need for approval crawls slimily in everywhere.

Rooted in fear, of people. Mala: 'Breathe out fear and breathe out love'. Paul Taylor 'You cant go on being afraid of people forever'. Fear of their anger, fear of expressing my own because I believe they won't hear it, won't listen, know they will just turn it back to me or be hurt by it. If I express pain, need, anger, they just go into their own reactive emotions, and the attention turns to their needs and mine are ignored or abused.... I am powerless. And in me festers a maelstrom of hate for myself and others.

So, I rant on about myself, beating myself mercilessly with speculation about my motives. Brutally honest.

A migraine follows all this of course. I lie there furious.

Such an anger and resentment, 'What do you want?' I rage at God, 'What do you want from me? All this endless work to improve myself and still I suffer this punishing pain, powerless. Nothing takes it away'.

I rage at my mother too 'You were left with nothing. I'll NEVER understand why Dad did that. We found you a flat that the heaven-sent employment insurance JUST paid for, we confronted its appalling smells and nicotine brown walls and ceilings for you, cleaned it and decorated it, spared you what you refused to face, and made it lovely for you. And you've neglected it shamefully, and made it a problem and a burden, when you could have looked after it with pride and left it to me with love. You wont even buy a bed for me. I have to sleep on the sofa and find my own bedding from the damp airing cupboard and wheeze with asthma all night.'

Gosh, that felt good, to write like that. So, I rave on.

'and the its never enough syndrome. When I was young, there was never enough for extras, no luxury, no spare, when I wanted that delightful second helping at mealtimes there was none. You made just enough. To this day I crave food, meat, excess. Passion. Passion was not a word I ever heard. I can never do enough to please you. There's only ever just enough money, and you always say the same you only ever had just enough. I've learned this belief. You are angry. I am angry. When I did go off on my trip to really just please myself, look at what I came back to, disaster and penury. I did NOT expect it, I was full of confidence and faith. I was SO shocked. Appalled at what God was putting me through. I do NOT deserve it. Am I so very terrible that I must endure so much and be so deprived??? Terrible people win all the prizes and then they aren't even happy. I HATE that.'

I can't express anger to others directly at all. I get so irritated and frustrated. If I do try to say what I am feeling it all gets put straight back to me, and I give in all over again, because a fight is just not worth it and I am afraid it will damage others. Dad all over again. I take too much responsibility because others won't or can't. It's a kind of self-centredness really. There was a novel, where someone said in agony 'it's my fault, it's me, if he dies it's because of me' and his wife said 'don't keep on grabbing centre stage'.

Yes.

Then I start berating myself about my motives when I do things, my agenda to show up other's inadequacies. It goes on forever, the 'stuff' pours on, feeding itself to more and more self-torture.

So many pages of diary all so painful. I have resisted looking at it all to try to summarise it for this account. For weeks I have resisted 'doing this bit!' It's truly horrible to see how I used to think. Interesting too that I finally sit down determined to address these dozen or so pages on the dark of the moon.

It is Samhain, the Dark of the Year, the pit of the year. I am in the Cauldron of Ceridwen, stirring it myself, with a horrible avidity.

10 November

But, I have brought with me to Cadgwith Carol's book, Shakti Gawain's 'Living in the Light' and this morning I opened it at random, and, amazingly, I find myself reading about **the way our lives reflect our relationship with OURSELVES.** *Nothing short of revelation*. I have worked so much with projection onto others and this last year on the way life reflects what *we judge* in the others too, but I have not realised that the world also reflects how we treat ourselves. As without so within and vice versa. This is a new idea for me and here it is just when I need it. *Of course*. How can I NOT trust.

She says:
'If you judge and criticise yourself, others will judge and criticise you
If you hurt yourself, others will hurt you
If you lie to yourself, others will lie to you
If you are irresponsible to yourself, others will be irresponsible to you
If you blame yourself, others will blame you
If you do violence to yourself others will do violence to you emotionally or even physically
If you don't listen to your feelings noone will listen to your feelings.'

I added some of my own, you can go on for ever:
If you find fault with yourself others will find fault with you
If you are disappointed in yourself others will be disappointed in you
If you are ashamed of yourself others will be ashamed of you
If you take on guilt you will be found guilty
If you drive yourself too hard you will be driven too hard
If you doubt yourself you will be doubted
If you ignore you own needs your needs will be overlooked.

And then of course:
'If you love yourself others will love you
If you respect yourself others will respect you
If you trust yourself others will trust you
If you are honest with yourself others will be honest with you
If you are gentle and compassionate with yourself others will treat you with gentleness and compassion
If you honour yourself others will honour you
If you appreciate yourself others will appreciate you
If you enjoy yourself others will enjoy you'

And :
If you are kind to yourself others will be kind to you
If you respect yourself and your needs and boundaries, others will respect you and your needs and boundaries
If you protect yourself others will protect you
If you recognise your quality, others will recognise your quality
If you forgive yourself, others will forgive you
If you are peaceful and accepting with yourself, others will be peaceful and accepting with you.
If you embrace yourself as you are others will embrace you as you are
If you give yourself credit, others will give you credit
If you put yourself first, others will allow you to be first

So, I laugh in gratitude and a new practice for the Celtic New Year begins. My relationship with myself.

SG also says 'when I communicate truthfully and directly everything I really want to say it doesn't seem to matter too much how the other person responds. I feel so clear and empowered from taking care of myself that it is easier to let go of the result.' And then, too, I don't have hidden festering needs/resentments. I remember how people say I am hard to help: I guess it must be so when needs are unexpressed. People are glad so often to help when it is clear what is needed, and when we ASK..

Yes, I will work to slough off the need for approval and control on the deeper levels (all too easy to SAY I'm doing this as a way of gaining approval...!!!) and yes, let's get to the deeper levels and let go in PRIVATE, let go the PRETENCES, keep it to myself and my God. Wayne Dyer says that the minute we TALK about manifesting our reality we get into ego.

BUT, let me be kind to myself too, and honour myself just as I am.

I am willing to say to myself and my God, I'm OK, I'm lovable, I am open to being helped to intimacy again. *Please, God and Goddess, I need your help.*

The sun just came right out and flooded in all over me and this journal. Ros said, 'Perhaps this is the moment it all changes'.

Good Samhain work.

The sun stayed out until a glorious sunset, which we watched from Mullion cliffs with a sherry.

I am putting together the ways the world reflects us.

Its getting clearer....see the Ingredients box in a page or two. Once we know this, we can watch our reactions and see what's going on.

11 November

Lying in the sun on my red rug on Polurrian beach while Ros gathers stones along the waters edge. The sea is glittering exuberantly. Hardly anyone is here.

Must note down a story that appealed to me: The man a few cottages down is frail and elderly but has bought a boisterous and beautiful golden Labrador. He cannot really walk it far enough so he lets it out to wander the cliff path, and doesn't know which pile of dogshit is his dog's. So he goes everyday to pick it ALL up. Interesting parallels with my tendency to take on too much, and then to be over-conscientious as well, clearing everything up because I don't have the boundaries to know what is actually my responsibility.

It is blissful here, a retreat place. To get here you go past 'Come to good' and 'Playing Place' and then start to soar across the Lizard plateau. Then drop suddenly down into the exquisite crooked leaning maze of Cadgwith, with its fishing boats pulled up on the beach and the steep, narrow and twisting road. Serpentine rock abounds, it's best experienced in the caves on Kynance Cove - like going into the womb of the Earth Goddess. They are glossy, dark green, purple, red-brown, like organs of the body. The beach is, my favourite aunt said, 'the best in the world': not that she had been out of Britain much! But she could well be right.

I've been practising walking up hills with my legs not my shoulders. Getting into my body. Stop 'shouldering' and 'shoulding' my way through life. I guess I'm out of touch with my legs/the earth. Always afraid my body will let me down – so weak I cant move. Ungrounded. Well I would be I've been 'flying for so long, ever since I left River Meadows really, and launched` myself onto the wings of the universe can I ride the great wings AND be grounded in Mother Earth?.

I guess my body when it 'lets me down' is grounding me, is doing that FOR me. Can I find a way to keep grounded without overeating or letting my body doing it for me so painfully? My body can get very lazy. SG says we have to enlighten the body. That makes sense. Light food and lots of exercise. I have such a resistance.
Need a pulsation of stillness and exercise.

I'm sitting outside vine Cottage with a cup of tea, feet up on the wall. Waves pound the rocks below, the trees the other side of the bay are bent by the icy NE wind. But here all is sheltered, calm, warm in the sun.

Concorde booms. Barriers CAN be broken.

December 1999

I send out Christmas cards for the Millennium with copies of the SG thing in it. It seems so important I want to share it.

I feel equipped now for the twenty-first century.

This was a major turning point. I got it, finally.

I'd read of it before but not GOT IT. I was so happy to type out SG's words after those on all the Samhain agonies. What would we do without all these great teachers working today?? Go on suffering. We are being offered the way out of suffering, I am very grateful to be alive right now, when all these truths are being brought out into the open.

RECIPE for IF SOMETHING DISTURBS US

If there is an emotional reaction, then it is showing us either:

1. how we **treat** others
2. how we **judge** others
3. what we **envy** in others
4. how we **treat ourselves**

So if we look to see which it is every time we are disturbed/angry/irritated etc, we can bring awareness to it. then we can accept what we find in ourselves. Then we can accept it in others and not get annoyed, but just let it be.

Of course don't forget this works for positive stuff too. If we admire, are awed by, adore....those qualities are in us!!!!

The world is a mirror. We can use it to identify and clean up our thoughts and feelings so that we attract what we want in our lives....   This is how we create our lives.

Some of the Higher Sea House community and friends at Glenn and Nancy's wedding. Top: Carol, me, Vince and Mary (whose car I used in the States), Andrew. Bottom: Evelyn, Jamie (Nancy's son) Glenn, Nancy with her son Nick, Her mum Nanny (my gardening role model), Lisa and baby John.

Chapter 4   A New Millennium 2000

A new millennium is too big to grasp really. In the old days I would have been pressurised for months before that I wouldn't have anything suitably big to do on such a night, and would certainly have thought of arranging something. The root of my incorrigible organising I suspect. After this year, still safe here in our Higher Sea family, I will just let it be what it will be. And if that isn't major progress I don't know what is.

Maybe now the high seas are subsiding, and we sail on higher seas in a different sense.

I reflect that I am extremely glad to have got all the Terrible Time over before this momentous date.

So, interestingly, with not a jot of thought or organisation, I find myself in the best possible place for millennium eve for the eccentric old mystic that I am.. Glastonbury Tor….

Silhouetted against the smoky orange glow of 700 flares is a silent procession of endless dark figures slowly, steadily, climbing the Tor in this last night of the twentieth century. It is a scene from 1000 years ago, 2000 years ago, timeless, unchanged. We have travelled back in time, and enter into an awed enchantment. At the top, in the midst of the smoke and the throngs of waiting pilgrims, drums beat, flames are thrown, juggled, swallowed, children run weaving between legs, cups are raised. We turn and see the panorama of bonfires spread around the levels below and ranged along the hills. It is warm, still, the earth is pausing before she births the new age. When the bells ring out from all the churches below, there is a great roar, and rockets launch out and everyone hugs everyone as wine spills from cups and overflows in a great and joyous libation for the sacred hill.

We walked up out of the twentieth century, into the Middle ages, and came down into the twenty-first century.

1 January 2000

We are all sitting around tearfully watching the Millennium celebrations all around the globe, lubricated by Cava. It feels like perhaps the first totally global simultaneous celebration, with single-pointed focus and attention worldwide, a great wave of love and hope and pleasure travelling around the planet with the first sunrise of the millennium.

7 January

This new millennium starts with a new job as Coordinator for Chard Festival of Women in Music.

The angel card for the year, picked at our winter solstice ceremony, is Love. Good start.

Like 1997, this is a year I'm happy to see slip away.

Shakti Gawain contributed my new mantra for the year: '*WHATEVER'.* WHATEVER HAPPENS IS FOR THE HIGHEST GOOD. She called her publishing house Whatever House!!! I say it all the time, especially any time anything is at all anxiety-making, difficult, puzzling , WHATEVER. Just that. Relax. Whatever happens is fine. Relax relax relax.

I had a tough patch in December when I panicked, penniless again with Christmas coming, and in fury took an angel card saying crossly to myself, it will probably be Trust!! *It was*. I laughed out loud, and I relaxed.

Next day, I had a call completely out of the blue from Angela at the Festival of Women in Music inviting me to be Coordinator. I knew I was ready for a challenge again now, and that this was the right role for me. I had had a feeling that something like this would happen, ever since the interview there in August for publicist.

The same day, an old friend rang to ask if I could teach English to a French boy for cash, starting immediately. So, I had a proper job for the new year AND cash for Christmas presents!

I am reading Paul Ferrini's 'Reflections of the Christ Mind'. Still struggling a lot at times and it is really helping.

He says: 'Forgive yourself. Forgive everything that you think is wrong by forgiving yourself for being in judgment. Look at every judgment you make with compassion for yourself and the person you are judging. If you feel fear, look at the fear, forgive yourself for feeling fear. It then gets out of the way, because you are dwelling at ease with what is. Heaven is here and heaven is now. You see what you choose to see: a world free of judgment and shining in its endless beauty. Had you not taken the journey into and through fear, you would not have known your innocence. An angel who has not fallen from grace is not capable of conscious creation'

There's the way to start the twenty-first century.

He also says that when someone acts inappropriately and demands your attention, you don't want to allow yourself to be manipulated, which would reinforce his behaviour. You give him what he REALLY wants, your love. Give it freely, do what it feels right to do, but no more, and don't worry that you aren't meeting his demands. Say yes to loving him but no to being manipulated. You don't judge him or separate from him, but you refuse to be a victim or victimiser.

This I found very very helpful.

17 Feb. Flower remedies reading from Carol

The composite remedy picked intuitively is 'grief'. In 2 days it will be the 3rd anniversary of Dan's death. I am speechless.

Other remedies are Mediterranean sage, for warmth comfort and wisdom, and for me symbolises wisdom about the Mediterranean – my love for the sun, for it all, for my husband and son(sun). Then there is firethorn to balance unstable fire energies, very right for me. Good for over-emotional involvements, expectation of over-high standards…!!! Pine cones for feelings of inadequacy, the excessive need to please, inability to express own true authority due to domination. Helps one to lose the chains!!!! Wood anemone for old, karmic, difficult to eradicate, problems, deep feelings of guilt and fear, old blocks. All of this is spot-on.

It is hard to understand how this kind of accuracy happens, whether it is divination cards, flower essences or astrology, or whatever. We can only wonder and be grateful.

Carol made up a mixture of these for me and I took it daily with a sense of personal ritual and awareness of each remedy, until it was finished.

Early March   Struggling with mum.

I find myself able to put into words the crux of the problem as I see it. I write a 'letter' to her in my journal. 'If I express my hurt etc at something you do, then you are so upset that the focus of attention shifts entirely to your pain and my having hurt you. So my pain is never seen or heard, only yours. You then get ill in some way from distress. And refer to how you have helped me in hard times. You have to be the centre of attention, and you are threatened if I am not in the best form and able to care for you.

I need now to be able to say what I feel when I feel it and have you attend and care. That's all. I don't wish to accuse you or change you or judge you. You have chosen your life and I let you be who you choose to be.

You do not need to be afraid of my feelings, we love each other and love contains everything.'

There is a NB to myself, 'When she cries, moans, whines, don't tell her what she can do to make it better. Just tell her you love her and are there.'

Note in margin, obviously from later: Been practising all this, it works brilliantly. And it wasn't long before I could let go of the need for her to hear me. *I could let go of needing her to parent me even at my age!!!*

I am reading 'Emotional Blackmail' by Susan Forward.

Useful useful useful.

When this works its just FAN-TAS-TIC. Lifelong shit can dissolve in moments.

'If you've fallen into a pattern of habitually putting yourself last until you exhaust yourself physically, mentally, emotionally, spiritually, financially....it's time to change.' I read this and thought, 'I've come a *long long way* from when I lived like that.' I felt SOOO good.
She tells us to write this out, so I did:

'I forgive you Sandra. You've done your very best in all the difficult circumstances of your life. You really care. I forgive you, my dear. I forgive you, I forgive you, I forgive you. You are free of guilt. There was never any malice. You only wanted the best for everyone, their happiness, to share your happiness, fulfilment and harmony with us all. I can bless the past and move with trust and love into the future.'

There are so many tools to help us recover. I know now how she uses weakness, neediness and pain to elicit attention. I know she is afraid of her own true feared and unused power – she is very psychic, very intuitive, very attractive. (Her cousin and his son are members of the Magic Circle...and her uncle a prominent herbalist). She has preferred the safety of the power of weakness over others....

15 March Dozmary Pool, Bodmin Moor

En route to the Lizard again. This is the place where Ninever, the Lady of the Lake, rose from the lake and holding aloft the sword Excalibur, which she gave to Arthur, saying, 'always remember that the power of Excalibur lies not in the sword but in the scabbard.' The female contains and keeps safe the power of the male.

Driving through bright spring sunshine and a few light showers from Somerset to the Lizard, Dozmary Pool is a time warp, a place apart. We arrive wearing sunglasses, and step out of the car to walk to the pool. As an afterthought I pull on my jacket. But then in astonishment I suddenly realise it is raining, cold hard rain, and seize my plastic anorak. I am drawn like a magnet to the pool, through freezing winds, sleet, fine snow, dark grey cloud and mist. There is no way I would wait out the weather, it is a compulsion to go and meet the pool in its full mystery. Three geese are there to meet us, and accompany us silently as we walk around. It is a world of streaks of ochre,

RECIPE FOR DEALING WITH EMOTIONAL BLACKMAIL

Step into their shoes.
Imitate, aloud, when by yourself, the ranting/whining/abusing/whatever. Exaggerate it, magnify it. What happens when you do this enough is: you find out how he or she feels. . ..which is NOT powerful, but helpless, scared. An emotional coward. A mask of bravado or desperate need. This behaviour then becomes less scary, it doesn't disturb you so much. You just feel compassion - and gratitude for not being like that...!!!

Once you aren't disturbed you can use another powerful technique which is to laughingly say something like 'no, I don't THINK so, good try though' to out –of-order requests. Or 'Hey, I thought we were talking about ME here? You old attention grabber you!' But you have to be in a calm, unjudgmental and almost amused state for this to work . Then, it can cut right through the bullshit and they'll often laugh too.

khaki and greys, with white light drawn ruler - straight along the horizon beneath the massed charcoal clouds. A timeless huddle of stone farm grows out of the marshy shore. All is shrouded in swathes of mist and rain and driving sleet. A broken wooden fence wades crookedly into the motionless water. It is a place of unearthly stillness amid the maelstrom of nature. I am reminded of a quotation I love 'the stillness between the waves of the sea'. I have a feeling of contacting and being passed a great power, and of humbly contracting to use this wisely and well, and of feeling a great gratitude.

I try to take some photographs but the viewfinder suddenly blackens. Never found out why.

I have stayed alone to really feel it all, but Fergus - Ros's very determined Chihuahua-has done his shepherd thing and refused to leave without me so he and Ros are waiting patiently at the gate. As we walk away, the sleet stops, the mist lifts, the sun comes out, and all is golden. We look at each other in astonishment, and run back to the car, drenched and frozen, to hot coffee, cheese bread and my own smoked mackerel pate. The journey continues as before in sun and light showers.

Looking back that night, it felt as though we had to penetrate the veils to reach the still power of the place. The containing of the power, a parallel of the scabbard and sword, 'power is no use without control'. When to use the sword and when the scabbard? Reminds me of my tongue.

In 2003 I returned to the pool in a large group. It was again full of stories. One of us had a story of her own here, she had been part of this place, painfully. The parking lay-by was unaccountably invisible and I found myself driving her right down to the cottage she'd lived in. We held a ceremony there, near the site of her pain, and she was able to talk about it, while held in a loving group.

During the ceremony I was focussed on the candle flame, and an image of a flashing circle of prisms of light formed and remained on my retina. It was like a diamond ring, growing and growing in brightness, not quite a complete circle. I had no real idea what it was about, but it felt a very precious gift, and even now I can see it clearly in my mind's eye.

In Cadgwith in March

Planning to give up the pub cooking job and concentrate on the festival. I can see it needs another day a week, there is just too much to be done. I'm writing lists of how I want my life to be, all the new things I intend to do.

To the Dome with Rhapsody

Who would have believed that Katherine, Damon and I would be parading Rhapsody – the 10ft Festival Giant, a lady conductor with flowing robes and hair, and a baton –at the Millennium Dome? Watching that stunning show that we saw on New Years Eve? Life never ceases to amaze me. (I had organised a Parade of locally made Giants as a part of the Festival street party, and we created her, with much pleasure and laughter, in the Higher Sea garage.)

June 17

Thinking about that resolution in Cadgwith, well, what actually happened was full-on Music Festival for two months. I spoke with Jules, my M&M client, about needing more time for it and she said 'you must ask for it'. So I did and I got it and needed every second. It became fulltime for the last month.

No journal written at all. But what a fabulous cornucopia of memories. This was something totally new, tremendously exciting. Spilling, sliding, shining, fizzing, biting. The concentration, the anxiety, the weight, the exhilaration, the flying. The people, the warmth, the goodwill, the running around endlessly. Management by running around. The notebook and pen always by the bed for night-time thoughts. But above all of course, THE MUSIC.

I remember walking fast down the street from one venue to another in drizzling rain, holding walkie-talkie and file, two young venue managers running to catch up with me, vigorously asking me questions as they held a large umbrella over us, a whole stack of queries and problems dealt with in moments. The walkie talkie interrupting us with yet more queries. I loved it, having answers, knowing what to do. It was one of the most powerful experiences of my life.

My favourite times were those bits before a concert when the musicians play the first notes in their sound test. Cables everywhere, everyone running around, a sense of urgency, and then with those notes, a total shift of energy and whoosh the sound fills the venue and they are away, breaking here and there with shouted comments, but the energy is building now, the excitement palpable.

And dancing to African band Abakush with a crowd of my friends come for the concert, in a roaring hall packed with people and crackling with energy.

It was a five day event over 12 venues including a street closed off for a stage, with musicians from all over the world who needed looking after and accommodating, 100 volunteers to train and organise, and lots of important guests, not to mention a stack of H&S stuff.

And at some point during the Festival Run-in, in a heightened state I guess, I realised the rightness of all things JUST AS THEY ARE. The whole huge variety of human life could not BE unless it was ALL there, all these myriad hang-ups, dysfunctions, abnormalities, even atrocities. It is all there for us to choose from, respond to, learn from, experience.......(I guess that should be in reverse order?)

I have always got so outraged amazed disappointed bewildered shocked hurt and fearful when observing others' behaviour and standards. I'll never find a partner, someone I could commit to.... unless I find someone similar and even then, we'll have different high standards (Jules's 'different fields of rigour') – how would he cope with my indulgent side?....

....My comfort eating/ slobbing around/ reading endlessly/ hunching over/ dragging myself up hills/ resistance to exercise/ depressing myself/ procrastinating/ dreaming/ and being nervous in parties where I don't know anyone and I am overlooked. All that. And with my history....all *that*. Tough stuff.

I guess the inveterate idealist that I have always been is changing?? Is this the Harmony that the music is bringing with it? Will I find a light touch on all that tough stuff? Will I begin to see the end of idealism's other side: disappointment and resentment?

And then, as the adrenaline begins to fade, decompression begins to hit.

I knew I had overdone it and I kind of expected some reaction. It blew in after a couple of weeks. Dizzy spells, nausea, headaches, and then a full-blown full-moon migraine and depression. Deep deep deep. Just surfacing on and off for days. Fragile and frightened.

I know Glenn and Nancy are off to the States soon and Maud and Martin (Carol's daughter and partner) move in. Unknowns again.

June 18

Walking in the garden, in the summer dusk, the lovely old house warm from the day's sun, all her windows golden-lit, all her rooms teeming with life, family life. A midsummer night's dream. A Merchant Ivory film. Nancy's family over from the States. I am only a peripheral part of it all but I am here, and not embroiled or entangled and that seems to be all I can do at the moment.

I am giving thanks for the successful Festival, and I offer, as I drift though the apple trees, my loneliness and fears up to the Goddess and I feel at peace.

August

But Festival Reaction was not done with me. Soon I was writhing at midnight with an earache I thought would burst my ear wide open, and Dr Andrew Tressider who lives opposite just happened to be the doctor on duty and he made me sit very very still in the kitchen while he extracted with a horrendously needle-like instrument a mountain of foul gunge from my ear canal. He then gave me some different antibiotics, and painkillers which knocked me right out, and left me to sleep. For days I surfaced to consciousness to take some more tablets and then was gone again.

That was the second bout of earache, and it was closely followed by a stack of bad migraines with vomiting, and accompanied by asthma and sinusitis and appalling weakness.

Ben and I went to France, in his car, camping. It was a lovely interlude for a week, being driven by my son. I was fragile but was OK except for a bout of sickness towards the end. We loved going over the big bridge at Nantes, crossing into the land of light and red roofs. We found a campsite, very busy, but amazingly there was a pitch right by the cliff, with steps to the beach. We hung out, reading, resting, walking.

By September I was still getting ill, with asthma, headaches, nausea etc. I despaired and went to the doctor. She did a load of tests and everything was OK. But she HEARD me. She took me seriously and she was thorough. I was very grateful and maybe all I needed was to be heard.

During all this messy stuff I had a confrontation with mum. Which was equally painful. But somewhere after the earaches I finally felt

free of the need for her to behave as I think a caring mother should. This began earlier in the year and came to a kind of fruition now.

I think this was a big step. It'll come and go, this feeling, I know, but once there, an insight will not usually be fully lost I find. I can leave her be and be grateful I have my mum. Just as she is. I don't need to compete with her to be the child. Took me till I am 54 to learn this. Sad.

I don't need to change, or fix her, I don't need to REACT so much to her. Oh blessed relief. I can love her. I can see the positives, see her elegance, style, natural class, artistry, eye for beauty. I can accept the whole mum. I can tease her. I don't need her to be my parent. I can parent myself now.

It must have been around that month that Rachel gave me a poem:

Wild Geese
By Mary Oliver

You do not have to be good
You do not have to walk through the desert repenting
You only have to let the soft animal of your body do what it loves
Tell me about despair
Yours, and I will tell you mine
Meanwhile the world goes on
Meanwhile the sun and the clear pebbles of the rain are moving across the
landscapes
Over the prairies and the deep trees
The mountains and the rivers
Meanwhile the wild geese, high in the clean blue air
Are heading home again
Whoever you are
No matter how lonely
The world offers itself to your imagination
Calls to you like the wild
Geese, harsh and exciting-
Over and over announcing your place
In the family of things.

Sitting there in 2005 typing this from my journal exhilaratingly high up on an Andalucian mountain, a guest of a Dutch woman, I suddenly remembered that big Belgian guy who always came to our Wine Barn who invited Miro and I to Poltimore House and got us drunk on cognac and I went on and on about my mum and he said to Miro 'My God, do you have to put up with this all the time?' or something like that and I was so wild. I thought, outraged, but I'm THE GOOD ONE. I'm the GOOD ONE, you've got it all wrong. I'm the one who has the terrible time with HIM'. And we went home and I was sick all night and just left it all. Yes, I just left it all, I couldn't move at all. Miro cleaned up for me. Role reversal. And it wasn't just hangover or alcohol poisoning it was the sight of a truth denied all my life. I went on denying it too, I'm afraid. Here in Spain in a valley that mirrors ourselves - a valley like Crestone, I am seeing very clearly just how difficult I was. This is a humbling place

Interesting.

Even more interesting is the fact that looking back that was actually the LAST of the migraines that had haunted me most of my life. They came up for the last time with a vengeance and I saw what I had to see, finally. Mum and I were pretty much fine after that. I started to lighten up at last.

It follows on from the insight during the spring, about everyone's peculiarities/flaws/wounds/hang-ups/complexes are just as they need to be for a fully varied world. There's got to be everything. I see that I don't need to change or challenge people. BUT I do have to do only what is good for ME for them – what feels comfortable for me. Boundaries, its all about boundaries. No point doing loads then getting all resentful cos they don't come up to scratch. No point sacrificing then being walked over, mocked, used, while I simmer with anger and frustration, disappointment and pain. Take care of my own needs. Love everyone as they are. 'Love and do what you will.' St Augustine.

I can value my own particular way of being complete with all its flaws. If I can accept and love others as they are I can love myself as I am too. Others can ask of me what they want and I will do as much as I truly want to do. No more. I can ask others for help on the expressed understanding that they only do it if they want to. People know I am truly happy to do what I do. It shows. I receive help but I know I am not being a nuisance – lifelong Stuff being addressed here. Wow. There's an amazing freedom in all this. And valuing myself, and being able to ask, I find people take me at my own valuation….

'Dwell at ease with what is'

16 September

I was an only child of caring parents. Privileged. I guess I never had to fight for anything. **I got what I needed.**

Except easy company, friends, laughter, banter and teasing and learning to deal with anger, and to fight and compete.

What I am now focussing on is EXPANDING my acknowledged needs. To stop saying, 'I don't need very much' 'I can live on only £550 a month' ' *Don't worry about me, I'm alright'*. I need a rich and varied life. Pleasures are needs, not something to try to do without. Unexpressed, unadmitted need, or FEAR OF NEED becomes neediness, which is repellent. It is shame about needs, so they are hidden, buried.

20 September

On sunbed on the lawn in morning sun. Music pouring out of the house. Golden hamstone walls glow in the sun. My toenails are gold too - new thing dating from Nancy's brother's teenage daughter's visit! First time ever I painted my toenails. *Can you believe that?* At 54. SAD. What have I been thinking of...

Wistaria tendrils flowing in soft wind. Containers spilling bright flowers. Scent of lemon balm. Butterflies. The odd wasp. The last heat of summer. My white wrought iron table and chairs , treasured since Bennetts. Maud and Amber (3 weeks old) in the French window. Amber wrapped in a blanket of squares. I actually knitted one, with great difficulty, when I had earache. (I can scarcely believe this, reading it in 2005, knitting is not something I do. it also occurs to me now that Amber – means healing - was born when I was struggling through illness to come to 'birthing' new understandings...)

Amber Tallulah Star was born here at Higher Sea House, appropriately in a birthing pool. I was in the house, and will never forget it, being so close to a birth.

I've been sorting out my boxes in the workshop. Found old letters. Ouch.

Letters to mum from when I was a small girl and later a young teenager. I remember when mum found them and gave them to me , how thrilled I was, and how PD and I pored over them with such gratitude. It was like being given back my little girl, because I have only three memories (painful) until I was 11. That was wonderful.

But re-reading the ones from myself as a Grammar school girl, I really saw how cruel and patronising I was, showing off my learning, my cleverness, my understanding, to my uneducated mother. Pretending I had lots of friends and was wanted. Hiding, always hiding, my loneliness. Taking refuge in the 'aloof' game. Also painful to read was a copy of a letter I sent to Dan, and his reply, which referred to a 'cascade of sermons'. Mum always said I was just like my father, forever preaching. He was isolated too. 'Don't get too cut off' were PD's last words to me.

Sermons. Solutions. Self-improvement. Answers. Ways to perfection. Ideals. Accounts of my insights and discoveries. 'I've had enough of all your discoveries;' said Miro. Seeking these, offering these, attempting these, reading and writing these. No fun I realise now, for those close to me. Forever 'fixing' or attempting to fix. So that 'All is Well'.

It all makes me cringe.

I am sighing with the recognition of it all, but then I hear 'Panis Angelica' streaming out of the open windows and smile with pleasure, and I laugh at myself. Remember, I say aloud, remember, *Acceptance*, it's all OK. I don't have to be perfect. And I go in to get a cup of tea.

Next I clear the garage and rescue Rhapsody, who has been lying there wounded like me all summer. She is now standing and conducting again. I speak to her. We explored expansion together, and both succeeded and failed. She has one final date and then I arrange a ceremonial burning for her. Her job is done. We watch her sparks fly into the night sky and say thankyou.

Autumn with a garden. I never had a garden really until now.

Work largely done, so much harvested, warm ground, onions strung (over tea and cakes on the lawn), marrows hardening in the sun, all the roots there for winter, courgettes taking over everything, runner beans rampant, brassicas coming on. New fence kept the rabbits out well. Oh yes. I want more of this in my life. *I want more time for this.*

Meeting the Feminine Face of God

All this work redressing the balance between male and female...empowering my feminine side, bringing harmony into my life, learning to be kind to myself, learning to accept people gently as they are, learning to mother myself....... But still when I speak to God I say

'Lord'.

It never occurred to me that I have only been talking with one aspect of God and it is the masculine, sterner, side. Just as I was always so hard on myself, full of criticism and judgment of myself and others. The patriarchal syndrome.

One day I tell my friend Yon that I would like to do more ceremonial work, and she tells me about a course in ceremony to be held in Glastonbury. Next day, at a party on Dartmoor, I mention this and another friend, Nanette, says, 'Well it just so happens I've got the brochure in my bag.... forgot to give it to someone. It's clearly meant for you'

And so I apply to begin the 'Heart of the Goddess' training as a Priestess of Avalon with Kathy Jones, and begin to discover and connect with the Divine Feminine. And softness, gentleness, tenderness begin to creep exquisitely into my wounded heart and life.

I have to pay by cheques. So I think, 'ah, if I need a cheque book one will come to me. I go into the local branch of the bank where I had opened a new account with before the bankruptcy, but that account had of course been frozen. I speak honestly to the manager. He looks me up on the screen and, amazingly, said, 'your bankruptcy does not show on the screen. Write to your branch, and say you would like to activate the account, and need a cheque book. I do this, and lo and behold one arrives in the post. And I am only half way though my three year insolvency. More magic.....it never ends....

And I remember when I begin to 'hear' Her Voice in my heart, and mind, and I felt this smile dawn on my face. 'Aaaaah' I breathed to Her. 'Aaaaah, yes, of course. Now I understand'.

I start Kathy Jones's 'Heart of the Goddess' Priestess training course at Halloween. I was nervous and self- conscious, but I knew it is going to be of huge importance to me. The ceremonies were of a quality and depth I've not known before – true sacred theatre.

The first ceremony was for Samhain, or Halloween. All souls.

HEART OF THE GODDESS TRAINING

Kathy Jones says: 'Students participate in a teaching and ceremonial cycle which mirrors the changing appearance of the Goddess as She moves through the cycle of Her seasons. During this year you will begin to learn about the Isle of Avalon and will enter its Mysteries.'

This course is profound, with high quality teaching, very intimate sharing among the group and truly spectacular sacred ritual and drama. After two years students can self-initiate as a Priestess of Avalon in a most beautiful and powerful nightime ceremony at Chalice well gardens. Priestesses serve the world in many ways, some high profile some quietly, unidentified in their communities, but just as powerfully.

SAMHAIN

This is the beginning of the Dark of the Year. Halloween, All Hallows, All Souls. It is the night when the veils between the worlds are thin and chaos reigns as the Celtic Goddess Ceridwen stirs her Cauldron. It is a time of confrontation and change, of letting go the old that no longer serves us well, and of rebirth.

It is the Celtic New Year, which celebrates the start of the long dormancy time of winter, of the time for looking inwards, quietening, facing our darkness, and from that place nurturing seeds of ideas and dreams and intentions for the spring. This is the time when we prepare to dive into our deepest selves.

I remember forcing my way, and being pushed, through a long twisting 'birth canal' of fellow trainees, in the pitch dark, and being ejected exhausted into a circle of cloaked and hooded 'Morgens' - oracles, all leaning over me and whispering seductively. 'Buy expensive perfume….sing every day… walk on the wet grass in the morning…make love at the edge of the sea…eat good chocolate…' and then I am wrapped up, given a chalice to drink from and hugged and welcomed and told that I am loved.

This is the start of a New Year in the Celtic Wheel of the Year. A new beginning.

I decide I need a small totally stress-free job to supplement my Hotbed Coordination earnings. (I have 'created' a continuing job for myself at the festival by cooking up a conference for women composers in the non-festival year.) I look in the paper that day and saw a 2 days a week post as housekeeper. I call and when I realise where it is I am flabbergasted- it is Cricket Court, the spectacular house in Cricket Malherbie that I've adored quietly for years. It is in that fantastic in the true sense of the word house that the power to create my own reality is fully cemented somehow, I know it for sure, just by the job coming when I choose it, being there in that wish-list house and in the time spent absorbing the atmosphere of that glorious circular library where Churchill, Eisenhower, and de Gaulle strategised in secret during World War 2. The house is a creation of the imagination for pleasure alone. I enjoy tending it and tidying up the myriad strewn and heaped sumptuous possessions of the gloriously chaotic young Australian woman who owned it. I relish spending time with someone who had the knack of making big money with ease. I breathed in the power and carelessness and the opulence.

And watched the gardener with a certain envy, out there in the weather. I should have known by then that envy is showing us what we want. But I did not think I was remotely fit enough.

11 November

Transformation game 11.11.00 Full moon

Dancing friend Fiona Parr facilitates us. Rachel, Jenny, Millie and I. All old friends reconnecting to do some honest hard work on ourselves, in Jenny's house. It's a good game to play with people you know well so you can give and get feedback. We have to decide what we want to change in our lives, what our Intention in playing the game is. We have decided to do two days, and we all stay there overnight. This makes for a very powerful time, as you continue to work with it all even in rest times. It's also a lot of fun!

A very profound game. I draw the same insight card as I drew years ago at Michael and Maya's: 'Thankyou for demonstrating conscious joyous living'

My intention is a bit longwinded but says what I had to say:

'I intend that I know deeply that I deserve to be strong and healthy, fulfilled, valued and abundantly rewarded, in order to be of service to the divine feminine.'

TRANSFORMATION GAME

This spiritual board game was invented at Findhorn Community, whose website says: 'Sometimes life is filled with blessings, insights, and a heart-felt sense of connection with people around us. Other times we stumble through a series of setbacks, accumulating pain, even falling into depression; and nothing we try seems to help us get out of it. Sometimes someone unexpectedly appreciates us or offers to serve us - or we reach out to help another. Sometimes miracles happen, pain is lifted, new directions open up, and the seemingly impossible occurs.
Just as life is filled with this rich variety of experience, so is the Transformation Game®, a fun and complex board game which offers a playful yet substantial way of understanding and transforming key issues in your life.'

It's a great tool, fun and exciting and revelatory, always astonishingly apt.

I have had a lot of illness ever since the Festival and I want to change that. The first awareness tokens I take on the physical level are health and touch, fitness, strength, detachment and perseverance!!!! Last insight: 'You exercise regularly and nourish your body with wholesome foods.' Well, I don't, enough, but it's a good reminder of what I've got to do!!!

Setbacks are envy twice, rejection and judgement.

Most significant moment: realising that I can ask for support in my self-doubt over social difficulties and unwanted/overlooked feelings. I do not need to hide these feelings in shame.

Most significant realisations: mainly already realised but clearly needs more work. I am stuck at the emotional level, and I need to forgive Miro and Mum. I do tend to judge and reject and then leave suddenly as a kind of punishment (Mum and Dad, Miro, Patricia Dyehouse's therapy, Paul Taylor's Zen group, Tutorial college, Exeter College...) Watch for self-doubt. Have a high self evaluation, walk tall.

I am full of rememberings and insights after this weekend. We are asked to write a poem for the Winter Solstice as part of our extensive homework for the Priestess Course.

WINTER FRUITS

Shapes emerging
winter's purge
Flaying flood and fear and wind
Earth is weeping

Naked stones
and bones
of mountain, man and moor
honed to the core

Winter will not let us hide
breaks through resistances and pride
pierces our resistances
and shapes of land and trees and selves
stand naked in the blast

Torrents roar
winds claw
Lay bare the gleam of
Winter's fruits

Bright knife edge

of truth
forged to patient strength and
humbled by awe

and

Clarity
drops
i n still t r a n s p a r e n c y a n d
Frozen filigree

And the fruits of winter shine across the wastes

I painted a picture to go with it, of a skeletal tree with hanging orange-red fruits.

In late November 2004 in Andalucia, I saw the persimmon trees looking exactly like my painting. I hoped they represented the harvest of all the struggles, here in this glorious place. Extraordinarily, John cut it down by mistake. I knew immediately that our dream would not come to fruition. But I kept an open mind nevertheless. When I look back on the year 2000 now I see A YEAR OF INSIGHTS. Insights after the fall and recovery. Lots of chaotic and masochistic thought patterns but progress. The pattern of the years emerges as I work on this book.

New Year's Eve

Another one, but things are on the up. On New Year's Eve I really like to write out what I've done that year and what I dream of for next.

So, this year I:
- Continued to relish living in community and learning to grow organic veggies.
- Organised a music festival showcasing music written by women, and introduced events including Julie Felix on stage.
- Paraded the festival giant at the Millennium Dome
- Was in a house when a baby girl was born
- Had some of the worst physical pain of my life and found that it resolved in what seems a final way, my relationship with my mother
- Created a perfect job for myself as organiser of Hotbed conference for women composers
- Began training as a Priestess of Avalon, and began to connect with the Divine Feminine

Next year 2001:

I will have to move home, I expect.
My intention for the year ahead is to find a home where I have community, views, garden to learn about and tend, veggies to grow, land, fireplace, beauty, stability. And I want time for all that. I take a Power Deck card for this move and I have an image of a Moongate leading to a path to the globe of Earth. I prop it up on my altar.

We will see...

Reading Astrology for the Soul by Jan Spiller.

I am North Node in Gemini.
This is 'A people-oriented lifetime'
Tendencies to leave behind are:
Self-righteousness
Aloofness
Assuming others know where they're at
Needing to be right
Espousing truth without taking others' views into account
Careless spontaneity
Talking oneself too seriously
Prejudging present on basis of past.

Achilles heel= self righteousness.
Really want: to be totally free to pursue Truth, to have adventures, to be spontaneous, to be right 100% of the time, to have that acknowledged and valued......

Need to: stop focussing on truth and start focussing on people.

Well. Ha!!!!!!!! How accurate is that!!!!!!!!

It says 'past lives were as spiritual teachers, and truth seeking has been the main motivation, people very neglected. Now the challenge is to rejoin society and stay connected to others. The pinnacle of Truth is lonely. Superior attitude prevents connection, and therefore there is a feeling of being undervalued.'

God, its all so true.

Has my 'humility' been a mask for an innate arrogance?? 'Where does all this over-humility come from': said someone on John Garrie's workshop.

So I add to my intention for 2001:
Get back to the 'interested in how things are, not how you want them to be' mantra. That says it all.

Stable Cottage

Chapter 5   Stability

To Stable Cottage Spring Equinox 2001

The move soon comes. The news that the owners were returning from Africa is a shock even though we all knew one day soon we would have to leave Higher Sea. It comes in mid-February. The date is the end of May: exactly when Hotbed is happening. No way can I move then.

BUT…. I arranged in the autumn that our actual lease ends on March 25 so that I could move out if need be before things really hotted up. How did I do that? I don't know, but it worked. The others negotiate a lower rent for the last two months so the owners do not have an empty property.

I sit at the dinner table with everyone – Glenn and Nancy are over from the States- and feel the profound cellular shaking which heralds big change.

Overnight I cast about my memories and up come the one of Maud and Martin going to see a cottage at Barley Hill Farm and pronouncing it too small. In the morning I call the owner Lora – we met her at her Herbs and Healing Event at the Farm - who says, yes it is still empty (4 months it waited for me!!!) and I could go straight up. I see it and I think 'YES'. I call Lora later as requested to confirm, from the middle of a Hotbed meeting at the Tacchi Morris Centre, and then go home and say 'All fixed'. Within twenty hours I am re-homed. Lora gives me a key bless her, and says 'Would you like to do the garden for the cottage?' 'Yes, except I don't know how to garden...but I can grow vegetables now!' 'Start with that then' says Lora. Bless her indeed.

'Aha' says Glenn, on learning I am off to Stable Cottage, *'Stability at last'.*

I give up Cricket Court – I am becoming bored with cleaning now. I am headed for gardening in return for my cottage for those two days. That feels much better. I remember the gardener I had envied... how fast things manifest! Now my perception of my fitness is changing. The last week there I sit on the terrace having my coffee and looking across the Isle Valley at Barley Hill dozing in the sun. It is Spring Equinox and it feels like a big move I am making.

...and so from that most delicious of houses I fly across the Isle valley and land at Stable Cottage for a rest (from flying!!!)....

I walk the land in bliss. Golden carp welcome me in a pool beside a **Moongate.!!!!!** (Just as on the card I drew for my new home. This I find really hard to believe, the magic seems to flow ever faster). So I know I am in the right place.

And as I stand looking at the House itself, a memory flies into my mind. When I was in Crestone and I heard from Glenn and Nancy that they were renting Higher Sea House with Steve and Sarah, I felt deep envy, and I saw in my mind's eye a picture of a gabled greyish Victorian house high on a hill with far reaching views. When I did arrive at HSH, I was astonished that it was a pink L-shaped thatched farmhouse in a valley!!!! But now.... Here it is. Exactly as I had seen back in 1998. I am home. The Higher Seas have brought me safely into land on Barley Hill.

Up at the top of the hill gazing at the vast sunlit views to the Mendips and Glastonbury Tor I sink to my knees in wonder and say aloud 'Where HAS the Goddess brought me now!!!!' I visualise a labyrinth and a ceremonial site there

I know now it is right to stop my therapy group at last – after four and a half years - before I move. Angelika said good leaving was perhaps the most important part. It is hard but I think that will be achieved. She is very supportive of me amid the hostility from the group which always accompanies a leaving.

Her final word to me is that I *do not need to sell so hard my way of being, I have only to be it*.

I say it often 'I do not need to sell so hard my way of being, I have only to be it.'

This is advice I work to always follow, though it's hard. The best advice I ever had maybe. She says that it's a matter of control....my main fear is of losing control. Such a luxury to receive advice sometimes, therapy is usually non-directional, which is exasperating at times..

Several people say they will miss my stories, always of how things 'work out'.
Angelika says it must have been hard for me in that group, who are I realise now rather wedded to their suffering. Also at the last group David says something I take as negative and I respond and the whole group choruses 'she got it the wrong way round again!' I find this immensely reassuring. It reminds me of John Gordon's first comment on listening to me in 1983 and my sad tale of unwantedness: 'so you've been fending people off all your life have you?' he said. 'No no, it's the other way round' I sobbed.

Even now I still have trouble believing this but I can see it is probably the truth and that I have one way and another given out signals which fend people off. The aloof defense game. It just comes across to me in my stuff as rejection by them. I remember Marion's very helpful observation that I came across as uninterested in people, because I was so quiet...because I felt no interest from others. Classic reflection. But, I'm getting there maybe? It's only ego, fear.

Kate says to me; 'I can't touch you but I am happy to sit beside you'. She wrote me a poem when I left, which I still treasure:

To Sandra

Dancing over rainbows
Sploshing with the rain
Grieving with the bleeding moon
Face to face with pain

Timid as a tendril
Fearless as a tree
Young as life
Old as earth
Great eternity

Rising with the dewdrops
Sploshing through the skies
Red as fire
Gold as life
Fearless, joyous, wise

With love Kate
I'll miss you. Take care. Journey well

It is still hard to let go of Higher Sea. I dread being alone again and living in a small very basic space after so much luxury. But as my friend Andrew said 'think of the outside space'. And so it proves. The outside space more than compensates, and the cottage becomes a much loved nest....and my very own space.

So begins the grounding process of gardening in return for my cottage (I was a total ignoramus) and of living on the ground in a stone cottage that looked as if it grew out of the earth. My witches cottage, with its chimney and its protective bay tree high on the edge of the secret and mysterious Blackdown Hills. Tall trees guard the land (116 acres) and deer, badgers and foxes can be seen at night. Owls hoot.

GROUP THERAPY

There is such value in expressing stuff honestly in a group with a trained facilitator. And it is eerily amazing how each person represents a part of our being. This always seems to happen in circles. Such mystery.

We can learn to recognise this, to accept each person and love them as they are, and receive the gift of their insights.

We learn to be grateful for our own problems when we see others'!

While we are learning, it is valuable. With any therapy, this is so. If we stop learning, it may be time to go.

When our intuition tells us to leave, and there is no doubt or confusion in our minds, then it is very important to leave calmly with confidence and love. There is a real danger of indulgence in negativity in these groups, I feel. People get stuck in pain and stay too long. We have to watch out.

At a party I say how terrified I am of being on my own again. 'I don't even have a cat' I say. I never dared get one for fear of having to abandon it later. And Cathy says "Would you like mine? I have to move to town' 'What colour is it ?' I ask 'Black'. 'Aah. What's his name?' 'Sprog. He likes a lot of laps.' 'Aah. Yes, yes I would'. So later on I drive across the Blackdowns to Wellington to be introduced and as Sprog walks meditatively in I know he is my cat. My night sky cat. He sits quite still for hours in the cobbled courtyard in the night, contemplating.

When I agreed to grow veggies, I also hesitantly agreed to weed the hillside water and rock garden. I didn't actually know which were weeds. Another deep end. Reminiscent of starting at the Tutorial College teaching A-level when I had never taught A-level before, and had not taught at all for countless years. Always in at the deep end. Anyway my friend Ann came to stay for the weekend and taught me weeds very effectively.

So that is all right. And Carol tells me seriously to not do one thing for more than half an hour, while I got used to the physical work. I took her advice and was very careful. Within a few months I am also avidly wielding some Felco secateurs that Ben gave me, (he has been successfully occupied as a landscape gardener for years...he decided, wise boy, to train after Dan died.... He said 'I'm going to grow things'. And he has never had to advertise for work.

My confidence is growing, and by the time I was taken off of veggie growing and put on the overgrown main gardens instead I was itching to get to them.

I embark on three years of becoming wild woman of the woods, or to use Lora's husband Bob's phrase, Barley Hill's resident garden gnome. I take to it like a duck to water. I can't look after the veggie garden too , no time, and am sad to see it begin to be swallowed up in weeds. *(I dreamt of it fully restored to walled garden glory, and lo and behold Chloe and Neil arrived and did just that so they could have a private garden, and I was able to share it and grow all my veggies again. We even got chickens. Fresh picked organic veg and free range hens.)*
The simple life claims me completely. High maintenance, complex lives with much property are simply draining, stressing, and make you insecure with fears of loss

In my simplicity, with fresh air and exercise, I am getting stronger and healthier all the time. Stresses have become manageable challenges. Fears are all but gone. I have a cat on my lap when I sit down exhausted, and who likes to perch on my side as I sleep. I wake to his weight and to his purr.

A great wave of tenderness washes through my being…. For myself and for the world.

I feel held in the arms of the universe.

I am completely free of migraines, have been since the autumn of 2000.

….and to date I still am. Thank God.

273

Hotbed May 2001

is my triumph. I have never felt so confident as I do during and after it. 100 women composers and songwriters, a great 4 day tapestry of events, workshops, concerts, a surge of connections and sharings. All in the magnificent setting of the Tacchi Morris Arts Centre in Taunton….all glass and light, with proper dance studios, theatre, and music rooms.

I am proud. There were lots of mistakes, but these helped people, it seemed, they said 'It was so inspiring to see how you all just kept going anyway, and everything was fine'. We don't have to get it all right. This is Angela's gift to me, I think, not minding when things aren't right. She is singularly undisturbed by criticism, and very accepting. A great gift.

Afterwards I listened to Angela and Richard talking about the concert being arranged in Tuscany and I wailed 'I want to go too' and they said 'well, then you must come'.

Volterra, Tuscany. June 2001

In Volterra I fall in love with Italy, of course!!!!!

Oh the passion of it all. The sunny lunches in the great golden piazza, birds wheeling around the towers, the laughter. There are jugs of red wine and I have not been able to drink red wine for years, it gave me headaches even to smell it. But there and then I knew I had to join in. And I did. And I was fine and have been ever since. I made a decision not to allow my past experiences to limit my present. I chose powerfully, unaware almost of what I was doing.

And oh, oh, that first bruschetta. Oh my God. Ecstasy. And Richard saying cheekily 'well, there's nothing quite like the first time…'

A feast, it is, of food drink music emotion and beauty. The box at the concert, we smuggle in a bottle of wine and drink it from the bottle and weep through the whole thing, it is so moving. Children bussed from all over Europe to sing.

And in a small piazza next day, choirs of English and German children singing to each other from different corners. And all the children together in procession around the town…singing their hearts out.

It is summer solstice while we are there and Jenny (my dear friend who came too!) and I conduct an improvised but substantial ceremony around the font in the Battistero of the church. After a while Angela and her Latvian vet Rainis come and join in, and soon tourists were arriving and are remarkably receptive to it all. At night we sit singing in a field with beer and cheese (also Latvian style) amid a thousand fireflies…..

And Florence on the way back just Jenny and I staying in the decrepit faded grandeur of the top floor of a Palazzo overlooking Piazza Santo Spirito. Picnicking graciously up there on the terrazzo, eating Italian goodies, with a woman composer and her husband.

I say in Volterra, **'The Music is healing me'**. And when I got back, Kathy Jones says to me, talking about my work for the festival: **'It's all about the music isn't it? The music is healing you'.** I only have to love the music. All the rest, all the organisation, I just need to do my best and then relax and leave it in the hands of the Goddess. Easier said than done.

July

Well, I looked at the photos of Volterra and said 'aaargh, look at me' and determined to lose weight. It's going well and pounds are dropping away. I've often been able to lose weight successfully but I never think I can do it before I start, I just love all the wrong things....fatty meat, cheese, bread, pain au chocolat....
I try to keep to 1000 cals a day, but have a meal or a day off here and there to confuse my metabolism. I have some staple foods which help, and I probably keep low fat cream cheese in business.

17 August

We just heard that Gribble Booth and Taylor have returned our unfairly disputed Higher Sea House deposit *by mistake*. Just like they once paid their rent *by mistake* in Queen St. when they were my tenant! Extraordinary. Both times it was clearly right that the money was paid. I'd love to hear the conversation when they tell our landlords what they have done!

18 &19 August The Dark Goddess

I am reluctantly on a Weekend workshop with Jane Meredith 'The Dark Goddess'.

I am sitting in the courtyard café at the Glastonbury experience, writing this. It is raining very finely so I am alone. I was brought here by the 'Inanna' card, chosen at the end of the Goddess Conference two weeks ago. I saw it and thought oh no I've done that. I don't want to dive into all that agony again deliberately, don't want to open up the wounds that are healing so fast with the music and the garden. But I have obeyed and here I am.

Yesterday, in slow deep ritual, face to face with the Dark Goddess – a very clear mirror under the cloth of the black altar at the centre of an elaborately constructed labyrinthine path. I didn't expect this, though I guess I should have, and I saw with shock my own terrible pain and I wept. I felt the pain burning the roof of my mouth, my eyes, my temple, and stabbing at my heart. Last night we left the workshop, to spend a night 'on the meat hook', as Inanna did in the underworld, until meeting again today.

I think it should probably be residential. Driving home in that space....and then at midnight I shut my door and slugs snails and a frog all got killed. I almost screamed when the door resisted and I pushed harder and harder and then I opened it again and saw the squashed remains of the frog and then the slugs and snails. It seems they all made for my doorjamb as I sat and paced with my agony in my dark place of fear and pain, and they were all there when I shut the door - I found my murderous self. I was struck still and silent with horror and shame curled me hotly into a ball.

MY FAVOURITE SLIMMING PASTA

Boil your favourite pasta, and stir in a good dollop of low fat cream cheese, so the pasta is well covered. Stir in some fresh ground black pepper, and a dash of cayenne pepper, then add some prawns, grilled mushrooms and chargrilled red peppers, and baby spinach leaves. It only takes a moment to heat through. The spinach will just wilt.

Serve straight away, not too well mixed, so you still see all the deep colours of the vegetables. You could add a few shavings of parmesan...it weighs so little its hardly any any cals, which is a godsend.

I also like tomato puree blended in along with the cream cheese. Grilled courgettes are good added too, or sundried tomatoes.

SMOKED MACKEREL PATE

Pull the skin off a packet of the fish and flake the flesh up. Add nearly half a normal tub of cheese and a big spoon of light mayo, a few shakes of Tabasco sauce, white pepper, chopped chives and parsley, juice of a lemon. Mix it up strongly so it's smooth. Use a blender if you like. Push down into a bowl, flatten top with a fork, and chill. This will last days and days for lunch with wholemeal toast or ryvita. No butter!

MORE ON LOW FAT CREAM CHEESE

Fill celery chunks with it, or smoked salmon, or red peppers. Or mix it with light mayo and low fat yogurt for a dip for crudités. Slice leeks thinly and fry softly with a tiny bit of oil, then stir in the cheese . Or melt the cheese, add some yogurt and heat through with lots of chopped herbs and pour over vegetables.

AND OTHER LOW CAL GOODIES

Veggies roasted with a little olive oil, or grilled veggies, with some parmesan. Casseroles made without sautéing onion, just throw everything in a pot in liquid and cook. Tins of chopped tomatoes or fresh tomatoes, make a good liquid. Jars of low cal sauces are useful too. Chargrilled chicken breast and lean bacon on top of lots of leaves. Fresh tomatoes and chopped onion and parsley on wholemeal toast, no butter, but plenty of black pepper.

Seafood griddled and eaten with low cal mayo with lemon juice stirred in. 'Instant' soups made by boiling up a stock cube and adding fine chopped veggies, herbs and maybe tomato puree. Blend or not as you fancy. If you have cooked chicken etc, add a little of that too.

....and it happens that this weekend its been two weeks that I don't know where Ben is and that triggers huge fears. I can't find him. His friends don't know either. It all compounds, as I have opened up the wounds, and past present and fear of future pains all pile up and overflow.

But in the early hours, perhaps three o'clock, I walk outside, and suddenly I lift my head and am shocked again by the stars, clear and brilliant, just as when Jane this morning took us on an inner journey and we emerged from the Gate of the Underworld into the night sky and the stars.

Inanna on the meat hook for three days and three nights. Christ on the Cross. The dark of the moon for three nights. So many stories tell of this theme.

I have drawn the Courage card for the weekend, and a card saying 'Don't procrastinate just do it'. I know I will have to let it all out in front of the group. Well, I do it. Jennifer helps by 'going' first and letting go right into her pain, and a chant rises **'Tell it like it is. Tell it like it is'**. Jane says to me, 'open your eyes don't go into yourself'. And I howl with my head up and my eyes wide open and I see the circle of eyes full of support and love and I find myself throwing myself onto the cushions and losing control and letting it all out. Big sounds pouring from me. Huge sounds. Shame, guilt, rage, fear, incomprehension at my aloneness, my losses, my unwantedness. My throat is wide open. Like my eyes. No thinking just the emotion. No pretending. No hiding. Arms around me, hands stroking me voices soft in my ears, strong gentle soft hands on my forehead.

Later in small groups, I have my turn to lie face down on the cushions again and the women say to me words I have asked them to say and much more. 'Sandra, you deserve the love of a good man' 'a strong competent caring man' 'a man who will enjoy you' 'no more guilt' 'no more shame'.

Reminded me of Sancreed Holy Well in 1997 the summer after Dan died. Rachel started crying for a lover who had drowned, and I was able to cry too, to howl, and wail, and sob. And we fell to the ground holding each other and everyone heaped themselves onto us and I felt all the weight and warmth of those bodies, the warmth of all that compassion.

It was the week Princess Diana died. We were in such utter disbelief. We walked to the nearest stone circle and held a ceremony for her, and for all our lost loves.

Anyway, back to the workshop....'*And when you have your first argument*' says Stella firmly ' *don't run away into the sea*'.

She sees me as a Selkie, says there was something fey about me, and I had drawn the seal card. Always there is that longing to retreat into the Spirit Sea when things are not as I feel they should be. That Glittering Sea that stretches through and beyond us all, the gold of the Divine immanent and transcendent, the Love that is our Home. The Spaces between, the potency that lies there immeasurable. But I am here to learn to relate to people this lifetime, not to the Divine. That Love will help me on the path, but I know I will always be tempted to slide into the Silky Sea and I will remember Stella's words when my man comes to me.

And John said to me as he watched me in the waves, 'you are so at one with the sea' 'I wish I could join you ' and Swithin said I want to take lessons so I can swim with you'.

25 August

I am sitting in Lora's conservatory, 'babysitting' George and Grace. This is the first weekend I am at home since the beginning of July. Heart of the Goddess course, Goddess Conference, Catering for Ros's 60th birthday, Mum's birthday for 3 days, the Dark Goddess. As well as the gardening. And lots of work for Jules.

I am very excited about the Scillies, where Ros and I are to stay in 'The White House' - a flat above the village bakery/shop/PO on a promontory with Tresco just across the water and the sea on 3 sides. And I can scarcely take in that I am going to Iceland in the fall with Philippa on the way to see Glenn and Nancy in Vermont.

With Ben in Bristol this week…delicious scampi and chips by the river, cappuccino in Millennium Square, 2 Imax films, so nice to share all that with him. And Ben bought me my dress for my Initiation. We saw it in Chandni Chowk and I was riveted. I had thought to get blue material and embroider it with oh so much, but Reality tells me no, I cant do this. So I buy this yellow and orange dress, and I will buy the gold mesh I saw and it will be a veil, and I will plait a golden Girdle, and my black velvet cloak that Miro bought me years ago, which carries memories of such humiliation and abuse and fear, will be transmuted by the event. I hid from a drunken lashing Miro, wrapped up in it all night in the barn after the Hunt Ball at Castle Drogo, shivering. I don't need all that drama any more.

Sacred drama now…..The Initiation is to be in the dark in Chalice Well gardens. I know it will be deep magic and the black cloak, my dark side, will be there in its power, unprojected, protected, recognised and harnessed. My pain is becoming my power.

It is a very still silent evening. The sun is down now and the young moon is white in the pinking sky.

8 September

I am sitting outside in the September sun, listening to the wind in the tall trees. This is one of the things I most love here at Barley Hill. Tall trees roaring but only a breeze in the garden whispering gently into my cobbled courtyard. Sprog sits in the open French windows watching everything stirring. Music drifts out - Vaughan Williams Mass in G Minor. I will pick vegetables soon and make soup for lunch.

The garden, the land, the great views, have become the mainstays of my life. I pour love into the neglected earth, and I excitedly clear tangles and jungles. By the top pond I cut back a mass of bramble the size of a garden shed and find a paved area big enough for a seat. One is brought up. Now I start taking my coffee up to this high seat and drink in the view across the top of the magical steep rock and water garden and the far vistas of glowing golden green of lush South Somerset. This garden is like fairyland to me, so densely planted with unusual trees and shrubs, grasses, heathers and herbs. In a little walled garden I uncover a sundial, a big circular brick edged bed, and beautiful brick segmented wheels for herbs. Down at the bottom are rock steps down to the lowest pond, and there are great Gunnera there breathing again as the mass of bramble, nettle and bindweed is cleared away. One day I start the garden in front of Wyn's window in the annexe. She can't see out of her window and the window is invisible from the path. Slowly I cut through, it's like the Sleeping Beauty, and I laugh as I cut, and finally I am revealing her face at the window, amazed as all the light floods in.

And every day I go and cut and dig my vegetables for my meals. All completely organic. How healthy a life can you get? Fresh air, exercise, beauty, a garden to restore, fresh picked veg. I am fortunate indeed. The weight is dropping off. I feel I am stepping out of a suit of protective fat that I saw as my only resource for so long. I no longer need the protection. I am emerging.

I have been sometimes criticised for smugness. I don't feel smug, but if this appears so, it is spiritual pride- 'the last thing to go' said Roshi John Garrie. I can only keep watching. That 'Watching Brief' again – the second title of a hundred for my book, which I will one day get going on again when the time is right. The first title was 'One woman's Diary of a Year lived as if it were her Last'. I think it wont be smugness or pride when there is gratitude and humility? An ongoing watching brief certainly, and living with a sense of the Moment.

"The one who binds to himself a joy, does the winged life destroy; but the one who kisses the joy as it flies, lives in eternity's sunrise." William Blake

11 September

Living with a sense of the Moment whatever the Moment brings....

I am in the greenhouse when Wyn rushes out. 'Have you been watching television?' she says. 'Go, quickly, go'
I run back and switch on to see the second tower fall.
All afternoon I watch in the same disbelief as that when Princess Diana died.

But there is no one to share this moment with.

I sit there alone watching history, watching apocalypse, and what comes to me amidst it all is a thought which pours into my body and soul, and there is most certainly no smugness in this 'I don't want to be alone while I watch the world end'.

My father preached about how we can face disasters, huge and small. He was so wise, why did he never check I was OK in my marriage?

Scillies with Ros October 6

'Don't worry. Dance.' From Janice Griffiths 'The Courtyard in August'

....and from some other unrecorded book 'he enjoyed life immensely without forcing it on other people' . That is a lesson for me.

ROASTED VEGGIES

I adore this. Use more or less any veggies, in nice big chunks, maybe different shapes for different veg. Potatoes, sweet potatoes, squashes, courgettes, carrots, turnips and parsnips -in big chunks not slices, quartered onions – red and white, whole garlic cloves, fennel, leeks...season well to your taste. I like salt, black pepper, dry mustard, paprika (lots) , cayenne, and dried herbs. Toss it all in quite a lot of good olive oil with bare hands until all of it is coated and the spices are distributed well. Roast in a hottish oven for coming on for an hour, turning occasionally, until tender inside, crisp, browned. Don't overcook and do check for seasoning.. You could try adding middle eastern spices too...cumin and coriander, ginger...experiment.
This is great alone or with meats. Or add lumps of cheese at the end, let them melt...I like crumbled stilton, or feta.

GRIDDLED VEGGIES

Slice thickly some courgettes, aubergines (salt them first and leave till the juice comes out, then rinse and dry), onions, red and green peppers, mushrooms. Heat a cast iron griddle pan with a little olive oil. Fry the slices till nicely striped and cooked, it'll take several goes I expect- keep the cooked slices warm on a big flameproof platter in a low oven. Arrange the platter nicely, and dress with a balsamic dressing, or a few dashes of olive oil, or sprinkle with crumbled goat cheese or feta or sliced mozzarella and brown under a hot grill.

CRUDITES

Arrange on a favourite big platter an array of sticks of raw veggies... celery, courgette, carrot, peppers of all colours, cucumber, apple, mushroom slices, cauli or broccoli spriglets, mini corns, fennel, sugarsnap peas, and in the centre put a dish or dishes of dip. I like to mix good mayo with some vinaigrette and plain yogurt and add a little Tabasco to taste. Or try sour cream and chives, or add cream cheese to the mayo mixture, or yogurt with some vinaigrette and lots of fine chopped fresh green herbs. You must mix these well. You can also add lemon juice and beaten egg white to good mayo for a foamy effect

NETTLE SOUP

The healthiest thing of all...(it's proven)...to cleanse you in spring...
Gather a carrier bag stuffed full of young nettle tips, just the top leaves, the bright green ones not fully spread open. Wash them then cook down just in the water left from washing in a large pan till wilted. Make a nice lot of roux, add some veggie **stock** and milk to make a sauce, then add the nettles. Then whiz a lot with a hand held bender until smooth and green. Add more liquid if wanted. Season well with salt, pepper, cayenne., and maybe swirl with cream....

Such an exhilarating journey. Running across to the helicopter in the noise and the downdraft. Looking down, not high up, so little between us and the land and the sea. And lifting straight up from the ground. And we go via St Mary's which meant TWO lift-offs. Then the tractor trailer to the quayside and the tiny boat to Bryher, and then, almost the very best, standing on the trailer behind the Bushells' tractor which is waiting to take us to the White House. We lurch along, hanging onto the bar at the front.

I am feeling wonderful, newly released from fat. I wear black trousers and sweater which actually reveal my shape, and I feel proud of that shape. I NEVER wore fitted clothes.

Then this flat – one huge room with wide views on three sides to the sea, and this very swish open plan kitchen. All rippling with light. Our own little path to the beach.

Sun and wind and glittering sand, swathes of white sand and dune grasses. The water utterly clear, the colour of the sand below and becoming a web of gold threads in the sunshine. Or the stones. This transparency, purity is the magic here. I walk around the island. The sea has stripes of turquoise and violet –just like Fiji. Castles. Humps of islands.

Badplace Hill. Still the powerful ceremonial site I remember form '98. That feeling of offering up. Then, it was the herald of my trip, and of the end of my Centre, of the Big Fall in 99. Now we are praying for peace, as America bombs Afghanistan after September 11th. Ros and I chanted, sent out sounds of peace into the winds. This magnificent place, very flat-topped, great slabs of flat stone, brilliant green grassy knolls around the clear shallow pool in the centre. The pool is shaped a little
like a vulva, and it comes to me now that this was maybe a place of Goddess worship on what is said to be the last remnant of the lost land of Lyonesse. Who knows…. I offer up my aloneness.

We sat afterwards watching a seal. She stayed watching us too, for ages, seemingly equally fascinated.

From our windows we look out at Hangman's Rock, with its gibbet. The TV news is ever more alarming. We feel in the Shadow of Death, the world poised at the edge of the precipice. The quote 'the 21st century will be a Spiritual century or no century at all' springs to mind. We feel the tide of fear flooding into the world….

It all makes these exquisite moments here in this magical place even more precious. As each day, we walk, or take the boat to other islands, eat cream teas, lie on the mica-brilliant sand, and savour the sublime 'Scilly days', then return salty, suntanned, and windblown to the escalating horror of the News. But we feel we have to keep an eye on it and accept the intensity it brings to our time out here. It is contradiction. Life.

Initiation 22 October

The initiation ceremony is nearly complete and we are gathered in silence at the Chalice Well head in the dark, to come forward to speak our vows one by one.

'...and he was in the hinder part of the ship, asleep on a pillow, and came and awaked Him and said 'Master, carest Thou not that we perish?'

A storm has struck, and the boat is filling with water, and the disciples are anxious. Jesus says 'Why are ye so fearful? How is it ye have no faith?'

Jesus has been speaking to multitudes all day, and he has set off for the other side of the lake, to take refuge.

He falls asleep. He is RELAXED. Utterly and completely. There are many examples of this is the records of his life and work, that he knew how to relax, how to stop.

That is what so many millions today don't know how to do. We live under great strain. The world is a difficult place in which to be at peace.

The anxiety of the world situation, the horrors we see on television, the news coming so directly to us, the struggle of men to keep going, the dread of unemployment, the relentless whirl of life... the storm is upon us, and our little craft is threatened.

This has developed the disease of Worry. It affects body and mind, we cannot turn it off.

We bring trouble home with us...'take it to bed and wake up with it'. Look at people with their set teeth and furrowed brows. Watch their fidgeting, their restless fingers. It invades holidays...everything.

All of this is WASTAGE.

People do not know how to relax. They say the mind is the problem. We must relax our minds.

Why could Jesus sleep in the storm? Because he was perfectly at one with nature and with God so there could be no harm in anything for Him. On the night of His betrayal he left His peace to us ' behold the hour cometh, yea, is now come, that ye shall be scattered, every man to his own, and shall leave me alone, and yet I am not alone because the father is with me.'

Here is the secret of relaxation...God is available for us, His Power is at our disposal.

Let us relax our bodies and open them passively to the influx of new physical forces.

Let us relax our minds and give God's peace the chance to enter in.

The vitality of God may become ours – as we trust Him, he works – new energy pours into our souls, which are rejuvenated and fear, worry, and our slavery to them disappear.

Christ knew this the last nights of his life.
David knew this when he was hunted by Absalom, yet he slept.
Peter knew this sleeping between two soldiers on the eve of his execution.
The Duke of Argyle fast asleep on the night before his execution knew this, yet his betrayer paced the floor in torment.

Let us know this too.

Put in a full day's work, then unbend, relax, recreate our forces, come to stillness and find communion with God. Let us do it consciously.

God is the strength of our lives. We do not believe this and we fail.

Strain is not ended by fighting it, but by SURRENDERING.   AMEN

My Vow as Priestess of Avalon:

'Lady of Avalon
I come to You
I come to You in Love. For the rest of my life.

I vow to tread my path with You as Your witness, Your priestess, Your celebrant, with love, passion and peace in my heart.

I vow to honour You and Your Mysteries with awe, humility and gratitude, and to rest in the not knowing of their Realities.

My path of service is to inspire and to empower transformation whenever I hear Your call, and to demonstrate conscious joyous living.

May I honour all that is as it is.

May I tread lightly on Your Earth

May I walk tall with the pride of You within and centred in compassion

May I live with grace and transparency of spirit

May I live free in myself, free in the world, free in You.

May I align my will with Yours letting go all resistances

May I remember that in fear, overwhelm or confusion I need only surrender to You that You are all abundance and strength, that You love me, and will always meet my needs, that life is all magic and we walk within its power always.

May I have courage to face my pain and 'Tell it like it is'.

May I see always the unspeakable beauty of the ordinary day

And may I always bow deeply before Your Cosmos and Dance

Blessed Be'

Kathy Jones standing solemnly at the wellhead, her whispered message to me '**always remember that you are loved'**

23 October

Remembering Ros's party, when her clairvoyant healer friend Teresa said after talking with me, 'I have been asked to give you a message.' I look at her. 'It is to tell you to **always remember that you are loved'**. My heart leapt yet again. She also told me I had reached a very high level in this lifetime and would be free to go where I chose when I died – 'to the stars'. I said 'Thankyou so much'. I was aware of my ego purring, but I think I managed to keep a leash on it. I told no one this. But it is important to be able to be proud and also hold in humility the paradox of being aware/unaware of our stage in the spiritual journey, and to know that every stage on the journey is of equal value. It is not the arriving, it is the travelling. Creation is for creation's sake, not for the sake of the end of the journey - us coming home to God again.

Today I am swept with the Knowing that I am indeed loved. I was just thinking, 'I will say this all the time as an affirmation, when I realised, 'I don't need to. **I know this'.**

And I am saying to myself, 'I am a Priestess' and my back straightens and my head lifts. And my hair goes on growing, it is really long now, and my body is emerging from fat. My mother said, 'I just came in and saw you from behind, and it was like you were young again, slim, with your hair long and tied back like that.' I feel this too. Starting all over again 'knowing the place for the first time' as TS Eliot said.

Beside these Knowings is another. It is a sense of **not seeking any more, not needing to know any more, of being free, of just wanting to Live, now that I have a sense of how to....just to enjoy being.**

This is the big knowing. The big change. This IS IT.

I look around at this particularly bright autumn, and feel richly succulent and ripe....
And I have treats planned. Such as....

Iceland and USA with Philippa at Samhain

It is easier now to leave Sprog. He knows the place, he has friends opposite, he knows I come back.

It's a wild morning, 6.45, as I wait for Andrew's lights to blaze round the drive through the pouring rain and pitch black. We plough through floods and buffeting wind and emerge in huge relief at the bus station in Taunton. The coach is here, but I have caught it. What a noble deed, Andrew.

So, I am sitting in the coach, off to Iceland and the US, with Philippa. I'm meeting her at Heathrow. Its nearly Halloween, the Celtic Samhain, and I am very aware that this is the Celtic New year. I feel rather new actually. I'm wearing my new grey handmade Jeff Banks coat, £10 at the Somerset Hospice Shop, a complex and challenging affair incorporating a pocketed and sleeved waistcoat, and scarves. It's the very devil to put on. It has a handwritten maker's name in it. I've brought my Australian leather hat, the US can take this get-up I think. Underneath are my new cheapo black trousers and top which make me look almost slim!!!!!

I've lost still more weight and have bought new fitted clothes. I was rather astonished when I saw myself in a full-length mirror the other day and thought 'is that me?' Since July I've lost a stone and a half. (Fairly strict 1000 cals a day using a Weightwatchers diet collected from the Daily Mail all summer, except one day a week I have 'off' and I indulge in such glories as fatty cold meat, cheese, bread, pate, all my favourite wickednesses foodwise.) I'm carrying a £14 wheeled Woolworths suitcase, a wonder of ease and lightness, and a new £7 bag with pockets. Altogether I feel great arranged in all my bargains.

Icelandair check-in is hosted by Aer Lingus, and I find there are connections with Ireland with the land of Fire and Ice and Independent People. We slide into two seats for a hand and arm massage before flying, glorious beginning. I sniff my arms all day. Apparently there was a big queue earlier so we are very blessed.

It takes a long time to leave behind the wild wet of Britain below us but just about when the wine arrives, the sun blazes in and I tune into a classical music station and Faure blazes in too. I am in a surprisingly intense state of ecstasy as I eat my stuffed fish in orange crumbs, and my mini Toblerone, to Faure's Pavane and keep thinking 'I'm flying NORTH'. I've never flown north before. It's a new direction. Iceland has so long drawn me. One man told me over the reception counter at the Centre that if I was a country I was Iceland...?? I wasn't very keen on that at the time.

Now I would say archly 'Ah so you can see the fire underneath can you?' Progress or what?

Philippa moved early to a vacant window seat and I can see she is experiencing the same euphoria.

And so in our bliss we arrive at Keflavik and a coach takes across the khaki and ochre wastes which call to mind Crestone. The land is new and raw, bare and encrusted with streaks of lichens and mosses, great flat expanses of grey lava fields exposed and ferocious amid the sludgey tussocks.

We are just panicking at the terminus – problems with the phone, when Bibi, short for Jacobina, (Philippa's neice's ex-boyfriend's grandmother(!)) breezes in to whisk us to a studenty, arty, attic flat with a glowing pale pinky chestnut wooden floor. It also proves to have student neighbours, one girl and a stack of men to judge from the shoes outside, who play very loud music and appear to knock over a few wardrobes in the middle of the night????

There is crying too, and shouting, and I lie in this delicious attic, in the warm, in this comfy sofabed, and feel safely ABOVE it all. There's some sadness too, though, I find, being above all those messy frightening passions.....

Golden Circle

8 hours seeing the wonders of south west Iceland. More and more I want to return and hire a car.
Gullfoss: the 'Golden Falls'. Staggering power. Clouds of rainbow spray, frosted rocks and grasses, spiky crystals wherever the spray has frozen, searing ice-cold wind and pure pure air. Every alveolus of each lung is scoured with blades of silver steely air. We are breathless with the stab of each in -breath.

These falls are the 3rd largest in Europe and said to be the most beautiful. So many levels, so complex. What I love are the great frosted gullies and gorges full of rainbows, the rocks iced with crystals like elaborate castles, the seething roaring whiteness.

Then as the coach approaches the Great Geyser, it erupts hugely, shocking the crowd into gasps, and we are very welcomed because it only erupts twice a day. Then we are running in for hot chocolate and cream and cakes, still chilled from Gullfoss.

We drift around, gazing into blue pools of welling steaming water, walking over slippy deposits of salts of all colours, and there in front of us, we see our long long shadows haloed with rainbows! A truly arresting sight. We stood unable to tear ourselves away, feeling even more welcomed.

Shokkur is a geyser of about 25 metres, and just before it erupts there is a large very beautiful welling dome of intensely blue glassy water. then this shockingly, movingly, gaspingly, thrust of water, so big, so strong, and a deep sound is drawn from my lungs and my head is thrown back and my toes curl. It is very sensual, very sexual. We watch three times and I feel I could stay for ever, gazing, waiting, gasping and it is so hard to move away.

More hot chocolate to restore warmth again and then we are off to Pingvellir, where the tectonic plates diverge. This means a lot to me, I taught tectonics for 9 years as part of Geography A Level and it was always my favourite bit of the syllabus.....Drama junkie that I am(!) This is also the place of the very first parliament and law-giving. The man who knew the law stood here and spoke the law from the heart by heart to the entire gathered population. I can see it all very clearly.

Our wonderful woman guide is probably exceptional, and we are so grateful for her gentleness, her smile, her great knowledge, for her sympathies with the pagan history of Iceland, with nature, and for her vivid recounting of the old stories.

When Christianity came to Iceland and it was decided to replace paganism with it, just as the decision was made there was a great eruption from the volcano and a huge and destructive spreading of lava. They asked themselves if it was an omen, but decided not. They said 'what has God got to do with volcanoes?' and they shut God off from nature. In later years after much successful harnessing of nature's forces - geothermal and water-as nature's masters they were just congratulating themselves when a rain of acid ash spewed over them and they had to retreat into the power station.

I loved the stories of the independent farmers, how each farm would have about 20 people, and was completely self-sufficient, making everything needed. Another story is of the visit of the King of Denmark, who wanted to meet an Icelandic farmer. One was found, but he said he took his hat off for no-one. The King agreed to this, and the two men met as equals and enjoyed each other's company, and met frequently after. The Icelandic farmer saw himself as presiding over his own kingdom of land, but he was always happy to open his doors to travellers. He visited the Danish King in Denmark too. The same King asked for a horse when the whole of the Golden Circle road had been built for his visit! He wanted to travel as the Icelanders did.

Our guide sang songs for us, and she also skilfully removed us from the 'pack' of coaches doing the rounds, which made all the difference.

The Blue Lagoon

Icy air slicing at naked skin, dashing across boarded decking to the milky-blue steaming morning waters. Sliding into the hot opaque silkiness, an involuntary aaaah gushes from my throat with my steaming breath. Powder-blue, surreal in its protecting swathes of steam, spread out over black jagged metallic lava which has welled from the centre of the earth: sprung from the heart of earth to show itself to us, to make new land, and through it well the healing waters, opaque with salts, depositing smooth glossy edges on the fierce lavas, in pastels and whites and golds.

Stillness, slowness, drifting, floating, in the hot waters from Gaia's belly, Gaia's womb. White-blue- clay-painted heads and shoulders motionless apparitions in the steam. Eerie. I look again and they are gone and others appear. Kind eyes show in clay-masked faces, hair plastered wetly, gentleness, softness.

Changing rooms of naked bodies, rows of hairdryers, high tech lockers, thick white towelling robes, pipes everywhere, great towering walls of lava bricks and glass. Hot chocolate sitting wrapped in robes on the decking drinking in warmth and the mesmerising sight through the glass wall.

In the distance floating beyond the plumes of steam from the invisible geothermal power-plant the volcano's shoulders strong, blue-grey. I am gazing to the horizon, to the mountains packed with unspeakable power. I feel in the presence of the stern face of God, and I feel the solidity of the power of the Icelanders control of the Power they guard. And spread at my feet the mercy of the warm waters, the Boddhisattva's compassion behind sternness.

Iceland was a very intense and powerful time, much like Colorado in 98 and Italy in June. Hard to really communicate these ecstatic times, but I can only be grateful, and also rather amazed at how I am financing them when I earn so very little. The flat in Reykjavik via Philippa, Ros paying for the flat on Bryher in the Scillies, Glenn and Nancy in Vermont, the special offer ticket.

Boston

Flying down into Boston through the night sky. At first just little glimpses of jewels through clouds, then more and more and then all the clouds were gone and I was out there flying with huge feathered wings through the clear cold still night sky over this vast jewelled black carpet. I can still see it. Twinkling glittering faceted sparkling glowing gems and fine gold and silver threads all spread out in a great web.

Dear Nanny's exuberant welcome, and her usual hair-raising whoosh through the traffic. At 75 she drives like a 20 year old, with huge confidence and panache and terrifying speed, dancing across the myriad lanes with bloodthirsty relish.

Now I am sitting propped up against a quilted rosy headboard looking out at the sunny leafy New England fall, the elegant clapboard shuttered houses dozing. My mug of tea has a hot air balloon on it. It is very quiet. The sheets are hand embroidered with pink daisies in fine cotton, with matching pillows.

A real power shower, and breakfast and then we are walking with a big and boisterous golden Labrador though the golden New England woods. Leaves fall like twirling golden rain with no hint of wind to dislodge them, they just fall, softly, all by themselves, ready to go. Bluest sky, great rocks around still ponds red-gold and green-gold with reflection. Berries and seas of crisp leaves.

Vermont

Right out of 'Little House on the Prairie' all barns and views and a hammock. I am swinging in it watching the waxing moon above the blue mountains in the east. Behind me sunset silhouettes the smoky Adirondacks in New York state.

287

America again, big, young, vigorous, brash, extrovert, expansive. Mammoth teaspoons and traffic cones and sandwiches, endless horizons....I need it.

Lying in the hammock again waiting now for the sun to rise, in my pyjamas and coat, scarves wrapped around my head. It doesn't, so I retreat to bed with tea and biscuits (gosh, *biscuits*!) and start to write, the sun is now pouring in on my page. I am very happy.

In Nancy's lovely clean dry house, I wrote:
My cottage is part of the earth. The damp wells up from the earth, as does, occasionally, the old horse pee from its long life as a stable. Spiders line each room with cobwebs. The fire breathes dust. Sprog leaks fur. My boots bring in mud. My nest seems lined with it all, a birds nest of woven natural materials, and it grounds me and I live in it happily, with blitzes now and again to keep it within limits.

But, oh, the joys of a spotless house.

Samhain (Halloween) Full moon

I am expected to lead the Samhain ceremony. Glenn introduces me as a Priestess of Avalon and I am given enormous respect as such, which is quite a new experience. Someone says their group hopes to be able to afford to bring 'people like me' over from the UK soon....??!! I guess, it's true, you are taken at your own valuation. If you dare to 'set yourself up' as something you are taken as that. I've never dared. It's a scary thing to do in many ways.

Its all been so full-on I've got exhausted again, so am lying in the hammock with the wind instead of climbing Mount Mansfield with the others!!!

Last night, at the exquisite circular straw-bale sanctuary built by Paul and Windsong. the circle dance was so beautiful, but I was anxious about managing the steps and drained of energy. So after the first slow ones, which I love, I withdrew and went out gently out into the dark wood surrounding the sanctuary. I walked through the lit gateway, around the lake, and began to walk the labyrinth, pacing slowly.

I felt very floaty and found I was imagining the scene from above.

The two circles. The circle of moving dancing energy, music, light and love glowing in the woods. And the dark circle of the labyrinth by the lake, with my still, silent, grey-cloaked figure moving into the centre, standing there motionless, then moving slowly out again. Feeling my sadness at being out of tune, out of step, but also glorying in my solitary role. It felt very poignant, and also painful.

I have been reading 'Communion with God' by Neale Donald Walsch. This feels like a big shift.
This morning some sea change. Feeling of Knowing it throughout my body as I read. That sort of shakiness. A vibrational shift.

Neale is saying:

It's all an illusion that we create. We powerfully and unconsciously set up situations for ourselves which will prove to us that old beliefs are right and we can say 'see? That's how it is for me.,.. it's not my fault.' Classic victim speak. 'Men are NEVER there for me' 'no one loves me' 'I always JUST get by' 'that always happens to me'.

Neale says 'Step out of the illusion. Live with it but not within it'. So you can witness it all. You are using illusions to create a localised contextual field within which you can experience and not just conceptualise one of the myriad aspects of Who You Are...USE this field. Consciously. Like an artist. Creating wonderful paintings....and extraordinary moments of grace.

For example to experience self as forgiveness, use the illusions of judgment, condemnation and superiority, by projecting these we create a cast of characters who will give us the opportunity to forgive....you are creating a contextual field in which to express/show up/ a certain aspect of the divinity within.

Advanced beings not only step outside they move away, putting the illusions behind them, and using the memory of them, their awareness of them elsewhere, as their contextual field.

I wrote down:

I chose and created the illusions of limited abundance – 'just having enough' – and of 'being alone' in order to fully experience my sufficiency, and to really know that I am always, often despite my own foolishness, looked after by God.

I chose and created the illusion of having no real mothering and of being personally and financially disempowered by a man to the extent of total loss of self esteem and then loss of property, credit, and solvency, in order to fully experience the process of mothering, parenting, and partnering myself, and to know that I am loved when I have nothing to give, and also to see my own goodness and strength. I chose the experience of living with joylessness and cruelty to see my own joy and kindness. I chose to be judgmental so I could attract people who would give me the opportunity to learn to accept and forgive.

How else would I know myself? Hard times, challenges, are a gift we give ourselves to see just how wonderful we are. Suffering is a path to God and a privilege....until we know we don't need it any more. UNTIL WE KNOW WE DON'T NEED IT ANY MORE...and we start to create our lives CONSCIOUSLY. Oh wow. I love this stuff.

Now, he also says, and this is a biggie:
There is NO MEANING TO ANYTHING SAVE WHAT WE GIVE IT. We *choose the meaning of* events in our lives. Life is meaningless.

No way, I say. I'm resisting it. It is making me feel lonely, I feel he is taking away all those messages from God that show up everywhere, that amaze me so endlessly.. I have been so so supported.

But......This is the MEANS by which we experience who we choose to be. We can decide what things mean. Don't ask WHY something is happening 'to you'. CHOOSE WHY IT IS HAPPENING.

This is what throws me completely, this is of immense significance.

WOW.. NOW THAT REALLY IS FREEDOM and POWER

Take the responsibility. All of it. Even for the meaning of what happens.

Make it up...give life its meaning ourselves, declare it, become who you choose to be in relation to it. Take care not to get into denial as you choose meanings though!

This really chucks out fear. It really is all up to us. Out of our decisions we define ourselves.

Happiness is a decision. Love is a decision. They are not reactions.

Actually its what I've always been doing, and it's what people find so hard to swallow. When Dan died, when I lost the centre and was bankrupted, when anything bad happens I have always ' seen the meaning' but actually what I was doing was choosing the meaning and people saw this and saw it as denial because I was looking for a meaning I wanted.

Typing this in Spain, I was excited all over again. Writing my book is a fantastic way to bring my journey together, to see it all of a piece and really apply all I have learned in the self-imposed tests of the moment. I can take it all further. I am writing the novel of my life. How did I choose to see what is happening right now? John being there so little? It means I wrote so much of this book. I would not have done it otherwise. It means we had time to get together more by phone, less demanding, working through stuff but with lots of SPACE between times together for processing, much less intense...I can see lots of benefits. I couldn't have been with him all that time anyway, I couldn't then have stayed in Spain for two years...he helped me a lot paying for overseeing his build, and later providing somewhere to live.

And I remember I chose the meaning of mum's dying.

And now in Vermont, I am choosing the meaning of Swithin's leaving. He said it meant, for one thing, that I am finishing this book and that I sold my house (right at the top of the market). He showed me what harmonious and peaceful loving can be like. He brought me to a deeper level of surrender and I can only be grateful for that and for the exquisite miracle of the *sacred sexuality we shared ... who knows, that beauty may come to us again..... with another. The trust is that we both created that in our lives and it moved us on and it can come again.....sustainably this time with the right partner.*

Life happens THROUGH us, not TO us. The journey is to mastery, to the wonder and glory of God in one's own body mind and soul, expressed in our lives. We understand all this at a cellular level, throughout the body.

A web..... a glittering sea of immeasurable energy, of love, that underpins all that is – immanent and transcendent - within and beyond - connecting everyone and everything in truth and beauty and unfathomable mystery.

'The Field' Lynne McTaggart calls it in her book on quantum physics and spirituality. Or to use Greg Braden's terms the 'Matrix'.

Lynne is an investigative journalist, whose research took her around the globe meeting top frontier scientists. This is revolutionary stuff – the stuff of sedition to the staid, conservative world of traditional science. In fact, many of the brave researchers here have been mocked, marginalized, had their funding yanked and so on, as they persisted in their work. *The Field* is about energy. This is quantum physics as you have never seen it before – as a life force that connects you, me, the planets and the past and the future. These scientists are making incredible discoveries that may link and explain such phenomena as remote viewing, distant healing, ESP, the role of intention in influencing outcomes, how homeopathy works and more. The link is *The Field*, short for the Zero Point Field, a universal quantum entity which most scientists have been ignoring for years. In fact, they have been subtracting it out of their work and their formulas – treating it as "white noise" that disturbs their hypothesis.

Montreal

We are off on a day out. Le cite de l'Isle. Mount Royal. Originally dedicated to Mary with a huge basilica exactly half the dimensions of St Peter's in Rome. It is called Mary Queen of the World Cathedral. Space, power, a vast and ornate central cupola, and *behind* this a powerful contrast, a simple figure of Mary in polished mid-brown wood, hanging seemingly in mid-air, against a backdrop of new moon and stars. Her bare feet point down delicately, one hand is held out poignantly and one is holding a golden globe with a cross (the earth and humanity's pain?). Her Face is compassion, humility, gentleness, simplicity, acceptance, grace. She wears a simple golden crown.

I light candles and I notice how few candles are lit here compared with other more ornate shrines. But here is the power. Why is she not recognised?

Another basilica to Mary, a gothic revival stunningly ornate building, Notre dame in Old Montreal, does not have the energy. It is full of tourists, flashing cameras, entrance fees, so different.

We had such fun, gazing at skyscrapers, the fabulous architecture, Chinatown, a highly stylish veggie restaurant in the centre with terrific sculptures, a dim atmospheric bar on the waterfront with the BEST chocolate truffle cake ever, being in Canada for the first time, driving along lake Champlain.

Found a lovely quote by Baudelaire and pinned it up. I like it best in the French:

'La, tout est l'ordre et beaute,
Luxe, calme et volupte.'

Lovely words– luxe...volupte....

mmmmmmmm.....

Christmas 2001

With my Mum – it was to be our last one together: I think we sensed it. The Methodist Church had been meeting in mum's sitting room for years, and there was a service there for Christmas. Mum and I prepared for it together. She was agitated, feeling unprepared as she is so weak now. 'We don't have enough advent candles' she said, distraught. 'Aha' I said 'it just so happens....' I had remembered the long plain white candles and glass candlesticks I had received in the Earth Mysteries random winter solstice celebration gift-giving. Mum marvelled as I produced them. I had wondered why they had come to me and now I knew.

It was a very poignant service for us. It was taken by an ex-president of the Methodist Conference, who appeared wearing long robes and an equal–armed cross pendant to take the service with full reverence in mum's sitting room.... We sang all the well known carols at the tops of our voices, unaccompanied, in that little sitting room. Mum sitting there trembling with pleasure. At the end I put out my angel cards and everyone took one, even (bemusedly) the minister. As always highly appropriate cards were drawn and everyone got quite emotional.

For her last ever Christmas present to me Mum gave me a poster enlargement of the 'Diamond ring' sun at the eclipse. She knows I love things like that. It also feels like a blessing of a new relationship when it comes. I told her I would like a partner one day.

When Ben and I set off up to the Moor for a snowy walk, she did her usual anxious 'phone in, let me know you're OK' and I was able so easily to laugh and say 'absolutely not mum' and she could laugh too and say 'thought probably not' and I could joke 'but you thought you'd give it a try'...and give her a hug. Breakthrough....so simple. But so huge and happy. WHY WHY WHY has it taken all my life to be able to deal with her anxieties and controls. To have it all acknowledged, out in the open, accepted, but with my boundaries in place.

Ben and I walked down Meldon in a blizzard, exhilarated.

QUANTUM PHYSICS

Is proving everything mystics have talked
of for centuries. The sacred and science
are converging, as I talked of when I
founded The Convergence Centre.
The 'field' or 'matrix' is the unifying
energy of all that is. It is found in the
spaces between, in the space within the
atom. It is immeasurable in conventional
science. It has been termed 'white noise'
and ignored.
This is a quantum area of no space, or all
space, and no time or all times – and it
seems to be where waves of energy and
information get exchanged. All that is
springs from this field of unlimited
potential.
The popular film 'What the bleep do we
know?' attempts to popularise this..
Yes it is being explained, but it also
remains a mystery.

December

So good to get home. Snowballs on the lawn. The sheep a dirty cream in the white orchard.

29 December

Driving back on deserted roads in the early hours from the Earth Mysteries dinner in Exeter. I am flying on great black wings under the white full moon, across blue-white fields of snow, dark blue hedges and woods, cobwebs of lights of small towns, scattered lights of farms amid the hills. It is 'the snowman' and I can hear the music in my head. Unspeakable glory. Silent night. I am utterly wonderstruck.

And driving there, the moon and Venus in the electric blue sunset sky, a strip of dark orange runs along the smoky black hills of the western horizon.

So many gorgeous events with all my friends, two weeks packed with them. Jenny's welcoming smoked salmon and samosa supper for Glenn, and the new Moon Sharing. Winchester, the Romanesque transept, lots of lovely Earth Mystery talk in the cathedral café, then the labyrinth on St Catherine's Hill. Making a fire up there in the dusk and watching all the city's lights appear below us, walking the labyrinth FAST for once, a sense of the ENERGY of transformation, dynamic rather than contemplative. A party at Angela's, and the Festival party, Glenn staying with me, Andrew and Lisa and the boys coming for lunch, so much laughing in my tiny kitchen. Companionship. I ask silently that a woman moves into the cottage opposite soon, a companion for me....

Then Glastonbury, talking about my travels for once over lunch. A rare thing, I always feel people don't want to hear. But Rosemary and Jenny and Sonja wanted to listen, and I found myself amazed at my own stories. The Goddess Temple glittering white for Danu and winter solstice, fabulous jewelled skulls on the altar. Bones, stones, bare branches hung with icicles. Then supper in Wells and the candlelit cathedral for the most exquisite concert of Christmas music. So much unspeakable beauty.

New Year's Eve 2001/2

Outside all is ice, white moon, crisp white grass, the air like sharp splinters in the lungs. Nothing moves. Nature pauses after her last outbreath of the old year. She waits, empty.

I am suspended in silent space, also pausing after my outbreaths, knowing the emptiness. Stars above, lights in the distance below me, a holy night.

My body has been saying all day 'stay home' and so I am. Jenny agrees and at midnight we agree we will both go outside and listen to the bells and drink a toast. Angela is still going to Wendy's, no iced-up lane negotiation needed for her. I dared to 'not go', to stay alone on this important night, to drink in the space before the new begins.

I sense a sea change not far off, as my three years of bankruptcy comes towards its end. I have adjusted with surprising ease to the simple financial life using cash, few bills, no credit, no borrowing. I spend what I have earned. I realise it all happened because of my lifelong fear of it. And I vow to myself that as the tide turns and abundance flows in to my life, I will keep my connection with the Goddess, I will keep my life simple, I will not fear AND I will not borrow unwisely.

So I stand outside in the cold clear night and feel the 'stripped' phase pass away. I thank Goddess for seeing me through it all, and for all the gifts it brought. What abundance I have had in my restricted life....riches are truly not material they are riches of experience.

I thank Her too for the new kindness with which I treat myself, after last year's revelations from Shakti Gawain and the Heart of the Goddess course. The practice has become deep-seated now, and I see more and more how Miro was the part of me that was so hard and cruel to myself, so irrational, tormenting. He has not surfaced in my life all year, although I know he is still in Exeter. I go there when I want or need to, but I don't often fear. When I do, I accept it and am kind to myself about it. It's understandable. I surrender it as best I can.

I thank her for the healing of the relationship with my mother.

I thank her for my lovely Ben, whose beautiful soul shines through his difficulties with life.

I thank her for the revelations in Neale Donald Walsch's book, and the confidence they gave me to choose both the meaning of the past and the nature of my future. It will be very different from my past, God willing.

I thank her for the Christmas present from my M&M client Jules: her book, 'the Moon: Myth and Image'. Inside she has written 'To a Real Moon Priestess'. What a gift.

I thank her for Angelika's final advice to me, not to sell so hard my way of being but to simply be it.

I thank Her for this year of new-found stability, of grounding in the Earth Mother, for the natural abundance all around me, for all the vegetables, for the land.

I ask her to help me to stand tall with Her presence within, and to help me remember I do not need recognition or approval but to just live my life my way, in love.

So at midnight I raise my glass alone but not alone to the newly met divine feminine, the great Mother

....and to the flow of bounty in 2002.

Battered but beloved photos of my mum, at 60 and 80.

Chapter 6   Abundance – My Mum

2002

January

Mum and I have agreed we can see no solution re the problem of her not being able to take care of herself eventually. She cannot transfer her house to me or even will it to me because of the bankruptcy. We can see that a Home would eat up her money in no time, and that I cannot stop work to care for her without too great a sacrifice. I know I simply can't do it. I am not proud of this but it is how it is. We are at peace now together, in acceptance of each other as we are, but it is a great strain at the same time. It is a dilemma that was worrying us a lot.

We are at least now able to talk about it. Previously, nothing was said and I felt she didn't really want me to have her flat. Or that I had to give up my life if I wanted it and do as she wanted….the price of having the flat…The last dregs of a lifetime of 'stuff' was still crouching there inside me eating at me. But then one day she did say 'it would help you wouldn't it if you had my flat when I die'. At first I couldn't respond properly, was ashamed to say yes, but eventually I could. Aaaaaaah…….And suddenly we could talk about it, and it was all so simple and easy. It is slow, this healing process. But we were almost there.

So we have decided to pray formally together, with a candle. 'We hand this situation over to You Lord and we trust You will look after us.' She speaks, and I speak, mum reads something from the Bible, and we have a quiet time, and then we both look up and we look into each other's eyes. It was done.

She says to me one day 'I admire how you have lived your life'. It reminds me of Dan saying once before he got really ill ' I admire how you manage your life'

She keeps going until my discharge from bankruptcy in March, though fading. I didn't often worry about the situation. I was getting more skilled at trusting.

Berne with Angela

We go for a conference (quite useless!) There is no snow, so we set off to find some... Memories of a little train chuntering up into a .white world. Hanging out of the window in ecstasy. Planning lots of railway journeys....

9 February

My money at the Festival (Angela is founder) has risen. Again I was able to ask for this. I really am moving on.

Today I have a new journal after so long. A sense of abundance comes with it. The last one has lasted nearly three years, three years of being in the financial wasteland of bankruptcy. And now, *in one month,* I will be out of it. I have to apply for a Certificate of Discharge. It has been very simple, and wholesome, using only what I earn. Work has appeared. The pride of travelling on money I have saved is quite something. How I managed to go to the Scillies, Iceland and the USA in the autumn I cant really say, but I did, thanks to Ros, Philippa, Glenn and Nancy.

And I have lost so much weight over the last eight months that I have just bought size 12 instead of getting stuck even in an 18... it's as if the fat was a resource, the only saved reserve I had. Once I was in my cottage and there was no-one to keep putting rich sauces and apple crumble in front of me, and the Discharge was only months away, the weight went. I have lost two stone.

I am earning a lot (relatively) now from the Festival, and I have been shopping! So, moving into new abundant times. I am sitting in my car by the river in Frenchweir, waiting for Jenny. We are going to walk along the river into town to have tea. I am concerned about how I learn to live in abundance without fear of loss. I am struggling with this. I recall Jules saying: money flows in and out like the tides.

I talk with Carol. 'It's the same process' she says. And so it is: the same process as for dealing with poverty consciousness and with the mum situation. Be grateful, love what I have, trust and surrender.

I read 'The Abundance Book'. 'I am a rich woman' I say 'I am safe in the arms of the Universe'.

18 April   My birthday

London with Angela and Ben.   Such excitement. Visiting a corporate entertainment barge underneath Canary Wharf and talking about a Foundation launch there ....then the Eye, dinner in Chinatown, then, dancing in the smoke of the Hippodrome in the early hours. What a way to become 56.

8 May

So much happens, life is so full, I am always meaning to write my journal but I never do. The fabulous week in Berne, Louise and Rob's wedding in Bickleigh castle before the great fireplace, the conference at divine Dartington, a birthday day in London, the week in Cadgwith with 5 other women in the bungalow with massive conservatory with view I had admired for so long from Vine Cottage. ...as always, life overflowing with treats. Tonight I am sitting by my log fire writing in it at last because my power is off, it has been on and off for days. And indeed, the usual reflection in action, I have been feeling very emotional and powerless, because of the escalation of the harassing letters my Mum gets from Miro. Thinking this, I have just realised the water pump is probably overloading the circuits - see what is going on inside and that will indicate what is going on outside......

But then tonight I felt a switch within, about the time I realised it was the water pump, I also suddenly impulsively called Terry the Chagford postman who does odd jobs for mum. I spoke to him about the endless flood of mad letters from Miro to Mum for me, which I have been paying to have redirected to his mental health worker to spare her receiving them. The redirection payment has run out and there are problems renewing. I am so angry about this, at this endless harassment. Terry said he can refuse them, using a red sticker saying 'gone away', which is of course true. What a gift. This seemed so momentous, all the pressure lifted off me. It feels like a sign that the harassment is coming to an end.

And indeed not long after that, I hear from several separate people that Miro had returned to Serbia. I take the news with surprising equanimity, but am pleased the next time I go into Exeter that I do not have to keep an eye open in case he is around.

I thought in Spain writing this in 2004, gosh, that's not long ago. It feels like a lifetime ago. He was in my life until only 2 years ago. No wonder there was never a man. How could there be? Once he was out of my life completely it began to feel a faint possibility. It seems I had to not only work so much on myself, I had to let go of Queen St, and endure the consequences and then I could just begin to feel free....

Mum is failing fast now I am released from bankruptcy. She had clearly consciously waited for my freedom. She keeps falling. Every fall seems to make her mind slip – mini strokes I believe. I am organising Hotbed 2002 and running up and down to Dartmoor to her. Several times she is put into hospital. Her wonderful support network in Chagford (especially her friend Angela who is certainly an angel) look after her. I will always be grateful to them.

I struggle with wondering if I should give everything up and move in with her, but knew I would go mad. I would not survive. She seems to accept this. She keeps slipping. One day she says, 'Miro has gone hasn't he?' 'yes,' I say 'he has gone back

ABUNDANCE

Focus first on the flow of spiritual abundance, not material

Forget the effect, except for the bubbling up gratitude for 'what is'. Money is not the supply, Spirit is. Money is the effect. When we concentrate on the effect we forget the cause and stop the flow.
Money is not the source
of our supply, substance, security, support, safety, or our abundance, richness, happiness, peace or joy. God is.
Focus on the Source not the channel; see the infinity of the Flow, the waves of Good, coming from every direction. See the abundance of nature. Wonder at it.
Use the Supply in peace, love and joy: support the Flow and it will support us.
Trust the flow, give generously, give money to charities, buy what you know is right to have.
But don't fall into the trap of doing that out of pride, then ego will block the flow of spirit which is the source.
Abundance is a gift.
Never be afraid of losing, or fear future lack...that will disconnect you and block flow.
Concentrate on connection and on gratitude.
Paradoxically...also take care to live within your means, and to take action when money is needed – but not in a martyred way. Be grateful you can work.... Don't use this magic as a cop out from work.
Yes, I know. Hard to grasp.
Take care spiritually AND physically
'Trust Allah and tie up your camel'....
Ease will flow....

home'. 'And you've got a job?' 'yes, I've got a job'. 'And Ben is alright' 'Yes, Ben is alright'. 'I don't want to leave you but you're alright now aren't you?' 'Yes I'm alright now'. And she nods, satisfied, and goes back to sleep.

I lean in and whisper intently *'I'm sorry it took me so long to be alright mum'.* She nods faintly again.

I do what I can. In May before Hotbed she falls badly and is admitted to hospital again. Her mind has slipped badly too and she has no idea mostly what was what and who was who. But she does know me, though she thinks I am young again. The staff tell me she must not live alone again. They also tell me (*how wonderful is that?*) not to try to look after her myself. They say it might not be long before she doesn't know me. They say that she could go on like that for years. I try to take no notice of all that negative stuff, just kept on going, and trusting. It is constant mental and emotional discipline. 'Whatever', I say, 'whatever happens is for the highest good, just trust'. This mantra has been a mainstay for a year now.

But it is an awful time, torn between work and mum.

Hotbed 2002 and The Musical Masquerade

Hotbed is greatly appreciated again, but the highlight for me is the concert at Hestercombe. These gardens have a formal Gertrude Jekyll area and acres and acres of landscaped lake and woodlands with temples and grottos and beautiful lakes. Our event is a Summer Musical Masquerade. People – 400! - bring picnics and dress up and wear masks. We positioned musicians and singers all around….so that the public drifted from sound to sound. It was spectacular.

After strawberries and champagne, there was a performance by a quartet with a harpsichord with the Orangerie terrace as stage, and for this my Ben and a young black man volunteer, lit the hundreds of flares placed around the stage and steps and lawn where everyone sat. It was very moving for me to watch them.

I drifted around in my long floaty frock blissed out by what we had all created together.

At the end I helped blow them out and my hair (I always had rather a lot of hair – only nowadays do I keep it trimmed - interesting symbology) caught fire (probably because I had too much champagne).

Care for Mum

Once I am free of Hotbed I am able to research care homes. I soon realise she would be best in one near me. I am told good rooms are like gold-dust. A ground floor en suite?…no way….! Angela tells me she's often visited one called Sunnyside and they were always hugging the old people…that sounds what I want so I call them and say what I need. 'Oh no, we're full dear' someone said cosily, but then another voice called out 'No, wait'. *Just that morning* someone had given notice of moving out…and so a newly-built room with bathroom on the ground floor was available and I took it for mum, terrified as I realised what a huge financial commitment it was. £1200 per month. But they were just wonderful and they did hug all the time and they truly loved mum. I felt I was on course but it was a very hard time.

One day Ben and I go, feeling quite ill about it all, nervous of how she would be, to Okehampton to travel up in the ambulance with her, but there was a mistake and it doesn't turn up. So it turned out that Mum makes the journey without us a day later when we are both working, and actually quite enjoys it to our and her own surprise. She got lots of male attention and she always loves that! I have been dreading it and it turned out that it was *not* something I had to do..... She was fine against all expectations, and lapped up all the attention. Ben and I wait for her at Sunnyside. I have brought all her favourite things up and arranged everything.

But it is all just absolutely heartbreaking.

Next morning early I walk in the heavy rain for an hour, weeping.

I have no journal for the time of mum's fading, and I have written about it later that year in the past tense...

She once said that once she couldn't be helping anyone any more she would not last long and she was true to her word. My dear dear mother took just six weeks to die. There was nothing really wrong with her. She had decided and she found her way. She ate little and had permanent diarrhoea. It was dreadful, but I got good at nursing, and I am glad I did. I spent every afternoon with her. It was a great and deep bond, that awful time taking her endlessly and painfully slowly across the two metres or so to the toilet. 'You see I told you you could do nursing' she said. Another time she said, 'I expect you are finding it all very interesting'. She knew me!

Indeed it was a new world to me, the care of the elderly, and I was as usual watching and listening and learning. She was occasionally lucid, and once said in great satisfaction that they didn't know what was wrong with her but she knew she wanted to 'go' and she was going to be able to go to heaven at last. I was, though I didn't know it then, witnessing conscious dying. She was doing it for me. She truly wanted me to have her money before it was all eaten up by fees, and before I exhausted myself with spending hours a day with her; the fact that she died is the measure of the depth of that wish.

Mum was admitted to hospital after only a month in the home. There I had to fight for her long-stated wish of non-intervention. Very difficult but I did it. I had to wait an hour and a half to talk with a doctor who could authorise it. She understood and I asked that the papers be changed while I watched. I wanted to be sure. She wrote 'KEEP COMFORTABLE ONLY'. I breathed a huge sigh of relief. Only the day before they had forced an awful and excruciating examination on her. I know because I was there the whole time holding her. But even that was meant to be because she was proud of her courage, and she'd always called herself a coward about pain. 'I was brave wasn't I' she said. 'Yes you were, mum' I said, 'you were very brave'.

Days passed. She lay there, a tiny shrivelled version of herself. She said, 'I'm going soon. I want to take you with me but I know I mustn't'. A pause, a sliver of hope, 'I mustn't?' 'No, 'I said ' I still want to be here mum, I want to live some more.' She nodded and accepted it.

Ages ago, I had arranged to go to Turkey with Angela, her teenage daughter Adrienne & our friend Gabrielle to stay with Belinda (an amazing lady in her late seventies) in her flat in Erdek on the Sea of Marmara. I said to my mum as she lay in hospital that I would cancel, no problem, go another time, I had loads of trips. She came to life, almost sat up, in agitation. 'Go' she said 'I want you to go Sandra'. It was the same voice I heard in the caravan on Dartmoor: her higher self speaking through. Eventually I said, 'Alright Mum. Ben will come in to see you.' She sagged in relief.

On her birthday she was 82. It was the day before I was going to the Minack Theatre and then the day after to Turkey. I brought her a little card of seabirds flying. She was very pleased with it. 'I saw seabirds' she said, 'I saw them flying right here'. She pointed into the middle of the room.

The nurses brought her a little cake. I will never forget how from her semi-coma she shot out a hand to grasp a piece and ate it with such tremendous appetite and gusto, then slipped away again.

It was to be her last food. Her last taste of the sweetness of life.

I sat with her for a while, went to buy the fizzy drinks for her she was asking for, then I kissed her goodbye and left for my trip. I looked back at her little body and almost drowned in love.

She looked like an angel, glowing and peaceful and still.

Minack

One moment I was totally focussed on that little yellow body on the hospital bed.

Then, suddenly, after sleeping all the way down to Cornwall in Rosie's Magic Bus, I woke as if from a long long nightmare to find myself transported to a seat in the Minack Theatre in bright sunshine with an impossibly turquoise sea below me. I was back in the world of life again.

We watched The Tempest and I marvelled at the rightness for this moment – a story about the integration of the Shadow self. In this performance, directed by a woman, (I *knew* it was before I looked afterwards!), Prospero embraces Caliban at the end. I felt such peace. Prue and I sat in the café with some of the cast and the director and talked about it all.

When I got back, late at night, there was a call from the hospital to say that as soon I left Mum plunged.

I called Ben and my cousin Terry. Ben said 'I haven't done much for Nana, I can do this'. I agonised about going, but the consensus of the nurses, Ben and Terry, and my gut feeling, was 'go'. Mum asked that I did and I had to respect that. She had waited until I was gone. She didn't know about the Minack, *she thought I had left for Turkey*. The nurses said people so often wait till they are alone to die. It's harder with people hanging on you.

So, I went. Looking back I think she was afraid she would somehow take me with her. Or that she wouldn't be able to go if I was there.

And I do feel I would have felt very alone in my cottage with it all, and very unsafe driving to and fro.

20 August Erdek, Turkey

On the 18th August, we all sat eating fresh fish on a restaurant boat in the balmy night air. All along the harbour in all the cafes men were roaring tumultuously at the football. We clinked glasses and toasted at every cheer. We toasted my mum.

At five oclock in the morning on the 19th there were great claps of thunder, exactly simultaneous with the prayer call from the mosque.

At twelve noon, Turkey time, Belinda said 'twelve o'clock girls, out of the sun', and we all, laughing at our obedience, wandered in to the thatched shack beach cafe that was our ' home' each long lovely beach day. And then, suddenly, there was a great wave which came right up the narrow beach and soaked all the towels and sent everyone running. It seemed to me strangely darker and hushed and I stood there quite still, watching the sea clutching at the top of the beach. It was rather biblical. They said perhaps it was a warship out at sea going too fast. I said to myself *'Mum?'*

Later that day the call came from Ben. Mum died peacefully at 10am. There is a two hour time difference. The wave came in at noon. She was clutching at me, perhaps.

I howled and wept, and they all clustered around me and wept too, and stroked and held me. Belinda said 'I couldn't cry when my mother died'. They poured me raki and I drank it gratefully. She and Gabrielle went out and bought two candles in glasses. We lit them and held hands around it. 'One for this life and one for the next' said Angela. They also bought a lily and a rose in a fan of pink pleated paper tied with ribbon.

Later that evening there were two very long prayer calls - usually at 5am and 5pm only. Belinda said without thinking, 'it's a special call, a lament, someone must have died,' and we all looked at each other in amazement.

It seems she chose or was chosen to die while I was away, while I was held in a circle of friends and not alone in my cottage. I wanted to be with her, but I was 'told' I didn't have to do that. Rather as Ben and I were spared the journey with her up to Somerset. I never cease to be amazed. The hospital told me there was no need for me to go home, there was nothing to be done. Ben has been into see her before and after she died. I would be home soon.

Next day I lay on the beach watching the seabirds against the blue sky, just like that 'last' birthday card I gave mum that she loved so much. 'Fly free Mum' I wrote in it. At first there's just a few; I look at them and I am seeing all my family in that other freer dimension. That's Mum I said to myself, that's Dan, that's Dad, then there were more that's Aunty Phyl I said , that's Nanny, that's Granny, that's the grandfathers I never met.....Aunty Betty, Uncle Eddie and so it went, the group of birds getting larger by the moment. What a reunion it was. She was a soul flying free, not trapped any longer in her poor racked body and mind. I watched the party in the sky for ages it seems, feeling so happy for her and for all of them I felt her triumph at being there, and her pleasure that she did it, she got to them, they had been calling her for years, I know. She waited till I was solvent again so I could inherit. She chose to go when I was here in this blissful place.

She managed it: at last she was 'taken by Jesus to heaven' as she so often begged to be. She was so angry with God that she was abandoned here in such discomfort and 'no use to anyone'.

Yesterday afternoon the rain and clouds went quietly away. They seemed to have come with the news of my mother's death. We could lie in the sun again, and drink beer as the sun went down into a violet softness. Eating lamb and aubergines, and then taking a chair and sitting by the water watching the moon rise. The harvest moon. Swimming in the dark translucent water. Playing sand fairies with Adrienne. Hunting socks and sandals distributed along the beach by a playful dog.

I did write some journal at the time for the last few days of the Turkish trip.....

Yesterday morning, waking to cloud, we took a bus ride, clattering into the blue-green mountains to a remote village where women sat plaiting red onions and an old woman in black swept the earth with a twig. (yes, a twig, not a bunch of twigs) We bought strings of red onions. Are we to carry them all the way to the UK?? Children gave us figs, wild mint, blackberries. A woman let down from her window a basket on a string for an onion.

This morning, oh, this morning. Most exquisite, delicate, of early mornings. Flawless. In a small boat we putter across glassy transparent water towards the narrow beach and row of thatched shack cafes; the empty glittering beach is new-raked, the cloudy olive groves spread from the sand to the cloudier layers of the mountains: a world new-minted after all the emotional journeys of the week. There have been many, not just mine: an intense time for us all.

Then on the returning boat.....
Waved off by the café owners from this little piece of paradise.
The boatman gestures to me to sit on the prow, and I slide astride the bowsprit, legs dangling in the warm milky water, head back against the mast. And the sky and the sea are flying around me and I am transported into the sublime. All is pure, clear, full of joy and of sorrow.

A seabird comes flying towards me and I look into its eyes and a tear leaves my eye and I say, choked, 'hello Mum, look at me'.

I feel visited, she has come to see me in my sorrow and my bliss.

She never could come to see me, only a few times, it was always me visiting her. But in her new freedom she visited MY place.

We are off home tomorrow, via Istanbul. My turning point. A new world is starting for me. How will I be without my mum?

We are both free now .

Istanbul

15 million people. I feel I just met Asia as a result of a lost taxi-driver. A new continent. A continent without mum. I felt so moved, touched a whole new continent within.

A million images flying colliding soaring sparking in my mind's eye. I can begin to glimpse India's impact and atmosphere now. We drove, weaving our way, fighting for space, through the tiny streets- through a roaring, singing firework of a city sizzling in colour sounds and smells. This city explodes in the mind, the heart, the soul, the body. It engulfs and floods your whole being. Narrow dark canyon streets of immensely tall ornate crumbling colourful buildings dressed with wrought iron lacework, full of men all over the street amid cars, bicycles, children, cats, with multilayered rows of washing strung high high above it all, and men dashing here and there weaving between cars, holding aloft silver and gold trays of tea glasses, and a man pushing a wooden display stand on wheels, and an old old bent man in a fez crossing unhurried before us calm in all the pouring jubilant chaos. Life cascades through the streets.

My feeling of this new continent in my life is, strangely in this world of no space at all, just that…..

Space.

How will I

Face

the

Space

No mum and her needs and demands and I can see it coming eventually, no work pressure.

23 August

I flew back to arrange everything.

What will remain with me is mum's face lying there in the lovely little chapel of rest at Sillifant and Sons in Exeter. I barely recognised her because her face was relaxed. She never could relax. She had found peace and it totally changed her face.

Her expression was absolutely *triumphant*. Satisfied.

She had done it, she had 'got to heaven'. She had done the right thing…she had managed to die leaving me her capital and flat, giving us that time to really come together as I nursed her but without causing either of us long-drawn-out suffering. It was an achievement and she knew it, not least because until recently she had I know found our relationship so difficult she was not wholeheartedly wanting to leave me such prosperity.

'I want everyone at my funeral to rejoice that I have gone onto heaven. Thank you all for everything.' Mum's minister read her words out at her funeral and we sang her chosen hymns and read her chosen reading; she was prepared for death to the last detail. Angela had bless her driven Ben and I down to Exeter in her sloe-purple Golf. My ancient red Polo would not have fitted the bill, especially as I had arranged for us all to go to the cathedral and light a candle for her in the Lady Chapel, and we had to lead the convoy of cars. Then, gradually, we all gathered in a beautiful room in the Royal Clarence hotel overlooking the Cathedral for a buffet. It was all graceful, elegant and stylish, just like her.

Friends from many times from her life were there, and all my Newell cousins who always manage to be there for us when needed. Just as their mum Betty, my mum's twin sister who died when in her 40s was there for me when I first had Dan.

Four friends were with Ben and I, and after everyone had gone, we lingered over more tea. Angela dealt with a over-friendly waiter who wouldn't stop telling us the tales of his time there by asking to see the ballroom, and then explaining to him that we needed to be quiet. And so at last we were left in peace to watch the sunset glow on the cathedral and the dusk begin to drop.

13 Oct Gara Rock Hotel Devon

This is my treat to myself after this year's long journey with mum.

Yesterday evening crouching over a little smoking smouldering pile of twigs and paper on the beach as the dusk settles on a clear sunny day and the sun sets gold. No red skies: an accurate forecast of today's first depression of the season, wild and wet and windy, swirling cloud and mist. I still managed to walk down to the beach and watch the waves for a couple of hours, then walked the cliffs in some trepidation for a further 2. I saw again from the other side (nice symbolism there) the gorgeous Salcombe beaches and the town clinging to its hillside.

Now I am watching Michael Palin's 'Sahara' and sipping liqueur. I have the sofa pulled into the big window so I can watch the wildness outside and feel so warm and snug and still. Lucy comes to join me tomorrow.

For quite a long time now I have woken up and bounced out of bed with pleasure at the new day. I don't remember experiencing this before, despite my increasing happiness of the last 2 years.

My new car sits gleaming outside. It's affecting me more than the house because it is in my life all the time. I say thankyou to mum at least every day. I talk to her a lot. I know she is pleased.

I am for the first time ever, wearing clothes that fit to my shape, showing my curves. I don't feel so ashamed of my belly. I don't have this longing to be flatter. I always wore clothes that went straight down but now I have stretchy things and I feel so womanly and actually proud of my shape. It's so new. But underneath all this I know I am getting too tired. I have a whole house to decorate. And the Festival is worrying me. I can't do it. I did tell Angela but neither of us could really face it.

24 November 2002 Bay View Bungalow Cadgwith

I am sitting…..

at last, I am just sitting.

On the cane sofa in this beautiful conservatory with the view spread out below me. I have lit a fire, made tea. The others will be here soon. The moon was nearly full and we watched it reflected in the sea as we ate our supper at the long conservatory table. I slept in the little sitting room where Jenny slept in the spring, with the doors open to the view. I lay watching it get light, but fell asleep again before the sun rose out of the sea.

I have just finished decorating the whole of No 7 Park Terrace in Chard. I am exhausted. My tenant has moved in. The long process is over and I can begin to take stock.

Suddenly I look back over the year and because I can, I crumple.

The power has been playing up. Interesting because I have none right now. We sat with candles, by the log fire. My body is stopping me in my over-fast tracks I think.

I sit still as the soft dark grows around me and lights in the huddled cottages below are deepening yellow. The smell of wood smoke curls up to me. The cliffs are strongly black now. The earth is soft, rich and full, heavy and replete with summer as she lies beneath the sky.

I lie with her, at rest.

5 December

I was very ill for two weeks. Quite frighteningly so, with a kidney infection, plus fever, weakness, vomiting, nosebleeds, heartburn (I'd never experienced that before - it was surprisingly bad for what sounds a mild complaint). Jayne brought me Gaviscom, which was a spectacular relief. I ate nothing for a whole week. I lost nearly half a stone. The doctor gave me two courses of antibiotics, and said I was probably anaemic. My hair was falling out too. I met the alarming vulnerability of being ill with no-one to care for me. But Lora, Jayne and Chloe saved the day. So I was all right. But I knew my body was talking to me. I knew I had to give in my notice as Coordinator of the festival. I knew in September I had to do this - I even told Angela - and I didn't. It as usual took illness to make me.

I tell Angela. It is New Moon. I feel a relief so big its proportions are still out of sight. I just couldn't dispel the anxiety about the Festival. Wendy says it is like an allergy. The chemical furore in the body leading up to, during and after the festival is enough to frighten the body into reacting against its impending repetition. Amazing but true, I think. I remember that fizzy feeling in the head that never went away. Event management is a nightmare really, especially when you are older and not in tip top form.

The first time I go into town I get a parking ticket, and a sympathetic traffic warden tells me to write and say I am an old lady and not well.....I suddenly feel a bit of fighting spirit welling up. I am NOT an old lady. Absolutely NOT. Next day I am definitely more myself and my hair looks less lank.

I will have a rest until after Tobago in January. Yes...Tobago....

19 December

I buy a fat Christmas tree, and it is lovely to lie on my sofa, and look at it and listen to carols.

Strange feeling, Christmas is here and I'm not going to mum's. I have time to sit with it and feel it and think of her and Christmasses past. Ben will come to share it with me here.

Its full moon and two evenings I looked up out of the window in the early dark and there suddenly totally unexpectedly the first time was the huge bright solstice moon right in the middle of my window.

On Christmas eve I wait in the chapter house of Exeter Cathedral for the Bishop Grandisson Christmas eve mass. It is such a favourite that people queue for hours. When we are finally admitted we can't believe it, we are in the second row at the very front.

This reminds me of that first Christmas after I left Miro. I was alone then, very fragile, but I queued patiently by myself and was shown to a seat in the very front, and watched as the great procession went slowly by and the rituals unfolded. Sacred theatre.

It made me feel on course.

As it does now.

MUM'S RECIPES

My grandmother wrote these...my mother used them all her life, and here they are

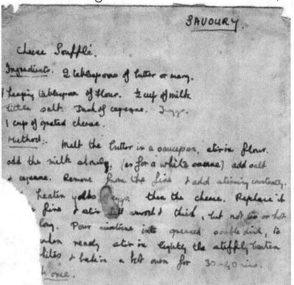

The missing bit : 'replace it on the fire & stir till smooth & thick, but not too hot or too long. Pour mixture into greased soufflé dish, to which when ready stir in lightly the stiffly beaten egg white and bake in a hot oven for 30-40 minutes. Serve at once.

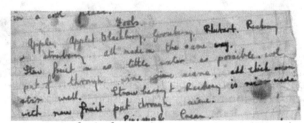

Mum used to make these fruit fools with cream AND custard. The set is better.

Junket and Caramel Cream were staples when I was a child. Bake the dish of cream caramel in a bain-marie, ie a roasting tin of cold water. This will give it a smooth bubble-free custard.

After Dancing the Maypole high on Dartmoor

Tobago, the waterfall pool, orange immortelle flowers
Scattered on the water Me floating in centre, with
Jenny, Sue just getting out.

Chapter 7   Into The Glory

2003

This year I have been asked to keep a diary of my ordinary life for the Priestess magazine, and I have copied some of it here. This path, the transformational path of the Priestesses of Avalon, has been so enormously helpful for me, connecting me to a softer more human, feminine, accepting divinity. It is earth-based, pantheistic, rooted in natural cycles, theatrical and colourful, and ….sacred theatre again of a very different kind but the same power at heart. What a contrast with the austere Zen work, but how wonderful are they both!! I feel it is so important to honour and RELISH IT ALL. Not everyone's way I know, but it is mine.,..

2 January late evening

Sitting by my fire, attempting to write over Sprog. The rain is pattering on the skylight, and the trees are roaring.

It is 2003 and I *don't* have to organize a Festival. It is taking time to know this! I have plenty of time. I can hardly believe I just wrote that. Me! I have plenty of time. To savour the simplicity and the beauty.

I've been walking often in the dusk - 'the magic hour' - taking in the space, the stillness, the silence, of Solstice in winter. I have never felt so much in touch with the energy of this time of year. I can feel the winter goddess Danu in the land, see her shapes, her vistas, her great perspectives. Time to see as I rest.

I've always been whizzy-busy from early December on, right through to June. Having to make an huge effort to hold Danu in my being so her spaciousness is not completely buried. This year I could really be with and celebrate the true nature of the Solstice and Christmas.

Reading Stuart Wilde's 'Whispering Winds of Change' (from Earth Mysteries group giveaway at Solstice celebration.) Perfectly reflects where I am beginning to find myself.

'We have to return to simplicity and enjoy the sheer wonder of finding ourselves human'

'Almost all yearning will have gone from your heart and you will know what works for you and what doesn't'

I am what I am. I am a slave to no one. Nothing has a hold over me, for I belong to myself. I know that I cannot fix the world, but I can offer an 'island of calm'

'Rest in the Now, using whatever comes to hand, waiting for those things you haven't got and forgetting that you ever wanted them'

'The simple worship of the Great Spirit and the Sacred Mother embodied in Nature - the tribes' quiet simple life far from ego, aligned to Nature through pantheistic religions with little or no dogma'

Every cell of my body is overflowing with gratitude. 'Emptying myself of everything but the joy of the moment'.

4 January

Everything very still, silent. Sitting on a rock in the hillside garden in bright sunshine, watching a fine fall of tiny crystals glittering in the cold air, falling so slowly, suspended, swirling. No clouds above, but some high wispy white ones moving away quite fast. The crystals- somehow crystals not snow – must have taken so long to fall the sky is blue above. The low sun is reflecting off the middle pool. The immanent sacred holds me.

5 January

Frozen ground. Frost crystals over a quarter of an inch. I cleared brambles. I love doing that. Creating new space. I feel so rich with time.

Sat 2 February

It is Imbolc, Bridie's festival of first light. I am sitting here in the Goddess Temple alone. I feel for the first time – I am a Priestess in the Temple of the Goddess. I am awed, humble and proud. And I am so glad to have this time to come and thank Her for the powerful space and silence of Her winter, and now for the first stirrings as Bridie passes over the sleeping land, waking the earth as she passes…. I can almost hear Her as She passes. Because I have been so deep in winter I can feel Her delicate coming.

The peace here is otherworldly, quite sublime. I brought the Festival team here in July. Niki said she felt a rare peace here and she took it with her as she traveled the US and Canada with her amazing one woman show. A remarkable tribute.

Just dipped into a magazine here. ' A deep subterranean river of earth-based spirituality with its myriad streams and tributaries, is re-emerging not a moment too soon.' I will quote this on the invitation to the Exeter Earth Mysteries group to a Spring Equinox ceremony in the Temple.

7-17 February *In Tobago in the Caribbean!!*

Unspoilt tropical paradise, another glorious face of the Goddess.

Rain forest studded with gold Immortelles dripping down steep hills to white beaches and coconut palms. A brimming, pouring feeling of 'World as Lover' (Joanna Macy's words) as I ride great waves kneeling in the prow of a tiny boat.

Dancing, dancing dancing at Buccoo's 'Sunday School' - beach bacchanalia! I danced with lots of Tobago men – what rhythm!- without misunderstanding- I thanked them and said I was going back to my friends. Best dancing of my life. Jenny and I felt we managed what could have been misunderstood rather well! I remember years ago when I was dancing rather wildly somewhere and felt so alone in my dance, and an old lady said to me, her eyes full of savoured memories… 'Go to the Caribbean my dear, there you'll find men who can dance with you…'. And oh I did, I did. I danced for hours, spinning whirling leaping gliding swooping.

It felt so huge to come on this trip, I booked it in blind faith nearly a year ago, and I was so nervous I forgot my passport, had to race back for it, and nearly missed my coach. Wyn, my neighbour drove me, racing excitedly, and caught the coach at the next stop…. Sue was on tenterhooks.

Sitting under a remote waterfall and floating in the natural pool as a confetti of orange Immortelle flowers drifted down on us. Fell in love with a village called Castara. Wooden shacks teetering on the edge of soft white sand, a sandy café literally overflowing with colour, fabrics, paintings and rampant plants called 'Heaven on Earth'

Jenny and Chris had been round the world and Sue and I met them in Antigua. We were dancing about at the top of the steps of a vast Boeing 777 to welcome them. The lovely BA staff had left us to it! Before that I had the pleasure of standing at the door,

(wrapped in the lovely hot air!) waving off the crew that brought us from the UK and welcoming on the new crew for the hop to Tobago. All quite momentous, .
(Many pages of diary follow...!)

26 February Shock.

The suddenness of death. My tenant, who I had begun to realise was mentally ill, has committed suicide.

On Sunday I heard. A friend said ' Go out in the garden and see what is coming up' and I did. I spent five hours gardening that day. Later the full moon shone in my window and magnified my maelstrom of feelings.

It has taken me until now for the vibration of shock to even begin to fade. I called to God and Goddess in total bewilderment. I let time pass and I felt the pain, and shame that this had happened to my tenant in my house. That this has come into my world again. I thought I was healing.

After a while I spoke of this to Angela, and said, 'I can only follow my usual recipe. Trust and surrender.' She said, very surprised at my shame, 'you don't have to own this'. I have too often 'taken on' responsibility where it is not mine. Then she said 'perhaps meeting you was her last chance, perhaps you were a gift to her'. And indeed Joan seemed to have sought me out to talk a great deal, but I felt I wasn't helping. But who knows perhaps some healing happened on a level I don't know. I had wanted my house to be a place of healing.

What Angela suggested was a whole new way of looking at things, and I felt that sort of cellular shifting right through my body that comes with big change. And I remembered reading recently that WE choose the meanings from events in our lives. We are THAT powerful. I recalled other people close to me saying similar things that I had felt it arrogant to 'hear'. Can I now know this in <u>gratitude</u> about myself?

Practically speaking, I am also grateful that my tenant did not do it in the house, and that she was moving out anyway and I have a company tenancy lined up, so I am not affected in that way. I think 'Enough of wanting a healing house. I just want a house that brings me income'. It felt a powerful thought, it's not so terrible to want abundance....

I have thanked my tenant's soul, lit a candle for her and prayed that she is at peace now. I will go through the house with love, incense, Tibetan bells.

5 March

A friend suggested I go with her to see the remake of the film 'Solaris'. A metaphysical love story set at the edge of the universe. The director says 'Even at the end of the galaxy we have to confront ourselves.' This ethereally beautiful film is about redemption after suicide! My friend didn't know about my tenant! I was sitting there transfixed in a brand new cinema, and out of the silence against the backdrop of the swirling violets and pinks of the planet Solaris came the words 'We are beyond all that now (alive or dead). Everything we did is forgiven us'.

8 March

The pace of growth is leaping now in the garden. I drift around it with my secateurs and a cup of tea, clearing branches that block the bulbs. I've been starting to desilt ponds and streams too – unblocking!! So growth can be freed and water (and emotions) can flow. How will this year unfold?

9 March Dartmoor

Deep in Dartmoor with fellow Priestesses Clare and Ciel yesterday. (What's the feminine of fellow??). After too large a Sunday Lunch we struggled up to the Stone Circle. But what had happened to the weather while we ate? Lashing horizontal rain. Finally we got there, saturated and huddling into ourselves. Some women and several dogs some distance away suddenly came and stood in the circle, not acknowledging us at all. Stayed there, ignoring us. Very weird for Dartmoor, people *always* say hello and didn't-expect-to-see-anyone-else-out-here-in-this……..

Eventually, after walking round the circle slowly 3 times, and still a dog sat right in the entrance and the women were still talking, we left, letting the icy wind blow us down the hill to Clare's warm cottage.. We knew we were not meant to enter this time. Soon after they all left too. Clare talked about the dog being the Guardian of the Underworld, and how the weather turned hostile whenever she took people to the circle…was the circle an entrance to the underworld? I began to think about how drawn I was feeling to that other dimension since my mother died. And now my tenant had taken refuge there. It feels so close, a whisper away. I felt I was being told, no, not now. Perhaps my closeness to the other worlds was part of what drew my tenant to me.

Round Clare's fire we shared in ceremonial space all that we had been feeling since we last met. It's just so valuable. We call ourselves Rainbow Beech, the rainbow part is the result of a rainbow *ending* on my car bonnet (it really did!) as I drove to our first gathering.

14 March

The Ceremony of Taking my Sunbed out of the Shed. Such a pleasure. Lying for the very first time in the newly born warm sun with a cup of tea and a book and Sprog rejecting my lap in favour of inserting himself between my face and the book. Suddenly there is no difficulty in doing my 14 hours of gardening a week..

16 March

War. It is hard to take in as I garden in the Idyll of an exceptionally lovely English Spring.

How can Life contain so much?

18 March

Rounding up walkabout sheep in my best coat and shoes. (Hole in the fence)

314

20 March

I took it in today. I watched a terrified woman journalist (so many women journalists out there) shaking so much she could barely get her gas mask on. In the background desert dust and men running and great shouts going up "GAS, GAS, GAS'. It was like those dreams where you need to run and are rooted to the spot. I felt what she was feeling. I was there for a moment.

I think of all the collective projections creating this war, and I watch in myself the different parts of me surfacing as they respond to it. There is definitely a part which seeks drama and which wants to 'get rid of evil'. This part has been small for some years, and I do not act from it, but I see it again now, and I remember all the 'wars' of my own rather tempestuous life. It was full of drama and conflict, agony and ecstasy, thunder and lightning. Colour. I explored that world and I am grateful for its richness and its lessons but I find my drama and colour in other ways now, thank Goddess.

In those days I lived for ten years on Dartmoor. It perfectly reflected my inner environment. I will always love the Moor, and I can see the Goddess of Dartmoor, so beautiful in her bleakness, wild and harsh, with her wind-flying grey hair streaming skeins of cloud, and her purple-grey heathery brackeny cloak, her arms outstretched, her buzzard circling and an adder coiled at her feet. Now, I live with the gentle Goddess of South Somerset, lying resting, half asleep in the green and gold Summerland, soft, warm, fertile and enfolding. Her robe is embroidered richly with flowers, birds, butterflies and fruit, and her hair is woven with ribbons and blossom. A basket of apples spills in plenty beside her and sheep sleep in the buttercups. I feel like painting these Goddesses.

21 March

Early morning walks these days in the exquisite hazy sun. Faint gleaming veil of mist. A young deer 50 yards ahead, stood, poised, large ears pricked, watching me, then walked slowly towards me. Suspended in time. No gap between me and nature for a moment. The he very slowly turned away into the woods.

Radio 4 talking about – 'the ritualisation of everything is necessary because everything has a spirit'. This is wonderful.

Later, the first butterfly of Spring. The extraordinary in the ordinary. Now, the silk soft poised dusk is still blue, even at 7 oclock. The early lemon tulips have closed their petals.

Rumi says – 'This is not a day for asking questions. Not a day on any calendar. This day is conscious of itself. This day is a lover, bread, and gentleness. More manifest than words can say'

I love this sooooo much. Reminds me of Joanna Macy's 'World as Lover, World as Self'. It's all out there, the Truth.

But Truth is not only beautiful, it is not only ecstasy, it is a fierce terrible beauty, a scalpel shining and slicing so sharply, such a fine edged blade it cuts as it touches, deeply, cleanly, drawing blood. It is a heady thing, when you let it in, and trust it. It is immaculate, impeccable. It does not let you down.

24 March Spring Equinox in the Goddess Temple

As an introduction to our Glastonbury work with Kathy Jones, for our group of friends, Clare and I took the circle (all sitting, relaxed, eyes closed), around the Wheel of Ana, which we had laid out with all its symbols, at the centre of our horseshoe of cushions facing the altar. There is a Goddess associated with each of the eight points of the compass. Clare and I took turns to describe, in full rich detail, what we saw *as each Goddess moved towards us as she was called to Her Temple*. We allowed silence between each. It was a profound experience I will not forget. We ended with Clare teaching us a Rumi moving meditation.....

"something ….is lifting…my wings…"

…..To Chalice Well and a picnic and good conversation with loving friends….and out in the clear air, one of us reads the Charge of The Goddess as we lie spread on the grass in the sun.

28 March

I am spread in the sun on my sunbed, with Sprog spread over me. The Chorus of the Hebrew Slaves pours out of the window. All is still and quiet here, everyone is out, the valley still hazy, the trees soft pearly smoke in the distance. Birds carrying bits for nests. Their song piercingly sweet. It almost hurts. I am diving into the moment. Soaring on the moment.

This is Spring and I am writing lazily in my journal not anxiously writing lists for the Festival.

It is probably too soon to say but I think something has shifted at the Festival. 7 of us are doing, with less hours each, what 3 of us did last time. I had a vision of this 'chunking' of work during the Goddess conference – I saw how things were done there. Again, strange but not strange how it has come about through events.
(My illness, and no-one to take over). Mysterious are Her ways…

10 April

Friends to stay and lots of picnics on sunny beaches…lots of nice things have been happening. Springy things. Theatres, playing with small children, Starla just walking, eating with friends, a kiln opening, painting…Mothers Day with Ben in Bristol in a trendy restaurant. And the great gift of him telling me how lucky we are to have no problems with each other, to have no needs from each other, so we can simply enjoy our times together…it is the first Mothers Day since Mum died, and we are free to go out!!

The red tulips are out. Very suddenly. And all the blossom trees are on the point of bursting. My birthday is on Good Friday this year. I don't recall that before. This year is to see a great rebirth…..? I feel a certain trepidation. Life is so good, but fear of loss sometimes creeps in, especially as the owners of Barley Hill are probably going to sell. I bring myself into the present, feel the gratitude for now, trust I will be looked after as I always have been, and accept and surrender my fears. It is a discipline, which after years of therapy and exploration, seems to me to become necessary to avoid indulging emotion. My watching brief..

I will spend my birthday in Stourhead gardens with Ben. It feels right. Late in Beltane I will be in the Lake District, at Castlerigg stone circle as the new moon shows herself. Images of Castlerigg have been calling me for a good few months now.

And now Ciel is inviting Clare and I to dance the Maypole at Beltane because she 'has poles outside'??... all will doubtless be revealed.

16 April

A month of sun. Today I made bread for the first time, and nettle soup. Felt such a connection with my father, who was a master baker. Then I baked *myself* in my bikini up on the hill, with the Sea Valley dreaming in the haze below. The luxury of solitude.

Sitting in a coffee bar in Street, in a comfy chair with a cappuccino, while my car is, amazingly, passing its MOT. Reading Goddess Within, which arrived today, and contains my Diary of a Priestess. I realize strongly that I want to invite others to share their diaries in the newsletter – what an insight into different ways of being a priestess. Who feels the urge to respond??

Writing this has somehow crystallized my own priestess experience, clarified for me who I am.

I had seen priestesshood as being ceremony- leading, teaching, community work etc, all on a large and organized scale, and felt this was not my thing. But it feels like my particular role is the quiet demonstration of the joy and passion of the simple life of connection with the Divine Feminine. Just ordinary living, but touching its extraordinariness.

I have in the past participated in two long, profound, facilitated Transformation Games (a Findhorn board game), and in both what came through was recognition for 'demonstrating conscious, joyous living'. It didn't really sink in that that is how I am a priestess – that unassuming, everyday ongoing practice of being gratefully in the moment with Spirit. At times, disciplined, but increasingly, luxurious.

Creating our own reality while simultaneously surrendering to 'whatever'. Holding the paradox. This, my truth, is my fundamental passion, and the journeying over a lifetime for this truth has been my deepest and most abiding preoccupation.

26 April

'Who was Jesus?' conference at Dartington with Millie and Mike and Andrew. Margaret Starbird was over from the US for it, a very modest woman, at pains to explain that her name is her husband's real one not a 'new age invention'. Some of the speakers moved me to welling tears.

THE CHARGE OF THE GODDESS

I who am the beauty
of the green earth and the white moon upon
the mysteries of the waters,
I call upon your soul to arise and come unto me.

For I am the soul of nature
that gives life to the universe.
From me all things proceed and unto me
they must return.
Let My worship be in the
heart that rejoices, for behold,
all acts of love and pleasure
are My rituals.

Let there be beauty and strength,
power and compassion,
honor and humility,
mirth and reverence within you.
And you who seek to know me,
know that the seeking and yearning
will avail you not,
unless you know the Mystery:
for if that which you seek,

you find not within yourself,
you will never find it without.

For behold,
I have been with you from the beginning,
and I am that which is attained
at the end of desire

Starhawk

The loss of the Bride of Christ is the fundamental flaw in Christianity: Marriage was obligatory for a Jewish man by the age of 20.

We are taken through the 'I AM' exercise. Everyone reaching to the ceiling of the great raftered hall, shouting as loud as they can 'I AM'. It is important not to add one's name, because that is limiting. This is a statement of eternal consciousness.

2 May Beltane

Twice, in the week leading up to Beltane –and I must say it's been a remarkably strong intensification of energy this year - I have been invited to share my passions, and I did…

First, I found myself live on BBC Somerset Sound, on a programme called Women on Top, for an interview which took a whole hour to go out with all the music in the breaks. It was for the Festival but I was also to be asked about myself and what made me tick, what excited me… And so, I took the chance, and I spoke my truth to everyone out there.

It was fantastic. The interviewer said it was the best interview she had ever done, and afterwards it took me quite a time, many out-breaths and two flapjacks to feel my feet properly. (Grounding is an endless practice for me). I spoke to those who still see themselves as victims, whether of men, institutions, employers, or their own emotions. I spoke of the disconnection from our land, from the mystical, from the sacred in all things and people, and of the overfull, over-fast lives it is trendy to live. I prayed I would manage not to say goddess or priestess…not the most appropriate for local radio!!…

Then again, at Clare's Beltane ceremony for the Earth Mysteries group in her new house, by the Beltane fire, we were all invited to engage with and share our passions. A glorious array of passions flowed…… songs, feelings about trees, a tai chi dance, stories, sounding and then laughing the chakras, and me speaking again about my own abiding passion from which so many other passions flow! I talked differently here, of course, and could go deeper. Talking about 'mental hygiene', of the outer showing us what is inner, about most suffering being unnecessary, of the possibility of a commitment to happiness, of the importance of taking 100% responsibility for our lives, and of honouring all that is as it is.

Both times, and always when I have to speak in public or I'm facing a challenging conversation, I ask Goddess to bring through the right words.

On Beltane morning Ciel, Clare and I danced the maypole - there are redundant telephone poles in the meadow opposite Ciel's amazing house. The owner left them because the buzzards like to sit on them. So there we were in a sunny but soaked Dartmoor meadow, singing and hopping merrily around in our wellingtons. And someone came by afterwards and took a photo for us, and that's quite a miracle out there. Lying afterwards, spread out, bare feet in the flowery grass.

9 May The Lakes

Wrenched myself back from the Lake District after 5 glorious mountain climbing days. 5 women and a dog in a minibus. Stayed at a Quaker centre with a yurt in acres of bluebell woods. A rough sculpture of stag and doe on a hillock affirms Beltane to us. Castlerigg is one of the most sublime sacred sites I have ever visited. People told us we'd never get it to ourselves, but we did. As we approached in the deep yellow light and long shadows of evening a group were just leaving, and then it seemed the energy expanded and the power grew and we were silent for a long time just being with it all. A great bowl of mountains, and the stones strong against them. We held a spontaneous ceremony there, toning and taking it in turns to shout 'I am' as loudly as we could while raising up our arms and faces to the mountains and skies.

12 May

From a wonderful little book 'Wisdom of the Christian Mystics':

'What does God do all day long?
He gives birth. From the beginning of eternity
God lies on a maternity bed
Giving birth to the All' – Meister Eckhart (14th C)

24 May

More poles...carrying a 10ft flagpole through the streets for the Festival. Very Beltane...

27 May

....out in the garden in my dressing gown at 4.20am waiting for the first bird of the dawn chorus – and there it is, a pigeon, faintly, then, pure and strong, a lone blackbird. By 4.30 the trees are full of song and the sky is lightening fast. The festival starts tomorrow.

29 May Hothouse

Well, here I am sitting in Hothouse at the Festival. I can't believe I can have time to write this while running a café/rehearsal/jamming/networking venue for performers?! I've finally perhaps licked the old 'alone with a restaurant' horror. (Dates from running restaurants for years with a lazy and unreliable husband). They all make themselves at home, and I don't have to do anything. So, right now, a buzz of Bulgarian, French and English at the red and white tables, and someone giving Indian Head Massage in a corner. Jayne came in – said, 'thought I'd touch base' - I am the base??! Gosh.   It feels a bit like being the calm eye of the Festival as it swirls around me. Stability. Last year I was flying around, spinning from one problem-solving to another, holding the energy of the whole.. Or am I just out on a limb? No matter, this is a great way to experience the Festival.

31 May

This morning Paula interviewed me at length for a paper she is presenting in a Canadian conference on 'Challenging the Status Quo' later this year. I realize afresh more about who I am, and my value. I like to be separate, seeing the whole of whatever .....

Sounds of Sally & friends rehearsing 'When the Devil Scratched the Earth' in the next room. Three of 'Noir Femmes' (big band of 15 black women) enjoying soup and talking animatedly in broad northern accents. This is what I love: the behind the scenes stuff. Angela rings, I dive to unearth my mobile, I can hardly hear her because of the cacophony of the junk band workshop playing in the Baptist church courtyard and giving rise to complaints from the sedate teashop next door. She tells me I just must get myself down to the street music, the atmosphere is fantastic. (I did! And it was!)

Someone drifts through from the field campsite, barefoot and with a huge instrument in a case. People are sitting out on the grass, coming in to get a cuppa now and again. More Noir Femmes coming in, lots of noisy hugs...great appreciation of the food. Now all 15 of them and the roar is swelling! I'm really looking forward to tonight and their concert!

Every now and then, I sit and type another sentence. I've always liked doing this, have often in the past had articles of this type published in various specialist magazines etc. I want to do more. And now I have this wonderful laptop that's just what I can do. Have laptop will travel.

Notice all the women have seen to their food with no trouble at all, but the male driver is completely helpless. Same with another man yesterday. Amazing to see how the stereotypes are so true.

It occurs to me now, in the midst of all this, that I could offer to come with my laptop and record my impressions of the Goddess Conference. This excites me. The richness of all the images I recall ...

The Festival dances on, a stunning vibrant tapestry of music '100% made by women', skillfully woven from all genres; medieval harp, hurdy gurdy and harpsichord alongside virtual soundscapes, rollicking rock, and exquisite voices, and the audience getting to their feet to dance as Noir Femmes reach their crescendo...

Organisation was pretty chaotic, with no overall control, but it was fine. It just doesn't really matter that lots of things didn't get done. Am I learning to let go at last?

Trust it is all happening as it should, that we are NEVER meant to overwork, though paradoxically sometimes it feels right to do so....ah mystery...

8 June

Gardening at top speed all week, high Festival energy still running strong. 'Decompression' takes a while and needs to be gradual. The garden is wildly exuberant, and I so adore it, tending it as it soars to solstice.

9 June

Kathy (Jones) rang today, just as I was lying on my sunbed re-reading Jane Meredith's 'Honouring the Dark Goddess' article and thinking, 'this path really HELPS'.

Thought I'd send it to a friend who's digging into herself right now, have already sent something Buddhist, but reading this again (came in the post today) I was struck by how very much more helpful it was.

Out of the conversation with Kathy comes a new project, conceived the other day when I typed 'have laptop, will travel'. I will write an article about the Goddess

Conference and try and get it into the alternative press. I'll get started on contacting them.

(Reminds me, must find those missing tentpoles – my beloved old tent only just did its job at the conference last year, trying to stay up without 2 poles. I guess I was pretty bowed as well, as my mother was in hospital and approaching her last days – how life does reflect our feelings)

The Goddess Conference 2003: Diary of a Priestess

Wed 30 July 7.30pm   Opening Ceremony

We are four hundred and more, waiting in the evening sun, in Glastonbury High street outside the Town Hall: the roar of chatter cuts off as we enter.

Past the slow strong drumbeat into the shadowy and plangent Mystery that is Avalon. Smoke hangs in shrouds and skeins, dim and numinous, the silent filing women are shapes disappearing into another world, timeless, merging the millennia. Distantly, faint gleams of rich gold altar cloths, great candles, amidst the slow dance of the incense and the pilgrims.

Suddenly, from the smoke, jolting every cell of my being, rear the willow arms of the Nine Morgens, stretched out above us reaching from their world to ours. Within their circle an inner circle of black hooded cloaked figures still as standing stones. The oracles, the shapeshifters, dwelling in the spaces between and within worlds.

 Fierce they stand, formidable, conjured from our deep unconscious, motionless.

All is still. Silent. The power is building, waiting. Smoke thins.

A gong sounds, reverberates. The circle of stones, ancestors, sisters, whirls into life, cloaks flying, as a voice soars, calls them from the ethers. Masked faces of crow and hawk emerge from the hoods. A frisson of energy shivers through my body. One by one the Sisters call in from the silence the mysterious, secret energies that are the Nine Morgens of the transformational Isle of Avalon.

There is a hush.

And there above the singers is an otherwordly, translucent figure in white with the lined, noble, stern face of an elder. The mike sends her astonishing, deep, sad and serious voice into every corner of the room. In the silences there is not another sound to be heard. I am transfixed by her transparency, her elder quality, delicate but fearsomely strong. She seems to have lived a thousand years.

Yet, when she descends to conduct her choir, suddenly she is packed with earthly energy and she dances and whirls, whipping round, arms upstretched, shouting, 'I am the Goddess' and then at the end 'You are the Goddess'.

Which is what we are all here to know. The Goddess is within all.

Thursday 31 July. Preparing for Her Mysteries

Last year I was a Priestess literally grounded in Earth. (Working in the earth 'cleansing' ritual, bare breasted and painted in earth pigments).This year I can walk the Wheel of the Year...

From Air.... on a white, windy mountain top, a sense of far vistas, through veils of feathers, past white clad beings smudging sage, into Danu's wintry sanctuary, into space. Air is Clarity, intelligence, intellect. And here we kneel to her and a mirror is revealed within...

Through Fire...the dark Assembly Rooms lit only by a labyrinth of flames, red/gold Priestesses offering baskets of red candles, each pilgrim walking or dancing the spiral, lit candles dancing with them, and in the fiery sanctuary burning a symbol of those habits that are no longer serving us. Fire is Enthusiasm, Passion, Transmutation and Alchemy.

And Water...a blue/green sea goddess welcomes us into the damp dank chill of the White Spring cave and we are stroked from crown to toes with water. We walk barefoot in the water as it flows across the floor, choose a shell in the cave.. 'the artist's shell' murmurs the Priestess to me....Water is Flow, Emotion, the depths..

And now finally to Earth, and we are whirled into the glorious noisy colour and merriment that is humanity on earth....Earth is stability, solidity, warmth of human kind. I recall a phrase of Anita Brookner's "and she stepped out into the bright dark dangerous and infinitely welcoming street". I am so happy to be here, painting feet, celebrating feet, watching the loving attention with which people decorate each others feet. Listening to the roar of chatter and laughter, feet stamping, of children's voices, a baby crying....

In this life journey, we experience the terrors of space and emptiness and flying that Air brings us, burn in the flames of the passions and pain of Fire, feel we are drowning in Water's waves of emotion and finally thankfully we feel the gratitude for being alive and conscious of this day, hearing the laughter and feeling our feet walking on the Earth, and we can play.

And later in the blue dusk, by the light of what seem to be thousands of candles, and with black Morgens eerily materialising and vanishing among the trees, Chalice Well gardens are the scene of communion and celebration.

Friday 1 August. Lammas.   Ceremonies of the Mysteries of   the Nine Morgens.

Tonight I am in ceremonial role in the Goddess Temple, holding a quiet space with Tiziana and Heather. I am dressed in flowing white chiffon (an old evening dress which holds bitter memories that will be cleansed tonight) with a circle of golden roses in my hair (my spiritual name is Golden Rose) and a plaited golden girdle at my waist. The Temple and the gold-hung altar are ablaze with candles and colour. There is a deep peace.

As I stand at the door of the Temple, and bow to each person entering, I am overwhelmed by the vast variety of people who come here, all ages, faces, shapes and stories. I am deeply moved as I look into four hundred plus pairs of eyes. Namaste. 'The Goddess in me greets the Goddess in you'…

Later I visit the Oracle of the Nine Morgens in the ancient stone fortress that is the Glastonbury Assembly Rooms.

In the dark, deep red candles glow faintly. It is silent. Faceless black figures with cleft sticks watch and guide. The Nine hooded Morgens are seated, hunched shapes in a circle facing outwards. One by one each pilgrim kneels at the feet of a Morgen and whispers of their yearning, their need, their desire, the questions in their heart. And listen to the Oracle speak to them.

It is deep and profound Magick, unutterably beautiful in its Mystery.

Saturday 2 August. Gorgeous Goddess Masque.

'It started in the loos'… my friends said to me over lunch on Sunday. Riotous preparations at the campsite shower block (a woman there with her children wanted so much to look like them and come too…we all need to do this…)….then the four wild women, (3 of them Irish, need I say more?) dancing down the street in their flowing robes and masks. Hecate, Freya, Maeve/Mab and the Dark Goddess. 'We were freed in our masks, beyond ourselves' 'and we were each separately introduced really loudly as we entered the hall and everyone clapped and stamped '. And finally, marveled Jenny, 'when we came out at the end that very instant the fireworks were set off in Glastonbury Abbey for the Jools Holland concert. It was like it was for us! …and a group of men going past clapped us'…

Ann said 'In the masks I could really see into everyone's eyes. Such colours I saw, that I wouldn't have noticed, when you are looking at a whole face' 'But that says something about you', I said, 'that you looked beyond the mask.'

Sunday 3 August. Procession to the Tor.

As I stand outside the Town Hall, watching the banners being carried out, and then, each placed over a woman, the nine decorated willow figures of the Morgens, it comes to me what we are doing, what we are celebrating today. I hear a voice, soft and deep, within me, saying.. .

The Morgens are come forth into the light. Out of the edges into the centre, out into the bright street. To be seen and recognized. Our most shadowy, feared and hidden selves out in the clear sunlight.

The conference this year is dedicated to them, to 'bring them forth from the mists of our forgetting'

They are the farthest reaches of our own shadows, and they hold the *keys to our healing and are the point of our power.*

If we find the farthest most cobwebby, sometimes deeply lovely, sometimes apparently foul and monstrous parts of ourselves, and honour them as *all the same, as they are*, bringing them out into the summer day, then we release our healing and our power. Eventually maybe powers such as the Morgens guide us to Mastery.... Oh dear, *mastery*, but 'Mistressy' won't do - what *can* we say instead?

Now, I am standing above the Vesica Pisces pool at Chalice Well. I am scribbling in my notebook, hearing the exuberant sounds of the Procession draw near, when, suddenly, the great double doors are thrown open and in BURST the Morris Men, who for the first time ever have led the procession, followed by dancing Morgens surrounded with banners. The voice speaks again

The men are coming in.

I climb the Tor, the long exulting procession winds its way up ahead of me, banners and Morgens flying. Just so would the pilgrims have climbed through the Millennia. I recall Millennium Eve, when 700 flares spiralled up the Tor, and I saw the dark hunched silhouettes of hundreds of climbing pilgrims against the smoky orange glow. I was transported then, back to the years 0 and 1000, and when we descended we left behind the Middle Ages and came down into the 21st Century.

At the top in the wide airy space the Morgens take their places in a circle.

The Morgens are come back to the Tor.

We call and welcome them in with immense and heartfelt power. Circles of it stream out from the Tor. A voice soars in a sudden silence.

'Thankyou Goddess for everything, thankyou Goddess you give me the best, thankyou Goddess for everything'. And massed voices fly again on the wings of the wind and the rays of the sun across the seas of Avalon and out into the awakening world. And the heap of fruit is shared and the juices flow and seeds are scattered. And I find myself at the centre around the juicy cloth full and overflowing of the song and the dance and the passion

'We are a people
at the full height of our power

Here is the place
and now is the hour

We recognize our sacred worth
(I was happily singing 'Earth" – that's good too!)
We have the power
To transform the Earth'

Shawna Carol's chant. I asked her to write down the words for me and she said, 'take it and use it' and gave me a wonderful hug.

On the way down, Irish Ann said to me 'we ring each other at least a few times a week, and we are practicing ringing friends when we think of them just to say 'I was thinking of you and I thought I would phone and tell you'. This is what it is all about.

As we journey from competing with each other for men, looks, shapes and status, to sharing, nurturing, enjoying each other and the feminine in ourselves.

To meet the Mystery that shimmers through the fabric of our world. To meet ourselves.

Harvesting First Fruits together under the wheatgold wings of the expansive and sumptuous grain Goddess Ker.

21 September   Autumn Equinox Reflections on a summer

I am sitting here working in Lora's study, and I can only sing an inner hymn of praise and thanks for this the most glorious of summers. And remember that feeling in 98 in Colorado of being amazed at my capacity for momentousness.

And abundance. My freedom is hard to take in….. and yet it also feels so natural and right. To live in this way, doing wonderful things and seeing wonderful people.

Rich with memories.

Wild camping on the beach. For 3 days 3 of us were out of the world out of time on remote Cogden Beach. Unwashed, white with salt, we lived with the sea kale, the fine shingle, the sea the sun and the long vistas of the Dorset coast. We swam, we made designs with the stones, we collected wood, we sat around the fire, we lay in a row in our sleeping bags gazing up at the stars. We cooked corncobs from my garden in their husks at the edge of the flames. Just a scattering of fishermen and their patient families, and after lunch a tiny 'rush hour' of walkers on the coastal path. We were undisturbed. Admired and envied rather.

That was the August bank holiday weekend that Liz joined Angela and I. The start of a great friendship. Just as we were stuffing things into the car, Liz rang Angela and said, 'what are you doing for the weekend?' She was just in the painful process of leaving her very unsuitable man. Angela said 'Camping, but all the sites are full, and the Post office lady said she's seen a few tents sometimes down at Cogden Beach…..we're going to risk it'. So Liz came too. It was when Liz brought me home, that she saw Barley Hill Farm in all its summery sleepy splendour and George just happened to be playing the piano and the sounds drifted out and she stood and took it all in and I saw her fall in love with it.

Soon after I heard that Chloe was moving out of her cottage opposite mine because Wyn was leaving her larger one at the back and they could take it over, so I rang Liz and said 'Well, if you want to come and live at Barley Hill you can.' And she plucked up all her courage, left her man and came to be my neighbour and companion.

And then there was a great high point for me….. standing on the terrace of the House of Commons with a glass of wine and a dinner jacketed man on either side and watching the full moon rise, apricot, in the summer dusk…. and talking to an eminent professor of Government over dinner in the Churchill Room. Which reminds me now of the power of the study at Cricket Court. (The War Cabinet met there, including Churchill and Eisenhower.) It was there that I really feel the belief in my ability to create my own reality firmed up. Since then I have had no migraines and the flow of my life has been so wonderful. After the dinner in the House of Commons, a few of us, rather inebriated, found ourselves happily wandering the corridors of power, looking for the way out, and eventually danced across the great courtyard under Big Ben and were merrily bid goodnight by the guards. It was extraordinary. That night was a long held dream come true.

Sitting on evening beaches eating fish and chips. Drinking two pots of tea and eating two cakes at the Bay Hotel at Lyme. Frolicking in the waves at Lucy's wonderful Great Mattescombe beach. Walking the cliffs. Lying wrapped up in a red blanket when the sun went in. Angela and I getting into a *very* unfriendly sea by saying, if we can do this, we can take the Foundation forward into whatever shape we choose...

Flying to America again, having a row of window seats all to myself, (both ways actually). And the front seats of the coach, both ways.... How about that...

Looking down on the wastes of Greenland, the vastness of Canada, the smoke of hundreds of miles of forest fire, seeing another jet streaming across the sky and thinking, that's me now. And writing in my journal I find I am writing what I would fear if I had another relationship. And, when a bout of very bad turbulence hit, thinking 'am I ready to die?' and realizing NO, I need to address that double page spread of feared scenarios which accompany thoughts of having a lover/partner. OK, I wrote, I decide to have a lover again before I die, and it will work and I will learn I can do it and not damage anyone or myself, in fact my life will be ENHANCED....

Feared scenarios if I have a lover:
- I would be squashed to invisibility again
- I would, with a good guy, behave BADLY
- Once in a sexual relationship the floodgates would open and I would become promiscuous
- I couldn't commit without perfection and a perfect guy wont want me...
- I'd take his stuff too seriously and go down WITH him (again)
- I wouldn't manage the anxiety of the fear of loss
- I'd lose my freedom, my life, friends, adventures, space, peace, my relationship with God and Goddess
- I'd lose control
- I'd try to control him
- I'd damage him
- I'd not manage to keep boundaries about my own needs
- I'd love too much, look after too much, disempower him (again)
- If he really knew how I am he'd not want me
- My spiritual life would frighten/alienate/amuse/disturb him

It's definitely time to sort that lot out..... I do NOT want to die before I do.

Vermont's Lake Champlain in summer, swimming in fresh water, so different, such a different way of feeling so cleansed. The still clear water on the stones. Lying on the sunbed *in* the shallows, watching children play. Swimming in rapids, the tension and the exhilaration. Glenn and Nick diving from 40ft rocks into the gorge. Picnics on the rocks. The serious heatwave which began the day I got there. The temperature still 96F at 7pm. The dinner table with its blue flowered cloth out on the grass to catch the faint breeze. The Cookout at the lakeside. The Burlington Boathouse – just sitting on the decking looking out at the lake and mountains and the boats going to and fro. Girly day out with Nancy, haircut at a salon on the lake, prawn dumplings for lunch, shops and giggles.

The Goddess Conference...well, have already written about that. But, the afterword, the inspiration that came to Moira to arrange a Goddess conference in Ireland with the Catholic nuns who guard the flame of Brigid. Bringing the worlds together. Will this happen too? I so want it to.

Walking the labyrinth at Gloucester Cathedral, with the exhibition of Millie's (Camilla Nock. RA) paintings, which to me are like a representation of DNA or code. It was the coming out that was so spectacular, because in Chartres in 98 we couldn't, we had to walk straight out. So Kathy said we were still in there. She felt we needed to go back to Chartres, but I felt that with intent and awareness, I could walk out of both at the same time. And it certainly felt BIG, that walk out.

Such a feeling of release and striding out into a new world. The world in which I intend to take a lover. (Always remembering, as Neale Donald Walsch would say, unless I don't). Clear intent, a decision, made up there in the Mid-Atlantic sky, with detachment as well as commitment. The usual balancing act.

Actually I think Kathy was right, and I did need to walk out in Chartres itself. And at the end of September 2007 Swithin took me there - on our way back from his 'enchanted castle' in the Dordogne to Paris and home, what a time that was! - to witness the sublime Son et Lumiere event which is only held then. That is an event I would tell everyone to go to. I promise you it is it mindblowing. I had no expectations about the labyrinth. I was well aware that it was mostly closed, but to my utter joy at 11pm that night, as we wandered in soaked in bliss and wonder from what we had witnessed, there it was, empty and open and waiting. I walked proudly straight in to the centre, I waited until S reached the centre and we meditated quietly for some minutes, and then I began, with such a triumphant feeling, such awe, to walk out, with S behind me. I said to him, 'I walked in alone ten years ago, and I walked out today with you'.
As we walked out of the great Cathedral doors holding hands thunderous music suddenly struck up.

Another day, in Liskeard, Ciel and Clare and John and I went to a multi faith pilgrimage to a 'lost shrine' to Mary. We did our thing while they did theirs, then we went and sat in a field and had a picnic.

And Clare and Ciel coming up here and eating lunch on the lawn, Starla sitting on all our laps, and having a ceremony in the woods, they were all blocked off with brambles

PEACE AND BLISS

Peace and bliss come when ' we do not care what happens' (Krishnamurti) when we trust (through experience) that whatever happens happens for our highest good. We cannot always know what is for our highest good, but our higher self or soul know and if we align our will with the soul's will we find peace.
Anxiety vanishes. And then bliss at what IS, experiencing what IS, flows into the space left when all the anxiety dissolves. And the IS is untainted by past pain or fear of future.
Gratitude swells within, and this love and gratitude for the present creates more and more of the same......
We choose, plan, desire, yes. But then we trust that if those choices are not for the best they will not happen. And we feel the gratitude already for what WILL happen.
The rewards of this simple process are unlimited.
The rewards of faith and surrender.

'And he carried me away in the Spirit to a mountain great and high, and shewed me the holy City of Jerusalem coming down out of heaven from God'

John sees a world at peace. Humanity at one with each other, all national hatreds gone.

Nations are separate. Yet in friendly cooperation for the common good. Evils and fears that have cursed mankind are burned up (v. 8). Social life is built on fine character – all life is under the rule of the Heavenly Father.

In the vision that John had on Patmos, this life is set out under the emblem of a city, the perfection of man's social life, a city of truth, beauty, goodness. It's a symbolic picture, this city symmetrical like a cube with streets of gold.

The symbols mean that human life shall be as safe as an old walled city, as pure as gold, as beautiful as the flashing jewels, and brilliant with light

Man has transferred this picture to Heaven, but it concerns our own world here and now – it has always been the dream of man. He knows he is made for a life grander than he has ever known. Let us cherish this dream still. Do not dismiss it as impossible and idealistic. Egrave it upon our hearts – make it a subject of our prayer and effort.

BUT this City is not of man's building, it has come down from heaven. It is Divinely founded and directed, God is in the midst of the city, man and God are in union with each other.

The Gates are open to all. There is no temple. All nationalism vanishes. It is a world at one with God. Think of the approach to the City, it is a beautiful conception. The City is One, but 12 gates give access , at all points of the compass – all embracing. Opposite EVERY people is a gate.

This is necessary because we differ greatly – mentality – habit- temperament – race – culture. God respects the differences – hence a gate is open nearest each people – we do not have to go far. The Holy city is not for one race or outlook. There dreamers, scientists, practical men, farmers, craftsmen…all with a different outlook.

All these, so different, cannot enter by one path, one gate.

The sceptical must have a reason, like Thomas, the mystical think in symbols like John, the practical are happy in service like Andrew.

Some enter by way of love, some by hot tears and penitence, some by simple belief, some by sudden conversion, and some by slow reflection.

Gates are open for all. But they are guarded. We must pass the Angel, and submit to the law of the City. We cannot enter as idly sauntering tourists, and we must enter one by one, not as a crowd. Some are kept out. (v8 and 27)

But we have to think further still. If we enter, we must go through, there is a tendency for us to hang around the gate, we mistake the gate for the City.

A sceptic must go through to reach faith. A mystic must go through to reach practice. The practical must reach mystical fellowship, the penitent must reach full joy. From ignorance to knowledge, from symbolism to reality…let us beware of incomplete onesided lives, let us work to find our wholeness.

AND Let us reflect that there is such a thing as a closed gate.   AMEN.

but we got through, and doing the I AM thing, it is so powerful, amazing to hear them both. Rare to be so completely unoverheard.

And yet more lovely things...the Fireworks Manufacturers National Championships at Plymouth Hoe with chips and ice cream, and a Jazz supper cruise down the River Dart – sitting on deck with a coffee watching the black tree-lined river slipping past, no lights, just dark water, then the forest of lights that is Dartmouth and Kingswear.... All with Rosie's wonderful Magic Bus.

Shakespeare in the Globe immediately followed by the three hours or more of Prokofiev's War and Peace at The Proms in the Albert Hall... what a day. I'll never forget walking into the upper gallery and seeing it all below me, and perching on a vertiginous seat, feeling like a bird, and then the overture, the voices soaring, tears jerking from my eyes...

And last but not least, gorgeous sunny days on my sun bed in the garden with a book, and evenings watering the garden, picking and eating veggies, and savouring the still night air. Sprog doing his night sky cat bit in the middle of the lawn. Mars the closest it's been for 60,000 years. The male is coming nearer.

A sense of riding the realms of bliss.

My father wrote a sermon about Heaven on Earth, based on John's Vision of the Holy City in Revelation, at the very end of the Bible. He speaks of wholeness.

I feel myself coming into wholeness, and I feel ready to meet a man from that strong place.

In the midst of this rising peace and ease I have been saying to myself

I AM OPENING

I have been saying to myself, the words came from nowhere.

I AM OPENING

And then a thought flashed through my head one day unbidden. 'I wonder what he'll be like?' Intense *curiosity* replaces that awful method of listing criteria. If I just trust....

October

I need to make a bit more money, to supplement the rent coming in from No 7. I need £250-300 a month. This long time not working, since Hothouse, is catching up with me. I have ideas but don't feel the urge or instinct to act. Then one sunny Saturday at Sally Gregson's Millhouse in the Mendips for a WRAGS workshop on plant propagation I overhear someone say that the local coordinator is leaving. I go home, email the director my CV, (which I just happen to have just updated for a jobshare Angela and I considered!). On Monday I speak with her and on Thursday I drive blissfully up though the sun to see her in the Cirencester Head Office. The pay is £280 per month for 10 hours a week. It occurs to me that I should have 'ordered' more money!!!!!!! My patch includes Cornwall so I get expenses paid trips! It also includes Highgrove so I shall get to see that; it's been on my wish list this year. I am now the South West's Coordinator for the Women Returners to the Land…. Women Returners to Amenity Gardening Scheme. It is part of the Women's Farm and Garden Association , which started the Land Army in the first world war. The government was so impressed with it it started the Land Army in the second world war. My mother was a land girl, no wonder she was always so fit physically. She would love what I am doing. I will be based at home which will be a new experience.

Tomorrow I am carrying on rescuing a garden in the Mendips, which also came my way quite serendipitously, so on my way back from the interview I treated myself to a hotel to save going home and coming back up again. As I drove into Weston super Mare I thought, 'I need a big room with all frills right on the sea, not too pricey.'

I immediately saw this big old hotel built up on the rocks, and sure enough there was my room, on a corner jutting into the sea, very characterful and spacious, with the sea smashing up to just below the big windows. Perfect. I made a cup of tea and lay listening to the sea, then I walked out into the suddenly wild night and found fish and chips. I put on the TV and as I lift a chip a golden eagle soars across the screen. This is living.

WRAGS and the Mendip garden sorted me out financially quite nicely. I never cease to be amazed….. The job is utterly delicious, it involves walking round all the best gardens and talking with gardeners. Today it is taking me up to London for a Forum, and I will see the Chelsea Physic garden. I sit on the train with tea and cake and the monochrome winter landscape, all soft grey rain and bare trees flashes past, the raindrops slanting across the windows.

Later that month I sat in bed propped up on pillows in a big attic room in Mousehole, overlooking the harbour and the Lizard peninsula. It has a big dormer window, a skylight, and a strawberry coloured sofa. And excellent breakfast I expect, in the Ship Inn next door.

I am remembering this time last year when I was in Cadgwith with Linda and Philippa, so exhausted and about to be really quite ill. And about to leave the Festival and feel the huge burden lift. The freedom and feeling of being rich with time lasted through to my birthday, and then one month's really hard work helping at the Festival paid for my summer. The best summer ever really. I am watching it get light over the harbour. The Christmas lights are being strung up. Seagulls fly past my window and I think of mum and another Christmas without her. I thank her, as I do each day, and feel the sadness too.. But all the pleasures of the Christmas season spread out ahead. Lights, carols on classic FM, our singing group part of a Christmas concert in a beautiful local church, choosing little gifts, getting cards, the whole thing.

I went to Shropshire with Rosie's Magic Bus, to see the Wolves Conservation Centre. Gorgeous man running it. He said, looking at me in my Yugoslav red embroidered wool jacket and new black hat, 'you look fantastic'….very satisfying.

When we got to the top of the hill, walking silently in the dark, we stopped, looked down over the still blackness of the valley of wolves, and we howled and the wolves and probably their keeper too howled back.

Magic in the Magic bus.

Angela, Linda and Liz from left, with Linda's yellow convertible.. Liz and I at Sennen

CHAPTER 8   OPENING

26 November

The days of glory draw in. Winter sets in. I have my wonderful women friends but there is still no man in my life. No man ever touches me or asks me out even.

Long talk with Rosie about asthma. Have come to a pause in WRAGS, and finished the Mendip garden while exhausted, and have ground to my usual halt, in bed for a few days drained and asthmatic. 'Asthma is about the heart chakra' she said 'it is weeping inside'. That's the first thing the homeopath John Gordon said about me back in the 80s. This year I've had a lot of asthma, and it is the year I have decided to seek relationship with a man again. I've also realized fully that my right ear's deafness is deafness to the male, not just a response to Miro. Rosie said, maybe the asthma has come up to the surface to be dealt with, now that my life is relatively safe and stable.

I healed my asthma almost completely with the chest-opening Zen work in the 80s, then Dan died and my chest closed up again, I bowed over in pain to protect my heart. Then the bankruptcy and the end of the centre kept it well closed. And the continued harassment in the form of the letters.

Only now, over a year after Miro left, mum died, and the bankruptcy was discharged, can I begin to open. It was earlier this year walking up Chard High Street, that I said spontaneously to myself almost aloud, *'I am opening'.* The heart chakra wound is perhaps coming up in its oldest physical form to be healed.

I know there is still bitterness there. I said heatedly to Rosie when talking of men....

'My dad died suddenly just as he was about to retire and left mum with nothing. When I was a young woman he refused to let me come home for a while even though I told him I was being subjected to mental and physical cruelty. He never enquired later...I overworked ridiculously for so long and my family didn't give a shit, just took advantage of me. My husband retreated into mental illness whenever things got tough and once jumped off a roof in front of my mother. He had a psychotic breakdown when I said enough. And when I did get a divorce my mum immediately got a bad back and became demanding. My elder son who had everything going for him also became mentally ill and committed suicide. My ex-husband harassed everyone out of the properties I ran because he couldn't, and bankrupted me. Then continued to harass me for years.' I was shocked to hear still the bitterness, feel the acid of it.

I also spoke like this to Lora, and she said tartly 'You'd better borrow back the book you lent me! You're still identifying with your past, with your story.'

Truth is, when it takes me over, I feel in that place that I don't know how to get past it. It's beyond me. I can only hand it over...

Soooo.... Get out the books again!!!....and I do get my calm back, and it's less and less often that I wind myself up like that with those words. Because that's what it is, its self-torture. **Thinking instead of experiencing the moment**. Opening up my wounds with my words. Caroline Myss talks about this in her book 'Why people don't heal and how they can'. She says: 'Beware of the temptation to see yourself unfairly treated. It is a prescription for disaster'. When we open up wounds and keep them open for attention we don't ever heal. We become attached to our wounds. She says 'Say, I got the lesson, then thank it and release it. Let the wound close over. Don't use it to manipulate others or indulge in self-pity.' I remember Paul Taylor saying to me acerbically in front of the whole group when I was complaining about my mother's self -pity and asking him what to do: 'look to your own self-pity'.

That old script.

Ah well, it all passed. I stopped paying that role. Didn't it take a time, though. Kept coming back and hitting me when I thought I was past it...

When I began to get the old script out of my head, what welled up into the silence piece by piece was a new understanding. This only really came together in the last few years. I had always worked much much too hard, partly from fear yes, but also to try to shame those close to me into doing more, into caring for me. That would have worked with me but of course it didn't work with them. I saw how irritating it must have been when I kept martyring myself, how what I was doing was a kind of emotional blackmail. I saw how they had all attacked as a means of defence and I had no idea what they were doing and wept in incomprehension and tried harder to please.... I saw how resentful and sour I was at all the love my husband received, when he did no more than he wanted to, and performed so well for company. How too too easy it is to take advantage of people who need approval and do too much to get it. And how I envied this and tried to

334

HAND IT OVER

When we just can't see a way through, no matter what it is.
We recognize we are powerless, and we can say so to our God.
We don't have to do it all ourselves.
This is a wonderful realization. It is trust in action.
We can do our best, then relax and in the space that suddenly expands within all the turmoil, it's amazing how answers can well up.
And how if we just accept the not knowing what to do, things start to change around us, all sorts of unexpected things happen.
Handing it over, I have always found, opens the door to miracles.
It is the time proven method used by the AA, and is as good for the addiction to suffering as for any other
We just have to really want
to feel better

get attention myself and became even more irritating. He wanted me to take care of myself, refuse to accept the abuse, and be the lovely woman I was, but I was not able to. And he was not able to give and show his love for me, out of his fear that if I recognized my worth I would leave.

The jigsaw fell into place. Slowly. There's lots I'll never understand but THAT'S FINE. I don't need to. I understand enough to relinquish blaming and to move on in compassion for the whole story. To put my story behind me.

The gardening must be helping, the singing and the yoga too, my lungs are telling me they are ready to let go. I am wearing pink and green, my new car is deep green, my bed cushions are green. I am learning the language of growing things.

I am beginning to know...A man will come, how will it happen?? Oh, new thought, how wonderful was that when I first spontaneously thought it!

December Italy, divine Italy

Italy is where the process had its beginnings. While there, I found myself making the unequivocal choice to live at least part of the year in the sun and in the Mediterranean culture. I have always wanted to and I am nearly 60 and if I don't do things soon I never will.

We stayed in an exquisite little hill village called Papiano, it was a thirteenth century castle and our tiny house was part of its nunnery. Linda had arranged it. So easy, such fun, four women, Linda, Liz, Angela, me. Liz and I liked to get up early and go and collect firewood and breakfast bread and croissants. Snow capped mountains. Greetings everywhere. 'Freddo, freddo!!!' they called to us laughing as we stepped out swathed in scarves hats and gloves. Assissi, Perugia, Montepulciano....in Assissi the dim, profoundly sacred numinous Lower Church and the soaring ecstasy of the brilliantly light and colourful Upper Church. The perfect symbol of the two aspects of the love of God. I stood for ages before the Franciscan relics, his actual robe, his actual sandals, I could not believe what I was seeing. It was like seeing being able to see Christ's robe, I had to be fetched by my ever patient friends. Then, a thin vertical slice of perfect sunset in a narrow basilica window, and from the terraces, the valley shrouded in mist.

Lake Trasimeno eerie, ethereal, all reflected reeds, grasses, still wading birds. The Piero della Francesca in the Perugia gallery, the crowded Christmas streets, fabulous stiltwalkers and the elegant white lights, tea and cakes in Sandri's café, the sumptuous market in the underground medieval city.

And Rome, whizzing around it in taxis. Vatican city. What struck me most was the maleness of St Peter's. It seemed to me to be all about power *over*. I could feel the nature of Catholicism. You couldn't walk directly down the central aisle to the high Altar, it was closed. It had no Lady Chapel that I could find. It was all size and no soul: it felt cold and it felt heartless. Interesting. SO SO different from the basilica of St Francis at Assissi.

I fell in love with Italy, with its language, and also with a ruined house on the hill. It had a tall bit and a shorter bit, was a distinctive shape.
Liz and I burrowed through brambles and branches to get in, braved the gappy rotting steps and floors and looked out at the view from the top. 'We're in love, aren't we?' said Liz. We plotted and planned. Roof terrace! Said Liz. Upstairs sitting room! Said I. Such excitement.

Then I got real, 'We can only think about this if a windfall comes from somewhere' I said.

But I came back to Barley Hill and I knew in my heart that my time there was ending: the golden carp had died while I was away, eaten by the heron, (I always felt that when the carp went so would I) and the sun was calling me, just as the hills had done in 1997. What will happen, I thought, appetites for southern sun curling greedily up within me?

The strange thing was, once I was home the first phone call I got was from my cousin Maureen telling me that Les, Aunty Phyl's companion, had died. And the thought came, Mum always said that that was her family home that Les took over when Phyl died, and by rights part of it was hers...and I remembered my words to Liz. But I knew Les had no time for me because I had no time for her: I had found her handling of everything very hard to stomach, and the day I went up to stay to be with Phyl, she had arranged for her to go into a nursing home, so she wasn't there!! I remember sitting with Phyl in the home, and telling her about the Centre, and she suddenly said, 'Why do you do all these things?' silence then understanding.' 'I suppose its because you like the challenge'. Her last words to me were 'I hope your mum behaves herself'. I loved her sharpness.

She was always something of a second mother to me. Apparently when I was 18 months old and we were living with her, I always knew when she was coming home from work, and used to go to the window. And when mum had her breakdown when I was 4, I was there a lot. I was often there. She once told me mum was 'all top show and nothing underneath'. Poor mum! But truth there too. No wonder it was hard for mum having a daughter who was obsessed with the depth of things. I believe now that we chose each other and agreed roles before incarnation, partly for just that reason, to show ourselves to ourselves. It makes it all easier once you see this process.

Winter solstice

We all gather at Mike and Millie's, the love we all have for each other glows in the firelight. My angel card for the year is *CHANGE*. I thought so, I said. That's what I've been feeling. Just when I've got so settled and peaceful. That seems to be how it happens. You get everything sorted in one world and you get 'instructions' to move to another!!!!

I still have this feeling, a sense of sweetness surging towards me. Sweetness of life, of love.
I AM OPENING

SWEET THINGS

CHOCOLATE AND GRAND MARNIER MOUSSE

Take a bar of the very best dark chocolate, at least 70% cocoa solids. Melt 175 g
of it gently in a bowl over simmering water. Beat in 3 egg yolks (large free
range eggs) and the stir in 2tbsp Grand Marnier liqueur. Whisk the egg white
till stiff, and enjoy the wonderful effect as you
fold them tenderly into the chocolate....
Chill and serve with cream and curls of the chocolate.

CARAMEL BANANAS

Sauté in butter 4 bananas sliced lengthwise - be very gentle and refrain from
turning more than once. Arrange them on a flat dish and keep warm
Dissolve 100g sugar in 150ml water and heat until golden brown – don't stir.
Pour half the caramel over the bananas, and eat with lots of good vanilla
icecream or pouring cream. You could make half the caramel in advance, spread
it over a baking sheet, then chill, and smash it up into shards for decoration.

CHAMPAGNE JELLY

You can cheat and use packet jelly or use gelatine. Make up two packets of lime
jelly with a bottle of sparkling white wine instead of the cold water. Or use
strawberry or raspberry jelly and sparkling rose. Pour into glasses or one big
dish. Chill quickly in the freezer to retain the bubbles within the jelly. Frost
some grapes...white for white wine, black for rose....dip grapes in egg white and
then into white sugar. Pile these onto the set jelly.
You can also make jelly up with claret, or with fruit juices, and add cut up
fresh fruit to the dish before pouring in the jelly. If you use gelatine follow
directions on the packet for quantities.

HONEYED APRICOTS

Poach ripe apricots till just soft in a little water, stir in good quality runny
honey to taste. Serve warm with yogurt. You can try this with apples and pears,
or peaches , and some ginger can be great added as well or instead...ground or
stem. Its also gorgeous with alcohol added- brandy or a 'matching' liqueur....

How will it happen? How will my lover come to me?? The curiosity is strong now.

New Year's Eve 03/04
Dancing in 2004

This year I felt myself opening. Slowly. And on New Year's Eve at Mike and Millie's again I danced and danced to Abba and other seventies music in the blue Italian dress that Angela and I bought between us. Dancing Queen. Into the new year with a great

Whoosh.......

I remember watching Sandra Poustie's legs dancing this in '78 or '79. She was wearing culottes and I was of course in the kitchen and could only see her legs. I always longed to dance it and tonight I did.

2004

Such a fantastic life, but ALONE, UNAPPROACHED and MYSTIFIED as to why. I could understand it if I was approached and found too earnest a soul ...or something... but I am always looked at but never touched it seems. My mother said the same about herself. She was widowed in 79 and was alone until she died in 2002. I DO NOT CHOOSE THAT PATH. I have too strong a sexuality.

February

I am very low. The 19th is the 7th anniversary of Dan's death. 7 years. I am very heavy and tired. Spring is coming too soon, and I am angry with the nettles and the brambles. I can't get warm, except in the bath or in bed in the mornings or sitting over the electric fire. Bank Overdraft won't go down, Weight won't go down. No results for my efforts. 'What's the point' feelings beginning.

Spoke about my loneliness and longing for a partner at the Valentine's Speaking Circle for Philippa's birthday. At Speaking Circles you get to stand up before a group and speak from the heart about whatever comes, and you are given FULL ATTENTION. You are also videoed, so you can see yourself ....something I've long thought a brilliant therapy. It is a deeply valuable exercise. I tried to get beyond words, and was quite touched when I saw myself on video. That was part of the party when Philippa and Michael arrived in a helicopter.....!!!!

I feel weak, asthmatic, overweight, lonely. Oh dear. And now a speeding camera flashed at me. I seem to be losing hope.

Next day, I re-read Caroline Myss's book about keeping our wounds open, and I noticed some pain in my right hand, and these two things helped me back up again. When I get pain it reminds me of what matters. I used to have so pain and trouble, and I know how fortunate I am now. Caroline Myss suggests having a short time weekly specified for acknowledging the negative stuff, then otherwise deliberately embracing the energy of love and gratitude for what is.

She talks about liberation from the power of life's illusions, that we can see that our greatest contributions are often the ones that carry no physical packaging: love, understanding, compassion, joy, optimism, acceptance, courage.

One night I have supper out with Glenn, Andrew and Lisa. We are talking deeply. The subject of my aloneness comes up. 'What concerns me', I say, 'is that I feel that it is not just a deep belief that I am destined to be alone, it is a Knowing. Maybe I brought it from a past life, because it's always been there, ever since I can remember. There's nothing that can be done, its how it has to be. That's my fear.'

Andrew suddenly said, 'there's a number for that. I saw it then, it flashed past. I don't know what it is but yes there's a number for it.' Andrew is something of a numerologist in a highly idiosyncratic way. He senses many things and can find a symbol which has been drawn in the air while he was out of the room. I respect his words, and I am just sitting there, quite still, taking in that there IS a way to overcome this block, that it IS just a block.

Gosh, I said. Yes. Yes.

6 March

Looking at my overdraft's history and seeing how it built because of Italy and the Wolves trip. And yet I KNOW it right I did these things. Looking back when I was needing work in October   I put a clear parameter on how much I needed and that was what came along! Exactly! It wasn't enough because I had not fully acknowledged my needs.. I need a full rich life, that costs money. Nothing wrong with that. If I had said a higher figure to myself would it have come along?? I now need a lump sum to sort me out and I will not put a limit on it!!!!

19 March

Highy pleasurable Annual Ceremonies of Getting the Sunbed out of the Shed, and of Hanging out the Washing for the First Time…. Warm sun, winds and showers.

But still. Yearnings. Low, empty, why can I not have a love of MY OWN?? I talk it through with Rosie. 'Englishmen may not be right for you' she said musingly 'go to Spain and see Carol'. 'Its already booked' I said, 'I got a free flight with the Daily Mail'. I go on being low, grey with despondency, and mystified as to why the right man does not appear. I turn spring away in my mind and in my heart, the whole world has its sap rising and I am alone.

I know now that yearning is an affirmation of lack and will keep away that which you yearn for. But perhaps I needed to feel it that spring, to acknowledge to myself and to others my wholehearted wish for a lover and

DESIRE

From Esther and Jerry Hicks' 'Ask and it is Given'

'We could describe the sensation of desire as the delicious awareness of new possibilities. Desire is a fresh free feeling of anticipating wonderful expansion. The feeling of desire is truly the feeling of life flowing through you. But many people, when using the word desire, feel something quite different. Desire for them often feels like yearning, for while they are focussed on something they want they are equally aware of its absence. And so, while they are using words of desire, they are offering a vibration of lack.

There is no feeling of lack in true desire. So keep in mind that whatever you ask it is always given – then desires will be pure and unresisted.'

When we live so close to our own desire we live equally close to God. True desire, true passion, that is, not greedy ego stuff.

But....Desire for the highest experience of life we can create....that is living in beauty And in truth

partner. Or perhaps the feeling comes strongest before the release from the pattern.

Beltane is approaching and some energy returns.

Reading Andrew Cohen 'teachings of liberation'. He's provided my new mantra:

Interested in how things are not how you want them to be.

This is proving to be a very useful one, as Shakti Gawain's 'whatever' was for so long. Things are better now, and I am coping less with anxiety than with feeling critical.

He also says that we *don't need to work it all out*. We can just finish with it. *Working it out is continuing with suffering*. We can just end working it out, accept. 'Renounce all the morbid gratifications and satisfaction that you derive from dwelling on the pain and agony of your past. It doesn't have to mean anything at all'.

'Then,' he says 'you will be released from the terrible burden of becoming - and that is peace'. 'Spiritual is the very nature of what you already are. There's nothing to do about it except Realise it. Once you have made this discovery its all over. Then there is literally nothing more to do'

I read somewhere 'need nothing, desire everything, choose what shows up'.

I remember St Augustine. 'Love and do what you will'.

I think of all the journals full of miserable tangles of introspection. Of looking and dwelling on my 'faults' and others 'faults'. On things being my fault or their fault. A lifetime of trying to find out who I am, what is wrong with me, how it all works, seeking answers and meaning. A lifetime of increasingly identifying with my story, my losses.

I write: all we have to do is be willing to love what is: see honestly, accept, surrender to what IS, and try not to NOT ACT FROM the aspects which are not serving us or others, which are not coming from love and compassion.

1 May

Beltane comes, I dance the maypole again. I drive Andrew and Millie down and we picnic on the moor on the way. I'm feeling better.

On May 1 as if in celebration of the Beltane energy, 10 East European countries join Europe. Expansion, integration on the world stage. It excites me, that Europe can get bigger and I only hope it gets looser, less regulated, less tight. I still find I am against the Euro for Britain. It reflects my ambivalence about relationship. I want to keep independent, individual, clearly bounded, strong….but I want the togetherness, the warmth, and the strength of the *group* too….now, if I could find a relationship that allowed both………..

SETTING AND PRESETTING THE SLICE

We choose what we see around us, what we look for, and we fill our minds and hearts with that. What we look for will be there. The positive becomes all, and the 'contextual field of suffering and negativity' is in the past, or elsewhere. We do not deny it, but we do not choose it now.

After a while we find that our lives are actually full of what we like, full of joy, and it is a surprise if something isn't wonderful and it makes us enquire curiously what thought of ours, what resistance, gave us that in our life. It is fun to sort it. Wonder, bliss and peace become second nature. We feel we will burst with it all.

We can make Choices not just for the future generally but just as importantly for the very next slice of our day, re-making them as we change activity and slip into the next bit, focusing clearly but lightly on what we want from each slice of day. This intention will be preset then for similar slices in the future. We can preset the tuning, the vibrational frequency – but **don't preset the thankyous!!!**. Soon our lives are full only of what we enjoy and all our frequent activities are preset for quality... We are looking for and seeing only the good we choose. And that good flows in, in resonance.

All week I am full-on with the play at the Warehouse Theatre - J.M. Barrie's 'Dear Brutus'. It is about second chances and magical woods on Midsummer Eve- how we would behave if circumstances had been different. It is deep, light and fascinating. I am doing the props. Appropriately for Beltane, I am 'flower maiden': I have to fill the stage with flowers, cut from a garden. I've been running around sourcing things, people are very helpful and generous.

Then on 11th May I go to Spain to see Carol and am staggered by the vastness of the scale of the place; the Alpujarras at the foot of the 12000' Sierra Nevada. At the beach, I fall over, and it is the highpoint of young Tallullah's day out. I am surprised because I haven't fallen over for a long time, and for me falling is always the mark of losing balance as something new comes my way.. Several times, I trip up. I think 'uh huh' 'what is going to happen?'

Then on my last day, sitting at a café table is a man. 'I like his face' I thought as we sat avoiding each others gaze. I notice his papers. 'Mom's Land' they say. I think, 'Ah, A Spanish American whose mother has left him land here'. Carol arrives and we all get talking and spend the day together. His name is John Cano. He keeps taking my hand very firmly to help me, and asks me many questions. His land is stunningly beautiful and there are two hoopoes and a white Beltane horse. He has worked on himself and is not afraid of showing his vulnerability. He has heart. He is a bit older than me.

At the end of the day he kisses me briefly but strongly and my whole body goes into shock. I haven't been kissed like that forever it seems: as a woman he wants.

I go home next day in a daze. On the plane the world below is clear as a bell all the way and I feel I am seeing my life so far unreel from above as we fly, Spain, France, the Channel Islands where I grew up, the south of England, London where I was born. It's like it must be before you die. I am so bemused my ears give me no trouble going down for about the first time in my life, which makes me even more bemused. (attention totally OFF my ears... so they are fine, interesting) I know this man 'has my name on him'. I know I will see him again. I especially like the way he says 'yes' and I find myself doing it, strongly pronouncing the s..

........*He was to make me feel a woman again and I will be forever grateful. And I still say 'yes' like him...*

Next day I perched on Angela's hospital bed, she had had a new hip. I said dazedly 'this man.......he kissed me......'

June

He called, he emailed....we got to know each other.

One day I open a letter to find.............. a cheque for £17000, and a letter from my aunt's comapanion's solicitors saying there is more to come. I am haring down to Angela's waving the cheque in a delirious stupor.

The legacy totalled £23000 altogether and I paid off almost all of my mortgage and all of my overdraft and still had some left. I was dumbstruck. It felt that my spending last year was justified.

Typing this now, I am electrified having just been reading my journal for March ' I need a lump sum'........it's so hard to believe. Can you see why I trust? It is a matter of experience now not faith. Also I've got frustrated today, and typing this out has put everything back in perspective. Made me feel much better.

August

Before too long John flies to England from New York and we are spending a day in each other's arms, on a boat up and down the Thames, in a hotel room with a view of the Wheel, and in a London theatre watching Mamma Mia, and standing up jigging at the end for a euphoric 'Waterloo'. Have I met my Waterloo? Remembering the new year, danced in to Abba, the overture for the year.....?

He blasts in his own inimitable style through all my barriers.

Part of the symphony.

Wrapped in each other by the fire in my cottage he reads Kahlil Gibran on Love to me.

Then said Almitra, "Speak to us of Love."

And he raised his head and looked upon the people, and there fell a stillness upon them. And with a great voice he said:

When love beckons to you follow him,

Though his ways are hard and steep.

And when his wings enfold you yield to him,

Though the sword hidden among his pinions may wound you.

And when he speaks to you believe in him,

Though his voice may shatter your dreams as the north wind lays waste the garden.

For even as love crowns you so shall he crucify you. Even as he is for your growth so is he for your pruning.

Even as he ascends to your height and caresses your tenderest branches that quiver in the sun,

So shall he descend to your roots and shake them in their clinging to the earth.

Like sheaves of corn he gathers you unto himself.

He threshes you to make you naked.

He sifts you to free you from your husks.

He grinds you to whiteness.

He kneads you until you are pliant;

And then he assigns you to his sacred fire, that you may become sacred bread for God's sacred feast.

All these things shall love do unto you that you may know the secrets of your heart, and in that knowledge become a fragment of Life's heart.

But if in your fear you would seek only love's peace and love's pleasure,

Then it is better for you that you cover your nakedness and pass out of love's threshing-floor,

Into the seasonless world where you shall laugh, but not all of your laughter, and weep, but not all of your tears.

Love gives naught but itself and takes naught but from itself.

Love possesses not nor would it be possessed;

For love is sufficient unto love.

When you love you should not say, "God is in my heart," but rather, I am in the heart of God."

And think not you can direct the course of love, for love, if it finds you worthy, directs your course.

Love has no other desire but to fulfil itself.

But if you love and must needs have desires, let these be your desires:

To melt and be like a running brook that sings its melody to the night.

To know the pain of too much tenderness.

To be wounded by your own understanding of love;

And to bleed willingly and joyfully.

To wake at dawn with a winged heart and give thanks for another day of loving;

To rest at the noon hour and meditate love's ecstasy;

To return home at eventide with gratitude;

And then to sleep with a prayer for the beloved in your heart and a song of praise upon your lips.

I drive him to Heathrow, it is like a flight, we sing a lot of the way, to West Side Story. That was his youth...the real thing. He weeps as we sing. Afterwards I sit on my sofa and shake for a day. Twelve and a half years of celibacy has ended.

September

One morning I wake with an idea fully fledged. The legacy enabled it. Pieces have just come together. Liz has said that her friends Jan and David are looking for somewhere to live for a while before going abroad....and I know they loved it here at Barley Hill when they visited. I know Liz would enjoy doing the garden, and having Sprog.

So I go to get Liz and tell her that all being well I plan to go and live in Spain for the winter….. and she says 'I just know this is all going to happen'.

It all falls into place. John says 'ask Carol if she knows somewhere we could stay'. I ring Carol, who says 'well, strangely enough this morning Rosi (another Rosi) said she was going to let her casita for the winter'. I ring Rosi and ask her what it is like. 'It has a fireplace, a roof terrace, a bath, hot water, views of the mountains, and costs 300 Euros a month'….she says. 'I'll take it' I say excitedly. And I tell John and he cannot believe it had taken only an hour to sort….(AND it turned out it was only 15 minutes walk from John's land and ruined cortijo). As I always say, how about that?

My WRAGS job offers to keep my job open for 3 months. Patricia is very understanding. 'At our age, if you find a man you need to go for it' she laughs.

John is sometimes uncertain. Unsurprisingly! And due to that I realize that actually, it doesn't matter if he comes to Spain or not, for the whole time or just occasionally, or not at all. I can afford – just - to live there on my rental income. I have friends there, and that's what matters.

So I go.... in terror and delight... for my time in the sun, and to love's threshing floor...

(For three months, and stayed two years).

I read this by Emily Bronte by chance just before I leave on one rainbow filled morning:

'and faith shines equal, arming me from fear'.....

348

High in the Sierra Nevada at O Sel Ling Tibetan Buddhist Monastery,
the Mediterranean in the distance

Chapter 8
......and the River runs through me

12 October 2004   To Andalucia

They say to live in the Alpujarras is an initiation, a baptism by fire, and I think the journey there was that Initiation, or it was a foretaste of the trials of the Threshing Floor of Love that was calling me....

I locked the door of Stable Cottage, took a last harrowing look at Liz 's cottage where Sprog had now stopped miaowing. I howled all the way from Barley Hill to Angela's, rain battering the car in the empathy I have come to so appreciate from Nature.

'Oh my' said Angela as I dripped in. And, after tea and a hot croissant, 'Here, take a card.... for your new life....'. And, for the third time in this story of one Spanish New Yorker, Andalucia, and me, the angel of 'Delight' glowed up at me. 'I don't know, you are just magic' she said. I said, but we all are, life is.

The rain stopped as we drove away in newborn sunshine and blithe innocence. It shone peacefully on the Pont Aven as she towered over Plymouth dock, and as we watched England fade away.

The light and the peace did not last long, and as the sun dropped we were all at once cast headlong into a dark heaving cauldron of ocean and wind.

('I am never seasick' I had said smugly. 'I'll show you how to breathe with the sea'.)

Not much later I was suitably humbled. Wanly and with considerable difficulty I got up off the floor of the loo, washed my mouth, and came out into the cabin. Hanging on tight to the lurching walls and slipping on the reeling floor. Huge booms echoed as waves hit the ship. 'I've blocked up the basin' I mumbled, as Angela sat on her bunk, clearly not at all sick despite my appalling noises from the bathroom two feet away.

Eventually I fell asleep, emptied and peaceful. Angela was wide awake, not sick but seriously terrified as the lurches and booming crashes grew worse by the minute. Too frightened to negotiate the miles of corridor, reluctant to wake me, but needing to talk. Just when she was at the point of real panic, a voice announced my car number and called me to reception. She - both relieved and worried - woke me and when I heard I was knotted and sick again with fear for my car and of what it might have done to other cars. So, both of us terrified for different reasons, we supported each other along the plunging passages. But the crew have been vigilant, and blocked my wheels, and I breathed again as I yanked the handbrake up more strongly. The receptionist tells us this is the first storm for this new ship, but that there is nothing to worry about. I left Angela with some friendly passengers and dived back to the horizontal again. I slept.

Then I heard the captain speaking and my mind flew awake. Before hearing his words I realise the boat is STILL.

'This is your captain speaking. The forecast was for Force 6 or 7 winds. This ship is built for Force 9. We are currently experiencing to Force 10, with 10 metre waves. I therefore have had no choice but to turn the ship around and have brought her with the aid of a local pilot into safe anchorage off Brest. If the winds drop we will resume our passage. If not we will reassess tomorrow morning, and I will make an announcement at 8am'.

Angela came in. 'Yes I heard' I said. In the blessed stillness we talked about it all and then dropped off to sleep. As I slipped from exhausted consciousness I felt the shocked ship breathing out as she rested.

Next day, defeated by a barrage of cyclones coming in across Biscay, we crawled around the coast of Brittany to the little ferry port of Roscoff. Heaving and rolling through the relentless seas hour after hour. I surfaced now and again from my prone position to walk the safer of the forbidden decks. The bow had a glassed in walkway all around. The waves crashed right over it all, streaming back down the glass before rearing up over us again. People told us the waves last night were smashing over the windows of *the bar,* which is on the *top storey.* They saw a ship in distress send up flares, and the lifeboat come out from Brest before the ship vanished. One game old couple ate their dinner unperturbed in the restaurant, bottles and china and people crashing all around them.

The high seas lasted till just before we reached Roscoff. As I lay shaking incessantly in the cabin, Angela stood out on deck and, with land so close, felt safe to enjoy the exhilaration of it all. A very different and humbling role for the arrogant sailor that I am!!!

Finally the sea abated and we stood together in the sunlight and prepared to dock in France instead of Spain….. The tiny distance had taken us until 4pm. We had taken 24 hours to cross the channel. It felt like forever. We just managed to buy a map of France- stocks were not surprisingly almost out- and pored over routes over a pot of tea.

In Brittany Ferries terminal thousands of haggard white faces streamed in to claim refunds. But the company knew just what to do. Long white-clothed tables dispensed endless tea, coffee and exquisite tiny croissants and pain au chocolat. Dozens of smiling staff at computers alphabetically labelled dispensed cash refunds in euros of the whole fare. All the white faces began to lift, conversations started, stories were compared, and the atmosphere lightened and energy began to flow. Cheerful French boys wove skilfully through the crowds bearing great trays of steaming pastries shoulder high. The roar of chatter rose. We stopped trembling.

And before too long we drove into the pretty town, took a room at the first nice hotel, and, fragile but heady with relief and dry land went out to walk and then to eat.

Over the smidgeon of red wine that our stomachs allowed, we talked about it. How Angela was saved from her panic attack in the nick of time by my not having fully put on the handbrake of my car. ' But you MUST have known you could wake me' I wailed. 'Of COURSE you could wake me'. How she loved the waves once she felt safe. 'But we're always safe' I said. 'Whatever'.

We talked of I shook so much all evening and all day, which reminded me of entering the Crestone valleys for the first time, and the evening of knowing I was going to have to leave Higher sea and move to Barley Hill. It was like having all the molecules shift about and settle into a new pattern. This time it was like a continuation of the shaking that began when John kissed me in Orgiva, that continued on meeting him at Heathrow, and then sitting all day shaking on the sofa after he left…. shaking is a big sign of vibration changing.. ..of new beginnings. Then we talked about how I got sick when I don't ever. I am reminded of the plane to LA from Denver, how I 'couldn't stomach' the big changes ahead. It somehow shows me that this too is a whole new story starting. I pray I don't have to go through more terrible times first, but really that's NOT my instinct this time. I hope.

I remember the card taken for this year of 2004 at Winter Solstice….'Change'…..
And the one at Ciel's in September…'Migration', and then in 'Pathways' shop later that month, 'A move to a new home is imminent. It will be a good move'.

Next day, once again in good spirits and blithe innocence we set off. They lasted through sunny Brittany's hills and forests and empty roads, and a good lunch in a Gastronomie Francaise restaurant in La Roche Bernard.

But that was the only respite allowed us, as the afternoon took us into the bleak and tangled roads and traffic of the Atlantic coast; and next day we battled with the endless lorries on narrow 2 lane motorways, and the sun abandoned us, vanishing into surging angry black rain-clouds. Soon we were driving, slowly, peering into the whiteouts of rain, mists, continuous lorry spray, and this rarely ceased until we reached Andalucia.

It was all so bad, we took care to treat ourselves very very well in-between laps.

Just before reaching the Spanish border, in numb exhaustion, having prayed for the rain to stop all day, I prayed, 'well at least can we have somewhere nice to stay please'. Very soon I glimpsed a hoarding for a hotel- 'Panoramic Terrace'- 'that will do' I said. So we followed the signs and came to a spectacular and very elegant hotel on the cliffs at St Jean de Luz with a collection of modern art. I was so numb I couldn't appreciate it for about half an hour, finally coming to with a pot of tea and biscuits in the lounge surrounded by sculpture and views. Angela again took my role and did the enthusiast bit. She also gamely swam in the outdoor pool, shivering in the cold wind as she got in and out: it was the horizon sort, and beyond it great waves crashed onto the rocks. In our room was a large painting of a 'peregrino' with his staff – a pilgrim on the Camino. I took a photo of it.

There are wonderful memories of the Guggenheim in Bilbao: we were quite blown away by it all, and I remember lying prone on one of the circular seats looking up into the atrium in disbelief soaking it all in. And Angela driving us literally to the door, and parking there! It was Sunday and we risked it as the whole street was lined with cars. Some Americans joined us and we compared traffic notes and debated happily whether to chance it. Plus we had the best tapas imaginable! Another foreign tourist was helping himself to them, because no one served him, you had to wait ages. He said it was the only way not to starve, and he paid at the end.

We felt strongly by then that this was our own Camino (friends had walked that earlier in the year). Shells started to appear at the Roscoff hotel and continued every stopping place right to this casita.

We reached Burgos, the crossing point of our journey with the Path, on Sun eve. There was absolutely nowhere to park, it was jammed with cars, & I crawled around looking for ages.(Lovely patient Spanish drivers didn't hoot me once!) But eventually we stumbled on a spot and then a really nice hotel.

We walked tiredly into the centre, and as we did I felt myself becoming tremendously energised. Angela was amazed, she was shattered and I had been too. We just took in the atmosphere and ate very local food in this place (random choice!) where all the arty types were congregating so we had a great people watch. The conductor of an orchestra and some of the musicians came in after a concert at the Cathedral, it was lovely. I was so high, I was astonished. We looked into Moritos tapas bar, that was an experience and a half....LIFE in capitals. The exuberance of Spain. It was just all SO beautiful, what a city.

The cathedral is stupendous, but dark, heavy, male, and ornate, bearing down upon you. But I loved the Mary Magdalen painting by a da Vinci pupil and the tryptych of her life and I wondered if it was portraying the bloodline of Christ, as she holds a child...?

We saw some peregrinos with their staffs in the morning, and I felt totally overcome with exhaustion just watching them. Such weariness and sadness overtook me. We eventually found some of the brass shells in the street (near the peregrinos hospital) and walked the Way just a little, and I was so pleased to do that, but all I felt was the weariness. And the gratitude that I didn't have to do it. I was rather disappointed with myself for a moment but it passed and we resumed our own motorised endurance test.

We pushed through it all steadily, and through horrific traffic around cities, (me feeding Angela rescue remedy in the middle of 6 lanes of racetrack around Madrid), endlessly supporting and encouraging each other. When we got lost (because I chickened out and left the motorway) and sat breathing heavily in a factory car park, we were directed in unintelligible Spanish and many hand signals but still incomprehensibly found the way...

To two nights in a hotel which had been the pleasure palace of the Cardinals...mmmmm

Well south of Toledo, the car alarmed us by coughing on the motorway – acceleration vanished for a moment – so we pulled off – and suddenly the weather really let loose and we sat parked for an hour in the midst of hammering rain, spreading lakes and rivers of blood red floods and great daggers of fork lightning. So, thanks to the car, mercifully, we were spared driving through that very worst spate of weather. That was actually my worst moment of the whole trip, surprisingly: I sat there in all that ridiculous drama, thinking, I don't any more care WHAT the weather throws at us, just SO LONG AS THE CAR GETS US THERE. I had a sudden overwhelming horror of having come so close and breaking down in this desolate place.

But the rain and the floods subsided a little and we splashed off again, me holding my breath in case the car was really in trouble. But that was the last of it and soon we were climbing in bright sun up to the pass into Andalucia, and one by one the Sierras passed before us, dramatic, hazy and rich with Southern colour, until we drove in a euphoric burst of energy over the Puerto de Suspiro del Moro and into the Alpujarras.

The journey was like a birth canal into a new life. It was pushing through veil after veil to reach this Andalucian Avalon. It was our Camino de Santiago de Compostela - two different friends walked it this year and we felt very close to them. All the way along, from the hotel in Roscoff to this casita, there was a trail of scallop shells, and they really helped.

So, 9 days after leaving home, we arrived at this delicious casita, and ran exclaiming around it.

Angela wrote on a card for me when she left:

'To Sandra, in memory of a journey undertaken in true friendship. Harmoniously, supportively, through real challenges.'

We were really proud of ourselves.

21 October   Here I am.

I am sitting typing this in the sun on the roof terrace, perched high above flat white Alpujarran roofs, chimneys, flowers. The terrace curls around a huge twisted olive stump. Animals and spirits wink at me from its knots and folds. The washing line with its pegs is astonishing against the bulk of the mountains - Sierra de Lujar, 6000feet.....
Scents of jasmine in the warm air. A blue pool glimmers through grey green olives below. And way below that the river's green snake winds through the dry land, Lujar

surging steeply up on the other side, a car or two slowly climbing the gash in its shoulder, out of the valley. To the north the vast Sierra Nevada heaves itself to nearly 12000ft, its shoulders dotted with tiny strings of white villages. All is white light, shapes, heat. Mary Oliver asks

"do you think there is anywhere, in any language
a word billowing enough
for the pleasure
that fills you
as the sun
reaches out
as it warms you"

22 October   Blessing the Land

This is what I wrote, in a little writing group, about the first ceremony on John's land- for full moon -just after my arrival. There was an eclipse of the moon that day, amazingly. **And I was told, to my bewildered wonderment, that the great circle of flat stones in front of the ruin is an 'era', a Moorish Threshing Floor,** traditionally used for ceremonies, and in local myth a witches' take off and landing place!!!!....

'High, expansive, numinous, a sacred place, the Sierras great cloaked and hooded beings ranged benevolently around. They watch and try to protect. And weep soundlessly at all the pain of the valley below.

This place stands high and level within the valley, it feels strong and open, but is dry and sad with long neglect and past agonies. The stone bones of the cortijo are forlorn but still standing, and the ancient ceremonial 'era' threshing circle is still strong beneath the weeds.

I am glad beyond measure to be here.

It is the magic hour. Dusk dropping bluely, soft in the clean mountain air. A kind wind. I touch it, thank it, and it strokes my face and lifts my hair as silently but swiftly I gather stones, and form a labyrinth in this potent place.

I place the last stone, a large one at the entrance, and I lay out an altar beside it and then as I stand upright in the new dark and spread my arms to the land and its sleeping spirits a white glow haloes a peak to the east and grows.

The white full moon rises solemnly in the strength and beauty of Taurus and Venus, released and washed clean by the morning's eclipse, and gazes down on the land.

I am still, meeting her.

My witness a local dog, sitting quietly watching.

Then, slowly, I light the central lantern, and place a light to mark the way across the dry streambed to the ancient olive near which I have made this labyrinth.

And soon there are faint voices and torchbeams, warm hugs, and quiet dark shapes huddle to light nightlights in jars, and a circle of light appears in the darkness, the white stone paths within it glowing faintly in the moonlight.

We hold hands in a circle, silent beneath the moon. The wind stops. The land hushes around us. I speak of our purpose here, to ask for blessings on this land, its spirits, its owner John Cano in New York City and our new relationship, and as I do a lovely young Canadian girl sees a shooting star. I also at John's request ask for blessings for his mother's family – named Fernandez -whose land this was, and to connect to the friends in England on Barley Hill who are right now tuning in to us all here and also asking for these blessings.

Together but leaving spaces between us, in drifts of incense, each ringing Tibetan bells as we enter, we walk the paths, to formally open this sacred space. I see it all as from above, the dark figures pacing in and out of the small lit circle at the heart of the great moonlit valley, surrounded by the vast solid shapes of the mountains. Two dogs watch, guardians of the gateway.

I see a figure dance off into the shadows, another sits in meditation and another lies on the scarred land, arms outstretched. I see myself moving in and out of the ruined house, touching the walls, the windows, the trees in the courtyard. I see each figure walking into the centre of the labyrinth alone with his or her personal quest. I see a figure kneeling and then standing arms outstretched at the centre.

I see us in a circle on the labyrinth, linking hands and thanking each other and the spirits of the land, thanking John, thanking the full moon veiled now in glowing thin cloud as we close our ceremony.

It is deeply magical, potent, and I am awed by it. Blessed.'

Towards Conscious Intimacy

I know just as deeply that I am in the right place at right time. I am brought here to a real physical 'love's threshing floor' as Kahlil Gibran put it.

I do feel the fear, but here I am Lord, here I am Lady, a whole person stepping forth into the unknown.....

I think it was Oriah Mountain Dreamer who said this:
' I find, in our time together, more of myself. And I find, in my time alone, more of the world'. Very true. And this...
'I have come to accept that no matter how much I am able to be with myself, no matter how much I like my own company, I still long to sit close to and at times completely merge myself with, another in deep intimacy. The completeness of self is found when we can be alone, AND when we can bring all of who we are to another, receiving and being received fully.

This is the sacred marriage: the coming together of two whole persons, who have each met themselves on the road....'

My adventure into intimacy, its initiation completed, feels blessed.

So I step forward....

EPILOGUE

February 2008

This is where I have decided to stop my story, in October 2004. The years that follow are a whole new one….would be a book in themselves.

I had - and still have - no idea of whether I will know the glories of the Sacred Marriage in this life, but it is my most earnest wish and aim. My only big ambition now in fact.

My Alpujarran adventure lasted a spell binding 'living on the edge' two years, and I returned (miraculously as usual the cottage was available) to Stable Cottage to yet more wonders….My journey since that challenging one in October 2004 has taken me with an endless flow of magic miracles and mystery through yet more explorations of life, of place and of love, and through new explorations of the coming together of sexuality, sensuality and spirituality. And a sublime and exquisite taste of conscious and sacred intimacy with my beloved S last autumn. The stories would take another whole book….what a movie that story would make!!!!!!!!

The wonder never fades. The amazement. In each moment we can experience everything anew. Like lovers for whom each glance, each touch, is so charged…when we love life, that is how it is….boredom doesn't get a look in.

This is luxury of course. We in the affluent world have the time to do this inner work, and we do it for everyone. We've made the journey through materialist success and found it empty without connection to the sacred. When enough people come to consciousness, the world will change and deprivation and atrocity will perhaps be a thing of the past. We really can create heaven on earth. This way of life becomes Second nature. The evolved human nature, Second Nature.

I notice now how many people are moving into new ways of being, in many ways. I notice how the world begins to come to silence together, as after the London bombings in the summer of 96(?) when there was stillness and silence in London, Paris, Madrid, Bali as big Ben struck noon…. 'we will not be broken' says the driver of the bombed London bus ie, we will not be driven into fear and reactions based on that. Wonderful, and o different to the States..

I had worked over so many years alone to become a whole person, with my joy and love of life and means of support independent of another person or set of circumstances. I could care for myself. So I felt free to explore intimacy from that strong place. I could stop becoming and be…..and hope to explore what Andrew Cohen calls 'The Conscious We'. When two people live together intimately and consciously. I still hope for that experience, a sustainable and sacred love.

But I must say it makes me both laugh and cry that in my late fifties and early sixties, silver-haired, lined and scarred, stooped and a bit overweight, I have lovers, but the beautiful woman in her forties who divorced her husband was so overlooked…..

But…..it all fits together, its all for the highest good. (Though I often think, laughing, but what a waste!!!!)

And, as I wrote these words yesterday, I was reflecting that THE ONLY NEGATIVE CHARGE I STILL FEEL IS AROUND MY FATHER. I can nearly accept and forgive but I am still a bit troubled by just not understanding how he as a good man could have let me down so. Still some bitterness is there.

Well, last night a man in the group of friends here in Vermont (who knows nothing at all of my story) was listening to me talk about the 'explosion' of my face into monstrous shapes (yes I know! I told you it would make a movie!!!) when deserted by Swithin, and looking at me very intently, and he suddenly came to stand in front of me and he said, 'was your father a religious man?' 'Yes, a lay preacher'. 'When your face exploded he was pulling something out of you, with the aid of this man'. Silence. 'He is looking down on you and can see (great sadness here in his voice) how your life has been, and he says HE IS SORRY HE DIDN'T STAND UP FOR YOU'.

Tears burst from my eyes.

I gazed at him at they spilled down my face. He went on 'Your mother says she wants you to dance now'. 'Your mother and father are holding hands, they haven't done that in a long time. They are looking down on you ....' I sobbed. I cant tell you what a relief it was to know they have seen how it has been, that my pain is acknowledged by them with sorrow. All my family had apologised to me except my father. And now he too had spoken to me from beyond the grave.

Later, still shaking, I told Glenn and Cami (Cameron is Nancy's chosen name - the divine window belongs to them!) that that afternoon I had been reflecting that my bitterness towards my father was the last piece still to heal but that I knew that I didn't have to work it out, just accept it..... and that I still was mystified about why my face 'exploded'. ' Oh so you were calling your father in' Glenn said, and Cami added 'Your surrender called him in'. Apparently Jim does this kind of thing occasionally, usually spontaneously. And I suddenly know that my father, acting through S, pulled out with S's terrible action the deep buried anger of generations of men in my father's family. The healing of ages of angry men has taken place through the betrayal by my beloved. Yes, I know .... but it feels right and we CAN choose our meanings... though I am always open to new meanings that come to me....

Whatever, now I really do feel a release and maybe now a man will appear who is not angry or bitter...a man who is free, we will see.

So now I have done what I came here to do, my book is written and I am a free woman. Family relationships, the Task we are all set, are resolved to the best of my ability; my dearest Ben has always been a gift to me, not a task, there has always been ease there.....

The last piece has been given me on my last day here, and now I write the last page.

I can put my Story down now.....

Yes, yes. I HAVE PUT MY STORY DOWN. In both senses. It is written, AND I no longer carry it. In writing it, and editing it, I have travelled a long way. I wrote...'I climbed out of all the shit'...I felt shame at parts of my story and I was still bitter. Now, as I edit this last page or two, at the point of publication, I have come through to feeling proud of my whole life, and grateful for it all, and that there was actually no 'shit' in the manner I meant it....only in the manner of my thinking. 'Lost in thought'. Lost in a cauldron of negative thoughts and feelings all feeding each other. I travelled this lifetime and also in the writing from shame to grateful pride and from fear to love.

'The self is made, not given. It is a creative and active process of attending a life that must be heard, shaped, seen, said aloud into the world, finally enacted and woven into the lives of others,' said Barbara Myerhoff. 'Yes yes exactly' I say as I read this. 'Ah I love that'

Leaving Vermont, I threw all the waste paper from my work into a big recycling dumpster, and got back into the car. 'Did you see the plane?' said Cami. 'Uh???' I said, 'turn round' she said. I did. RIGHT NEXT TO THE DUMPSTER WAS A SMALL AEROPLANE – a private one owned by the lakeside estate I had been staying on.

I said ' right. I've left the rubbish behind and now it's time to stop looking at it and see the plane and fly'.

(Believe it or not those are the last words of narrative I typed in this book. I remembered the event and added it in....just as I send the manuscript off to be printed...)

Time to Relish and Cherish. There is only Now, and Now I love and enjoy and am loved and enjoyed. I repeat that to myself. There is only Now, and Now I love and enjoy and am loved and enjoyed. I am not in demand, I am not successful, not in the world's eyes, but I have no need of such things. I used to long for it. I was told that when it came I would no longer need it or even want it....that could well be true. Time will tell.

This life is without doubt orchestrated. It is a symphony. An opera, a play. We compose it, sometimes formally, sometimes in improvisation. Sometimes it is composed for us and we can only surrender, only align our will with the divine.

What do we choose for the next act? It is up to us. Choose and then surrender. The surrender is the key.

Power and humility in a dance of grace.

We can do all this consciously. But we have all always been doing it anyway, unconsciously – and creating havoc instead of harmony! To do it consciously is an act of great power, and we are protected from this by unconsciousness until we develop the responsibility and humility to use the power wisely. But then...then ...we Relish and Cherish every moment.

The individual experiences itself cut off from God and fearful in its loneliness, terrified by creation, and it creates suffering, conflicts, wars and atrocities from all its fears.

Until we each one by one reconnect to the Sacred through diving into stillness, silence, the Now, our selves, Communion with Nature....Until we each one by one lovingly tame our frightened egos and come to awareness of ourselves as a part of God and of everything. We learn that experiencing takes up more awareness than thinking, and we can let go the torments of thinking and simply experience each moment.

We find the control - so we can let go of control... so we can surrender! Paradox is everywhere and when we find it we are near the truth.

We need to fully Individuate in order to become aware of our Connection and our Divinity. We need to feel complete in ourselves, be free of any attachment or expectation to fully feel the field of infinite possibilities. Our Connection is our Source of everything we need. Our Connection is Liberation.

This is the great story of humanity, and the evolution of humanity is very possibly taking a leap right now as we watch. To the second human nature, until that becomes 'Second Nature'. And the world ego, in the pain of its separateness and its fear, fights for its life, and horrors and atrocities pour forth even as the silent revolution gently spreads from person to person in a wave of love and grace across the planet.

This may not happen, but it also may. We can only work on ourselves and help where we feel a passion to do so…..these are pivotal times. There is real urgency in our inner work now.

As we each learn the dance

And one day the whole world will dance the dance. Ride the realms of bliss. Laugh the cosmic laugh and play in all creation.

But meanwhile the field of infinite possibilities dances on…...glittering in the sunlight…laughing and beckoning…..

But it is time take my leave of you, with this moment now….and the best pudding of all

I AM SITTING IN THE MOMENT

I am sitting in the moment

poised in the wave

I ride the wave of space and time, I dive into it and feel the depth within, I fly on the currents of love through wind and water and see all passing below and around

Love. Only love.

I gaze from the peak of the wave, where shall I go, where draws me now? I gaze from the trough of the wave into the turmoil around me, what have I drawn to me now.

I choose, but I am beyond choices. I surrender from my power. Whatever. Whatever.

I have chosen what is here. I choose what comes, what crosses my path.

No why. Love. Only, love.

Riding the waves of life, waves pour from me and pour to me, and pass under me and over me and through me. I am all of it, in love with all, and I am still in the midst of it and I am in stillness in the midst of it.

I sit on, I fly on, I swim on. In praise. Only, in praise.

In my spirit my body dances, beyond gravity, beyond boundaries, and adores itself as it leaps and turns in the air and my hair flies out and my back arches and my head is thrown back in glory.

As I sing to my Creator and to Creation. To the glittering sea of love that links it all.

And I sing to my Creation and to all the possibilities that dance for my being. To the threads, to the patterns and the majesty.

I fly to the mountain tops and I lie with the earth

......and the river runs through me '

THE END

TIRAMISU

I once took the marscapone and ladyfingers on a plane to a faraway place to make this for a lover.... This is the ultimate dolcissimo if it's made with love and tenderness and a dash of fiery passion...rich, potent, moist...

Beat 2 egg yolks very well with 2 tbsp Marsala or good brandy and 2 tbsp caster sugar. Set over a pan of simmering water and continue to whisk, until light, pale, fluffy and holding a trail from the whisk...Whisk a bit more off the heat.
Beat 250g marscapone cheese and 3 tbsp caster sugar then add 2 more tbsp marsala or brandy and 2 tbsp dark rum and beat in. Blend tenderly into the zabaglione (egg mixture)
Whisk 300ml double cream softly and stir it in. Mix 100ml strong good coffee and 2-3 more tbsp of Marsala or brandy
Arrange half of the ladyfingers (sponge fingers or savoiarde, preferably homemade) carefully in a large beautiful glass dish, and soak in half the alcoholic coffee. Spoon over them half of the gorgeous creamy mixture, then the rest of the fingers, the rest of the coffee, then finely grate a a 150g bar of very very dark (over 70%) chocolate and sprinkle half of it over the sponge....
Spoon over the rest of the creamy oozy concoction, and lastly and lovingly a thick layer of chocolate....
Chill for a few hours.
Bring out after dark
onto a warm Mediterranean jasmine scented terrace
with a bottle of Tia Maria or Kahlua

and **one** beautiful spoon

MY BOOKSHELF

I have simply listed the books on my bookshelf. There have been countless others.

Gill Edwards	Stepping into the Magic
	Wild love
Eckhart Tolle	The Power of Now
	Stillness speaks
	A New Earth
Stuart Wilde	The Quickening
	Whispering winds of change
	Life doesn't have to be a struggle
Gabrielle Roth	Maps to Ecstasy
Ajahn Sumedho	Cittaviveka
John Garrie Roshi	The Way is without Flaw
Marianne Williamson	The Return to Love
Masaru Emoto	Hidden messages of Water
Paul Ferrini	Reflections of the Christ Mind Series
Neale Donald Walsch	Conversations with God series
	Communion with God.
	Happier than God
Wayne Dyer	Getting in the gap
Esther and Jerry Hicks	Ask and it shall be given
	The Attraction Factor
Lynne Grabhorn	Excuse me your life is waiting!
Andrew Cohen	Enlightenment is a secret
	Creating Heaven on Earth
Osho	The Book of Secrets
Thich Nhat Hanh	The long road leads to Joy
	Teachings on Love
	Creating True Peace
Riane Eisler	Sacred Pleasure
Roger Housden	Ten poems to Change your life
	Soul and Sensuality
Shakti Gawain	Living in the Light
Caroline Myss	Why people don't heal and how they can.
Oriah Mountain Dreamer	The Invitation
Susan Hayward	Begin it Now
Notebooks of Paul Brunton	Healing of the Self: The Negaives.
Lesley Garner	Everything I ever learned about Love
Paulo Coelho	Manual of the warrior of Light
	The Alchemist
	Eleven Minutes
	The Pilgrimage
Kathy Jones	Spinning the Wheel of Ana
Robert Powell	The Blissful Life
John Moore (Editor)	Make Believe
Anne Dickson	A Woman in Your Own Right
Jules Cashford	The Moon Myth and Image
With Anne Baring	The Myth of the Goddess
Timothy Freke	The Wisdom of the Christian Mystics
Lynne McTaggart	The Field

WEBSITES

Some sites of authors/teachers mentioned in my story

www.http://

masaru-emoto.net	Messages in Water
soulwindows.co.uk	Dance to the Heart
gabrielleroth.com	5 Rhythms dance
eckharttolle.com	
krystal.cnchost.com	Cutting the Ties that Bind
kathyjones.co.uk	PriestessTraining/Goddess Conference
drwaynedyer.com	
nealedonaldwalsch.com	
livingthefield.com	
mrfire.com	Joe Vitale's Zero Point Theory
hooponopono.org	
greggbraden.com	
plumvillage.org	Thich Nhat Hanh's centre
en.wikipedia.org/wiki/John_Garrie	about John Garrie Roshi
haracombe.talktalk.net	Paul Taylor, Sati society
tanmaya.info	Tanmaya - Reiki Master
livingmagically.co.uk	Gill Edwards
lesleygarner.com	
stuartwilde.com	
paulocoelho.com	
paulferrini.com	
janemeredith.com	dark goddess workshops
rianeeisler.com	author of Sacred Pleasure

Thank you for sharing my journey with me. I am now back in my Somerset idyll.....living very simply and with great pleasure in the unspeakable beauty of the ordinary. I commend this and any other path which takes us to our connection with the Divine, however you visualise It, and the rich full tasting of life and love.

If you too are journeying in magic, reclaiming your power, and learning to truly love, and serve, I hope you have as much fun with it all as I have.... Because, this way of being is, when all is said and done.... fun. Awe-inspiring at times, agonising at times, but mostly...fun.

I can be contacted on my Blogsite: thepuddingisintheproof.blogspot.com or at thepuddingisintheproof@googlemail.com

All Blessings.   *Sandra Hartley*